Date Due

NOV 2 6 2007			

Double V

Double V

The Civil Rights Struggle
of the Tuskegee Airmen

Lawrence P. Scott
William M. Womack Sr.

Michigan State University Press
East Lansing
1994

All Michigan State University Press books are produced on paper which meets the requirements of American National Standard of Information Sciences—Permanence of paper for printed materials ANSI Z39.48-1984.

Michigan State University Press
East Lansing, Michigan 48823-5202

02 01 00 99 98 97 96 95 94 1 2 3 4 5 6 7 8 9

Library of Congress Cataloging-in-Publication Data

Scott, Lawrence P.
    Double V : the civil rights struggle of the Tuskegee Airmen / Lawrence P. Scott, William M. Womack, Sr.
          p.   cm.
    Includes bibliographical references and index.
    ISBN 0-87013-347-0
    1. United States. Air Force—Afro-Americans—History. 2. Air pilots, Military—United States—History. 3. World War, 1939-1945—Participation, Afro-American. 4. World War, 1914-1918—Participation, Afro-American. 5. Afro-Americans—Civil rights. I. Womack, William M., 1916–   . II. Title.
UG834.A37S36   1994
940.54'4973—dc20   94-20704
                                                                         CIP

Photographs reproduced in this book courtesy of the Tuskegee Airmen Museum, Detroit, Michigan.

Dedicated to the Memory of
Freddie Hutchins
Cornelius Coffey

Contents

Contents

Acknowledgments

We wish to extend our appreciation to the following for sharing their time, hearts, expertise, knowledge, and resources

C. Alfred Anderson
Theodore Berry
Omar P. Blair
Willa Brown-Chapell
Broadus Butler
Gilbert Cargill
Herbert Carter
Cornelius Coffey
Woodrow Crockett
Lemuel Custis
Ret. Gen. Benjamin O. Davis Jr.
Walter Downs
Charles Dryden
Leroy Gillead
William Holliman
Robert Hodge
Harold Hurd
Fred Hutchins
Clarence Jamison
Alexander Jefferson
Elmore Kennedy
Phillip Lee
Nancy Leftenant-Colon
Rufus Mitchell

Ira O'Neal
Robert Pitts
Wardell Polk
E. E. Richardson
Edith Roberts
John W. Rogers
Harry Shepherd
Harry Stewart
Roger Terry
Ret. Gen. Lucien Theus
William Thompson
Jenny Washington
Spann Watson
John Whitehead

Special thanks to:

Angela Scott
Dorothy Scott
Shirley Pyke
Barbara McCauley
Laurel Malson
Norbert Phillips
Al Cole
Richard Macon
Tuskegee Airmen Inc., Detroit Chapter
Tuskegee Airmen Inc.
Rufus Davenport Jr.

Foreword

These are the Brave
These men who cast aside
Old memories, to walk the blood-stained pave
Of sacrifice, joining the solemn ride
That moves away, to suffer and die
For freedom—when their own is denied!
Roscoe Jamison
As quoted in *Dusk of Dawn* by W.E.B. DuBois, 1940

Although the subject of this poem was the African-American soldier in World War I, its relevance rings true for the African-American soldier who, in World War II, risked his life fighting in foreign lands for the freedom of others while democracy escaped him in the land of his birth.

The members of the African-American Pursuit Squadron, 332nd Fighter Group, and 477th Bombardment Group, better known as the Tuskegee Airmen, felt the great sting of this paradox. Despite the handicap of racial segregation and the denial of basic rights granted to all Americans under the Constitution, these young men became mathematicians, scientists, and engineers competent in the operation, navigation, and maintenance of the most sophisticated aircraft in the world. The Tuskegee Airmen, although limited in number due to segregationist policies in the War Department, were among the best that America could offer to the war effort.

It is very important for readers of this book understand that the Tuskegee Airmen were the by-products of a racially segregated society and early twentieth-century civil rights movement initiated by the Niagara Movement and fine tuned by the National Association for the

Advancement of Colored People and the African-American Press. These men were well aware of their role. They knew that the future success of the civil rights movement was inextricably tied to their success in combat in the skies over Europe and in their conduct at segregated training bases at home. The engineers of the movement were also aware that the success of the Airmen would not only help eliminate questions about the loyalty of African Americans to the United States, the success of the Airmen would help belie, at the core, the basis for racial discrimination in America—white supremacy.

In the spring of 1945, during the latter stages of the European Campaign of World War II, the officers of the 332nd Fighter Group assisted in the destruction of the Nazi military industrial complex in Europe while the members of the 477th Bombardment Group planned and implemented non-violent protest against the Army Air Force's segregationist and discriminatory policies. In April of that year, 60 officers, some of whom were combat veterans, were arrested in their attempts to enter, non-violently, a segregated officers' club at Freeman Field in Indiana. A few days later, 101 officers, after refusing to sign an order relegating them to segregated quarters, were arrested and charged with refusing a direct order from a superior officer, a charge, upon conviction, punishable by death. The 101 officers were flown to another base and kept under guard to await their fate.

The Freeman Field protest and the success of the Tuskegee Airmen in combat served to illuminate the immoral, politically expensive, and counterproductive nature of segregation perpetrated by the Army Air Force and condoned by the War Department. Consequently, the NAACP and other players in the movement pushed for the elimination of segregation in the armed forces; in 1949, the Air Force became the first branch of the armed forces to initiate the desegregation of its units, five years before the Brown decision that outlawed segregation in public accommodations.

It is important for readers to remember that the non-violent protest enacted by the Airmen at Freemen Field predated the Shreveport and Montgomery bus boycotts of the early and mid-1950s and the lunch counter sit-ins and freedom rides of the 1960s, all of which are considered to be historic benchmarks in the story of the modern-day civil rights movement.

The members of the civil rights movement and all Americans owe the Tuskegee Airmen a debt of gratitude.

Benjamin L. Hooks
Past President of the NAACP

Introduction

As America mourned the death of President Roosevelt on 12 April 1945, another tragic event, which occurred the same day, went completely unnoticed. The U.S. Army Air Force, in a move unprecedented in the history of the U.S. Army, arrested 101 African American pilots, navigators and bombardiers for disobeying a direct order from a superior officer. The officers were charged with violating the 64th Article of War—a crime that, in wartime, carried a penalty of death upon conviction. The 101 officers had risked their lives by refusing to sign an order that would have placed them in segregated housing and recreational facilities unbecoming of American officers and gentlemen. While Harry S Truman took the oath of office of president of the United States, the 101 officers were secretly flown to an air base inside Ft. Knox and placed under arrest in their barracks, surrounded by twelve-foot barbed wire fences and armed guards.

These 101 officers, and what happened to them, personify the near-schizophrenic struggle for civil and human rights in a democracy during the struggle for survival in defense of democracy in a foreign land. While America and its European allies were waging war against the fascism and racism of the Axis powers, the 101 officers and other black officers and enlisted men involved in combat were attempting to achieve two victories—to stop Hitler overseas and to stop racism in America.

Thousands of young African-American men volunteered to fight for their freedom with hopes that their example of patriotism would change the national disposition toward African Americans. This mode of protest reached its zenith during World War II, when the African-American community organized around the idea of a double victory—

1

victory at home, as well as victory abroad. The African-American press, and specifically the *Pittsburgh Courier*, endorsed and cultivated the concept of a double victory into a rally cry and logo: "Double V." The *Courier* promoted the "Double V" campaign nationwide with "Double V" buttons, posters, bumper stickers, clubs, dances, and other fundraising activities for the war effort. The *Courier* and other African-American publications, to the best of their limited capability, kept black America appraised of the struggle for victory overseas and victory at home. We therefore felt that "Double V" was a historically appropriate title for our publication.

Since the story behind the arrest of the 101 officers and the adventures of other aviators who preceded them is an illustration of a long-running battle for civil rights, we have expanded the title to: *Double V: The Civil Rights Struggle of the Tuskegee Airmen.*

Double V chronicles, for the first time ever, a part of the civil rights movement in which African-American aviators played critical roles. The book recounts the struggle, from 1914 to 1947, of the African-American pilots, men and women, who overcame racial barriers just to fly airplanes. *Double V* will document how they removed the barriers to success and how, in the process, they provided the foundation for the modern day civil rights movement.

We selected pilots as the main characters because they were among the best America had to offer, and because they had the most to contribute. They were adventurous, courageous, and talented. They were the natural leaders. During the period covered in the book, most African American pilots were college-educated and had private pilot's licenses. Those men who flew in World War II were well-versed in the sciences and mathematics and were the most educated pilots in the Army Air Force until the Army relaxed its education requirements.

All of the chapters are based on facts confirmed and verified by extensive research of published and unpublished works, oral histories from the airmen, the black press, and government documents. The book is meant to be entertaining, as well as disconcerting, in detailing the predicaments in which the aviators found themselves. Many events are exposed to the public for the first time. Some events are revisited for the first time in fifty years. The reader will be amazed at the exploits of the pilots and inspired by their courage in facing adversity.

I n the summer of 1914, Europe's great powers were engaged in the final stages
of a nineteenth-century struggle for economic dominance over untapped
resources and markets in Africa and Asia. Yet, the very acquisition of colonies in
these faraway lands contributed to growing hostility among the colonizers, themselves, chiefly Great Britain, France, and Germany. To protect their interests,
European governments assembled large armies and navies to threaten rivals,
should they encroach on what were perceived to be vital national interests; they
then wove webs of secret agreements and treaties to secure allies for themselves,
should a war actually break out. By the fourteenth year of the twentieth century,
the competition for colonies and the race for global hegemony reached a flash-
point. Any spark might ignite the incendiary byproducts of unchecked imperialist
ambitions into a worldwide conflagration.

But the actual event that led to open hostility was neither a colonial dispute in
Africa nor was it precipitated by one of the great powers. World War I began in
the Balkans when the heir to the throne of the Austro-Hungarian Empire, Archduke
Franz Ferdinand, and his wife, who were visiting Sarajevo in July 1914, were assas-
sinated by a Croatian nationalist. In response to the murder, an incensed Austrian
government sent Serbia an ultimatum containing an overt military threat; with its
future in danger, Serbia called into play a secret military alliance it had with Russia.
Austria-Hungary's ally, Germany, perceiving that its interests were threatened by
Russia's military mobilization, saw no alternative but to go to war. France, Russia's
secret ally against Germany, immediately activated its military and prepared to
attack. Seeing that it was threatened in the east by Russia and in the west by
France, Germany immediately invaded France through neutral Belgium. Great
Britain, perceiving itself to be a guarantor of Belgian liberty, next entered the war
on the side of France and Russia. Even in the Far East, Japan, which possessed its
own imperialist ambitions, declared war on Germany and seized its colonies. Of the
West's great economic powers, only the United States remained neutral.

Chapter I

By Any Means Necessary

Plans for war defined the waves of national enthusiasm that swept over the European peoples during the summer of 1914. Soon after the events at Sarajevo, governments mobilized their massive military resources and prepared to defeat their respective enemies. Most Europeans thought the conflict would be over in a matter of months; almost none foresaw a struggle that would drag on for four long years, that emperors and kings would be dethroned or that millions of lives would be sacrificed on the battlefield.

The handful of Americans living in France found themselves in a precarious situation. Notwithstanding the fact that they were surrounded by an enthusiastic French citizenry, it was clear that their lives might be at risk if they remained in the country. Their dilemma was underscored when the United States government issued a formal statement outlining its policy of neutrality and encouraging American citizens living in Europe to return home. The issue was, however, a simple one for the French government; young foreign males living in that country were given a choice; they could leave France or they could join the French Foreign Legion.[1]

One enterprising young American thought of an alternative. Norman Prince, who happened to be vacationing in Paris when the war came, petitioned the French government for the establishment of an American squadron within the French Flying Corps. Prince, the son of a wealthy businessman, was a student pilot and viewed fighting for the French as both romantic and a payback for help France gave to the United States in the Revolutionary War. According to Arthur Whitehouse, author of *The Years of the Sky Kings*,[2] Prince recruited all of the American men he could find, including two African Americans,

Eugene Bullard and Robert Scanlon. When Prince first approached the French authorities with his plan and a list of volunteers, the government officials rejected the idea of an American squadron, citing the American policy of neutrality and the lack of flying experience among some of the volunteers. Prince was told that individuals with enough flight experience could volunteer for service in the French Flying Service, and that he should return to the United States for more civilian flight training. All of the other men on the list who had little or no flying experience were given the option of returning to the United States or joining the French Foreign Legion.[3]

Prince returned to Boston to continue his flight training. All of the other white men on Prince's volunteer list, Victor Chapman, William Thaw, Kiffin Rockwell, Bert Hall, and Elliot Cowden, joined the Foreign Legion.[4] These men were, for the most part, adventure seekers and romantics. The war, and the impending danger, attracted them, and service in the Foreign Legion was their right of passage. If some of these men had chosen to return home, they could have led productive and successful lives. For the two African Americans, however, the options offered to them were as attractive as playing Russian Roulette. Both options—life in America or life in the Foreign Legion—offered little consolation. Either choice could result in death for both men.

At the start of World War I, African Americans in the United States had little protection from unscrupulous whites in the executive, judicial, and legislative branches of the federal, state, and local governments. Although African Americans had a right to protection and fair treatment from the three branches of government, as stipulated in the fourteenth and fifteenth amendments to the United States Constitution, oftentimes they were denied that protection.[5]

From the end of the Reconstruction period to the beginning of the new century, over 2,450 African Americans were lynched in the United States, most under the suspicion of committing a crime, or tried and convicted by biased and hostile all-white juries. According to John Hope Franklin, in *From Slavery to Freedom,* over 1,100 African Americans were murdered by white mobs in the first thirteen years of the twentieth century. Very few of the organizers of these mob murders were ever arrested or convicted by the judicial systems in the areas where the lynchings occurred.[6]

Eugene Bullard and Bob Scanlon both realized that America in 1914 was not a healthy place to be if you were a young, ambitious, African-American male, striving to participate in all of the liberties granted to American citizens. Both had ventured to Paris to escape racial oppression and violence and to participate in the liberties denied to them in America.

Not much is known or written about Bob Scanlon, other than that he was a heavyweight boxer who supposedly fought under the name of Bob Armstrong, and that he found his way to England, where he met Jack Johnson, who was, by then, in self-imposed exile.[7] Johnson invited Scanlon to join his boxing troupe as a sparring partner. It was reported that Johnson admired fast machines, especially fast automobiles. While he was in England, it was not unusual to see him speeding on area race tracks with professional race car drivers or speeding around the city of London with the latest and most expensive sports car available.[8]

Johnson's need and respect for speed and excitement affected his employees, and especially Scanlon. The young prize fighter wanted to fly an airplane. It was reported by the NAACP's December 1915 issue of *The Crisis* that Scanlon had built his own biplane and had flown it over London.[9] If this occurred as reported, in the years preceding World War I, then Scanlon may have been the first known African American to build and fly an airplane. When Johnson defended his title in Paris, France, against Jim Moran in 1914, Scanlon accompanied him. Shortly after Johnson's fight, Germany invaded France and Johnson and his troupe hastily left France for England. Scanlon, who had difficulty finding Johnson in the panic that engulfed Paris, missed their departure and was, therefore, stranded.[10]

Eugene Bullard arrived in Paris in 1913, after a seven-year odyssey that took him from his hometown of Columbus, Georgia, to Virginia, Scotland, England, and then to France.[11] Bullard's father was a descendant of slaves from the French colony of Martinique and, as a child, he was told stories of how the French treated their slaves with more kindness than the British or the Americans. He was told that an African could live like a man in France. His father's stories took on new meaning when the young Bullard experienced the terror of mob violence in Georgia, when a lynch mob of masked men came to his house looking for his father. Bullard, as recounted in his unpublished memoirs, inserted in a book written by P. J. Carisella and James W. Ryan entitled *The Black Swallow of Death,* made his decision, while his entire family hid from the lynching party, to leave Georgia for France.[12]

By most accounts, the young Bullard was between eight and eleven years of age when he ran away from Columbus.[13] His sojourn from Columbus took him to various cities in the South, where he took on odd jobs to earn money for his journey to France. He survived by working as a stable hand and as a race horse jockey. After two years of this nomadic life, Eugene arrived in Newport News, Virginia, selected a cargo ship, and hid in a lifeboat. Fortunately for young Bullard, the vessel, a German cargo ship, was headed for Europe. He was discovered when the ship was at sea and was forced to work in the galley.

Eugene was put ashore to fend for himself in Aberdeen, Scotland. He survived in the seaside trading town by dancing for money and acting as a look out for gamblers.[14] He somehow latched on to a traveling amusement show and ended up in Liverpool, England, working at a gymnasium for prize fighters.[15] He became interested in boxing, and secured a manager by the name of Aaron Brown, who went by the fight name of the "Dixie Kid." Young Bullard participated in several boxing matches in Liverpool and London, England, and once fought in North Africa and in France.

While based as a boxer in London, Bullard met Jack Johnson and Bob Scanlon. All three happened to be residing at the same boarding house.[16] Johnson and Scanlon were among the first adult Negro males to take an interest in the teenaged Bullard since he had left home. Johnson shared boxing secrets and, by example, the material facts of life, lessons that Bullard would never forget. Although there is no data to verify that Bullard was aware of Scanlon's experience, it appears reasonable that Bullard knew of Scanlon's flying activity and, possibly, participated in the construction and in the flying of the plane.

With his limited boxing experience, Bullard performed only once in France and shortly after the fight, his boxing troupe returned to London. Saddened by his lost opportunity to stay in France, his longtime goal, Bullard investigated ways of returning to France. Bullard received his chance when a traveling minstrel troupe in London allowed him to join them for their next set of shows which happened to be in Paris, in late 1913.[17] Young Bullard had finally made it to Paris, and now he tried to secure some boxing dates for petty cash. He ended up doing odd jobs between fights and was in Paris during Johnson's championship fight with Moran and was there when World War I began.

Paris was where Bullard wanted to be, where his father had said he could live like a human being, with some respect. African Americans could move around Paris relatively free of the daily humiliation of forced segregation that they encountered in America. This lifestyle, for many African Americans who visited Paris during the early part of the twentieth century, was thought to be a relief, if not an enlightening experience. Consequently, the decision whether to return to America in 1914, or to remain and fight for democracy for a former slave-trading country that now treated descendants of slaves with a modicum of decency, was emotionally difficult, yet intellectually simple. Eugene Bullard and Bob Scanlon would join the French Foreign Legion and fight on behalf of France. They rationalized that they probably had a greater chance of surviving a foreign war in a foreign country than surviving in America.[18]

Unlike any other war in the history of man, this particular war would be the first to feature the utilization of weaponry of mass destruction. Chemical warfare, fire cannons, guns with 80 millimeter shells, tanks with cannons and machine guns, and airplanes with machine guns and bombs would be used extensively in offensive maneuvers designed to kill thousands of people. Millions of lives would be lost on several continents.[19] Young Bullard and Scanlon had no idea of the magnitude of the human violence and the loss of life they were to witness, but they had tasted enough freedom in France to take the chance of dying for her.

In October 1914, Bullard, Scanlon, and, according to *The Crisis* magazine, approximately ten other African Americans volunteered for service in the French Foreign Legion.[20] They received training for the next month and then were assigned to the Marching Regiment of the Foreign Legion. The French Foreign Legion was an organization that operated with an army of misfits, criminals, and men who sought adventure. The Foreign Legion was made up of several nationalities, representing several races. Although the Legion had no policy of segregation of the races, men of common nationality or race were often assigned to the same division. All of the African Americans, including Bullard and Scanlon, were assigned to a division with Moroccans.[21]

By December 1914, this division reached the battlefront and was engaged in a skirmish to capture the Artois Ridge, a crucial part of the German rail system. Early in 1915, the division was engaged in hand-to-hand combat over Hill 119 in Souchez and the Labyrinth near the Alsace Front.[22]

Later that summer, the Marching Regiment was merged into the 1st Regiment, and Bullard and Scanlon, along with other African Americans, were, again, placed in a separate division with the Moroccans. Later, in the fall of 1915, the division was involved in an intensive and bloody battle at Champagne, which included heavy shelling and machine gun fire. There were many losses in the 1st Regiment and in the Moroccan Division. According to *The Crisis*, all of the African Americans were killed.[23] It was later reported, however, that Bullard was alive.[24] *The Crisis* reported that Scanlon died after being shot by a German while he assaulted German soldiers with his fists.[25] Bullard received a head wound from shell fragments, and he claimed in his memoirs, that he and Scanlon were the only African Americans in the Moroccan division to survive the Champagne conflict.[26] Bullard also reported seeing Scanlon alive as late as 1940.

Shortly after the battle at Champagne, the French Foreign Legion was disengaged and its soldiers, including Americans, were released and given the option to volunteer for service in the French Infantry. White Americans, however, who had expressed an earlier interest in flying were invited to volunteer in the French Flying Corps. A few Americans received pilot training, and some eventually served in the French Flying Corps.[27]

By this time in late 1915, Norman Prince was back in France, flying as a bombardier for a French squadron, but he continued to pursue his dream of an American Volunteer Squadron in the French Flying Corps. He enlisted the aide of the director of the American Volunteer Ambulance Service, Edmund Gross. Mr. Gross was very receptive to Prince's idea and arranged meetings with influential members of the French government and the American ambassadors. Once the French officials and representatives of the American government were convinced that international laws pertaining to neutrality were not violated with the establishment of an American Volunteer Squadron, the preliminary plans for such a squadron were approved. The Vanderbilts agreed to furnish $20,000 for the flyers' pay, uniforms, furloughs, and medals. Mr. Gross was appointed the fiduciary agent.[28]

By March 1916, the white Americans who had been approached in 1914 by Norman Prince, and those who had volunteered for the French Foreign Legion and the Flying Corps, were transferred to the newly established Escadrille American, N. 124. These men, William Thaw, Elliot Cowdin, Bert Hall, Victor Chapman, Kiffen Rockwell, and James McConnel, would make up the nucleus of what would become the renowned Lafayette Escadrille.[29] Eugene Bullard and Bob Scanlon, the two African Americans approached by Prince, were not invited or transferred to the Escadrille American. There was speculation that Gross did not care to have African Americans in his employ.[30] When there were African Americans available in Paris to drive ambulances, he chose not to hire them. There was also speculation that the members of the new flying squadron, many of whom were from the South, would protest the presence of African Americans with equal status. Consequently, Bullard and Scanlon volunteered to be transferred to the French Infantry.

The two African-American veterans of the French Foreign Legion were assigned to the 170th Infantry of the French Army, and Bullard was promoted to Corporal. Their regiment consisted of Moroccans and Algerians. The French, at this point in the war, enjoyed the luxury of the full participation of African men from French colonies, who fought in defense of France. Although France, unlike Germany and Great Britain, who did not pay Africans to fight other African men in their respective East African colonies, according to W. E. B. DuBois in "An

Essay Toward a History of the Black Man in the Great War," the French did employ a great number of Africans on the European continent during World War I. Approximately 310,000 African men from the French colonies fought on French and Belgian soil.[31]

By March 1916, the 170th Infantry had moved to Verdun and was engaged in the most ferocious assault by the German Army at that time in the war. Germany's objective was to terminate as much enemy manpower as possible. The 170th was attacked by the German troops in a town called Vaux, nestled in the mountains of d'Haudremont. Under intense shelling, the shelter that housed a part of the regiment was hit and collapsed, and Bullard, according to his memoirs, received a head wound and lost a good many of his teeth.[32]

Later in the month, the 170th was ordered to defend Fort Douaumont, in Verdun, from a German offensive. Bullard was assigned a machine-gun set up outside the Fort. The action, as Bullard described it in an article by Will Irwin in the 15 July 1916 issue of *The Saturday Evening Post*, was perpetual, with waves of Germans being cut down by machine-gun fire and waves of German troops replacing those cut down.[33] Bullard's machine-gun unit was overwhelmed, and they had to make their way back to the fort. Along the way, they had to move from shell hole to shell hole, away from the German gunfire. The German advance was so fast that Bullard was forced to hide in one shell hole, where he surprised a German soldier by jumping out of the hole and shooting the soldier in the chest.

By the time he arrived at the fort, the Germans were firing their large guns at it. Later that night, as Bullard slept, a shell exploded in the house, killing or wounding most of the men. Bullard received a thigh wound and head cuts, but was able to leave the compound to search for medical assistance. When he returned with the medical help, he was cited the French Order of the Day, which is an honorable mention for the *croix de guerre*, for securing medical help for other men while he was, himself, wounded.[34]

Bullard was ordered to a makeshift military hospital to be treated for his leg and head wounds. While he was recuperating, Bullard received the *croix de guerre*. He also received his disability discharge from the 170th Regiment. He was faced with yet another situation where he had to choose between returning to America and remaining in France. While in the hospital, he was fortunate to meet the area commander for the French Flying Corps, who was visiting wounded men from his squadron. When asked about his future plans, Bullard told the commander that he would like to be a pilot.[35] The commander promised that he would assist Bullard in gaining admittance to the Flying Corps.

In October 1916, Bullard began his training as an aerial gunner and, shortly afterward, was transferred to the flight school in Tours. By May 1917, he had received his pilot's license. He was transferred to Chateauroux for advanced training on more sophisticated French fighter planes, such as the Caudron G-4 and the Nieuports N-24's which were the primary planes used by the Flying Corps. According to historian and journalist J. A. Rogers, France had already employed Africans as pilots and antiaircraft officers, but Bullard became the first known American of African descent to qualify as a military pilot.[36]

Bullard was kept in advanced training for four months, an unusual amount of time for a certified pilot in the French Flying Corps. He spent most of his time as a quartermaster in a barracks for Americans training on French planes. He saw several white American pilots who arrived after him matriculate through the advanced program, while he remained a quartermaster. In his memoirs in *The Black Swallow of Death,* Bullard stated that he believed that Edmund Gross of the Ambulance Service did not want African Americans in the French Flying Corps for fear that the corps would assign Bullard to the famed Lafayette Escadrille, therefore destroying the myths of African inferiority that the Americans had promoted in France.[37]

Bullard's assumptions were probably accurate. As soon as the first African-American combat soldiers arrived on French soil, white officers, including some commanding generals, such as General C. C. Ballou and others began to degrade the African as a soldier and depict him as a rapist, a natural criminal, cowardly, and unintelligent, not unlike the Senegalese troops used by the French command. The French army, appreciative and in great need of American assistance in the war, had to be tolerant of American racial bigotry, and therefore obliged, in Bullard's case. The French army, however, was also aware of the heroic efforts of their Senegalese, Moroccan, and other troops of Africa. The French Army Corps and the French Flying Corps needed assistance from every capable source, regardless of color, and when that need became critical, they insisted on that manpower. Consequently, in August 1917, Bullard was sent to the front lines to Escadrille Spad 93 of the French Flying Corps.

France's only African-American pilot began flying missions and sorties for the French Flying Corps. He was involved in several dogfights with German aircraft and was credited with destroying two and inflicting heavy damage to a third.[38] Bullard managed to escape injury on several occasions, proving that he was as adept as any French or Allied pilot at handling complex machinery.

By the time Bullard had completed his initial flight training, the United States government had declared war on Germany and had dispatched the administration of its Air Service of the American Expeditionary Force to Paris. The Air Service Operations, under the command of Brig. Gen. Benjamin Foulois, had no American planes or equipment and, therefore, Spads and Nieuports were purchased from the French. In addition, the Air Service had arrived with only 112 pilots and 300 enlisted men, most of whom had no combat experience.[39]

Over a one-year period, from 1916 to 1917, the French Service trained and used over two hundred American pilots.[40] By the fall of 1917, when Bullard was flying combat missions, over 150 of the Americans were still available to serve the United States, and were interested in commissions in the American Air Service. All of the white American pilots then serving in the French Service Aeronautique (French Flying Corps), were offered commissions, contingent on successful completion of physical examinations. Of the 150 pilots who were still available, 94 accepted commissions in the Air Service, 26 took commissions in the Navy, and 32 chose to remain with the French escadrilles.[41]

Although he had fled the bigotry and brutality of America, Bullard applied for a commission in the Air Service. Unfortunately, Bullard never received a reply from them. He could not understand the rationale for the rejection from his home country, in light of his status as a pilot in the French Service Aeronautique. He had combat experience, and he was a certified pilot, using the same planes that the U.S. Air Service was purchasing from French airplane manufacturers.

The only rationale that Bullard found legitimate was that the Air Service command did not want any African-American pilots. Certainly, the Air Service could have benefited from Bullard's experience and expertise. What Bullard may not have known was the extent of the irrational bigotry in the Air Service that permeated the War Department and the American Expeditionary Forces Command. The role of the African-American combat officer would be systematically degraded and eliminated over the duration of the war and during the postwar period.

The pain of being rejected by his home country was buffeted by the high regard that the French had for Bullard's services. He continued to fly for his Escadrille. After the rejection, however, Bullard never again considered the United States as his country. He flew for France until November 1917, when he was discharged from the Service Aeronautique over a disagreement with a superior officer.[42] After Bullard, there were no known African-American pilots in the Allied

Forces for the duration of World War I. Bullard was demoted to the French Infantry, 170th Regiment, where he served out the war as a stevedore and a quartermaster.

The significance of Bullard's accomplishments can best be appreciated by a comparison with his African peers in America. When President Woodrow Wilson signed the Congressional Declaration of War against Germany on 6 April 1917, there were 20,000 African-Americans soldiers on active duty in the regular army and the National Guard regiments.[43] About 10,000 of these soldiers were members of four units within the regular army: the 9th and 10th Cavalry and the 24th and 25th infantries. The balance of the 20,000 African troops served in colored national guard regiments in various states.

The first unit called to service in the United States after the declaration of war was the First Separate Battalion of the District of Columbia Infantry National Guard.[44] This all black unit, commanded by an African-American officer, Maj. James E. Walker, assembled for instruction on 25 March 1917. Their instructions were to guard the White House grounds, the Washington, D.C. water system, and the power plants of the Washington, D.C. area from possible foreign sabotage.[45] Shortly after the declaration of war, young African-American men flocked to induction stations to volunteer for the draft. In a matter of weeks, the four regular army units reached their manpower quotas. By 5 August 1917, all seven of the colored national guard regiments were activated for service.[46] They were the First Separate Company, Maryland; the First Separate Company, Connecticut; the First Separate Company, Massachusetts; the Ninth Separate Battalion, Ohio; the Eighth Illinois Regiment; and the Fifteenth New York Regiment.

After Congress passed the Selective Service Law on May 18th of the same year, 740,000 African men (approximately 8 percent of the total registration population) registered for the draft. According to the first Negro special advisor to the Secretary of War, Emmet J. Scott, in *Scott's Official History of the American Negro in the World War*, 36 percent of all African Americans who registered on registration day were certified and inducted into the U.S. Army. During the course of the war over 370,000 African-American men were drafted, and approximately 200,000 participated in the hostilities in Europe.[47] The existing regular army units were kept intact, but were, oddly enough, kept out of combat in the war. The colored national guard units were either merged into Infantry regiments or were assigned to the two African divisions set up by the War Department.

There was evidence to suggest that the War Department desired to limit the role of African Americans in the war. This particular disposition was inconsistent with England and France's positions on utilizing every possible source of manpower. England and France, both into the fourth year of the war, had lost thousands of men, and were desperate to use all of the troops that America could muster, regardless of race. Although the War Department eventually approved the brigading of African-American regiments with French units, it elected to exercise control over its African-American soldiers, with no clear agenda other than to discredit and demoralize them.[48] Several actions support this contention.

First, the War Department kept the four African regular army units out of the war. These soldiers were combat-ready and had excellent service records, and the War Department may have been fearful of their potential for success. The War Department was also weary of the 24th and 25th regiments' reactions to hostile white officers. In Houston, in 1917, after receiving long-term abuse and threats from local whites, unarmed African-American soldiers of the 24th Infantry retaliated by securing guns and killing seventeen of their alleged tormentors.[49] Also in the minds of the War Department was the alleged attack by African-American soldiers on hostile whites in Brownsville, Texas in 1906.

Second, Col. Charles Young, the highest ranking African-American officer in the regular army with command experience, was forced to retire shortly after the United States declared war. The War Department cited high blood pressure as the reason for Colonel Young's retirement.[50] The prevailing thought in the African community was that the War Department was planning an African-American division and did not want Colonel Young to command this unit. It was standard War Department procedure to promote colonels in command of a division to the rank of general in time of war. Colonel Young protested his forced retirement by riding horseback from Ohio to Washington, D.C. The War Department persisted, and Colonel Young saw no action in the war. The War Department did recall him to active duty, however, five days prior to the Armistice, to command the Ohio National Guard. The second ranking African-American officer with command experience in the regular army, Capt. Benjamin Oliver Davis, was assigned to duty in the Philippines with the 9th Cavalry and temporarily promoted to lieutenant colonel.

Third, even with the planning of an African-American division, the War Department made no provision for the training of African-American officers in its fourteen Officers' Training Camps. Members of the civil rights community, led by Dr. Joel E. Spingarn of the NAACP, and by the African-American student body from colleges and universities such as Howard, Lincoln, Fisk, Atlanta, Morehouse, Hampton, Virginia Union, Morgan, and Tuskegee, formed a Central Committee of African College Men to vigorously protest the segregation and exclusion of African Americans from Officers' Training Camps.[51] The Central Committee and the NAACP lobbied Congress and the War Department for admittance into the Officers' Camps. Finally, the War Department, in an attempt to minimize any opportunity for German propaganda to split the American people, relented and requested names of African-American officer candidates from the African-American colleges and universities, with the intent of establishing a Negro Officers' Training Camp.

Although a segregated training camp for officers was inconsistent with the NAACP's integrationist doctrine, and a target for Negro newspapers against another "Jim Crow" establishment, the NAACP, the Central Committee, and the African-American community rationalized that a separate officers' camp for African Americans was better than none. They felt that they had won the first fight in the war. The War Department established a Negro Officers' Camp at Des Moines, Iowa. Over 600 African-American men were commissioned as officers; none, however, with a rank higher than captain.[52] Very few of these men were ever to command African-American troops in combat.

Fourth, the War Department established, in an unprecedented and unorganized fashion, two African-American divisions, the 92nd and the 93rd. The 92nd was composed of four regiments, the 365th, 366th, 367th, and 368th, which were manned primarily by enlisted men. Unlike soldiers in any other American Expeditionary Force's unit, the men in the 92nd division were trained in seven different training camps across the Midwest and the East, and were never trained together, or even brought together as a division, until they were in France.[53]

The 92nd's Table of Organization was staffed with a bigoted white command structure disrespectful and intolerant of African-American enlisted men and, especially, African-American officers. The commanding officer, Gen. C. C. Ballou, allowed the white officers to verbally abuse the soldiers with racial epithets and unnecessary threats. When African-American officers graduated from the Negro Officers' Training Camp, they were assigned to the 92nd division camps. These officers endured humiliation from the white officers, and even General Ballou, himself, who issued "Base Order #35" to restrict the social interaction of the African-American officers of the division with the white citizens and to reinforce segregated customs of the towns where the camps were established.[54] According to reports in *Scott's Official History of the American Negro in the World War* and DuBois's "History of the Black Man in the Great War," General Ballou was not above embarrassing the

African-American officers in front of African-American troops, which served to undermine the officers' effectiveness.[55]

After the 92nd Division arrived in France, on 20 June 1918, General Ballou instituted "Base Order #35" restrictions for the officers. His white officers proceeded to plant myths and falsehoods among their French allies about the African Americans' alleged threats to rape white women. There were fourteen rape trials during the 92nd's tour of duty and only one African American, who was not an officer, and was not assigned to the 92nd, was found guilty and executed. In addition to the social restrictions and attempts to discredit African-American officers, Ballou's command set up "Efficiency Boards" to determine the quality of the officers in the various units. Over fifty African-American officers were demoted or reassigned, simply on the basis of race, and fifty new white officers were shipped in to replace them.[56]

The division completed their training in early August 1918 and were sent to a "quiet sector" in Vosges, where they encountered little German resistance. In late September, they were ordered to the Argonne Forest to play a secondary role in the Allied push to corner the Germans in their exodus out of France. One regiment of the division, the 368th, was ordered to participate in the offensive. Since the regiment was not equipped for front-line fighting, the regiment, according to Maj. M. A. Elser, commander of one of the combat battalions, was to provide "combat liaison duty" with a French Division and another white American Division.[57]

The 368th, however was ordered to front-line battle with no artillery support, no grenades, no signal flares, no maps, no general instruction, and only sixteen shears strong enough to cut through German barbed wire. Elser's battalion attacked without any directive or objective, and his unit was met with heavy machine-gun fire. Elser's battalion was forced to retreat after two days, and Elser was hospitalized for "shell shock." Another battalion, under the command of Maj. B. F. Norris, was sent "over the top" but it, too, fell victim to the German machine-gun, mortar, and artillery attacks, and was forced to retreat. In the ensuing retreat and confusion there were heavy losses, and many men suffered from being gassed.

When these battalions were relieved, Major Norris charged his African-American line officers with cowardice and abandonment of position, and ordered a court martial. All officers were acquitted by General Headquarters.[58] The damage caused by the attempted court martial, however, had festered and left many white officers secure in spreading the myth that African-American soldiers, in general, and officers, in particular, were unfit, on the basis of race, to serve in wartime.

The 93rd Provisional Division, unlike the 92nd, was composed of regiments established from the colored national guard units. The 369th Regiment was formed from the 15th New York; the 370th Regiment from the 8th Illinois; and the 371st and 372nd Regiments from the First Separate Battalion, District of Columbia Infantry; Company L, Sixth Massachusetts Infantry; the First Separate Company, Connecticut; the Ninth Separate Battalion, Ohio; and the First Separate Company, Maryland. These units were already commanded by African Americans, and had military experience.[59] This division also had its regiments trained in different camps, but unlike the 92nd, the regiments were never officially organized into a combat division and, therefore, the separate regiments went to Europe as separate and unattached fighting units of the American Expeditionary Forces.[60]

These African-American regiments, needing less training than enlisted men and officers of the 92nd, were part of America's answer to France's need for troop reinforcements, and were shipped to France as early as January 1918. Once the regiments arrived, they were attached to French Army Corps units. The African-American regiments, however, were forced to learn how to operate French equipment and to learn French military instruction. This was not easy, and took longer than expected, and, consequently, placed many black troops at a distinct disadvantage, which proved fatal.

The first fighting Negro Regiment, and one of the first American fighting units to reach France, was the 369th. The unit had been training in South Carolina when a skirmish between the soldiers of the 369th and the employees of a local hotel ensued. After the confrontation, the local government asked the War Department to relocate the regiment to another area. Rather than moving the 369th to another camp to complete their training, the War Department decided to send the 369th overseas.[61]

They arrived in France in January of 1918, were immediately brigaded with a French Army Corps unit, and spent the next several months learning French weaponry, French military commands, and other forms of French military life. The 369th were engaged in their first major battle in September of 1918, at Champagne. They suffered heavy casualties. Over 200 men were killed and several hundred were wounded by gas and shrapnel. The blame for the dead and wounded was placed on the so-called inefficiency of African-American officers and, therefore, five officers of the regiment were transferred to the 92nd Division.[62]

The 370th Regiment, formerly the 8th Illinois Colored National Guard Unit, was the most experienced unit in the proposed Provisional

93rd Division. The unit had African-American field officers and company officers with military service in Mexico in 1916, and was the only combat unit commanded by a African American, Col. Franklin A. Dennison.[63] The 370th arrived in France in late April 1918, and was assigned to a French Division. The unit fought with three French divisions in St. Mihiel and the Argonne Forest. The unit succeeded in capturing German strongholds, such as Mt. Dessinges and other occupied territory, including those in Belgium. They held an entire sector on the Canal L'Oise et Aisne without help. As in the case of other African-American combat field officers, the unit commander, Colonel Dennison was eventually reassigned, sent back to the United States, and replaced by a white officer.[64]

Fifth, only 40 percent of the 200,000-plus African-American men in the American Expeditionary Force in France were involved in combat. Approximately, 60 percent of the African Americans in the AEF overseas were used as common laborers or stevedores.[65] These men built roads and bridges, loaded and unloaded tons of cargo, buried the dead, and assembled automobiles, trucks, ships, and airplanes. The work was very tedious and was completed under duress in less that desirable conditions. Most, if not all, of the men were draftees, and were supervised, primarily and often brutally, by southern white officers who, according to the War Department, were best suited to command African Americans.[66]

Sixth, the War Department did not allow African Americans to serve in the Air Service and the Marine Corps.[67] The Navy only accepted African Americans as cooks and valets. Therefore, Bullard, had he remained in Georgia, would probably have been drafted and assigned to an African-American labor regiment. Having chosen to remain in France, Bullard had acquired a position that both African Americans and white Americans coveted.

Despite their lack of coordinated training, the bigoted white commanding officers, the imported "Jim Crow" regulations, the mass allegations of rape, and the systematic humiliation and elimination of African-American officers, Bullard's African-American peers in the American Expeditionary Force duplicated his success in battle. The men of the 369th spent a record 191 days on the front lines against the Germans. The 369th, as a regiment, received the *croix de guerre* and 171 men received citations for the *croix de guerre* and the Distinguished Service Cross. The 371st and 372nd regiments proudly received four citations for the Legion of Honor, the *croix de guerre* for the entire regiment, and twenty-six citations for the Distinguished Service Cross. The 370th Regiment boasted twenty-one citations for the Distinguished

Service Cross, one citation for the Distinguished Service Medal and over sixty citations for the *croix de guerre*.[68]

After Armistice Day, 11 November 1918, when hostilities ended, Bullard chose to remain in France. It may have been a wise decision. The African Americans who served in the Negro division and regiments of the American Expeditionary Force returned home to a heroes' welcome, especially in the African-American communities. The adulation was short-lived, however. African Americans, especially World War I veterans, were subjected to mob murder and other forms of mob violence. In the last year of the war and the year immediately following the war, over one hundred African Americans were lynched. It appeared that democracy escaped those African Americans who fought for democracy in France and in America.[69]

Bullard returned to boxing, and developed an interest in the jazz music he heard from other African Americans who chose to remain in France. He became a drummer in a jazz band and was able to persuade the Montmartre nightclub owner of Zelli's to hire his band, which he called Zelli's Zig Zag Band. In the mid-twenties, he was the owner of his own club, called Le Grand Duc. It was at this club that Bullard extended a helping hand to American Negro musicians in Paris. He provided employment for fledgling stars, such as Florence Jones, and was at the Paris docks when Ada "Bricktop" Smith arrived to work in his club. Langston Hughes worked at Le Grand Duc as a busboy.[70] His club became the top after-hours place for Negro entertainers, and attracted a rich international clientele, including John Emerson, Anita Loos, William Leeds, the Dolly Sisters, and other celebrities.[71]

Bullard married a wealthy French woman, Marcelle Straumann, in 1923, and became the father of two daughters. The early thirties brought depression and hard times for his family. He and his wife divorced. She died a short time later.[72]

He opened another club and gymnasium called L'escadrille. When the Nazis occupied Paris in 1940, however, they discovered Bullard's involvement in the French Resistance and confiscated his club, forcing him to leave Paris. Unfortunately, he was forced to leave his daughters with his Resistance contacts.[73]

He joined the French Army and fought at Orleans, where he received a shrapnel wound in the back. He was smuggled by the American consul out of France to Spain, and through Portugal. From Lisbon, he caught a passenger boat back to New York and, upon arrival, was hospitalized and treated for his wound. He spent the next several months working as a longshoreman to raise enough money to get his daughters back. He finally reunited with his daughters in late 1940. He spent the next several years at odd jobs in New York, and made several trips to Paris to reclaim his nightclub. Although he received small compensation, his businesses were lost.[74]

He spent his remaining years in New York involved in various forms of employment, including a two-year stint in the RCA Building in New York, from 1957 through 1959. He even appeared on the NBC morning television program "Today," with host Dave Garaway.[75] His life did not go without rewards. In 1954, he was chosen by the French government to light the "Everlasting Flame" at the Tomb of the Unknown Soldier, and he received a total of sixteen medals and awards.

Bullard was admitted to a New York hospital in August of 1961, suffering from a serious illness, and died in October of the same year. He was buried with honors in Flushing Cemetery in a plot set aside for French war officers, a touching tribute to a man who gave so much to a country that, in his mind, stood for freedom.

Due to the racial policies in the American press, Bullard's war exploits went virtually unknown, outside of Paris. Although he was mentioned briefly in *The Crisis* and in a few biographies and history books on World War I aviation, Bullard was an anomaly, even to the Negro community. Since there were few Negro war correspondents in France, and those there were primarily covered the American Negro regiments, his presence and actions went unnoticed. The U.S. Air Service's rejection of Bullard almost guaranteed that Bullard would not have the opportunity to succeed in an all-white air service and, therefore, young African Americans would not get any notions of joining the air service. Those few African Americans who knew of Bullard, such as Howard University scholar Rayford Logan and Negro newspaper editors, such as Robert Vann of the *Pittsburgh Courier* and Robert Abbott of the *Chicago Defender*, would strenuously argue on behalf of young African Americans interested in applying for what was to become the Army Air Corps of pre-World War II.

Notes

1. P. J. Carisella and James W. Ryan, *The Black Swallow of Death* (Boston: Marborough House, 1972), 71.
2. Arthur Whitehouse, *The Years of the Sky Kings* (Garden City, N.Y.: Doubleday and Company, Inc., 1959), 146-47.
3. Herbert Molloy Mason, *The Lafayette Escadrille* (New York: Random House, 1964), 46-54.
4. James Norman Hall, *High Adventure; A Narrative of Air Fighting in France* (New York: Houghton Mifflin Co., 1929); xi-xxiii; Mason, *The Lafayette*

Escadrille, 46-54; Alexander McKee, *The Friendless Sky: The Story of Air Combat in World War I* (New York: William Morrow and Company, 1964), 99-107.

5. John Hope Franklin, *From Slavery to Freedom*, 3d ed. (New York: Vintage Books, 1969), 439-55.

6. Ibid., 434-40.

7. Arthur Whitehouse, *Legion of the Lafayette* (Garden City, New York: Doubleday and Company, Inc., 1962), 310-11.

8. Jack Johnson, *Jack Johnson In the Ring and Out, Autobiography* (London: Proteus Publishing, 1977), 57; Randy Roberts, *Papa Jack: Jack Johnson and the Era of White Hopes* (New York: The Free Press, 1983), 192-93. Bob Scanlon may have fought under the name of Bob Armstrong.

9. W. E. B. DuBois, "The Color Line," *The Crisis* 11 (December 1915): 65.

10. Whitehouse, *The Years of the Sky Kings*, 146.

11. Carisella and Ryan, *The Black Swallow*, 37-67.

12. Ibid., 26-35.

13. Ibid., 34-35; Mary A. Smith, "The Incredible Life of Monsieur Bullard," *Ebony* 23 (December 1967): 120-28; John Gatski, "Enlisted History: Eugene J. Bullard, The First Black Combat Pilot." *Sargeants Magazine* (January/February 1988): 42-43; "Obituary," *New York Herald Tribune*, 14 October 1961, 42.

14. Carisella and Ryan, *The Black Swallow*, 57.

15. Ibid., 61.

16. Ibid., 62-63; Roberts, *Papa Jack*, 119-20, 192-93; Johnson, *Autobiography*, 57; Gatski, "Eugene J. Bullard," 42-43; Smith, "The Incredible Life of Monsieur Bullard," 125.

17. Carisella and Ryan, *The Black Swallow*, 69-70; Smith, "The Incredible Life of Monsieur Bullard," 125.

18. Carisella and Ryan, *The Black Swallow*, 69-70.

19. W. E. B. DuBois, "An Essay Toward a History of the Black Man in the Great War," *The Crisis* 18 (February 1919): 63-90.

20. W. E. B. DuBois, "The Color Line," *The Crisis* 11 (December 1915): 65.

21. Carisella and Ryan, *The Black Swallow*, 81.

22. Ibid., 91.

23. DuBois, "The Color Line," 65; W. E. B. DuBois, "The Horizon," *The Crisis* 17/18 (January 1919): 137.

24. DuBois, "The Horizon," *The Crisis* 16 (January 1918): 145.

25. Ibid., 137.

26. Carisella and Ryan, *The Black Swallow*, 112-13.

27. Whitehouse, *The Years of the Sky Kings*, 146-47; McKee, *The Friendless Sky*, 99-100.

28. Hall, *High Adventure*, xi-xxiii; Mason, *The Lafayette Escadrille*, 46-54.

29. McKee, *The Friendless Sky*, 99-100; Hall, *High Adventure*, xi-xxiii.

30. Carisella and Ryan, *The Black Swallow*, 161.

31. DuBois, "An Essay Toward a History," 64.

32. Carisella and Ryan, *The Black Swallow*, 120-25.
33. Will Irwin, "Flashes from the War Zone," *Saturday Evening Post*, 15 July 1916, 12.
34. Ibid., 12.
35. Carisella and Ryan, *The Black Swallow*, 138-39.
36. J. A. Rogers, "Your History," *Pittsburgh Courier*, 9 September 1939, 7.
37. Carisella and Ryan, *The Black Swallow*, 156-58, 161.
38. Ibid., 187.
39. Carroll V. Glinis Jr., *The Compact History of the United States Air Force* (New York: Hawthorne Books, Inc., 1963), 72, 80-81. Herbert Molloy Mason, *The United States Air Force: A Turbulent History* (New York: Mason Charter, 1976), 53, 60-64.
40. Mason, *The United States Air Force*, 60-64.
41. Ibid., 61.
42. Carisella and Ryan, *The Black Swallow*, 198.
43. Emmet J. Scott, *Scott's Official History of the American Negro in the World War*, 2d ed. (New York: Arno Press, 1969), 32.
44. Ibid., 35.
45. Ibid., 36.
46. Ibid., 34.
47. Ibid., 32, 67; DuBois, "An Essay Toward a History," 64, 81.
48. DuBois, "An Essay Toward a History," 67-68.
49. Franklin, *From Slavery to Freedom*, 460; W. E. B. DuBois, *Dusk of Dawn: An Essay Toward an Autobiography of a Race Concept* (New York: Schockon Books, 1968), 252; Scott, *Scott's Official History*, 94; James H. Brewer, "Robert Lee Vann, Democrat or Republican: An Exponent of Loose Leaf Politics," *Negro History Bulletin* 21 (February 1958): 100-3 in Bernard Sternsher, ed., *The Negro in Depression and War; Prelude to Revolution, 1930-1945* (Chicago: Quadrange Books, 1969), 244.
50. DuBois, *Dusk of Dawn*, 248-51; DuBois, "An Essay Toward a History," 67-69; Scott, *Scott's Official History*, 82-89.
51. DuBois, *Dusk of Dawn*, 248-51; DuBois, "An Essay Toward a History," 67-69; Scott, *Scott's Official History*, 82-89.
52. Scott, *Scott's Official History*, 90-91; DuBois, *Dusk of Dawn*, 251.
53. DuBois, "An Essay Toward a History," 69; Franklin, *From Slavery to Freedom*, 458; Scott, *Scott's Official History*, 130.
54. DuBois, "An Essay Toward a History," 70; Scott, *Scott's Official History*, 96-97.
55. DuBois, "An Essay Toward a History," 70.
56. Ibid., 71.
57. Ibid., 80-81.
58. Ibid., 81.
59. Scott, *Scott's Official History*, 34.
60. Ibid., 215, DuBois, "An Essay Toward a History," 72.
61. Franklin, *From Slavery to Freedom*, 460-61.

62. Scott, *Scott's Official History*, 213; DuBois, "An Essay Toward a History," 73.
63. Scott, *Scott's Official History*, 215.
64. DuBois, "An Essay Toward a History," 78.
65. Ibid., 64; Franklin, *From Slavery to Freedom*, 461-62.
66. Franklin, *From Slavery to Freedom*, 461-62.
67. Ibid., 458.
68. Ibid., 462-65; DuBois, "An Essay Toward a History," 76, 78, 83; Scott, *Scott's Official History*, 130, 203.
69. Franklin, *From Slavery to Freedom*, 480-82; Scott, *Scott's Official History*, 347.
70. Smith, "The Incredible Life of Monsieur Bullard," 125; Langston Hughes, *The Big Sea: An Autobiography of Langston Hughes* (New York: A. A. Knopf, 1940), 157-87.
71. Hughes, *The Big Sea*, 157-87.
72. Smith, "The Incredible Life of Monsieur Bullard," 125.
73. Ibid., 127; Carisella and Ryan, *The Black Swallow*, 229-36.
74. Smith, "The Incredible Life of Monsieur Bullard," 128; Carisella and Ryan, *The Black Swallow*, 247-48.
75. Smith, "The Incredible Life of Monsieur Bullard," 128; Carisella and Ryan, *The Black Swallow*, 256.

Chapter 2

Phoenix

Even the racism and segregation in Chicago that precipitated the riots of 1919 could not stop a twenty-six-year-old Negro manicurist and chili parlor owner from chasing her dream of becoming a pilot. Like Eugene Bullard, Bessie Coleman was a forward thinker who embraced the new and dangerous vocation of aviation at a time when Negroes and women, and especially, Negro women, were not taken seriously. Like Bullard, Ms. Coleman's achievements were obscured by geography and racism. Ms. Coleman's success was also limited by a short lifespan, and by sexism. Bessie Coleman died in a plane accident in 1926.

Bessie Coleman was born, circa 1893, in Atlanta, Texas. According to the memoirs of her sister, Elois Patterson, Bessie was well-read and an excellent student, good enough to attend Langston Industrial College for one semester. Although Ms. Coleman earned her tuition and board by washing and ironing laundry, she could not afford to continue at Langston.[1] Just prior to World War I, she moved to Chicago to stay with a member of her family and enrolled in the Burnham School of Beauty Culture. At the Burnham School, she successfully completed a manicurist course and secured a job at the White Sox Barbershop in the Loop. Not long after, she opened a chili stand on the south side, on Thirty-fifth and Indiana, to supplement her income.[2]

While working at the White Sox Barbershop, Bessie met many white men of note. Veterans of World War I, professional baseball players, businessmen, and probably men with some knowledge of aviation. If she met veteran flyers from the American Expeditionary Force, they probably would have talked about Eugene Bullard, the only African American who flew combat planes, and one who had a flamboyant reputation around Paris. Whether this was the case or not, Bessie decided to learn how to pilot an airplane.

Bessie tried to gain admittance to several flight schools in the Chicago area. Chicago, in 1919, was not ready for a Negro woman pilot, and no school would risk its reputation by becoming the first flight school to admit a Negro, especially a woman. After being rejected by all of the schools in the Chicago area, Ms. Coleman, at the suggestion of one of her customers, met with Robert Abbott, the publisher and editor of the *Chicago Defender*.[3]

Abbott was very supportive of Negroes attempting nonstereotypical careers. The Chicago editor was truly an integrationist. He encouraged Bessie to pursue a career in aviation, but to seek instruction in France, where a Negro woman would be treated with more respect and tolerance. He also advised Bessie to learn the French language.[4] Abbott secured names and addresses of flight schools in Paris for Bessie.

To prepare for the possibility of going to France, Bessie took Abbott's advice and studied French. She also applied to aviation schools in France. When she received her first acceptance letter, she closed her chili stand, resigned her manicurist position, and left for France.

Ms. Coleman arrived in Paris in 1920 and began flight training at one of the larger flying schools, reportedly under the watchful eye of a German Ace who was employed as a test pilot by the Fokker Aircraft Company. By the end of June 1921, Bessie had earned a pilot's license, granted by the Federation Aeronautique Internationale, the only known Negro woman to hold such as license at that time.[5]

According to the Negro press releases, she gave flying exhibitions in most of the European capitols. After her brief tour of exhibitions, Bessie returned to the United States to start a barnstorming tour of flying exhibits.[6] Unfortunately, she could not secure sponsors willing to take her as a marketable flying act. She faced discrimination and sexism while attempting to rent planes. She eventually returned to Paris, where she received advanced instruction in acrobatics and parachute jumping.[7]

By the time she returned to America in 1922, she was under contract with David Behncke, the future founder of the International Airline Pilot's Association.[8] Behncke immediately booked her in an air show in Chicago, highlighting her as the only Negro woman pilot in the world who could also parachute. According to her sister's memoirs, Ms. Coleman put on a dazzling show, flying figure eights, other acrobatic moves, and parachute jumping. Dr. A. Porter Davis, a Negro physician from Kansas City, and one of the first African Americans to earn a pilot's license in America, flew to Chicago to see Bessie fly.[9]

It was during this period that Ms. Coleman spoke of starting a flying school in Chicago for Negro men and women. She realized that Negroes in the Chicago area might not have the capital to invest in such a facility, equipped with planes and mechanical equipment. To raise funds for her idea, Bessie went on a tour of air shows across the country. Most of her shows were segregated. In preparation for an air-show in her home state of Texas, however, Bessie refused to perform unless all customers entered by the same entrance.[10] Her wish was granted, since she was the star attraction, and the customers entered in the same door. Once inside, however, the Negroes and whites were seated in separate sections.

During the next two years, Bessie took on jobs ranging from flying stunts to test piloting new model planes, and advertising. It was during an advertising flight for Firestone Rubber Company in Santa Monica, California, that Bessie suffered her first serious plane accident. She reportedly suffered three fractured ribs, a double fracture of one leg, and facial lacerations. She was forced to recuperate in California for several weeks.[11]

After recovering from the accident, she returned to Chicago and did not attempt to fly for over a year. During this interim phase, she met Ida B. Wells, noted journalist and editor of the Negro newspaper, *The Chicago Bee*. The women had much in common. Both were involved in nontraditional careers usually set aside for men, and both were uncharacteristically courageous.[12] Wells gave Bessie encouragement and pledged her support in Bessie's plans for starting an aviation school for Negroes who were locked out of the white flying schools in the Midwest.

Bessie returned to flying in 1925 to raise more money for her school. She also started a series of lectures on aviation to Negro audiences. She impressed on these audiences that aviation was a new and growing industry, with room for Negroes to participate, if they took advantage of the chance to learn the technology. In late April 1926, Bessie was in Jacksonville, Florida for one of her lectures and exhibitions. She was to perform for the Jacksonville Negro Welfare League, Community Chest. Whites also wanted to view the event and, therefore Bessie demanded, and was granted, an integrated audience.[13]

The day before the event, Bessie and her friends and business associates, including her public relations director, William D. Wills, went to a Jacksonville restaurant. According to her sister's memoirs, and articles from the press, Bessie found Robert Abbott dining in the same restaurant. After pleasantries and introductions were exchanged, Abbott, allegedly, in a private conversation, confided that he did not like the company she was keeping, referring to Mr. Wills. Abbott advised Bessie not to fly with Wills the next day.[14]

On the following day, Bessie took a practice flight with Wills without her parachute, which according to her sister's memoirs, was very unlike the safety-minded Bessie.[15] It was unclear in the newspaper accounts who was at the controls, but the plane was flown to an altitude of 3,500 feet, went into a nose dive, and rolled over, tossing Bessie to her death. The plane crashed into the ground, killing Wills instantly. Before rescuers could get to the bodies, a bystander lit a cigarette and threw the match to the gasoline soaked ground, which ignited and caused the plane to explode.[16]

Various newspaper reports of the accident, including accounts in *The Chicago Defender,* claimed that the mechanisms governing the controls were jammed by a wrench. The official investigation claimed that the mechanism controlling the "stick" was "faulty," which caused the steering controls to "jam."[17]

Bessie's death and funerals, one in Florida and the other in Chicago, were widely publicized in the Negro newspapers.[18] Her death created a tremendous gap that was not to be filled for several years. Clearly, she was years ahead of her time, with an avocation for an industry that was in its infancy. Ironically, she ended up a martyr. Her death brought more attention to aviation in the Negro community than all of her previous activity. The time was right, in 1926, for someone to take up the fight to encourage the Negro to ignore racism and discrimination and get involved in a new, exciting, and dangerous vocation.

In 1921, while Bessie Coleman was learning her craft in Paris, a young man from Trinidad arrived in New York City. Hubert Fauntleroy Julian, a confident twenty-four-year-old, was immediately drawn to and taken in by the West Indian community in Harlem, especially the Jamaican community.[19] At that time in history, the West Indian community, as well as a significant number of African Americans in New York, were part of the Black Nationalist movement, which was orchestrated by a Jamaican, Marcus Garvey. By 1921, the seven-year-old organization, called the Universal Negro Improvement Association (UNIA), under the auspices of Garvey was at full strength, with a reported membership of 500,000 people.[20]

Garvey preached about being black in positive terms. He stressed to Negroes of dark complexion that they were as beautiful as any other group of Negroes, or any other race. His organization sought to magnify anything black. Africa was depicted, for the first time to many Negroes, in a positive mode, as the birthplace of science, mathematics, the arts, and philosophy.[21] It logically followed that the two independent nations controlled by Africans, Liberia and Ethiopia, would be depicted as the homeland for Negroes. Ethiopia was exalted as the holy land, because of its religious significance in the bloodline of King Solomon and direct descendant Regent Ras Tafari Makonnen. Garvey stressed that Negroes would never receive justice in America, and should consider repatriating to Liberia or Ethiopia. Garvey actually entered into negotiations with Liberia for a homestead for the UNIA within the American Protectorate.[22]

In addition to lecturing, Garvey, the self-proclaimed provisional president of UNIA, had initiated some real-life organizational units within his nation. By the time Julian arrived in New York, there were many UNIA organizations, such as the Black Starship Line, the Universal African Motor Corps, the Black Eagle Flying Corps, the Black Cross Nurses, and the Universal African Legion, a makeshift army.[23] Julian became a member of the Universal African Legion and took an interest in flying. After securing flying lessons in 1922, Julian received his student license and became an officer in Garvey's Black Eagle Flying Corps. It is not certain how many planes, if any, were owned by the UNIA, but planes could have been rented.

During this period, Julian developed a reputation as an expert flyer and adventurer. He acquired the skill of parachute jumping and exhibited the skill at every opportunity around New York. The New York newspapers dubbed him the "Black Eagle," and Julian never disputed the new moniker. On one occasion, when he did not have a permit to give an exhibition, Julian jumped from a plane circling Manhattan and opened his parachute just in time to reach the roof top of an apartment building without injuring himself. The police, who witnessed the spectacle, followed the flight of the parachute and positioned themselves on the ground, where they thought they could capture Julian. When Julian landed on the roof instead, the police, dumbfounded, had to climb several flights of stairs to the roof in order to catch him. By the time they reached the roof, Julian was gone. He emerged a few minutes later, in Harlem, to a round of applause.[24]

In America, naturally, Marcus Garvey had critics, especially the NAACP, and enemies, but none so powerful as the United States government. It was estimated that within two years, from 1919-1921, Garvey's organization had collected over $10 million for the Black Star Line, but had only spent $1 million developing it. In 1923, Garvey was indicted by the U.S. government for mail fraud, convicted, and sentenced to five years in a federal prison in Atlanta, Georgia.[25] Garvey attempted to run the UNIA from prison, but the movement would never be the same. In 1927, after serving two years, Garvey was pardoned by President Calvin Coolidge and deported to Jamaica as an undesirable alien. After a vain attempt to resuscitate the UNIA in London, Garvey died in 1940.[26]

With Garvey neutralized and the UNIA fractured, Julian had no organization to sponsor his flying and parachute-jumping exhibitions. It was at this point in the young aviator's career that he was forced to become more of a showman and an entrepreneur than an expert. In 1924, for example, Julian proclaimed that he was preparing to fly to the Liberian homeland. At that point in history, no one had ever completed a nonstop flight across the Atlantic Ocean alone.[27] Undaunted, Julian managed to secure enough money from fundraising efforts among UNIA members and sympathizers to acquire a Belanca plane, which he called "Ethiopia I."

Julian planned his takeoff from Flushing Bay for 4 July 1924. Through publicity and self-promotion, Julian was able to draw 15,000 spectators to this event. After a shaky takeoff, the bold aviator managed to get his plane in the air for a few minutes. Unfortunately, he could not gain enough altitude, and the plane stalled and glided into a crash landing in the mud, in front of a disappointed crowd.[28] Although he was injured, Julian was not deterred. After recuperating, Julian was back giving flying exhibitions and parachute jumping, and he pledged to renew his efforts to fly the Atlantic Ocean.

Julian's opportunity for international notoriety came in the summer of 1930, when he was invited by Ras Tafari Makonnen, then Regent of Ethiopia, to prepare the miniature Ethiopian Air Corps exhibition to be held as part of his coronation ceremony.[29] Ras Tafari's father, who was the king, was very ill and the younger Makonnen was to inherit the kingdom of Abyssinia. Although Makonnen had commissioned French and English advisors to develop his Air Corps, he was weary of Europeans and more disposed to working with men of color. He was supportive of the Pan African Congress' efforts and appreciative of the UNIA's reverence of his nation's status as one of two independent African nations. Makonnen, in contrast to the other leaders of African nations under European dominance, reached out to African Americans to assist him in changing the economy, educational system, military, and health care infrastructure of his nation.[30]

Hubert Julian, still a citizen of Trinidad, had little difficulty in getting to Ethiopia. He was actually invited by the Ethiopian government, through Malak Bayen, then a student at Howard University and a commissioner within Makonnen's nation. Julian accepted the offer and prepared for his trip to Ethiopia. To supplement the travel expenses provided by Bayen, Julian, as reported by the *Amsterdam News*, solicited

money from the public by presenting himself as an emissary of Ras
Tafari Makonnen.[31] This misrepresentation was not appreciated by the
Ethiopian government.[32] Commissioner Bayen was ordered to publicly
repudiate any claims that Julian had made while presenting himself as a
representative of the Ethiopian government. The Ethiopian government had just received a preview of what they were about to experience
with the "Black Eagle."

By September of 1930, however, Julian had impressed Ras Tafari
Makonnen with his flying ability and his parachute-jumping exhibitions.
Taken by Julian's talents, Makonnen commissioned him as a colonel
and commanding officer of the Ethiopian Air Corps and honored him
with the Gold Order of Menilik.[33] Julian became a celebrity in Ethiopia
and, reportedly, behaved like one.

In early November 1930, Ras Tafari Makonnen was crowned
Kodamawi Haile Selassie I, King of Ethiopia, at a $3 million coronation
ceremony in Addis Ababa. The ceremony was attended by foreign dignitaries representing several European and Western countries.[34] The
festivities gave Selassie the opportunity to show foreigners and his
Ethiopian subjects the progress made toward modernization in
Ethiopia. One of Selassie's most prized possessions was the brand new
Imperial plane, a de Haviland Gypsy Moth. The airplane, to be proudly
displayed to the visitors at the coronation, was not to be flown without
explicit instructions.

Julian, who was reported to view himself as the second-most popular
person in Ethiopia, could not resist the attention and the acclaim he
would receive for flying the King's new plane. Ignoring explicit instructions from the King regarding the plane, Julian took it out and proceeded to put on his usual flying exhibition. This time, however, he lost
control of the plane, and crash-landed within full view of the King, his
court, and visitors, destroying the imperial plane.

Fortunately, for Julian, he was not seriously hurt. Unfortunately,
Selassie, angered and embarrassed over Julian's apparent lack of discipline and respect, had the "Black Eagle" dismissed from Ethiopia.[35]

Julian returned to New York, disappointed, but not deterred from
displaying his flying and parachute-jumping ability. Unfortunately, however, some individuals in New York now doubted his flying ability, after
the widely publicized fiasco in Flushing Bay and the accident in Addis
Ababa. Rumors were circulating in New York and throughout Negro
America, that Julian was primarily a parachutist, and was a "fake flyer."[36]

This rumor would have bothered most pilots, but this type of con-
jecture only served to enhance the publicity and promotional aspects
of Julian's exhibitions. Julian had long since acquired, through his

association with the UNIA African Legion, a sense of confidence, bordering on arrogance. He presented himself as if he were royalty, which is exactly the image that Marcus Garvey wanted his followers to project. Garvey lectured on black love of self, not black self-hatred. He also spoke of self-confidence and self-determination. All of these attributes were apparent, at least on the surface, with Hubert Julian. The "Black Eagle" sold himself.

On 13 August 1931, the proud Julian removed all doubt about his flying ability. In front of a crowd of 3,000 Negroes, flying a Ballanca biplane in Wilmington, Delaware, Colonel Julian put on an unforgettable show of stunt flying and acrobatics. For an encore, he performed a double parachute drop from 2,800 feet.[37] With his usual flair for self-promotion and the dramatic, Julian told the crowd, afterward, that he was the only Negro in the country who had earned a pilot's license from the United States Department of Commerce.[38] This, of course, was not true. He also proclaimed that he planned to qualify as one of the entrants for a long-distance flight record, flying from Los Angeles to New York. He never made the flight.

Present at the exhibition was W. A. Davis, editor of *The Amsterdam News*, who professed himself to be among the doubters of Julian's ability. After viewing Julian's work, however, Davis admitted that he was proud the race had someone of Julian's talent involved in aviation.[39] Despite himself, the "Black Eagle" served as a role model for young Negroes interested in aviation.

Notes

1. Eloise Patterson, *Memoirs of the Late Bessie Coleman Aviatrix: Pioneer of the Negro Peoples in Aviation* (Washington, D.C.: Library of Congress, 1969), 7; Associated Negro Press, "Practice Flight Fatal," *Pittsburgh Courier*, 7 May 1926.
2. Enoch P. Waters, *American Diary: A Personal History of the Black Press* (Chicago: Path Press, Inc., 1987), 198; Patterson, *Memoirs*, 7.
3. Waters, *American Diary*, 178.
4. Patterson, *Memoirs*, 2; Waters, *American Diary*, 149, 150, 198.
5. Waters, *American Diary*, 198; Associated Negro Press, "Practice Flight Fatal," *Pittsburgh Courier*, 7 May 1926; Marian Foster-Downer, "Three Funerals Held for Aviatrix," *Pittsburgh Courier*, 14 May 1926.
6. Associated Negro Press, "Practice Flight Fatal," *Pittsburgh Courier*, 7 May 1926; Foster-Downer, "Three Funerals Held for Aviatrix," *Pittsburgh Courier*, 14 May 1926.
7. Waters, *American Diary*, 198.
8. Patterson, *Memoirs*, 2.

9. Ibid., 2; Waters, *American Diary*, 198.

10. Waters, *American Diary*, 98; Patterson, *Memoirs*, 3-4; Associated Negro Press, "Practice Flight Fatal, *Pittsburgh Courier*, 7 May 1926."

11. Associated Negro Press, "Practice Flight Fatal," *Pittsburgh Courier*, 7 May 1926; Patterson, *Memoirs*, 4.

12. Foster-Downer, "Three Funerals Held for Aviatrix," *Pittsburgh Courier*, 14 May 1926.

13. Patterson, *Memoirs*, 5. Waters, *American Diary*, 199; Foster-Downer, "Three Funerals Held for Aviatrix" *Pittsburgh Courier*, 14 May 1926; "Recalls Exploits of Brave Bessie Coleman on Tenth Anniversary of Tragedy," *Chicago Defender*, 9 May 1936; Janet Harmon Waterford, "Race Interest in Aviation with Advent of Bessie Coleman, *Chicago Defender*, 28 March 1936.

14. Patterson, *Memoirs*, 4.

15. Ibid., 5; Associated Negro Press, "Practice Flight Fatal," *Pittsburgh Courier*, 7 May 1926; "Recalls Exploits of Brave Bessie Coleman on Tenth Anniversary of Tragedy," *Chicago Defender*, 9 May 1936.

16. Patterson, *Memoirs*, 4; Associated Negro Press, "Practice Flight Fatal," *Pittsburgh Courier*, 7 May 1926.

17. Associated Negro Press, "Practice Flight Fatal," *Pittsburgh Courier*, 7 May 1926.

18. Foster-Downer, "Three Funerals Held for Aviatrix," *Pittsburgh Courier*, 14 May 1926; "Recalls Exploits of Brave Bessie Coleman on Tenth Anniversary of Tragedy," *Chicago Defender*, 9 May 1936.

19. William Scott, "Hubert F. Julian and the Italo-Ethiopian War: A Tragic Episode in Pan African Relations," paper presented at the African Studies Association Meeting, Houston, Texas, November 1977, 4.

20. Franklin, *From Slavery to Freedom*, 491.

21. Ibid., 490; Scott, "Hubert F. Julian," 4-5.

22. Franklin, *From Slavery to Freedom*, 490.

23. Ibid.

24. "Champion Daredevil Parachutes to Tenament," *New York Daily Star*, 5 July 1924.

25. Franklin, *From Slavery to Freedom*, 491.

26. Ibid., 492.

27. Scott, "Hubert F. Julian," 6.

28. Ibid., 6; "Julian Always Good Copy," *Pittsburgh Courier*, 2 February 1936.

29. Scott, "Hubert F. Julian," 7-8; Associated Negro Press, "Herbert Julian on the Way to Abyssnia," *New York Amsterdam News*, 24 September 1930.

30. Scott, "Hubert F. Julian," 7; Hans Bromberg, "Abyssinia-Italy Strife May Start War," *Pittsburgh Courier*, 5 January 1935.

31. Associated Negro Press, "Abyssinian Official Repudiates Julian," *New York Amsterdam News*, 27 August 1930.

32. Ibid.; Scott, "Hubert F. Julian," 8.

33. Scott, "Hubert F. Julian," 9.

34. Associated Negro Press, "Tasfari Crowned Emperor Selassie," *New York Amsterdam News*, 5 November 1930.

35. Ibid.; Scott, "Hubert F. Julian," 71; *New York Amsterdam News*, 5 November 1930; "Deported," *Chicago Defender*, 8 November 1930; Lovis Morand, "Crown Ethiopian Emperor," *Chicago Defender*, 8 November 1980.

36. "3000 See Julian Stunt Flying," *Pittsburgh Courier*, 15 August 1931.

37. Ibid.

38. Ibid.; Doctor Porter A. Davis of Kansas City received his pilot's license in the mid-1920s. Julien, at that time, had only a student license. Monroe N. Work, "Occupations of Negroes. Licensed Negro Aviators," *The Negro Yearbook, An Annual Encyclopedia of the Negro, 1937-1938* (Tuskegee, Alabama: Tuskegee Institute, 1938), 280.

39. "3000 See Julian Stunt Flying," *Pittsburgh Courier*, 15 August 1931.

Chapter 3

Giant Steps

The early thirties were painful years for many American citizens. For Negroes, however, they were even more so—it was physically unhealthy and psychologically debilitating even to survive in America. Even more remarkable, then, were the survival tactics and the resiliency exhibited by the Negro community. The hard times developed men and women of character and daring, individuals who pushed at life's outer seams and frontiers to achieve freedom. This was especially true of those who wanted to fly airplanes.

There were several individual Negro men and women who performed daring feats as pilots, parachutists, and wingwalkers for Negro crowds. Leon Parris, a Haitian, was the first man of African descent to fly long distance, over 2,400 miles, from New York to Haiti, in April 1932.[1] Hubert Julian still excited crowds at air shows. Women pilots, such as Marie Dikerson of Los Angeles and Janet Waterford of Chicago, were extending the tradition started by Bessie Coleman.[2] These individuals who dared to live beyond the limitations imposed by white society, served as role models for other young African Americans.

Two men responsible for the first concerted effort to teach aviation skills to the Negro community were J. Herman Banning and William Powell. The nation's first Negro aero club was formed by these two men in Los Angeles in 1929.[3] J. Herman Banning was from Ames, Iowa, and was educated at Iowa State University. He became adept at repairing cars and motorcycles and went into the business of selling them. He eventually became bored with the speed limitations of land vehicles and sought a career in aviation. He received his flight training at Fisher Flying Field in Des Moines, Iowa, and received his private pilot's license in 1924. While taking flight instruction, Banning was one of the first

African Americans to build his own airplane and to test the product himself.[4] Shortly after receiving his pilot's license, Banning left his auto business and headed for California to make a living flying cargo and giving air shows.

William Powell, a native of Oklahoma and a World War I veteran officer, owned a gasoline station in Chicago in the 1920s. At his full-service station, Powell repaired motorcycle and automobile engines. When his business began to fail, Powell left Chicago and settled in Los Angeles to become a business fixture in the fledgling Negro community in Southern California.[5] Not long after arriving in Los Angeles, Powell met J. Herman Banning, a fellow auto mechanic and entrepreneur. Through Banning, Powell developed a interest in aviation. Although Powell was not a personal acquaintance of Bessie Coleman in Chicago, he, like many auto mechanics and upwardly mobile African Americans, was affected by her courage and artistry and sought to emulate her. Banning gave Powell flying lessons and, shortly thereafter, Powell received his pilot's license.[6]

Bessie Coleman's death, in 1926, affected Banning and Powell. Not long after Coleman's tragic accident, they attempted to interest more African Americans in the Los Angeles area in aviation. Banning and Powell both had a strong sense of community worth and responsibility to the race. Banning, especially, who would later write about his feelings on why the world could not deny the Negro, was aware of the potential in the untapped resource of wealth and creativity flowing in the minds of Negroes.[7]

By the end of the twenties, Banning and Powell had succeeded in forming the first organized Negro aviation group, which they named the Bessie Coleman Aero Club, in honor of the late aviatrix.[8] The Bessie Coleman Aero Club attracted Negro men and women, mechanics and would-be pilots. The aviators were able to find some land, which they converted into an airport they named the Bessie Coleman Airport. They repaired old airplane engines, converted automobile engines, and designed and built their own planes from spare parts.

The Bessie Coleman Aero Club, under the watchful eyes of Banning and Powell, assisted members in acquiring flight instruction and the necessary flight time to qualify for a pilot's license. The Club participated in air shows and flying exhibitions sponsored by and given to both white and integrated audiences. The Aero Club's primary interest, however, was to increase the interest in aviation among Los Angeles Negro youths. In Los Angeles, on Labor Day 1931, the Bessie Coleman Aero Club gave the first known, all-Negro air show given and sponsored by a Negro organization. The show featured flying acrobatics, wing walking, and parachute jumping, all performed by Negro experts.[9]

After the air show, the Aero Club expanded membership and continued offering instruction to members seeking pilot's licenses and experience in airplane engine mechanics. Other, more experienced, members participated in airplane races and cross-country flights for distance records. The Aero Club in Los Angeles had developed such a reputation among African Americans interested in aviation, that Col. Hubert Julian went to Los Angeles to persuade the group to sponsor him on the first transcontinental flight attempted by a Negro.[10]

Julian's proposed flight was well publicized. The "Black Eagle" took advantage of every promotional opportunity. He even had the temerity to name his plane the "*Pittsburgh Courier*," in honor of the popular Negro newspaper. This announcement made the cover page of the 5 May 1932 edition of the *Courier*, ensuring that at least a quarter of a million readers were aware of the trip. When Powell rejected Colonel Julian's solicitation, the two became engaged in an argument. Shortly after the skirmish, Julian announced that he was canceling the flight because he had received news that his wife had fallen gravely ill after childbirth.[11]

One of the most publicized long-distance airplane races involving the Bessie Coleman Aero Club was William Powell's attempt to win a cross-country air race. Powell and his co-pilot, Dick Wells, entered the Pacific Division of the Cord Cup Transcontinental Handicap Derby. They were racing against fifty-four white pilots to Cleveland, Ohio—a 2,369 mile trip. This was the first time African Americans had competed in an air race of this distance.[12] The prize was the Cord Cup, $10,000 in gold, and two new cars. The two pilots took off in a Lockheed Vega from Los Angeles on 25 August 1932, headed for Cleveland. After three days, the men were among the top twenty flyers in the race, and continued so until they experienced engine trouble and were forced out of the race near El Paso, Texas.[13]

Although Powell and Wells were disappointed, the Bessie Coleman Aero Club was especially proud of their effort. Not long after the aborted attempt by Powell and Wells, Julian began preparation for a transatlantic flight, this time set for 1933.[14]

Banning and a mechanic, Thomas Allen, already prepared for an air race, planned for a transcontinental, coast-to-coast flight, from Los Angeles to New York City.

Banning and Allen took off without fanfare, or much money, from Los Angeles on 21 September 1932. They flew an airplane with an eight-year-old engine that gave a maximum output of 100 horsepower.[15]

Fortunately, Allen was a master mechanic, and experienced with international air races. There were no problems encountered on the first leg of the trip. On the second leg, however, they experienced rough flying around the mountains and valleys leading into southern Texas, in approximately the same region where Powell and Wells were forced down a month earlier. Banning's adept flying and Allen's knowledge of the plane's mechanical tendencies got them through the difficulty, and they landed in El Paso without injury or damage to the plane.

The other problems Banning and Allen encountered were related to money. Since they had left Los Angeles with only twenty-five dollars between them, there were many times during the trip where the two had to decide whether to spend money for fuel or to eat. The fuel for the plane took priority over food. On one occasion, in New Mexico, Allen had to sell his spare suit and a watch to pay for enough fuel to make the next leg of the trip.[16] Fortunately, Banning had flown to some of the destinations before, and therefore there were friendly whites at various locations in Arizona, Oklahoma, Texas, Missouri, and Ohio who either fed them or gave them fuel, food, and a place to sleep. Where there were no friends, the two pilots had to sleep in the plane, in a barn, or even in an abandoned railroad boxcar. The pair did not experience much bigotry, because most of the attendants at the airports were in awe, and were respectful of their talents.[17]

The flight had a few treacherous spots. The two had to fly by their instruments in heavy fog for fifteen-minute intervals. They were fortunate they did not crash into mountains. The pair also ran into dangerous weather in the Allegheny Mountains and were forced to land in Cambridge, Ohio. After a brief stop in the Pittsburgh area, the aviators flew the final 313 miles of their 3,613-mile trip. They landed in Valley Stream, Long Island, New York, on 9 October 1932. The actual flying time was 41 hours and 27 minutes. J. Herman Banning and Thomas Allen were the first African Americans to successfully complete a transcontinental flight, and their feat was highlighted prominently in the Negro press.[18] The two flyers were honored with a parade in Harlem and were given a reception at the Marlboro Cafe.

The Negro community's exultation was short-lived. Banning, at age 33, was killed three months later, on 5 February 1933, during a flying exhibition at an air show in San Diego, California.[19] Ironically, he was not the pilot and his partner and trusted mechanic, Thomas Allen, was not at the air show. Allen had left for his home after he had heard a bad weather prediction for the air show date. Banning decided to do the air show, which was to feature a few acrobatics by Banning and a parachute jump by his passenger, Marion Daugherty. Banning had difficulty getting a plane to fly. Reportedly, the instructor at the Airtech Flying School in San Diego would not loan Banning one of his planes unless Banning allowed one of the Airtech advanced students to pilot the plane. The instructor felt that Banning was not a capable pilot, despite the fact that Banning had several hundred hours of air time and owned a transport pilot's license, which, at that time, was the highest rated license.[20] An airplane mechanic from the Naval Air Station in San Diego was chosen as the pilot.

Against his better judgment, Banning allowed the student pilot to fly the plane. Banning would make the parachute jump. This error in judgment proved fatal. After the pilot guided the plane to an altitude of 400 feet, he lost control and went into a tailspin. Two thousand spectators watched in horror as the plane crashed into the ground. The impact fractured Banning's skull and caused internal damage. He was pronounced dead one hour later, in a San Diego County hospital. The pilot, Albert Burghardt, was seriously injured, and feared dead at the time.[21]

The news of Banning's death, similar in many ways to that of Bessie Coleman, shocked the Negro community, and was viewed with a similar sense of loss. In the spirit of J. Herman Banning, Powell and the Bessie Coleman Aero Club continued the work of expanding Negro interest in aviation. By 1935, Powell had published a book entitled: *Black Wings* that chronicled the pioneering days of the Negro experience in aviation and the Bessie Coleman Club had expanded to seventy-five members including six whites and two Mexicans. Powell also secured a position with the Los Angeles School Department as an instructor of Aeronautics.[22] In addition, the Aero Club boasted a membership of at least seven Negro women, who carried on the legacy of Bessie Coleman. They were Gwendolyn Morton, Bridget Walton, Latina Wyatt, Marie Dikerson, Ann Jefferson, Willie Anne Sims, and Zola Benjamin.[23]

Less than two months after Banning's death, Colonel Julian sought to regain the spotlight vacated by Banning. Julian announced that he was planning to fly nonstop from New York to Paris, in half the time it took Lindbergh.[24] His manager, Lonnie Hicks claimed that Julian would take the New York to Newfoundland to Paris route sometime in June 1933. Hicks and Julian attempted to make money promoting the transatlantic flight by placing the plane on exhibit and by charging interested persons a fee to view the plane. Hicks touted the plane as being more powerful than the one used by Amelia Earhart in her transatlantic flight to Ireland in 1932. This time the trip was canceled because Julian did not have enough financial backing.

While Powell and Banning were promoting aviation in the Negro community in the West, a young man from Pennsylvania, was also trying to fulfill his childhood dream of becoming a pilot.

From an early age, C. Alfred Anderson, of Byrn Mawr, Pennsylvania, wanted to fly airplanes. While he was living with his grandmother in northern Virginia, he would run away from her house to find the airplanes that made the whining noise so attractive to his ears. His interest in airplanes was a single-minded obsession. So intense about planes was young Anderson, that persons started to refer to him as crazy, for Negroes could only dream of flying airplanes in those days before World War I. His running off to see the airplanes was disconcerting to his grandmother, and eventually she also tired of his constant talk about flying. Eventually, she sent young Alfred back to his mother in Pennsylvania.[25]

Alfred's dreams of flying never abated. As a young man, he convinced his parents to allow him to take flying lessons, In the early twenties, however, there were no whites in Byrn Mawr who would give him lessons. Anderson realized at a young age that the only way he was going to learn how to fly was to buy his own plane and teach himself. He actually went door to door, borrowing money for his airplane. He needed $2,500 to purchase a Velie Monocoupe, but he could only raise $2,000.[26] His fundraising effort was remarkable, considering the harsh economic times of 1929. Most African Americans in his community were fortunate to earn $70 per month. Loaning someone money to purchase an airplane was the last expense on the minds of his benefactors. Some, however, were dreamers like Anderson. One man, Morris Massey, a coal yard worker, gave him $500. His father was also instrumental in assisting young Anderson in his goal of acquiring an airplane. The senior Anderson was able to persuade a maid, Elsie Billingsley, who worked with him, to contribute $500 toward the cause.[27]

Anderson attracted another benefactor, his father's employer, a Mrs. Wright. Anderson's father was the caretaker of the Wright Estate, which included a private school for girls and a farm. Mrs. Wright received word that the senior Anderson was looking for investors in his son's venture. On hearing of Alfred's plans, Mrs. Wright gave Anderson's father the remaining balance of $500 needed to purchase the airplane.[28]

Although Alfred Anderson now had his own plane, he still had great difficulty in finding instructors to teach him the rudiments of flying. He convinced one white pilot to give him a few lessons. This gentleman, unfortunately, was killed in a plane accident shortly after giving Anderson his first lessons. Anderson also had difficulty in finding airport hangars where he could store his plane. Fortunately, a Negro dentist, Dr.

Winters, invited Anderson to use his farm property for practice. Dr. Winter's property also provided storage for his plane.[29]

Teaching oneself to fly can be a dangerous proposition. Anderson soon discovered the danger, on a trip to Dr. Winter's farm. On that particular occasion, the aspiring pilot received a huge gash on his forehead when he crash-landed his plane. The mishap did not deter Anderson, however. He successfully taught himself how to fly and pursued a transport pilot's license, which was the most advanced license one could obtain in 1932.

While practicing for his transport license, Anderson was fortunate to receive instruction from a man named Ernest Buhl.[30] Mr. Buhl was a recent immigrant from Germany and took a special interest in instructing the young Negro pilot. When it appeared that Anderson would receive an unusually difficult check flight by the Department of Commerce official, Mr. Buhl advised the official that any bigotry on the official's part would not be tolerated, and that he would report any acts of racism witnessed during Anderson's qualifying flight. Because of Mr. Buhl's support, Anderson was able to secure his transport license and became the first Negro since Bessie Coleman qualified to carry passengers in an airplane or to fly for an airline.[31]

Shortly after receiving his transport license, Anderson's father died. As a consequence of this untimely death, the young Anderson inherited his father's job as caretaker of the Wright Estate. Not long after Anderson started working for the Wrights, his employer, Mrs. Wright, died, and her daughter-in-law inherited and administered the estate. Anderson's new employer was not as gracious as her mother-in-law had been, and did not have much respect for her Negro employees. When she became aware of Anderson's acquisition of his transport license, she fired him, insisting that he use his transport license to earn a living.

Even the Depression could not dampen Anderson's enthusiasm for flying. To feed himself and to help his family, Anderson went to work for the Workers Progress Administration (WPA), laying sewage pipes. The young pilot spent every minute of his free time away from work flying his plane. Another Negro interested in flying sought a partnership with Anderson. Albert Forsythe, a surgeon from Atlantic City, was intent on buying an airplane, to show the Negro world what was capable with an airplane. Forsythe found Anderson working in a sewer drainage ditch and told him that the work was not suitable for a young pilot.[32]

It did not take Forsythe long to convince Anderson to form a working partnership. Anderson assisted Forsythe in his search for a plane. Ironically, Forsythe purchased an airplane from Anderson's former flight instructor, Mr. Buhl.

In 1932, the pair became the only Negroes in the Northeast to com-
mute, by plane, from Philadelphia to Atlantic City several times a
month.[33] Starting in 1933, the pair extended their trips to cross-country
and transcontinental flights, all consistent with Dr. Forsythe's plan for
record breaking and eye-opening exploits.

Their first major excursion was a round-trip transcontinental flight
from Atlantic City to Los Angeles. The trip was a record-breaking event
for African Americans, eclipsing, by seven hours, the one-way transcontinental flight of J. Herman Banning and Thomas Allen in 1932.[34] The
only directional equipment the men had was a compass. There was no
navigational equipment. A Rand McNally road map served them, until it
blew out of Forsythe's hands on the way back. At night, they used airport
beacons and flashlights to find their way.[35] They were met in Los Angeles
by 2,000 proud African Americans, many of whom were there as the
result of an excellent public relations effort by Bill Powell's flying club. It
was Powell's acknowledgment of a remarkable accomplishment.[36]

Although the flight received notoriety in the Negro press from Los
Angeles to New York, it paled in comparison to the adventure encoun-
tered by Anderson and Forsythe on their flight to South America. This
flight, taken in 1934, was a goodwill flight, financed primarily by
Forsythe, a member of the Tuskegee Institute, Class of 1913, to prove to
Negroes on both continents that Negroes could accomplish the same
feats as white pilots.[37] The trip was also sponsored by the Interracial
Goodwill Aviation Committee of Philadelphia and Atlantic City.[38]

The two airmen took off from Atlantic City and stopped at Tuskegee
Institute to have their plane christened the "Spirit of Booker T.
Washington."[39] While Tuskegee President Robert R. Moton was not ter-
ribly interested in aviation as a vocation, as evidenced by his rejection in
1934 of a proposal submitted by a Tuskegee alumnus and pilot, John
Robinson, he was quite impressed with the courage and skills of
Anderson and Forsythe.[40] One person at Tuskegee was interested. The
dean of the Veterinary School, Dr. Frederick Paterson, a friend of Dr.
Forsythe, was contemplating a flying school at Tuskegee. His ideas were
preliminary in 1934, but were crystallized by the exploits of Anderson
and Forsythe and spurred on by the student flying club initiated by J. C.
Evans of West Virginia State College for Negroes.[41]

The Goodwill aviators were to land in twenty-five different countries
bearing an official scroll to be signed by all of the government officials.[42] However, unlike flying in the United States, there were no air
fields with runways in the Caribbean. Often, the two had to circle towns
for several minutes before they could land. When they did land, it was

usually on a street or a playing field. In Nassau, they landed in a street lined with cars with their headlights turned on to simulate a runway. In Grenada, they landed on a race track.[43]

On the way to South America, there were some close calls. While landing in Trinidad, the airmen flew into powerful tailwinds. When they tried to take off the next morning, the tailwinds forced them to head toward land, instead of heading out toward the Caribbean, where they would have been pulled into the water. Their plane was weighted down with souvenirs and other cargo, and on take off, the winds forced the plane down in a populated area. The plane caught the top of a Bamboo tree and crash-landed in someone's front yard. The men were unharmed, but the plane was heavily damaged and the trip was aborted.[44]

When the men returned to Atlantic City, they were feted with a parade in Newark, preceded by a breakfast of chitterlings. This flight was also chronicled with photographs in the Negro press nationwide. The plane was showcased to the public in an exhibit at a golf course in Ardmore, Pennsylvania, sponsored by the Main Line Branch of the InterRacial Goodwill Aviation Committee.[45]

The widely publicized flying exploits of Julian, Anderson, Banning, Powell, and Parris, were indicative of the technical talent of the race, when given a chance to participate in any vocation and, therefore, were beneficial to younger African Americans with the same dreams. Coleman, Powell, and Banning notwithstanding, a few of the former pioneer Negro aviators were driven by personal and individual aspirations that were not necessarily related to civil rights protest or the development of Negro aviation.

In Chicago, in the early thirties, two Negro auto and motorcycle mechanics chose aviation as an avocation and pledged to develop a cadre of young Negro aviators who would change America's perception of Negro capability in the field of science and technology.

Cornelius Coffey and John Robinson came to Chicago in the late twenties to pursue careers in motorcycle and auto mechanics. Coffey, a reserved young man, already owned repair shops in Detroit and was expanding his ventures to Chicago. Robinson, outgoing and charismatic, arrived in Chicago in 1929 with a vocational degree in mechanics from Tuskegee Institute. Robinson had developed, in a short time, a reputation in Chicago as a motorcycle stunt rider. The two met while residing at a local YMCA and developed a friendship based on common occupations and aspirations for flying airplanes.[46] Coffey was instrumental in securing a job for Robinson at Elmwood Park Motor Sales, where Coffey was employed as a mechanic.

The two young men had difficulty gaining admittance to flying schools in the area, so they decided, first, to acquire a plane and, second, to secure flying lessons from accredited flight instructors who were not bigots. At the Elmwood Park site, Coffey and Robinson collected spare auto and motorcycle parts for the reconditioning of their first plane, a Waco #9.[47] When the construction of the plane was completed, the two men moved into a room at Acres Airport, where they could take their flying lessons and acquire enough hours to qualify for a private pilot's license. The two did repair work on automobiles and motorcycles that belonged to the airport officials and patrons. In lieu of pay, the owners of the Acres Airport let Coffey and Robinson use the airport as a base to accumulate their air time.[48]

When Coffey and Robinson secured their pilot's licenses, they attempted to enroll into master mechanic's courses in several aeronautical schools, including the Curtiss-Wright School of Aeronautics. Their applications were sent in by mail with an application fee to the Curtiss-Wright School. Curtiss-Wright admitted, by mail, the two to the master mechanic's course. When Coffey and Robinson arrived for the class, the administrator of the school, L. M. Churbuck, told them that a mistake had been made and that they could not be admitted to the class. Churbuck feared student reprisals against the Negro students. His worst fear, however, was student withdrawal from the school. Consequently, Churbuck offered to return the application fee to the two prospective students, but they refused to accept the money.[49]

Robinson and Coffey then began to work on an alternative plan to get into the school. Their employer, a Mr. Mack, offered to cover the legal costs of a lawsuit to gain admission into the school. Robinson, however, being the most combative of the two, took the route of direct action, by approaching Mr. Churbuck. After several meetings, Churbuck compromised and gave Robinson a job as a volunteer janitor and student helper.[50]

In a few weeks, Robinson had won the confidence of the instructors and the students with his skills. With the threat of a lawsuit and Robinsons's exhibition of mechanical skills, Mr. Churbuck relented, and allowed the two men to be admitted to the master mechanic's course. The white students, however, would not accept Robinson's new status, nor another Negro in the class, and they therefore made it very difficult for Coffey and Robinson. On several occasions the men were provoked, but did not partake in contentious behavior. The instructor, Jack Snyder, caught wind of the student plot and threatened action against the students if they persisted. Eventually, Coffey and Robinson were left alone and they completed the course in two years, at the top of their class.[51]

Soon after graduation, in 1931, from the master mechanic's course at Curtiss-Wright, the two men convinced Mr. Churbuck to open the school to a class of thirty-five Negro students. Robinson and Coffey, with the assistance of *The Chicago Defender*, one of the country's leading Negro newspapers, recruited enough men and women interested in flying to initiate a class of thirty-five at Curtiss-Wright. Fearing friction from the white students, Churbuck ordered classes for Negro students to be held at night.[52] Coffey and Robinson were hired as assistant instructors for the class, and for other classes held during the day. One of the classes assigned to the Negro instructors was one that included Chinese students.[53] These students were sent to Curtiss-Wright after the Japanese attack on Manchuria in 1931. They would later become the nucleus of the Chinese Royal Air Force in China's defense against Japanese aggression, which was to occur throughout the thirties.

From the group of interested Negro students, Coffey and Robinson started the Brown Eagle Aero Club. The Club was based at Acres Airport and provided the students at Curtiss-Wright with the opportunity to practice their skills in flying and airplane mechanics. The group was forced to move to another airport, however, when Acres Airport was sold to a land developer. The Brown Eagle Club surfaced at Robbins Airport, just outside of Chicago, in a town called Robbins, Illinois.[54] Robbins was an all-Negro community and was governed by a Negro mayor by the name of Keller. When the Aero Club moved to Robbins Airport, its runways were covered with weeds and tall grass. In addition, the old airport had dilapidated airplane hangars. Mayor Keller assisted the Aero Club in the reconstruction of the airport, by having the grass removed and by providing gravel and cinders for the runways.[55]

Mayor Keller helped in other ways as well. The neighboring white villagers and towns people did not like the idea of Negroes flying directly over their houses and, therefore, when members of the Aero Club landed in one of the towns adjacent to Robbins, the law enforcement officials would arrest them. Invariably, Mayor Keller, or his police chief, would rescue the pilots from jail.[56] Mayor Keller's support gave the Aero club a sense of security at Robbins Airport. Members of the Club could focus on sharpening their skills, instead of worrying about racial obstacles.

Robinson, Coffey, and other student members of the Brown Eagle Aero Club, such as Janet Waterford and Harold Hurd, purchased construction material for the airplane hangar, which the Aero Club built themselves.[57] At that time, in late 1931, the club possessed three planes, two owned by Coffey and Robinson and one purchased by Ms. Waterford. Another member, Earl Renfroe had purchased his own private plane.

Unfortunately, Robinson's plane was wrecked by Chinese students, who had borrowed the plane to build up pilot hours. Disaster also struck in 1933, when the hangar built by the Club members collapsed in a winter storm, destroying all of the planes housed inside.[58]

In the aftermath of the disaster, Coffey and Robinson searched for another airport. Because of their color, the two pilot/mechanics were refused space in several Chicago area airports. Finally, they were able to secure a secluded spot at the Harlem Airport on the south side of Chicago. They reconstituted the Aero Club and renamed it the Challenger Aero Club, and later, the Challenger Air Pilots Association.[59] In order to raise money to rent planes and pay rent at the new flying address, the group resorted to an assortment of fundraising tactics which included dances, dinners, airshows, and airplane rides. Eventually, enough money was raised to replace most of the planes that were lost in the storm of 1933.

As the Challengers prospered and attracted more young African Americans in the Chicago area interested in flying, Coffey and Robinson had ideas of developing aviation in the Negro community on a national scale. By 1934, Coffey and Robinson had developed excellent reputations as pilots and mechanics. Curtiss-Wright was so impressed with Robinson's flying skills that they employed Robinson to deliver planes to be used in other states for the Curtiss-Wright Air Service.[60] The work experience at Curtiss-Wright afforded both men the opportunity to learn the finer points of operating an aviation school and a flight service. Both men, and especially Robinson, believed that they could recreate the Curtiss-Wright experience at a Negro College that owned huge acres of land and a vocational program featuring automobile engine mechanics and welding. With Chicago as the hub, they believed a Negro flight service company could prosper in the Midwest and the South.

Since Tuskegee Institute had a strong program in auto mechanics and welding, and owned enough acreage for an airport, Tuskegee was selected as the first Negro College to approach with the idea of initiating a flying school. Robinson also felt that his student affiliation with Tuskegee would be an advantage. Robinson, who was a chauffeur for the dean of men, Captain Alvin Neely, was able to get an appointment with President Robert R. Moton of Tuskegee Institute.[61] The trip was timed with the graduation of the senior class of 1934, and was therefore a homecoming for Robinson. Coffey and another member of the Challengers, Grover Nash, were to accompany Robinson. The trip was also to a be a demonstration of the aviation skills of the trio, being the third-longest cross-country flight ever undertaken by Negroes. Robinson felt that the flying demonstration and his status as an alumnus, would be enough to convince President Moton to start an aviation school at Tuskegee Institute.[62]

In early June 1934, the trio started the trip to Tuskegee, Alabama, with two planes. Coffey and Robinson flew in a two-seater International, and Nash flew in the Buhl "Pup." The International, at Robinson's insistence, carried an extra fuel tank of 108 pounds of gasoline. This added weight concerned Coffey, who thought that the extra pounds would cause difficulty in takeoffs and landings.

As Coffey predicted, the tandem ran into trouble on a takeoff in Decatur, Alabama. The men had landed on a Decatur golfcourse to refuel the Pup that Nash was flying. In order to ensure a smooth takeoff, Coffey marked off the field that was their runway and tagged the spot where Robinson was to lift off. All of the flying instruments were in the back of the plane with Robinson, and therefore he was in control of the flight of the plane. The rudder bar, stick, and throttle were controlled by Coffey, who was stationed in the forward seat. Right above Coffey's legs was the fuel tank, held up by two makeshift straps that were added by Coffey shortly after an air accident in Chicago, when the tank fell on one of the Aero Club pilots and broke his legs.

Coffey walked halfway down the runway and placed a wooden stick and a white rag on the stick and told Robinson that when they attempted to take off, he was going to signal when they reached the stick and if the plane still felt heavy, Robinson was not to take off. Coffey had advised Robinson to wait until the afternoon, when there would be a breeze that could help lift the plane into the air. Robinson was very concerned about being late for their appointment at Tuskegee.[63]

In a short while, Nash took off without incident. Robinson and Coffey initiated their takeoff, and when they reached Coffey's marker, the plane, in Coffey's opinion, still felt too heavy to take off. Robinson ignored Coffey's frantic signaling, indicating that they were past the marker, and continued toward a fence that formed the border of the golfcourse. Robinson pulled the plane up just seconds before hitting the fence, but, to their horror, the plane just hung in a semistall in the air, and headed toward some houses near the field.

One of the houses that they were headed toward was a two-story house with a chimney. The tail of the plane was much lower than the height of the chimney, and therefore the front of the plane cleared the chimney, but the tail of the plane did not. The stabilizer and elevator were torn off, up to the fuselage, and the top brace wire was the only thing that held the stabilizer and the elevator onto the right side of the plane. Coffey, fearing a crash, loosened his belt. He could then see the landing gear, and he noticed that both wheels were turning. He looked back to the tail and saw that the elevator and stabilizer were gone. He pointed out the damage to the tail to Robinson and Robinson, instinctively, cut the power to the airplane. The plane started to dive, so Coffey switched the power back on. It was his intention to fly the plane until they could find a suitable place to land.[64]

They noticed a cotton field nearby and guided the plane to what they thought was a safe approach to a landing. There was a tree in the middle of the cotton field, however, and they were headed straight for it. Fearing a head-on crash, Coffey pulled up on the stick to get altitude and took his feet from under the gas tank. The plane's left wheel hit the top of the tree and the airplane swung around, crashed, and cartwheeled, shearing off both wings. Amazingly, no one was hurt. Nash, who witnessed the aborted takeoff and the crash, landed his plane and went to rescue the two pilots.[65]

Naturally, the plane crash attracted people to the scene. They were astonished at the sight of the airplane and the damage, but were more curious about and interested in the Negro pilots. The owner of the cotton field, however, was not impressed with the damage caused by the plane crash. He would not let the three pilots off of his land until they paid $125 for the damage to his cotton field. Fortunately, Robinson knew friends, who wired the money, enabling the three men to continue the trip.[66]

Coffey urged Robinson to take the Pup to Tuskegee and keep all of the appointments. Coffey and Nash were to meet with Robinson at Tuskegee. Robinson made the appointments, but was rebuffed by President Moton and the Tuskegee administration in his attempts to convince his alma mater to initiate a flying school. Robinson was so disappointed and bitter over Tuskegee's lack of interest that he left Tuskegee without his airplane.[67]

Although Moton and his administration did not elaborate on their reasons for rejecting Robinson's offer, the pilots from Chicago surmised that Moton and the Tuskegee administration were cautious in their adoption of modern vocational training, especially vocations that were considered highly technical, nonagricultural, and within the domain of white men. Coffey also speculated that Tuskegee Institute, which had a delicate relationship with whites in Macon County, Alabama and those living in Tuskegee, did not welcome the idea of planes flying all over the Tuskegee community, possibly angering the whites.[68]

Coffey and Robinson returned to Chicago and focused their attention on expanding and strengthening the Challenger Air Pilots Association.

The Challengers had grown to over thirty members, and the group began giving air shows, featuring flying demonstrations and parachute jumps. One of the members of the Challengers, a parachutist by the name of Fisher, urged the group to seek membership as an Air Reserve squadron within the Illinois National Guard.[69] In 1935, however, the state of Illinois was not accepting African Americans into the National Guard, not to mention an Air Reserve squadron. The group persisted and was finally awarded a state charter as a Military Order of Guard, Aviation Squadron. The charter was, in a sense, a symbolic gesture from the state of Illinois approved by the War Department. It gave members of the Challengers similar status to the state militia. The squadron had no administrative connection with the Illinois National Guard.[70]

The squadron, however, was given permission to designate one plane as Military Order of Guard property. The MOG insignia was placed on the plane. Members of the Challengers were given quasi-military positions. Coffey was a lieutenant colonel, Robinson a lieutenant colonel, and Fisher had the rank of major. Other members of the group, such as Harold Hurd, one of their first students at Curtiss-Wright, were made lieutenants. Although the MOG Aviation Squadron was symbolic, its significance was in the acknowledgment of the respect given to the competency of the Negro flying organization. Also significant was the fact that the Chicago MOG was the first Negro aviation squadron designated by a governmental body.[71]

Concurrent with the establishment of the Chicago MOG was the escalation of hostilities between Ethiopia and Italy. The Negro press, with their experience covering the Pan Africanist movement activities of W. E. B. DuBois and the Nationalist movement of Marcus Garvey in the twenties, covered the events evolving in Ethiopia with a natural affinity for the ebony Empire ruled by Haile Selassie. Although several European countries and the United States had business interests in Ethiopia, it still remained one of the few African nations not colonized by whites and, therefore, a legitimate sovereign African nation readily identifiable to the Negro masses. The Negro press, particularly *The Pittsburgh Courier, The Chicago Defender,* and *The New York Amsterdam News,* helped in the shaping of Negro public opinion regarding the proud, but virtually defenseless, country fending off a fascist regime led by a so-called madman.[72]

Italy was interested in gaining a colony in East Africa. Acquisition of an African colony would give the Italian leader, Mussolini, and the country the prestige and the wealth enjoyed by other European nations. Ethiopia was not interested in being a colony, although many countries, especially England, held business interests in the African country.

Selassie feared an invasion from Mussolini's troops. To head off the Italian fascist, Ethiopian troops were deployed on the border of Walwal. It was at Walwal that the Ethiopians and Italians clashed, with the Ethiopians charging the fascist troops with invading Ethiopian territory.[73] In January 1935, the Ethiopian government petitioned the League of Nations to intercede in the conflict. While waiting for the League to act, the Ethiopians led several guerrilla attacks on Italian troops encroaching on Ethiopian borders. Seventy-eight fascist troops were killed in an ambush on the Somalia-Ethiopia border. In reaction to the ambush, Mussolini ordered 230,000 troops and eighty aircraft to the Eritrea-Ethiopia border, and fighting between soldiers stationed on both fronts broke out.[74]

In February, the League of Nations intervened and persuaded both warring countries to honor a ceasefire and to establish a neutral zone within Ethiopia, claimed by England.[75] In the ensuing months, the league fashioned several arbitration overtures to the warring countries.

From the beginning of the Italo-Ethiopian conflict, the Negro press chronicled as many war-related events as possible. Although most did not have correspondents in Ethiopia, the Negro newspaper organizations relied on information from the various Ethiopian consulates and embassies established in the United States and the news received from the white press wire services. There were Ethiopian consulates in New York, Washington, D.C., and Chicago.[76] Operating on behalf of these consulates were advocate groups such as the International Council of Friends of Ethiopia, operating out of New York, the United Aid to Ethiopia, which had chapters in several cities, including Chicago, and the Ethiopian World Federation. These advocacy groups raised funds and coordinated resources for the Ethiopian cause.[77]

Naturally, Robinson, Coffey, and the Challenger Air Pilots Association were empathetic, and were attracted to the Ethiopian conflict, which they viewed as an opportunity for African Americans to participate in defending their brothers and sisters in the African diaspora. The Challengers, most of whom were already accomplished pilots and mechanics, felt their designation and experience as a Military Order of Guard Aviation unit provided the expertise needed to assist Ethiopia in the development of an Air Force. At least seven Challengers planned to serve as a volunteer air squadron for Ethiopia.[78] Since the United States had announced their official policy of neutrality, permission to volunteer for military duty with Ethiopia was discouraged, and in most cases, viewed as illegal. Therefore, the possibility of the United States government granting visas to a group of Negroes interested in fighting for Ethiopia was next to impossible.[79] The group decided that it would be more viable to offer the services of Robinson, who was considered by many in the group to be the most experienced and gifted pilot.[80]

When Robinson offered his services to the Chicago chapters of the Friends of Ethiopia and United Aid to Ethiopia, he was enthusiastically received, but the answer from the Ethiopian government was less than encouraging. Fresh in the minds of the Ethiopians and their leader, Haile Selassie, were the ill-mannered antics of Hubert Julian, the only Negro with American ties who volunteered for service in Ethiopia. To ensure no further embarrassment, the Ethiopian government asked Robinson to supply a list of references.[81] Only when Selassie was satisfied with Robinson's references, was the pilot invited to Ethiopia as a guest of the emperor.

By the end of April 1935, Johnny Robinson was in Ethiopia, acting as a consultant in the development of the Royal Air Force. Julian had preceded Robinson by a few weeks, but was not assigned a position in the Ethiopian Air Force. French, English, and Swedish mercenaries were also commissioned to train Ethiopian pilots and were on location prior to Robinson's arrival. Once Robinson displayed his flying skills, he won the emperor's confidence. By midsummer, Robinson was flying as Selassie's special emissary, delivering messages to the various Ethiopian outposts.[82]

To the surprise of many, the resilient Julian was back in Ethiopia by late March 1935. The colonel, with his inimitable style, was back in the good graces of the emperor.[83] The "Black Eagle" was assigned to a remote outpost to train infantry, and was recommissioned as a colonel. By early August 1935, Julian had impressed the Ethiopian emperor to the extent that he was reinstated as the commander of the Royal Ethiopian Air Force.[84] This promotion was allegedly not well-received by Robinson and the other aviation consultants. Robinson had been aware of Julian and his exploits for several years and, therefore, did not have much respect for him as a leader. In 1934, Julian had come to Chicago to interest the Challengers in investing in his annual attempt at a transatlantic flight. Julian requested the use of one of the Challenger planes at a rental rate that was, reportedly, unacceptable to Coffey and Robinson. Consequently, Julian's offer was rejected. Julian, angered, broke off negotiations and ordered the men from his room.[85]

A confrontation between the two charismatic and prideful Negro pilots over the leadership of the Ethiopian Air Force was inevitable. In August 1935, an argument ensued between the two, and it erupted into a fist fight. Selassie, embarrassed by the confrontation, and untrusting of his European consultants, was forced to make a decision between the two Negro pilots. Because of Julian's past history with the Ethiopian government, the emperor was predisposed to believe the fight was provocated by Julian, and therefore Julian was relieved of his command and sent to another remote village, in Ambo, Ethiopia, to prepare infantry troops for combat.[86] Robinson became the only logical choice to command the Air Force. Robinson became Emperor Selassie's official pilot and Chief of the Royal Ethiopian Air Force.[87]

By September, the League of Nations had voted on a covenant that charged that any act of aggression by Italy or Ethiopia would be viewed as an act of war against all members of the League of Nations.[88] Italy would not vote on the covenant and Great Britain and France moved to display a show of force in the Mediterranean. The United States, a non-member, employed a formal position of neutrality and a weapons embargo.[89] By the end of September 1935, Selassie had rejected protection from Great Britain and France, due to the political cost. Italy refused to participate in peace talks on the covenant and ordered its citizens to evacuate the consulate in the Ethiopian capital of Addis Ababa. Mussolini, however, assured Great Britain that there would be no aggression against British ships in the Mediterranean.[90]

On 2 October 1935, Mussolini declared war on Ethiopia, and fascist troops crossed the internationally recognized neutral zone.[91] In response to the Italian aggression, Emperor Selassie filed formal complaints with the League of Nations. Although there was a covenant signed by all league members, except Italy, the league members, including Britain and France, did not intervene in the Italian hostilities. Selassie was forced to order the defense of Ethiopia.[92]

On 3 October 1935, the Italian Air Force bombed Aduwa, Ethiopia, catching most of the population by surprise.[93] After the first set of bombs were dropped in the night, many of the city's residents sought shelter in the Red Cross Hospital headquarters. The Italians reportedly bombed the area that included the Red Cross shelter, killing several civilians.[94]

John Robinson was in Aduwa when the bombing occurred. He had been given orders to fly classified government dispatches to the Eritrean front, near Aduwa. This was his first war experience and, fortunately, he had arrived without seeing Italian planes along the way. During the bombing, Robinson was forced to retrieve his airplane and move it to a secure and camouflaged area. The Ethiopian Air Force could not afford to lose any planes. After the bombing, Robinson continued his mission, but on his return to Addis Ababa, Robinson, according to *The Exchange Telegraph* report acquired by the *Amsterdam News*, was engaged in combat with two Italian planes. It was reported that Robinson got off several rounds and managed to outmaneuver the Italian pilots and escape without injury to himself.[95] This encounter marked the first time an African-American pilot, serving an African nation, was engaged in air combat.

Colonel Robinson did not encounter any other enemy planes until the week of 10 December 1935. This time, Robinson was headed to Dessye, Ethiopia from Addis Ababa, delivering medicine to civilians and soldiers on the front, when he spotted a Italian bomber. The Negro pilot attacked the unsuspecting bomber with machine-gun fire. The bomber was badly disabled, but fortunately for the bomber, Italian fighter escorts chased Robinson away. Robinson was able to escape without injury, although his plane was damaged.[96]

Concurrent with Robinson's dogfights, was the arrival of American Negro journalist and historian, J. A. Rogers. The popular columnist was on assignment for *The Pittsburgh Courier*. Rogers provided *Courier* readers with battlefront photographs and reports from Ethiopia.[97] Many of these stories were syndicated to other Negro publications, such as *The Amsterdam News* and *The Chicago Defender*. Eventually, all of the Negro weeklies carried Rogers's stories.

Rogers was able to travel to different battlefronts for his photographs and stories, courtesy of Colonel Robinson. Rogers credited Robinson with having "balance and good judgment," traits that were admired and respected by Emperor Selassie.[98] Colonel Robinson was equally impressed with Rogers and was ecstatic to see and converse with another American Negro. The timing of Robinson's air exploits could not have been better. Rogers reported the air duels to the *Courier*, and those stories, unheard of in the Negro race, were featured on the front page of the Negro weeklies. Rogers described Robinson as heroic, and handsome in his uniform, which included gold epaulets and the colors of the Ethiopian crown.[99] There were pictures of Robinson in his airplane and in his full uniform, identifying him as Chief of the Ethiopian Air Force.[100] The *Courier* stories from Ethiopia made Robinson an unlikely hero in the American Negro community.

By the end of 1935, Robinson had so impressed Selassie with his flying skills, integrity, and loyalty, that he persuaded the emperor to approve the induction of six additional pilots from the Challenger Air Pilots Association into the Ethiopian Air Force.[101] At the time of the request, most of the French consultants had fled Ethiopia and, therefore, had presented the Ethiopian Air Force with a shortage of pilots. To adequately equip the new flyers, Robinson was granted permission to order six new planes from the United States. The U.S. government had enacted an embargo on war materials and equipment, however, and the sale was canceled. Robinson ordered the planes from England, at a cost of $30,000.[102]

Coffey and six other members of the Challengers, including Harold Hurd, Earl Renfroe, Albert Cosby, Dale White, Clyde Hampton, and one woman, Willa Brown, sought passports to Ethiopia. The neutrality policy of the United States presented an insurmountable obstacle. This policy prevented American citizens from volunteering with military organizations representing countries at war. Consequently, the Chicago flyers were never allowed to travel to Ethiopia. Robinson was forced to carry on with a skeleton Air Force, aided by Swedish consultants.[103]

Unlike Robinson, Julian was not held in high regard by the Ethiopian government. While on his assignment, training and drilling rural recruits, Julian was reportedly working on several schemes to embezzle money from the Ethiopian Army. According to the American Negro newspaper reports, Julian was constantly borrowing money from Americans in Ethiopia, and living on credit. It was also reported that Julian attempted to defraud the Ethiopian government by double billing the Ethiopian Army for equipment he claimed he bought with his own personal funds. He also complained, according to the Negro press, that he was owed eight months worth of backpay. When the army checked its payroll, it was found that Julian was in debt, due to nonpayments on several pay advances.[104] To make matters worse, Julian claimed that he was planning to marry Selassie's only daughter. Julian, by then an embarrassment to Selassie, was summoned to Addis Ababa, where Selassie, via a letter, requested his resignation and asked him to leave the country.[105]

Colonel Julian sailed for France on 17 November 1935. He had no money, but was able to persuade the Captain of the French liner to defer collection of the travel fee until they arrived in France, where Julian was to secure funds to pay for his trip. Once in France, however, Julian managed to evade the French police authorities who were intent on collecting the travel fee. Julian managed to tell white reporters, in an impromptu press conference, that he had penned a sixty-eight page manuscript entitled *Why I Resigned from the Abyssinian Army*. The book was supposed to reveal the Ethiopian atrocities and massacres witnessed by Julian. The book was to include photographs taken by Colonel Julian, from his own camera.[106]

There was suspicion at the time that Julian was paid by the Italian government to spread negative stories about Selassie's regime in order to diffuse the negative reaction to Italian aggression. This suspicion was reinforced by the $1,250 retainer Julian reportedly received from the Italian Consul in Paris, and the expensive clothes that Julian was sporting. Many members of the Negro press also believed that the Italian agents assisted the former chief of the Ethiopian Air Force in his escape from the French authorities. It appeared to the Negro press that the Italian agents provided money for Julian's trip back to New York on the luxury liner *Aquitania* in exchange for his support in their propaganda effort in the United States and the Negro community. Throwing a romantic spin to his story, Julian claimed that his new found fortune was the result of his relationship with an English woman of title.[107]

As soon as he landed in New York, in early January 1936, Julian gave a press conference. Resplendent in top hat, cane, morning suit with tails, and an eye moniker, the adventurer gave the press vivid and wild stories of Ethiopian tortures and other atrocities. So dramatic and graphic were Julian's accounts, that the Italian agents decided to create some diplomatic distance between themselves and the Negro showman.[108] Members of the Negro press and the community were not amused. Most of the Negro newspapers depicted Julian as an enigma, something short of a traitor to the Ethiopian cause, and, therefore, a traitor to the Negro race. To many in the Negro community, he was portrayed as a selfish con artist, and an embarrassment.[109]

When Julian decided to go on a lecture tour, reportedly sponsored by the friends of the Italian government, Negro groups sympathetic to the Ethiopian cause, such as the Friends of Ethiopia, led by Willis Huggins, and other organizations, petitioned the State Department to get Julian deported, on the grounds that the pilot was a threat to U.S. security.[110] Although there was no evidence that the State Department acted on the petition, Julian left the country for France in mid-January of 1936; and when he returned later in February of the same year, he was detained at Ellis Island.[111]

Later in June 1936, when the Italians overran Ethiopia, Julian announced to the Negro press, to no one's surprise, that he was an Italian subject and had changed his name to Huberto Fauntleroyana Juliano. He sailed to Italy for a tour of duty. He was to join the other Ethiopian defectors in Italy—Chieftain Ras Guysa and Malaku Bayen—to assist the Italian government in their occupation of Ethiopia. With this announcement, Julian was dismissed in the Negro press as a traitor to the human rights struggle. Whatever he contributed to the development of aviation in the Negro community was forever trivialized.[112]

In later years, Julian, in his biography, offered that he, in reality, was drawing attention to himself to divert attention from his plan to assassinate Mussolini. Although he claimed that he and Bayen were to meet with Mussolini, the opportunity for an assassination never occurred because, according to Julian, Mussolini's assistant canceled the meeting. As his career exhibited,[113] Julian had an answer for everything and always planned his escape routes.

Notes

1. Floyd J. Calvin, "Harlem Publisher Backs Cross Country Hop," *Pittsburgh Courier*, 12 March 1932; Floyd J. Calvin, "Leon Paris," *Pittsburgh Courier*, 26 March 1932; Floyd J. Calvin, "Paris Reaches Cuba," *Pittsburgh Courier*, 30 April 1932; "Aviator Arrives in Haiti," *Pittsburgh Courier*, 7 May 1932.

2. "Julian to Name Plane `High Courier,'" *Pittsburgh Courier*, 7 May 1932; Eleanor Barnes, "Costs of Flying Has Reached High Altitude, Says California Aviatrix," *Pittsburgh Courier*, 7 May 1932; "Fly With 'Em," *Pittsburgh Courier*, 22 July 1932.

3. Vaughn Hardesy and Dominick Pisano, *Black Wings: The American Black in Aviaton* (Washington, D.C.: The American National Air and Space Museum, Smithsonian Institution Press, 1984), 7.

4. J. Herman Banning, "The Day I Sprouted Wings," *Pittsburgh Courier*, 23 August 1932.

5. Interview with Cornelius Coffey, 1 February 1991, Chicago, Illinois; Banning, "The Day I Sprouted Wings," *Pittsburgh Courier*, 23 August 1932.

6. "Banning Dies in Air Crash," *Pittsburgh Courier*, 11 February 1933.

7. J. Herman Banning, "A Fugitive from Justice," *Pittsburgh Courier*, 31 December 1932.

8. Hardesy and Pisano, *Black Wings*, 7.

9. Ibid.

10. Lawrence F. Lamarr, "Aviators Race to Cleveland," *Pittsburgh Courier*, 27 August 1932; Barnes, "Costs of Flying Has Reached High Altitude," *Pittsburgh Courier*, 7 May 1932.

11. "Aviator's Wife Very Ill," *Pittsburgh Courier*, 13 February 1932.

12. Lamarr, "Aviators Race to Cleveland," *Pittsburgh Courier*, 27 August 1932.

13. "Where Trail of Plane Ended," *Pittsburgh Courier*, 10 September 1932.

14. "Col. Julian Plans Hop from New York to Paris," *Pittsburgh Courier*, 25 March 1933.

15. "Daring Aviators Near Goal," *Pittsburgh Courier*, 1 October 1932.

16. Bessye J. Bearden, "Two Fly Coast to Coast in an `Old Plane,'" *Chicago Defender*, 15 October 1932.

17. "Aviators End First Cross Country Flight," *Pittsburgh Courier*, 15 October 1932.

18. Ibid.; Hardesy and Pisano, *Black Wings*, 9; Bearden, "Two Fly Coast to Coast," *Chicago Defender*, 15 October 1932; "Fly From Coast," *New York Amsterdam News*, 12 October 1932.

19. "Banning Dies in Air Crash," *Pittsburgh Courier*, 11 February 1933.

20. Ibid.

21. "Blame White Flyer in Query of Banning's Death," *Pittsburgh Courier*, 18 February 1933.

22. "Californians Take Lead in Aviation," *Chicago Defender*, 23 May 1936; William J. Powell, "Leaders Should Encourage Field of Aviation," *Pittsburg Courier*, 15 May 1936; "Letter to the Editors," *Pittsburgh Courier*, 15 May 1936; Associated Negro Press, "Powell Leads Teaching of Brown Airmen," *Pittsburgh Courier*, 15 May 1936.

23. "Californians Take Lead," *Chicago Defender*, 23 May 1936; Associated Negro Press, "Powell Leads Teaching of Brown Airmen," *Pittsburgh Courier*, 15 May 1936.

24. "Col. Julian Plans Hop from New York to Paris," *Pittsburgh Courier*, 25 March 1933.

25. Interview with C. Alfred Anderson, 10 June 1990, Tuskegee, Alabama.

26. Ibid.

27. Ibid.

28. Ibid.

29. Ibid.

30. Ibid.

31. Ibid.; "Licensed Negro Aviators," in *Negro Yearbook, An Annual Encyclopedia of the Negro, 1937-1938*, edited by Monroe Work (Tuskegee, Alabama: Tuskegee Institute, 1938), 279; "Philly's First Transport Pilot," *Pittsburgh Courier*, 5 March 1932; Enoch P. Waters, *American Diary: A Personal History of the Black Press* (Chicago: Path Press, Inc., 1987), 200.

32. Interview with C. Alfred Anderson.

33. Ibid.

34. "Forsythe-Anderson Arrive on Coast after Record Flight, *Pittsburgh Courier*, 22 July 1933.

35. Interview with C. Alfred Anderson.

36. Ibid.

37. Ibid.

38. Hardesy and Pisano, *Black Wings*, 16.

39. Ibid.; Interview with C. Alfred Anderson.

40. Interview with C. Alfred Anderson. In June of 1934, John Robinson inquired about establishing a flight school at Tuskegee. Moton rejected the proposal.

41. Interview with C. Alfred Anderson.

42. Ibid.

43. Ibid.

44. Ibid.

45. Hardesy and Pisano, *Black Wings*, 16.

46. Janet Waterford, "The Real Story of Col. John Robinson," *Chicago Defender*, 5 April 1936; Interview with Cornelius Coffey.

47. Interview with Cornelius Coffey.

48. Ibid.

49. Ibid.

50. P. L. Prattis, "Ethiopia's Black Condor: The Story of John C. Robinson, Who Set His Heart on Becoming an Aviator—by a Man who Knew Him," *New York Amsterdam News*, 26 October 1935.
51. Interview with Cornelius Coffey.
52. Ibid.; Janet Waterford, "Robinson Organizes Brown Eagle Aero Club in Effort to Interest Race on Flying," *Chicago Defender*, 12 April 1936; Interview with Harold Hurd, 10 October 1990, Chicago, Illinois; Interview with Cornelius Coffey.
53. Waterford, "Robinson Organizes Brown Eagle," *Chicago Defender*, 12 April 1936; Interview with Cornelius Coffey.
54. Interview with Cornelius Coffee; Interview with Harold Hurd.
55. Waterford, "Robinson Arouses Race Interest in Aviation," *Chicago Defender*, 19 April 1936; Interview with Cornelius Coffey; Interview with Harold Hurd.
56. Waterford, "Robinson Arouses Race Interest in Aviation," *Chicago Defender*, 19 April 1936; Interview with Cornelius Coffey; Interview with Harold Hurd.
57. Ibid.
58. Ibid.; Hardesy and Pisano, *Black Wings*, 9-11.
59. Interview with Cornelius Coffey; Interview with Harold Hurd.
60. Waterford, "The Real Story of Col. John Robinson," *Chicago Defender*, 5 April 1936.
61. Prattis, "Ethiopia's Black Condor," *New York Amsterdam News*, 26 October 1935; Interview with Cornelius Coffey.
62. Ibid.; Interview with Cornelius Cobbey.
63. Ibid.
64. Ibid.
65. Ibid.
66. Ibid.
67. Ibid.; Associated Negro Press, "Tuskegee Graduates 183 at Commencement," *Pittsburgh Courier*, 2 June 1934.
68. Associated Negro Press, "Tuskegee Graduates 183 at Commencement," *Pittsburgh Courier*, 2 June 1934.
69. Interview with Harold Hurd.
70. Ibid.
71. Ibid.; Interview with Cornelius Coffey.
72. J. A. Rogers, "Italians Retreating," *Pittsburgh Courier*, 18 January 1936; "Ask League to Uphold Its Edicts," *Chicago Defender*, 22 September 1935; "Pro-Ethiopian Parade to be Protest Call," *New York Amsterdam News*, 27 April 1935.
73. "Italo-Ethiopian War Events Told," *Chicago Defender*, 12 October 1935.
74. Ibid.
75. Ibid.
76. Franklin, *From Slavery to Freedom*; Interview with Cornelius Coffey.
77. Franklin, *From Slavery to Freedom*, 574.

78. Interview with Cornelius Coffey; Interview with Harold Hurd; Associated Negro Press, "Col. Robinson Orders Six New Planes for Chi Flyers to Fight for Ethiopia," *Chicago Defender*, 4 January 1936.
79. Associated Negro Press, "Col. Robinson Orders Six New Planes for Chi Flyers to Fight for Ethiopia," *Chicago Defender*, 4 January 1936.
80. Interview with Cornelius Coffey; Interview with Harold Hurd.
81. Ibid.; "J. A. Roger's Exclusive Interview with Col. Robinson, Ethiopia's `Brown Condor,'" *Pittsburgh Courier*, 4 January 1936.
82. "Italo-Ethiopian War Events Told," *Chicago Defender*, 12 October 1935; J. A. Rogers, "Rogers Takes Death Ride," *Pittsburgh Courier*, 4 January 1936.
83. "Col. Julian Restored to King's Favor, *Chicago Defender*, 22 September 1935; Scott, "Hubert F. Julian."
84. Scott, "Hubert F. Julian," 15; "Col. Julian Turns Back on Ethiopia," *New York Amsterdam News*, 23 November 1935.
85. Interview with Harold Hurd; Interview with Cornelius Coffey.
86. Ibid.
87. Ibid.; "Ethiopian Air Chief," *Chicago Defender*, 31 August 1935; "Col. Julian Turns Back on Ethiopia," *New York Amsterdam News*, 23 November 1935.
88. "Italo-Ethiopian War Events Told," *Chicago Defender*, 30 November 1935.
89. Ibid.
90. Ibid.
91. Ibid.
92. Ibid.
93. Ibid.; "Robinson Tells All in the Bombing of Adowa," *Chicago Defender*, 12 October 1935.
94. Ibid.
95. "Negro Fighter in Center of Adowa Fight," *New York Amsterdam News*, 12 October 1935; Associated Negro Press, "Salassie Air Chief Eludes Italians," *Chicago Defender*, 12 December 1935.
96. J. A. Rogers, "Col. Robinson Stages Air Duel in Clouds with Enemy Planes," *Pittsburgh Courier*, 14 December 1935.
97. Ibid.; J. A. Rogers, "Rogers Paints Vivid World Picture," *Pittsburgh Courier*, 14 December 1935.
98. "J. A. Rogers Exclusive Interview with Col. Robinson," *Pittsburgh Courier*, 4 January 1936.
99. Ibid.; Rogers, "Rogers Paints Vivid World Picture," *Pittsburgh Courier*, 14 December 1935; Rogers, "Rogers Takes a Death Ride," *Pittsburgh Courier*, 4 January 1936; J. A. Rogers, "Little Rains in Ethiopia Have Halted Il Duce," *Pittsburgh Courier*, 18 January 1936.
100. "Leading Mountain Attack," *Chicago Defender*, 28 April 1936.
101. Associated Negro Press, "Col. Robinson Orders Six New Planes for Chi Flyers to Fight for Ethiopia," *Chicago Defender*, 4 January 1936.

102. Ibid.
103. Interview with Cornelius Coffey; Interview with Harold Hurd.
104. "Col. Julian Turns Back on Ethiopia," *New York Amsterdam News,* 23 November 1935.
105. Ibid.; "Col. Julian Admitted Zaphiro Scares Him," *Chicago Defender,* 2 February 1936; "On Way Home," *Chicago Defender,* 30 November 1935.
106. Edgar Wiggins, "Col. Julian Has Story," *Chicago Defender,* 21 December 1935; "Col. Julian Sold Out for $1,250, Alleged," *Pittsburgh Courier,* 11 January 1936.
107. "Col. Julian Sold Out for $1,250," *Pittsburgh Courier,* 11 January 1936; "Rumors Revived as Julian Joins Italians," *Chicago Defender,* 14 June 1936.
108. "Col. Julian Sold Out for $1,250," *Pittsburgh Courier,* 11 January 1936.
109. Ibid.; Scott, "Hubert F. Julian," 19.
110. Scott, "Hubert F. Julian," 20; "In Defense of Col. Julian," *Chicago Defender,* 11 January 1936.
111. Defender Press Service, "Black Eagle Admitted to U.S.," *Chicago Defender,* 8 February 1936; "Julian Can Only Blame Himself," *Chicago Defender,* 2 February 1936.
112. Scott, "Hubert F. Julian," 21.
113. Ibid., 22.

Chapter 4

The Movement

Remarkably, in 1936, there were over one hundred licensed Negro airplane pilots.[1] Chicago, with over 30 percent of the Negro licensed pilots in the country, continued to be the center of Negro aviation. These forward-thinking men and women of the Challenger Air Pilots Association, led by the experienced Cornelius Coffey, were of the best the Chicago area could offer. By late 1937, the Challengers had thirty-five members, several of whom had private pilots licenses, limited commercial licenses, and amateur licenses. Coffey and Dr. Earl Renfroe had transport licenses, the highest rated license. The club also owned five airplanes and leased two more. The Challengers still attracted doctors, dentists, nurses, lawyers, educators, and other professionals. A significant number of the club members were employed by the WPA.

These citizens, as evidenced by their involvement in the Chicago Society for Aid of Ethiopia and by their attempts to join John Robinson in combat in Ethiopia, were conscious of the Negro's condition on the African continent and in Chicago, and were willing to fight for freedom in both communities. Many members of the Challenger Club were active in the Chicago branches of the NAACP, the Urban League and various other civil rights and civic groups. Members of the club were involved in the Urban League's "Jobs for Negroes" campaign in Chicago, where African Americans boycotted white-owned retail outlets dependent on Negro consumers that did not employ Negroes.[2]

In February 1936, Chicago played host to the first Negro National Congress. This particular conference, the brainchild of John P. Davis, a lawyer and architect of the Negro Committee on National Recovery, featured the convening of 900 individuals representing several civil rights, civic, fraternal, sorority, and labor groups, including members of

61

the Challengers, together for the first time since the NAACP-backed
Amenia Conference in 1933. The purpose of the congress was to forge
unity among diverse organizations on goals such as unionism, adequate
and equitable relief from the "New Deal" programs, civil and political
rights, equality in economic opportunity, suppression of lynching, and
the abolition of segregation.[3]

Although this Congress was independent of any political party or per-
suasion, members of the Communist party did participate in the
regional Congress activities, and most had joined the local NAACP and
Urban League branches. As a result of the Communist infiltration into
their organizations, producing a fear of backlash from funding sources
and other philanthropic interests, the NAACP, and especially the Urban
League, proceeded to distance themselves from the party and the
National Congress. This very basic fear of Communist association and
affiliation led to the death of the National Negro Congress in 1940.[4]

One of the highlights of the National Negro Congress was the
appearance of Col. Hubert Julian. The "Black Eagle," fresh from being
detained at Ellis Island for attempting to enter the United States without a visa, entered the hall where the Congress was being held, royally
attired with his trademark cane. His timing was horrible. Colonel Julian
arrived the night after Lij Tansfaye Zaphiro, first secretary to the
Ethiopian representative in London, gave a stirring speech appealing
for aid for his country, then at war with Italy. Colonel Julian was noticed
immediately by the commander of the Brooklyn National War Veterans
Association, E. L. Sullinger. Mr. Sullinger began shouting "traitor, traitor," and asked the chairperson of the session, John Davis, to eject
Julian from the Congress. The shouting continued and included many
more conferees. Davis was forced to act on the disturbance. He asked
Julian for credentials verifying his registration at the Congress. When
Julian could not produce credentials, Davis asked him to leave. The
"Black Eagle" was escorted out by the police.[5]

The unanimous disdain for the reputation of Colonel Julian, which
was not enhanced by the Negro press releases and speeches from
Ethiopian representatives such as Zaphiro, was juxtaposed with the reverence exhibited in the Congress and in the Negro press for John
Robinson. The "Brown Condor's" courage and conviction, and his association with Cornelius Coffey and the Challenger Air Pilot Club of
Chicago were beyond reproach.

Under Coffey, the Challengers actively recruited women. By 1936,
two women were officers in the organization. As a policy, the Air Club
admitted one women for every ten men.[6] One woman, Willa Brown, was
to play a pivotal role in the development of Negro aviation.

Ms. Brown was recruited in 1935 by John Robinson, before he left for Ethiopia. They met in a Walgreen's Pharmacy in Chicago. Robinson, who was attracted by Ms. Brown's physical attributes, and very interested in getting acquainted, successfully sold Ms. Brown on the idea of joining the Challenger Club. Ms. Brown was a teacher of business administration at Roosevelt High School in Gary, Indiana.[7] She was a woman who enjoyed action and excitement, and found the Challenger Club stimulating. Flying became her avocation and she divorced her husband, secured a student pilot's license and devoted herself to expanding and promoting the Challenger Club.[8]

The problem of lack of visibility in certain parts of the Negro community affected the Challengers in the same manner that it affected the local branches of the NAACP. The Negro masses of Chicago had no idea that African Americans were flying airplanes in their area, and were certainly unaware of an organization of Negro flyers. Up until 1936, the Negro press, including the local *Chicago Defender*, carried few stories on Negro aviators. With the exception of Robinson and Julian, both of whom were featured infrequently in the Ethiopian campaign coverage in 1935, the Negro press did not give much ink to Negroes involved in aviation.[9]

Aviation required specific skills and money. Those African Americans who were involved were well educated professionals in other fields, highly skilled and successful mechanics from the Negro middle class, or were associated with the Negro middle class. The Challengers, members of the Negro middle class, tended to identify and socialize with other Negroes of the same class. To foster Negro interest in aviation, the Challengers had to expand their visibility beyond the Negro middle class. They had to develop a strategy to attract the Negro masses of Chicago.[10]

The primary reason for developing the vocation of aviation in the Negro community was that the field of aviation was still relatively new, and although opportunities in aviation in 1936 were rare for African Americans, positions in aviation mechanics, traffic control, commuter services, transport services, and positions in the Army Air Corps as ground crew members and pilots, were strong possibilities for African Americans in the future. Robinson and Coffey could visualize the future and made plans for the establishment of an aviation school, complete with ground school, mechanics, and pilot training. To accomplish this goal, they needed both money and visibility.

To attract publicity and raise funds, the Challengers relied on the business management and public relations expertise of Willa Brown. The group soon realized that without mass publicity the usual fundraising fare of chicken and fish dinners, dances, and air shows would only bring in a limited amount of money. They had to develop a more effective way of attracting attention and raising funds.[11] Willa Brown, chairperson of the Challengers' education committee and a member of the advisory board, planned ways to increase the group's visibility in the Negro community, until Felix Kirkpatrick, a new member of the Challengers, recommended that she see Enoch Waters, then the coordinator of editorials for the *Chicago Defender*.[12] Kirkpatrick, one of only two African Americans at the West Point Academy, had been suspiciously dismissed after his freshman year because of demerits given by upperclassmen. The *Defender* covered his appointment to the academy and carried a story on his dismissal.[13]

The business acumen and supreme confidence of Willa Brown was quite evident when she arrived unannounced and without appointment at the *Defender* newsroom. Reportedly disarmed by Willa's beauty and verve, Waters spent a short time listening to Willa's pitch for the Challenger Air Pilots Club. Waters, attracted by the news value of the event and by his personal interest in Ms. Brown, was persuaded to cover the air show for the *Defender*.[14]

Willa Brown's visit to the *Defender* newsroom was the public relations masterpiece needed to propel the Challengers into national prominence. Enoch Waters was so impressed with the flying expertise of the Challengers, that he persuaded the publisher of the *Defender*, Robert Abbott, and the editor, John Sengstake, to allow the *Defender* to cosponsor air shows with the Challengers. Persuading Abbott was not difficult since he reportedly had known Bessie Coleman personally, and had supported her in her attempts to pursue a flying career. Also, promoting Negro aviation was good business sense. Aviation was still a novelty in the country, especially among Negroes. Robert Abbott, being a staunch integrationist and a savvy businessman, supported Negro involvement in nontraditional vocations. In 1936, aviation was very nontraditional, and their coverage of the field would attract readers to the *Defender*.[15]

In addition, the *Defender* began printing a series of stories on Negro aviators, not only in Chicago, but also those operating in other parts of the country. Janet Waterford, of the Challenger Club, contributed several articles featuring Bessie Coleman, Johnny Robinson, Earl Renfroe, and other pioneer pilots.[16] The *Defender* covered the experiences of William Powell and the Bessie Coleman Club, and the Craftsmen of Black Wings in Los Angeles. Other Negro newspapers were receptive to the exploits of the Negro pilots. The *Pittsburgh Courier*, in particular, was supportive of Negro aviators. The *Courier* dispatched journalist J. A.

Rogers to Ethiopia to report on the hostilities between Ethiopia and Italy. Rogers interviewed Robinson extensively and his stories were carried by the *Courier* and other Negro weeklies.[17] The *Courier* also featured James Peck, a native of Pittsburgh, who served the Loyalists as a fighter pilot in the Spanish Civil War.[18] Robert Vann, the publisher of the *Courier* was, like his peer Robert Abbott, always supportive of the inclusion of African Americans in the field of aviation.

By 1936, the circulation of the Negro newspapers had reached the 380,000 mark with a readership rate of one million. The largest of the papers, the *Defender,* the *Baltimore Afro-American,* and the *Courier,* were national editions, with heavy circulation in the Northeast, Midwest, and South.[19] The Negro press, with the assistance of the Associated Negro Press, led by Claude Barnett, was the only mass communication tool, other than a few film production companies owned by and readily available to the Negro and, therefore, was the best mass medium to publicize events of national significance. John Robinson was a national figure. He was the only American who risked his life to fight for the last African empire. The homecoming of John Robinson would be an event perfectly suited for promoters of aviation, and the perfect media event for the Negro press.

The "Brown Condor" (the name given to Robinson by the press) was forced to leave Ethiopia in May of 1936.[20] The great Italian offensive, the alleged defection of various Ethiopian tribal leaders, and the unwillingness or inability of the League of Nations to provide relief had Emperor Selassie on the run, and the situation was untenable for Robinson. The rainy season provided Robinson the opportunity to flee the country. Cornelius Coffey sold one of his airplanes and sent Robinson money for the return trip to the States.[21]

Once it was known that Robinson was on his way back to the States, the Negro press, especially the *Defender,* the *Courier,* and the *New York Amsterdam News,* plotted strategy for getting the "exclusive" on Robinson's escapades in Ethiopia and his plans for the future. The *Courier* had already had an exclusive interview with Robinson in Ethiopia, but the *Defender's* David Kellum caught a ride on a Coast Guard patrol boat and met Robinson on the German luxury liner *Europa* for an exclusive interview, prior to its docking in New York Harbor.[22] The *Amsterdam News* was content to plan the welcome celebration, in conjunction with Claude Barnett of the Associated Negro Press, United Aid for Ethiopia, the African Patriotic League, the UNIA, and other organizations.[23]

When the *Europa* docked in New York on 22 May 1936, John Robinson disembarked from the ship to a roaring crowd of 2,000

African Americans from Harlem. A welcoming committee of several men immediately hoisted Robinson onto their shoulders and carried him to the reception room. After endless handshakes and endless kisses, the "Brown Condor" addressed the group in a modest manner, thanking the people for their warm reception and stating that he was glad to be home but would rather be fighting with "His Majesty" Selassie back in Ethiopia.[24] He was driven by a motorcade to the Harlem YMCA on West 135th Street. At this affair, many dignitaries gave speeches in honor of Robinson and the efforts of Ethiopia. Robinson, himself, emphasized that there was still work to do in Ethiopia and that there was a great need for doctors, nurses, and medical supplies to treat the thousands affected by the poison-gas bombs dropped by the Italian Air Force. He also stated that he intended to start a flying school to interest more African Americans in aviation and to train more Negroes for service in Ethiopia, and that to accomplish this feat, he needed a new plane.[25]

The following day, the *Amsterdam News* editorialized Robinson as a modest, unassuming hero who "will do big things in aviation which will reflect credibility on the Negro. His type needs the boosts rather than the glib dramatic posers who bring us such humorous headlines and accounts in the white press."[26] Colonel Robinson was also the guest of honor at a fundraising banquet at the Rockland Palace where over $300 was raised, and more pledged, for an airplane for Robinson to use in his new aviation school.[27]

John Robinson's own flying club, the Challengers, and the local *Defender* were not to be upstaged by New York. Willa Brown, with assistance from other Challenger members and the *Defender* staff, orchestrated a bombastic welcome party for John Robinson in Chicago. Robinson's homecoming was the club's, and the *Defender*'s, best opportunity for more visibility and business.[28] Willa Brown managed to secure a meeting room with a balcony at the Grand Hotel. She also arranged to have an evening banquet fundraiser at the Binga Arcade Building catered by the most exclusive restaurant on the South Side of Chicago.[29] The Challengers hoped to raise money and to secure enough pledges to purchase another plane.

When Robinson stepped off the TWA plane at Chicago Municipal Airport, he was mobbed by hundreds of persons who had broken through the police lines. He was showered with kisses and flowers. There were also several photo opportunities for the dignitaries at the airport, members of the welcoming committee, including the Challenger Club; Robert Abbott; Claude Barnett; W. T. Brown, honorary mayor of the South Side; former congressmen Oscar DePriest; Dr.

Julian H. Lewis, president of the Society of the United Aid of Ethiopia; members of the Eighth Infantry and the Military Order Guard; and many others.[30] After about fifteen minutes of exaltation, members of the welcoming committee gave short speeches of welcome and thanks to Colonel Robinson. The "Brown Condor" was escorted to a flag-draped open car and was the guest of honor in a parade with a 500-car motorcade with motorcycle escort that extended all the way to the Grand Hotel. Colonel Robinson was presented by Claude Barnett to a swelling crowd of 20,000 persons. The overwhelmed aviator told the crowd, as reported in the *Defender:*

> I am among people that I love. I yet regretted very much that the war ended the way it did. I had hoped of course that Ethiopia had been victorious in her struggle to maintain her standing in the family of nations. This was impossible because of the League of Nations failed her in addition thereto, the very people upon whom Ethiopia depended believing them to be the most patriotic of the tribes turned traitor at the most crucial moment.[31]

The banquet for Colonel Robinson was, in many ways, a resounding success for the Challengers. There was enough money raised to make a profit for the Challenger Air Club. The club was able to complete payments on one plane and was able to put a down payment on another lightweight plane.[32] What they did not gain in profit, they gained in visibility. Present at the banquet was Mrs. Annie Malone, founder and president of Poro College, a music school in Chicago. Mrs. Malone was so impressed with Colonel Robinson's efforts in Ethiopia, and with his plans for an aviation school in Chicago, that she offered one of her coach houses on 4400 King Drive to Robinson and the Challengers to use for ground school instruction.[33]

With John Robinson back in Chicago, the agenda for the Challenger Air Pilots Club was full for the remainder of 1936 and into 1937. First on the agenda was the establishment of an aviation school; second was the establishment of a plane rental service; and third, was a small airline, commuter, and cargo service.[34]

Robinson immediately embarked on a speaking tour throughout the Midwest, the Northeast and the South. His goals were to raise money for the aviation school, to encourage support for Ethiopia, and to raise interest among Negroes in the field of aviation.[35] Most of his visits, especially those to Pittsburgh, Kansas City, and Washington, D.C. were sponsored by the Negro press in those cities. In cities in the South, where there were no local Negro newspapers, the lectures were preceded by advance stories by the Associated Negro Press in the Negro weeklies that were distributed there. The lectures proved mutually beneficial for Robinson, the Challengers, and the Negro press, both financially and from a public relations point of view. Lectures given in cities with a Negro aviation club were preceded by an aerial circus by Robinson and his Challenger Club members along with local aviators. The flyers and parachute jumpers and the sponsoring organizations would charge admission for the aerial show and the Negro press would have a sensational story to print with pictures of big-name celebrities who were attracted to the spectacle.[36]

These visits to different areas of the country, and the subsequent positive feedback, convinced the *Defender*'s Enoch Waters to suggest that the Challengers establish a national airmen's association among Negro pilots and other advocates of Negro aviation. Following his advise, Willa Brown, education chairperson and the unofficial business manager of the group, solicited interest in the idea from Negro aviators from around the country. The response was so positive that the National Airmen's Association of America was chartered in 1937, with branches in most major cities in the country, except in the deep South.[37] The association attracted such notables as C. Alfred Anderson, Dr. Eugene Forsythe, William Powell, Dr. A. Porter Davis, Willie "Suicide" Jones, James Peck, and others. The first charter members of the NAAA were: Enoch Waters, Cornelius Coffey, Willa Brown, Harold Hurd, Janet Waterford, Marie St. Clair, Dale White, Chauncey Spenser, Charles Johnson, Grover Nash, Edward Johnson, and George Williams.[38] The *Defender* donated office space and a mailing address for the NAAA.

The *Defender* and the Negro Associated Press circulated every type of story and aviation event featuring Negro pilots and parachute jumpers, to every part of the country, to both Negro and white press publications. Soon it was common to see feature stories with accompanying photos about Negro aviators in most Negro weeklies.[39] The Negro press, the Challengers, and the NAAA were responsible for developing the Negro interest in aviation to such an extent that young African Americans were selecting aviation as an avocation and were applying to the Army Air Corps for cadet training, something unheard of and unimagined in the previous decades of the twentieth century.[40]

Shortly after the development of the NAAA, Coffey received his transport license. The club now had several members with instructor ratings and two with transport and commercial ratings. The pilot and mechanic ratings would ensure the club's certification as a flying school. Dr. Renfroe was the other member with a transport license but his availability for cargo delivery and commuter service was limited, due to his dental practice. Coffey and Robinson, full time mechanics, had more opportunity to accept cargo delivery and commuter service jobs. Mrs. Malone, at the advice of Robinson, purchased a Gullwing Stinson that Robinson piloted when Mrs. Malone traveled on business-related trips. Coffey strongly encouraged Robinson to secure his transport license. Coffey had received word through his pilots' network that the state of Illinois was cracking down on renegade pilots without proper license to carry passengers. Coffey knew that Negro pilots would be more conspicuous than whites. Robinson knew of the danger to himself and to his partners. When he arranged short-term flights for clients, he would navigate and Coffey would do the flying.[41]

A few of the commuter jobs were quite adventurous, and Coffey had to rely on his ingenuity to survive. On one occasion in 1937, Coffey was flying on one of the promotional tours in Mississippi when he developed problems with his crankshaft. The problem occurred on takeoff at a Jackson, Mississippi, airport. Coffey realized that he had to land the plane with the engine off, on a "dead stick."[42] He did not want to ruin the crankshaft and its bearings. A Negro named Crawford, who worked at the airport, saw Coffey's plane coming in for a landing with a dead propeller. Sensing trouble, Crawford drove out to meet Coffey, once he landed. Coffey convinced Crawford to tow his airplane to a hanger where he could check the damage. Coffey diagnosed a blown out bearing, which could indicate a broken crankshaft. To find out, he would have to check the cylinder master rods and crankshaft. Crawford, who had not seen or heard of a Negro airplane engine mechanic, inquired whether Coffey knew what he was doing. Coffey persuaded a skeptical Crawford to help him find a few 2' x 4's, and with these, they constructed a workbench. To Crawford's surprise, Coffey then began to dismantle the airplane engine. Coffey sent Crawford to get some kerosene to clean the engine parts and some gasoline needed to test the engine repair.

While on his errand, Crawford must have disclosed to individuals at the gas station and at the hardware store that a Negro was repairing an airplane engine, because a crowd of whites came to gawk at Coffey while he worked on his plane. They watched in disbelief as Coffey dismantled the parts for Crawford to clean in the kerosene and wrap in newspaper for protection against dust. The white people, who had never seen a Negro pilot, or dreamed that there could be a Negro airplane mechanic, began to heckle Coffey, saying "that darkie don't know what he's doin' with that airplane."[43]

Coffey continued, unperturbed, and discovered, by checking the cylinder rods and turning the prop, that the crankshaft turned but the accessories to the crankshaft did not, which meant that the crankshaft was broken. Coffey would have to tear down the entire engine, put in another crankshaft and rebuild the engine. Crawford again asked Coffey whether he could do it. Coffey informed him that he was trained to do it, and that he could.

Coffey contacted a man in Chicago by the name of Jack Snyder. Mr. Snyder owned an outlet for used spare parts for plane engines. Snyder airmailed a crankshaft and two master rods, bearings, and gaskets. As soon as Coffey received the parts, he put in the crankshaft and master rods and began rebuilding the engine. Persons in the crowd kept shouting "call the junkman, call the junkman. You don't have the sense to know what you're doin'."[44] Coffey did not respond.

Within four days of his forced landing, Coffey had completed the repairs on the engine and was ready for testing. He taught Mr. Crawford how to use the switch and to turn the throttle. Coffey blocked the wheels, placed a booster magnet on the floor, and wired it to the engine to give it a hot start. Coffey gave Crawford the signal to boost and switch on the engine. Then Coffey spun the propeller and yelled "clear," giving Crawford the signal to hit the throttle. According to Coffey, the white crowd stared in disbelief as the plane started on the first try. Coffey enjoyed the moment of triumph, and walked in back of the plane, in full view and close proximity to the crowd, and loudly announced that they would let the plane run for about an hour, shut it off, and then look for oil spots on the ground.[45]

One hour later, Coffey checked for oil spots, found none, and put the engine cowlings back on. Crawford topped the fuel tank with gasoline and Coffey took the plane up for a successful test flight. When he landed, Coffey offered Crawford a ride. Crawford respectfully declined, with a contented smile.[46]

By late September 1936, the John Robinson National Air College and School of Automotive Engineering, probably the first of its kind for African Americans in the country, was chartered and presented its first orientation to interested students and distinguished guests of Chicago. Using the buildings donated by Mrs. Malone, the School offered all phases of aviation ground school, including airplane engine mechanics. Flight instruction was provided by certified flight instructors of the Challenger Club at Harlem Field. Coffey provided the instruction for the automobile engine repair, which supplemented the airplane engine repair and rebuilding course. The vocational training was augmented by the instruction of French and Spanish languages provided by Homer Lewis. All of the courses and equipment were approved and certified by the Illinois Department of Commerce.

The Negro press, civil rights organizations, and Negro aviation all came of age in 1936. In order to prosper, each entity needed the others. There was a lot of crossover in the membership of these organizations and, therefore, they all became aware of and sensitive to the upward mobility and gains of the others. As one entity benefited from mobility, so did the others. John Robinson, founder of the Challenger Air Pilots Club, provided the Negro press and Negro America with a bona fide hero with the stature of Joe Louis and Jesse Owens. News about heroes sells newspapers, and the more newspapers sold, the larger the circulation. The increase in readership provided greater opportunity for the civil rights organizations to educate the Negro masses on issues of importance to their lives.

John Robinson's involvement in the Ethiopian conflict raised more interest within the Negro community in the political status of African-ruled nations than any other activity since Marcus Garvey. Once their attention was focused on Ethiopia, the Negro community, and especially the Negro press, began to question the role of the League of Nations, its lack of support and protection for Ethiopia, one of the last self-ruled nations in Africa, and what that lack of action signified.[47] The NAACP, with concurrence from the Negro publishers, questioned the role of the United States and the League of Nations in allowing the invasion and suppression of an African-ruled nation. The inaction of the United States and the Roosevelt administration caused the NAACP and the Negro publishers to ruminate that America was ambivalent in its support for Ethiopia because the Ethiopian conflict involved Africans.[48] The Roosevelt administration further exacerbated the situation by publicly admonishing Germany's racist and horrific treatment of its Jewish citizens, while ignoring the civil rights bills and antilynching legislation proposed to protect the ten million American citizens of African ancestry.[49]

This inconsistency in the Roosevelt administration's position on human rights forced some of the Negro publishers, key players in his victory in the 1932 presidential election, to reassess their support for Roosevelt in the 1936 presidential campaign. Robert Vann, publisher of the *Courier*, resigned his post as assistant attorney general in the Justice Department because of Roosevelt's inability or unwillingness to openly support antilynching legislation and other civil rights bills.[50] Vann felt that his position in the Roosevelt administration, granted as a result of his support for Roosevelt in 1932, would put him in an awkward position of political indebtedness to Roosevelt, despite the president's civil rights record. Cognizant of Vann's strategy, and fearful that Vann's action might affect other Negro publishers and the civil rights organizations with influence over Negro voters, Roosevelt began, for the first time during his first term, to proclaim in his campaign speeches that there would be "no forgotten men or forgotten races" in his government programs.[51]

The Roosevelt administration rewarded African Americans for their support in 1932 by appointing several Negroes to prominent positions with the executive and judicial branches of government. During Roosevelt's first term, hundreds of African Americans were hired into Civil Service jobs.[52] Roosevelt's patronage convinced many Negro publishers, Negro politicians, and civil rights leaders, that life with Roosevelt was better than life with the lily-white administration of Herbert Hoover, and probably better than the life promised by Alf Landon, Roosevelt's opponent.[53] Roosevelt's other ace-in-the-hole was his wife, Eleanor. Mrs. Roosevelt was a staunch supporter of Negro civil rights, and spoke out against lynching. Her support and friendship with influential Negro leaders, such as Walter White and Mary McLeod Bethune, was to her husband's advantage.[54]

Although Roosevelt won the election in 1936 with the endorsement of the *Courier*, other Negro publications, and Negro voters, the Democrats would not take the Negro vote for granted, as long as Robert Vann and the Negro press were viable purveyors of the Roosevelt administration's policies and actions on issues affecting the health, welfare, and civil and voting rights of African Americans.

It was during the 1936 election that Vann became, arguably, the most feared Negro politician in the country. The Negro attorney and businessman from Ahoskie, North Carolina, was instrumental in bringing a significant number of the traditionally Republican Negro voters to the Democratic fold in 1932.[55] Vann was a practitioner of political independence, playing what he called "loose leaf politics," a strategy whereby Vann would use his newspaper to report and analyze events affecting the lives of the Negro community and "watch dog" the reactions of the political parties to those events.[56] Instead of blindly endorsing a political party or candidate, Vann advocated research and analysis of a candidate's position on Negro issues before selecting the candidate, especially a candidate competing for national office, who would serve as an advocate for the Negro.

What made Vann's "loose leaf" strategy so effective was that he could shape Negro opinion with one story that would often be carried by all of the other Negro newspapers in the country. Fortunately for Vann, the publishers and editors of the competing Negro newspapers, such as Robert Abbott of the *Chicago Defender*, shared his political views. Although the *Defender* endorsed Hoover in 1932 and Landon in 1936, it did so, with reservations, out of traditional respect for the party of Lincoln.[57] By 1936, however, the *Defender* editorials on national issues affecting Negroes mirrored those of the *Courier* and other Negro newspapers usually followed suit. This communications network, assisted by Claude Barnett's Associated Negro Press, gave Vann the tremendous political independence that he felt the Negro community needed in order to receive respect and support in the struggle for racial equality.[58]

Chosen as a delegate-at-large from Pennsylvania to the 1924 Democratic national convention, and selected as a delegate-at-large to the 1936 Republican national convention, Vann was so feared as a political power broker that he was the only Negro, at that time, ever to be elected delegate-at-large for both the Democratic and Republican national conventions.[59] The publisher of the *Courier* was also among the few African Americans ever given influential positions within two presidential administrations representing different political parties. Vann had been appointed by Pres. Calvin Coolidge as chairman of a commission assigned to investigate racial tensions in the Virgin Islands in 1926, and in 1933, President Roosevelt appointed Vann as special assistant attorney general.[60]

In the remaining years before World War II, Vann would use the *Courier* as a barometer of Negro opinion and as the bellwether for Negro civil and political rights in America, including the rights of African Americans to participate in nontraditional occupations, and especially in aviation.

Notes

1. Monroe Work, ed., *Negro Yearbook, An Annual Encyclopedia of the Negro, 1937-1938* (Tuskegee, Alabama: Tuskegee Institute, 1938).
2. Interview with Harold Hurd.
3. "Randolph Heads Negro Congress," *New York Amsterdam News*, 22 February 1936.
4. Leslie Fishel, Jr., "The Negro in the New Deal Era," *Wisconsin Magazine of History* 48 (Winter 1964): 111-26.
5. "Col. Julian Ousted by Angry Delegates," *New York Amsterdam News*, 22 February 1936; "Call Julian Traitor," *Chicago Defender*, 22 February 1936.
6. Interview with Cornelius Coffey.
7. Ibid.
8. Waters, *American Diary*, 196-97.
9. Ibid., 196.
10. Interview with Cornelius Coffey.
11. Interview with Harold Hurd.

12. Waters, *American Diary*, 195.
13. "Kirkpatrick Returned from Academy, Tells of Dismissal," *Chicago Defender*, 11 January 1936.
14. Waters, *American Diary*, 195-96.
15. Ibid., 201-3.
16. Waterford, "The Real Story of Col. John Robinson," *Chicago Defender*, 5 April 1936; Waterford, "Robinson Organizes Brown Eagle," *Chicago Defender*, 12 April 1936.
17. Rogers, "J. A. Rogers Exclusive Interview with Col. Robinson," *Pittsburgh Courier*, 4 January 1936.
18. James Peck, "Goodwill Aviators Run into Plenty of Trouble," *Pittsburgh Courier*, 20 May 1939.
19. Brewer, "Robert Lee Vann," 102, in Sternsher, *The Negro in Depression and War*, 228-29.
20. David W. Kellum, "War Ace is Welcomed by Harlemmites," *Chicago Defender*, 23 May 1936; "Ethiopia Airman Returning Home," *New York Amsterdam News*, 11 April 1936.
21. Interview with Cornelius Coffey.
22. Kellum, "War Ace is Welcomed by Harlemmites," *Chicago Defender*, 23 May 1936.
23. G. James Flemming, "Col. Robinson Acclaimed As Ethiopia Hero," *New York Amsterdam News*, 23 May 1936.
24. Kellum, "War Ace is Welcomed by Harlemmites," *Chicago Defender*, 23 May 1936.
25. Ibid.
26. Flemming, "Col. Robinson Acclaimed As Ethiopia Hero," *New York Amsterdam News*, 23 May 1936; "A Hero Returns," *New York Amsterdam News*, 23 May 1936.
27. Ibid.; "5000 Pay Tribute to Robinson, *New York Amsterdam News*, 30 May 1936.
28. Waters, *American Diary*, 203.
29. Interview with Cornelius Coffey.
30. David W. Kellum, "Twenty Thousand Greet `Brown Condor' on Return," *Chicago Defender*, 30 May 1936; Associated Negro Press, "Chicago Hails Col. Robinson," *New Amsterdam News*, 30 May 1936.
31. Ibid.
32. Interview with Cornelius Coffey.
33. Ibid.
34. Ibid.; Associated Negro Press, "Robinson Wants Negro Air Line," *New York Amsterdam News*, 27 June 1936; Waters, *American Diary*, 204.
35. "Col. Robinson to Open Tour," *New York Amsterdam News*, 6 June 1936.
36. Waters, *American Diary*, 203-4.
37. Ibid., 201-3.
38. Ibid., 201.
39. Ibid., 202.

40. Lt. Benjamin O. Davis Jr., graduate of West Point, class of 1936, applied for a commission in Army Air Corps and was rejected due to the absence of Negro squadrons in the Air Corps. Benjamin O. Davis, Jr., *Benjamin O. Davis, Jr., American, An Autobiography* (Washington, D.C.: Smithsonian Institute Press, 1991), 44.
41. Interview with Cornelius Coffey.
42. Ibid.
43. Ibid.
44. Ibid.
45. Ibid.
46. Ibid.
47. Franklin, *From Slavery to Freedom*, 574.
48. "Pro-Ethiopian Parade to be Protest Call," *New York Amsterdam News*, 27 April 1935; "10,000 Protest Mussolini," *New York Amsterdam News*, 28 September 1935; Editorial, "Roosevelt and the Fascists," *Pittsburgh Courier*, 3 Octover 1936.
49. Kelly Miller, "The Mirror," *New York Amsterdam News*, 30 November 1935.
50. Brewer, "Robert Lee Vann," 100-3.
51. Allan Morrison, "The Secret Papers of FDR," *Negro Digest* 9 (January 1951): 3-13, in Sternsher, *The Negro in Depression and War*, 224-29.
52. Franklin, *From Slavery to Freedom*, 530-34.
53. Brewer, "Robert Lee Vann," 100-3.
54. White, *A Man Called White*, 168-69; Mary McLeod Bethune, "My Secret Talks with FDR, *Ebony* 4 (April 1949): 42-51, in Sternsher, *The Negro in Depression and War*, 53-65.
55. Brewer, "Robert Lee Vann," 100-3.
56. Ibid.
57. Ibid.
58. Franklin, *From Slavery to Freedom*, 562-63.
59. "Vann Gives Answer to Dems," *Pittsburgh Courier*, 28 October 1940; "Courier Editor Seriously Ill," *Pittsburgh Courier*, 26 October 1940.
60. Ibid.

Chapter 5

The Negro Aviator
and the Military

By 1937, the threatening Nazi movement displayed aggression by overtaking Austria, the Japanese invaded Manchuria and Indochina, the Italians occupied Ethiopia, and the Axis pact was signed by all three countries. The colonizing countries of Western Europe, particularly France and England, began to prepare for war.[1] Although the contiguous United States was not immediately vulnerable to attack from Axis members, it had a vested interest in its Negro "protectorates," such as the Philippines, Hawaii, Midway Island, Haiti, Puerto Rico, Cuba, Panama, and Liberia.[2] In response to the aggression of the Axis powers, the War Department secretly devised a troop mobilization plan that could be implemented, if forced into war.

In 1937, the U.S. regular army troop strength was at 165,000, and less than 2 percent, or about 3,000 troops, were Negro. All of the Negroes were concentrated in two cavalry regiments and two infantry regiments, with service units attached.[3] By 1931, Negro troop strength within these four regiments had been reduced, as a result of a 1926 congressional allotment for the expansion of the Army Air Corps.[4] The Air Corps allotment was acquired by extracting funds from other branches of the army. The reduction in allocation forced a downsizing of the four Negro regiments, causing a reduction in force. Therefore, Negro troops suffered a disproportionate reduction in force, when compared with white troops, because they had no other options in the regular army. In addition, Negro soldiers who were mustered out were barred from entering the Air Corps.[5]

According to the 1937 Mobilization Plan, the War Department called for a increase in the quota of African Americans in the regular army. According to Ulysses G. Lee's "Employment of Negro Troops in World

War II," the plan recommended that Negroes and whites be mobilized in proportion to their respective populations. If there was a mobilization effort, African Americans would be guaranteed at least 9.5 percent of the population that constituted the American troop strength.[6] To accomplish this, the War Department would have to add more Negro units in order to have an army proportionately representative of the Negro population in the country. The army would have to recruit and enlist more Negroes than whites, initially, on the designation of an emergency mobilization, in order to have a racially representative quota of Negroes.[7]

African Americans would be assigned to Infantry, the Cavalry, Artillery, Harbor Defense, Service Battalions, and Overhead Battalions.[8] However, there were no plans for separate Negro combat units above the designation of regiment. Allegedly, the War Department feared that Negro combat battalions could be attached to white units where Negroes were not wanted by white officers who practiced bigotry or by those who benefited by it.[9]

Many officers in the army, the majority of whom were from the South, believed in the stereotypes perpetuated by the Army War College studies of the Negro soldier produced in the previous decade, and the War College Reports of 1936. The War College studies and reports were, primarily, unscientific surveys and interviews of white officers who commanded Negro troops in World War I.[10] According to the studies, African Americans soldiers were "child-like," "careless," "shiftless," "irresponsible," "secretive," "superstitious," "unmoral and untruthful," and "more likely to be guilty of moral turpitude." The Negro soldier was also branded as "a comic," "emotionally unstable," "musically inclined, with good rhythm," and "if fed, loyal and compliant."[11]

The most damaging findings in the so-called studies were those that depicted the Negro soldier, especially the officer, as "lacking in physical courage and psychological characteristics" which made the Negro soldier "inherently inferior" and caused the Negro soldier to "lack confidence in his colored officer."[12]

The study also concluded that the Negro was intellectually inferior to the white man because his brain weighed thirty-five ounces contrasted with forty-five ounces for whites. This particular finding provided the army with a convenient and "scientific" explanation for the poor scores on army intelligence tests given to Negro inductees. Since the majority of Negroes scored in the lower percentiles, the army believed that the Negro soldier could only perform labor duty.[13]

The studies simply reflected the ignorance of men purporting to be intelligent officers. Despite strong evidence and support of the gallant service of Negro troops provided by General Pershing, Commander-in-Chief of the American Expeditionary Forces, and by Emmet Scott, Special Assistant to the Secretary of War, the War College studies provided the rationalization for white corps commanders and chiefs committed to limiting, if not eliminating, the opportunities for Negro soldiers within the army and navy, and especially within the Air Corps.[14]

The 1937 Mobilization Plan also included a provision that would require Negroes to be mobilized into arms and service units in the same ratio as white troops. The War Department knew that this would be a controversial provision, since the majority of African Americans who had served in World War I were limited to common labor and road building. Segregated arms and service units would also be maintained, and the only Negro officers would be warrant officers and chaplains. There would be no additional Negro officer candidates, over the number needed for the segregated units, unless there was a loss in the number of officers available at mobilization time.[15]

Another provision required African Americans to be assigned to service command and War Department overhead installations in a percentage "not less than" the percentage of Negroes in the total male population of military age within the corps area where the bases were located. The same provision called for Negroes to be assigned to overhead installations in arms and services units in a percentage "at least equal" to the percentage of African Americans in the male population in the area of the installation.[16] This provision was not as progressive as it appeared, since most of the installations and bases where African Americans would be assigned were in the South, an area with a large Negro male population.

Since another provision required the army to assign African Americans to arms and service units in the same ratio as whites, the army would have to add new Negro arms and service units in order to attain the same arms and service assignment ratio as that for white troops. There were no provisions for the addition of new Negro arms units in 1937. The army could conceivably have added new Negro service and overhead units and could have assigned them to southern installations. Therefore, the majority of the Negro troops inducted at mobilization time in 1937 could have been assigned to service and overhead duty.

The Army's Mobilization Plan of 1937 was the first War Department effort to seriously consider the Negro soldier's role in mobilization for war since 1931. War in 1937 was more of a possibility than war in 1931. In light of the contentious reports of the Negro troop effectiveness in World War I, which were utilized in the development of the 1931 Troop Utilization Plan, a few commanders in the War Department were sensitive to the Negro community's response to the employment of Negro troops.[17]

The War Department learned, through its experience in World War I, that there must be a consensus of allegiance and purpose among its population toward the elimination of the enemy force. The enemy must be readily identifiable, and the reason for fighting the enemy must be unequivocal. In World War I, the Negro population, as reflected in the Negro press, was not galvanized in its support for fighting for their country against Germany because of German atrocities against the United States. It was galvanized in its support of fighting for America because the Negro community felt that the sacrifice of life for their country, despite their second-class citizenship, was a sacrifice for freedom and democracy within America.[18]

In addition, there were no Negro officers in the War Department or in G-1 (Personnel) from whom to solicit advice. Fear of the unknown quantity of Negro mass support and fear of embarrassment from a negative Negro response convinced the War Department to issue the provisions to only a select group of commanders. Publication of the Mobilization Plan of 1937 was postponed, and a press blackout on the Mobilization Plan of 1937 was issued.[19]

The Air Corps portion of the 1937 Mobilization Plan did not include a utilization plan for Negroes. Most of the required provisions within the Plan that pertained to African Americans contained escape clauses, such as "unless conditions require modifications of national defense, when applicable, where desirable for training or other purposes," and "so far as practical."[20] One provision required that all African Americans be assigned to Negro organizations, except in cases where they would be "pooled."[21] The War Department and the Air Corps interpreted this provision and the other clauses as loopholes to use in exempting the corps from accepting African Americans. When prospective Negro candidates applied to the Air Corps Cadet program, they were told, usually by the adjutant general:

> The Congress has created several units of the Army exclusively for colored troops but no colored tactical units of the Air Corps have been authorized up to this time. Consequently, no provision has been made by the War Department for units to which the colored race could be assigned to after their completing the prescribed course of training to become military pilots. Accordingly, favorable consideration cannot be given your application for flying cadet appointment at this time. The supporting papers which accompanied your application are returned herewith.[22]

By the time John Robinson had taken command of the Ethiopian Air Force in late 1935, the Air Corps was in the final stages of completing its most expansive peacetime reorganization and buildup in its twenty-year history. A General Headquarters Air Force (GHQAF) was established by the War Department and given a commanding general who reported to the Army's Chief of Staff. The general of GHQAF would be in charge of training, organization, and operations of the Air Corps. The army retained the Chief Commanding Officer of the Air Corps, but he was assigned the responsibility of personnel, equipment, and other related logistics.[23]

The ten-year reorganization, which started in 1926, included a change in the strategic use of airplanes in military activity. Military aviation, which was observation-oriented before the reorganization, had become a combat-oriented organization. The army created nine new pursuit groups and three new bombardment groups. The addition of the new combat units provided the Air Corps with thirty-six new pursuit and bombardment squadrons. The observation groups were reduced in number. However, the 1936 version of the Air Corps provided more options in military aviation, and therefore created a demand for more pilots and support personnel.[24]

Even a personnel shortage did not alter the Army Air Corps' policy of rejecting qualified Negro applicants on the basis of race. It was quite ironic that, in 1937, all of the Air Corps installations on foreign soil were located in the Philippines, Hawaii, and in Panama—all U. S. "protectorates" populated by persons of color.[25] Negro citizens, regardless of qualifications, were denied equal opportunity to participate in the Air Corps in defense of their country, because of their color.

When the War Department submitted projected costs for the 1937 Mobilization Plan to Congress for appropriation in the 1938 fiscal year, the Negro press gained access to the specifics of the Mobilization Plan and its utilization of Negro troops. Once it became clear that the War Department did not have its recommended quota of African Americans in the armed services and did not have any plans for assigning Negroes to the Air Corps, the Negro press, especially Robert Vann's *Courier*, began to publish a series of editorials critical of the Roosevelt's administration and the War Department's policy in the use and the extent of Negro utilization in the army.[26]

The *Courier* chose a unique tactic. Instead of relying on the bigotry and racism argument, the *Courier* criticized the Roosevelt administration and Congress for taxing Negro citizens for the appropriation of the War Department's Mobilization Plan, which did not utilize African Americans in a manner commensurate with the Negro tax base. Vann's editorials maintained that if 10 percent of the nation's population was taxed for army appropriations, then they should be represented in 10 percent, or 20,000 positions, within the army.[27]

Things heated up when the Air Corps requested an increase in officer candidate strength of 2,092 but the request did not include Negro officers or candidates. The rationale for this increase in officer strength given by GHQAF's Gen. Frank M. Andrews was that the country was short on trained personnel, and that it took years to " impart the skills necessary to operate the modern airplane efficiently." He reiterated that the "persons we have are highly skilled in flying, navigating, bombing and shooting. They are at least the equal of any in the world. It is numbers that we lack."[28] Vann's editorial staff took note of this speech and commented that, despite the shortage, the Air Corps, incredulously, continued to bar highly qualified African Americans from cadet training, and that the Air Corps training was more exclusive than West Point and Annapolis.[29]

Throughout the early months of 1938, the *Courier* continued to accuse the Roosevelt administration and Congress of taxing African Americans while denying them the opportunity to serve in the Air Corps and other units within the army. One of the remedies suggested by the paper was the creation of a Negro division.[30] This Negro unit would incorporate an air squadron, tank battalion, signal corps, and an artillery regiment. The paper later acknowledged that such a division was not feasible in the current army structure.

The *Courier*'s "taxation without representation" strategy was very effective. Vann's paper received nationwide support from its subscribers and readers. The *Courier*, with a circulation of about 200,000 and a readership over one million, then took full advantage of election-year politics and their reader support by sending letters, under Vann's signature, soliciting nationwide endorsement of full utilization of the Negro within the army and navy. The employment of Negroes would include assignment to all of the arms and service units, including the Army Air Corps.[31]

The endorsement letter was sent to city mayors, state governors, U.S. representatives, U.S. senators, church leaders, college presidents, Spanish-American War and World War I veterans, and to prominent newspaper publishers. The response was so positive and overwhelming that the politicians, especially those congressmen from the Northern and border states with a large electoral vote, began advocating the *Courier* position on Capitol Hill.[32]

In March 1938, Hamilton Fish, a congressman from New York and former commanding officer of the all-Negro 15th National Guard of

New York, conferred with Robert Vann and Vann's associates in Pittsburgh to discuss the drafting of a bill that, if passed, would designate a Negro division, full Negro participation in all army units, including the Air Corps, and a quota of Negro nominees to West Point and Annapolis. Congressman Fish, cognizant of the true Negro contributions to World War I, endorsed Vann's proposals and, in April 1938, submitted three bills, known as the "Courier Bills," in the House of Representatives. The bills, officially known as H.R. 10064, H.R. 10065, and H.R. 10066, would, if passed, bar discrimination against the appointment of Negro officers and enlisted men in all units in the regular army, create a quota of Negro cadets to the army and navy military academies, and designate a Negro division, respectively.[33] All three bills were referred to the Military Affairs Committee.

Shortly after the introduction of the "Courier Bills" in Congress, the NAACP and its special counsel, Charles Houston, publicly endorsed the proposed legislation. The NAACP endorsement was critical, in that the support from the civil rights organization was national in scope, yet effective enough at the local level to get the attention of politicians from various parts of the country. Indeed, part of the NAACP's agenda in 1938 and 1939 was persuading the War Department to break the color bar in the Air Corps and the navy.[34]

Concurrent with the introduction of the "Courier Bills" Vann set up a national steering committee to bolster the lobbying effort necessary to guide the bills through the House and Senate. The ten-person committee consisted of Negro individuals from business, education, law, and social work.[35] Their first objective was to advocate equality and nondiscrimination in the designation of assignments in all units of, first, the army, then second, the navy. The steering committee worked from a program featuring "Ten Cardinal Points For Army and Navy Equality." The "Ten Cardinal Points" published in the *Courier* were:

1. We deserve jobs in the services;
2. We pay for the jobs in the services;
3. Our fighting record should be rewarded;
4. We seek the test to prove our merit;
5. We need education just as the whites;
6. We seek a chance to shatter prejudice;
7. Our loyalty is an American tradition;
8. Americanism is test of our fighting men;
9. We want to glorify America before the world; and
10. We want to inspire future Black America.[36]

Members of the steering committee were Robert L. Vann, editor of the *Courier*; Emmet J. Scott, secretary and treasurer of Howard University, confidential secretary to Booker T. Washington, and former special assistant to Secretary of War Newton Baker; Oscar De Priest, former congressman from Cook County, Illinois; J. Finley Wilson, Grand Exalted Ruler of the Improved Benevolent Independent Order of the Elks of the World; Charles C. Diggs, member of the Michigan state legislature, and mortician from Detroit; A. L. Lewis, founder and chairman of the board of directors of the Afro American Life Insurance Company; Eugene Kinckle Jones, executive secretary of the Urban League and of the National Conference of Social Work; George S. Schuyler, author; A. T. Walden, Atlanta lawyer and World War I veteran; and F. W. Ransom, president of Mme. C. J. Walker Manufacturing Company.[37]

The general targets of the steering committee were the representatives and senators from states with large blocks of Negro voters. The primary target, however, was President Roosevelt, who remained silent on the equality of Negro utilization in the armed forces. Vann and the steering committee members knew the president, by executive order, could create a Negro division in the army with all the necessary units except the Air Corps. Roosevelt could also order an allotment of enlisted men from the 24th and 25th Infantries to the Air Corps for training, or order the Air Corps to recruit officer candidates from Howard or Wilberforce universities, the only Negro universities offering reserve officer training.[38] In addition, there were several hundred young Negro pilots with flying experience from whom to recruit for cadet training.

The situation became even more absurd when, in June 1938, a bill authorizing the president to permit citizens of U.S. republics and "protectorates" to receive free instruction at professional schools administered by the United States, namely, West Point and Annapolis, was introduced. Most citizens of the republics and protectorates were of color, and a significant number of them were of African ancestry. The bill was introduced to foster "friendly relations between America and the Latin American countries."[39] Congressman Fish and other members of the House, while not against the bill, were quick to point out the inconsistencies between the special treatment given to foreign students and the government's unwillingness to admit American-born Negro citizens to the military academies. Several House members stated that the president, by executive order, could increase the number of African Americans admitted to West Point and Annapolis by eighty per year.[40]

It appeared to Vann and the steering committee that the only other option for change was legislation. At the urging of Vann's steering committee, Congressman Fish requested that the House Military Affairs Committee review the "Courier Bills" at its earliest convenience.

1938 was also an eventful year for the Challenger Air Pilots Club and the National Airmen's Association. Coffey and Robinson parted company, for reasons that were not widely known to the public. There was speculation that John Robinson had not followed Coffey's advice about securing a commercial pilot's license. Coffey was concerned that authorities in the Commerce Department would eventually discover that their flying school was providing flight instruction with an instructor that did not possess the proper credentials. This particular transgression could disqualify the school, and it could lose its charter.[41]

There was also the matter of Willa Brown. It was Robinson who was first attracted to and who recruited Willa for the Challengers. While Robinson was in Ethiopia, Ms. Brown developed a relationship with Coffey, out of respect and admiration for his skills as an airplane mechanic and a pilot. When Robinson returned from Ethiopia, the three may have entered into a love triangle, which may have ended when Coffey married Willa in 1937. Coffey and Ms. Brown, then the new owner of a private pilot's license, received a charter to open their own flying school, called the Coffey School of Aeronautics. The school was located at Harlem Airport. The curriculum of the flying school was identical to the previous venture with Robinson, except that auto mechanics were not offered. The majority of the Challenger members elected to stay with Coffey.[42]

Robinson went on to be an instructor of aviation at Poro College, and later was a technical consultant to an airplane mechanics training program funded by the National Youth Administration (NYA) at Chanute Field in Rantoul, Illinois.[43]

With Harlem Airport as its base of flying operations, the Challengers and the NAAA put on a series of dazzling air shows, featuring scintillating flying stunts and acrobatics and death-defying parachute jumps. The highlight of the air shows were record-setting parachute jumps by Willie "Suicide" Jones. At Markham Field, on 1 September 1938, Mr. Jones jumped from a plane at 29,400 feet. The previous record was held by a Russian, who left his plane at 26,500 feet.[44]

Another highpoint for the Challenger Club, although not related to a flying show, was the selection of Challenger member Grover C. Nash as the first Negro to fly airmail service in the Chicago area. Nash, who owned a limited commercial pilot's license, was commissioned to fly the airmail between Chicago and Matton, Illinois, as part of National Air Mail Week, held during the week of 19 May 1938.[45]

This event, although symbolic in its significance, was highly publicized and brought recognition to the existence of Negro flyers around the country.

The Challenger Club also became interested in a new development in Washington. On 17 September 1938, President Roosevelt authorized the use of $100,000 from the National Youth Administration for the implementation of experimental programs in aviation instruction, to be provided at colleges and universities throughout the country. The program, called the Civilian Pilot Training Program (CPTP), was to be administered at thirteen institutions of higher learning during the following academic year.[46] Negro colleges and universities were not selected in the experimental program. Consequently, very few Negro students would participate in the experiment. The CPTP would consist of ground school, consisting of seventy-two lectures and thirty-five to fifty hours of flight training at civilian airports. The program was to be administered by the Civil Aeronautics Authority.[47]

The CAA and the Army Air Corps made it clear that the CPTP program had no connection with the military. This was clearly a subterfuge. The Air Corps had training contracts with private flying schools to train cadets in the primary phase of flight training.[48] The military flight instructors received their instructors' rating at the private flight schools. The only difference in this program was that the primary training would be conducted on college campuses, by college faculty, who, undoubtedly, were hired from a CAA certified flight school. The other hidden factor in favor of the Air Corps was that the Corps could have early access to officer candidates, who, as it turned out, were in great demand. The Air Corps' shortage of quality officers could be alleviated by the CPTP project.

The Roosevelt administration and the CAA claimed that the CPTP was part of the concept of governmental involvement in education. The White House perception, which was carefully promoted, emphasized that the program would serve as a primer of life's work or would enable people to use airplanes for personal travel.[49] The program also allegedly brought the students in touch with a new technological concept that was to play an integral part in the lives of Americans.

The ground school portion of the course included history of aviation, civil air regulations, navigation, meteorology, parachutes, aircraft and the theory of flight, engines, and instruments and radio uses and forms. The flight school courses consisted of three stages: Stage A provided a minimum of eight hours of dual instruction featuring taxiing, air work, takeoffs, landings, and other maneuvers. Stage B included primary solo—a minimum of three hours solo, with a one hour dual check given randomly. Stage C consisted of advanced solo—a minimum of fifteen hours solo and eight hours dual check ride given at random.[50]

Over 300 men were chosen to participate in the experimental program. A small number of African Americans enrolled in Northern colleges and universities were among the 300 men selected for the initial run.[51]

President Roosevelt was quietly developing a civilian cadre of flyers for future utilization in case of a war emergency. In late November 1938, the Negro press became aware of President Roosevelt's intent to ask Congress, in his State of the Union message in January 1939, for America's largest military appropriation ever.[52] World events were pushing America away from the neutrality and isolationist policies of the twenties and early thirties. German forces had moved into Czechoslovakia and Austria, and were poised to take Romania, Greece, Yugoslavia, the Netherlands, and Belgium. The Nazi party had also terrorized the Jewish community, and in November 1938, initiated a brutal attack on Jewish persons, businesses, and synagogues.[53] America's friends, England and France, were gearing up for war with Germany. President Roosevelt envisioned America involved in another world conflict, and wanted a rearmament package that would enable the country to mobilize in case of attack.

Robert Vann and the *Courier* seized the opportunity to emphasize that the country's 1940 fiscal year appropriation, the largest ever and the largest appropriation to be paid, in part, from taxes paid by African Americans, did not include the addition or new utilization of Negroes in the army and navy. The Negro press continued to stress the "taxation without representation" strategy, and added the accusation that the president and Congress were more concerned about the human rights of European citizens than the rights of American citizens. Columnist George Schuyler pointed out that while America should be shocked and angered over Germany's treatment of Jews and other religious groups, the Roosevelt administration should express the same outrage over the hundred African Americans lynched and beaten in America during the Roosevelt administration's tenure.[54]

On 12 January 1939, President Roosevelt presented his "Adequate National Defense Plan" to Congress. This rearmament plan would cost the taxpayers one-half billion dollars. Included in the plan would be an increase in the number of planes built and an increase in the number of officers and enlisted men in the Air Corps. The authorized strength of the air arm would be increased to 5,500 planes, and the number of enlisted men and officers would be increased to 65,000 and 3,203 men, respectively.[55] The "Adequate National Defense Plan," like all others before it, did not include any new plans for Negroes. This plan, however, did offer some possibilities for private civilian flight schools, such as the one owned by Cornelius Coffey in Chicago. The defense bill, which was presented shortly after President Roosevelt's speech, included an allotment that would allow the Air Corps to send their pilot candidates to civilian flying schools accredited by the CAA and selected by the military.[56]

This window of opportunity was not lost on Vann's steering committee, or on the National Airmen's Association and the Challengers. In 1939, the Army Air Corps was not contracting with any Negro flying schools, since none were accredited as military training centers. Therefore, the next step in the journey toward full participation in the Air Corps would involve the forging of a coalition of the Negro Press, Vann's committee, and the National Airmen's Association of America. The first order of business was getting the Coffey school on firm ground by obtaining more equipment, and attracting more instructors, students, and, most importantly, political support.[57] Each organization realized that the attainment of CAA and Air Corps accreditation for the Coffey school or any other Negro organization was predicated on a united front, reinforced by competence, preparedness, and political clout. This united front would remove all legal obstacles to the utilization of African Americans in the Air Corps. This acknowledgment was made publicly in the 25 February 1939 issue of the *Courier* by Earl Renfroe, member of the National Airmen's Association and an officer within the Challengers.[58]

The NAAA and Vann's coalition hired a civil rights activist and political consultant, Edgar Brown, to lobby influential politicians. Brown, who was also president of the U.S. Government Employees Association, conferred with the NAAA, Vann, and his committee members and set out a course to persuade politicians to include Negroes in the Air Corps.[59] The NAAA lobbyist and Emmet Scott, a member of the steering committee, gave testimony to both the Senate and House Military Affairs committees on behalf of the coalition and the Negro community. In addition, Brown and members of the NAAA met with Mayor Kelly of Chicago, with the purpose of convincing him to use his political influence to persuade Senate and House members from Illinois to support the inclusion of African Americans in the Air Corps. The other favor asked of Mayor Kelly was that he lobby the Illinois senators and congressmen for their support in the selection of Chicago, and particularly Coffey's flying school, as an aviation training contractor for the Air Corps.[60]

In mid-March 1939, the Senate Military Affairs Committee voted to support the "National Defense Appropriation Bill" and the Air Corps expansion. The Senate committee agreed to amend the Air Corps expansion portion by recommending that one Negro school should be given aircraft and flying equipment for the training of colored pilots.[61] This amendment was considered a compromise between senators who supported full and equal utilization of African Americans in the Air Corps and senators and the Air Corps and War Department generals who advocated for an all-white Air Corps, and not a social experiment.

The first amendment was provided by Sen. Styles Bridges, a Democrat from New Hampshire. Senator Bridges proposed to the committee that the Secretary of War lend aircraft and equipment to Negro colleges to train Negro Army Air Corps pilots, mechanics, and other personnel who would have been trained at Air Corps training centers.[62] Southern senators argued that there was no provision within the appropriations bill forbidding the Air Corps from contracting with Negro schools or refusing African Americans training opportunities. Therefore, in their opinion, the amendment was unnecessary. Sen. Styles Bridges and Sen. Charles L. McNary (D) Oregon, considered the rationale for the objections to the original amendment to be subterfuge.[63]

Senator Bridges's amendment was voted down by voice vote. However, Sen. M. M. Logan, (D) Kentucky, introduced a compromise that absolved the War Department from the responsibility of and commitment to admitting African Americans into the Air Corps, while leaving the door open to the possibility of Negroes qualifying, at some future date, for admittance. The Logan compromise would enable Congress to give the Civil Aeronautics Authority the authority to designate certain Negro schools for aviation training. The War Department, according to the compromise, would be responsible for accrediting the Negro schools.[64]

The Logan compromise was edited and bolstered with another amendment presented by Sen. H. H. Schwartz (D) Wyoming. The Schwartz amendment authorized aviation training and the allocation of equipment to civilian aviation schools providing military training to at least one Negro school for the training of Negro Air Corps pilots. Although the committee members initially accepted the Schwartz amendment, ranking members, under pressure from the War Department, altered the amendment authorizing the Civilian Aeronautics Authority, instead of the Air Corps, with the responsibility for administering the training of Negro pilots.[65]

The Schwartz amendment was adopted by both the Senate and House and was attached to Section 4, the nondiscrimination boilerplate of the National Defense Appropriation Bill. The bill was passed and signed into law by President Roosevelt in early April 1939. Although the wording of the Schwartz amendment was somewhat ambiguous, and the Air Corps felt there was no legislative mandate to train and admit Negro pilots, the coalition of the NAAA, Challengers, and Robert Vann's steering committee claimed a victory in gaining that first step toward full utilization of the Negro in the regular army, and especially in the Air Corps.[66] The next step for the coalition was the admission of Negro applicants to army flying schools.

The school most mentioned as a candidate for the CAA-authorized Negro pilot training program was Howard University.[67] At the time, Howard offered courses in applied science and had a ROTC unit. The NAAA, Robert Vann, and Edgar Brown, however, supported Coffey and his flying school, in Chicago. The coalition's lobbying effort in Chicago paid dividends. Congressman Everett M. Dirksen, (R) Illinois, successfully amended the bill for continuation of funding for the Civilian Pilot Training Program. The Dirksen amendment prohibited racial discrimination in the administration of the CPTP. None of the benefits of training or programs would be denied on account of race, creed, or color.[68]

The CPTP bill, authored by Clarence F. Lea, (D) California, would provide aviation training, administered by the CAA, to 15,000 civilian pilots between the ages of 18 and 25, at a cost of $5.6 million over a one-year period. The training would occur at CAA-certified facilities, such as civilian flying schools, colleges and universities, and individuals.[69] The bill was presented by Lea as a result of the success of the experimental college program initiated in the Fall of 1938. During that academic year, over 80 percent of the 330 men selected to participate in the CPTP experiment passed the course and obtained their private pilot's licenses.[70]

In the spirit of the National Defense Appropriations Bill, passed earlier in April 1939, the CPTP bill, if passed, would provide for the selection and preliminary training of a large group of pilots who could be tapped in case of a war emergency. For the first time in history, Negro colleges and universities with engineering schools and access to air fields could apply for participation.

To punctuate the victories gained from the Schwartz amendment to the National Defense Appropriation Bill and the Dirksen amendment to the CPTP Bill, the National Airmen's Association of America planned a flying demonstration that would illustrate the competence and qualifications of Negro pilots. The 3,000-mile demonstration flight that would take place in early May 1939 would include air shows at ten different cities, including Cleveland, Pittsburgh, Washington, New York, Baltimore, West Virginia State College, Dayton, and Ft. Wayne, with the trip ending in Chicago.[71]

Two members of the Challenger Club, Dale White and Chauncey Spencer, were selected to make the trip. White was to be the copilot, and Spencer was selected as the navigator. The original plan called for the two gentlemen to fly to these cities and meet with local NAAA members for the purpose of encouraging the airmen to persevere and presenting them with a special invitation to the first national conference of the NAAA, to be held in Chicago in August of 1939.[72]

The agenda in Washington was to include meetings with lobbyist Edgar Brown, Congressman Dirksen, and, if possible, other members of the Senate Military Affairs Committee who would be responsible for introducing legislation that would open the doors to pilot training and other technical positions within the Army Air Corps. The immediate goal was to secure an aviation training contract with the CAA for the Coffey School of Aeronautics.[73]

The NAAA encountered difficulty in raising money for the trip. This apparent lack of financial commitment from local organizations and NAAA branch chapters was enough to discourage the men from making the trip. However, White and Spencer were determined to followthrough with the flight, as scheduled. Spencer, then an employee in the WPA, was able to obtain, through a co-worker familiar with wealthy African Americans in Chicago, $1,000 from the Jones family of Chicago. The Joneses were among the most successful Negro entrepreneurs in the Midwest. The Joneses owned a chain of Ben Franklin retail outlets and several tracts of real estate in Chicago.[74] With the NAAA contribution, personal funds, and the $1000 from the Jones family, White and Spencer were able to rent an old Lincoln-Page biplane. The plane had no lights, brakes, or flying instruments, other than oil and speed gauges. Spencer and White dubbed the plane "Old Faithful."[75]

The adventurous pair left Harlem Airport on 8 May 1939. About thirty minutes into the flight, the gas lines ruptured forcing White and Spencer to land in Auburn, Indiana.[76] After a short layover for repairs, the men started off again, headed for Pittsburgh. While flying over Ohio, *Old Faithful* experienced engine failure caused by a broken crankshaft. With the engine loosing oil pressure and vibrating uncontrollably, White successfully landed the machine in a cornfield in Sherwood, Ohio. From Sherwood, they called Coffey, who, with assistant Ben Hale, arrived on the scene to install another crankshaft.[77]

Two days later, the two were off again to Pittsburgh. Since the plane did not have any lights, they were forced to land at dusk in Morgantown, West Virginia. When they landed at the airport and disembarked from the plane, the crew chief at the airport refused to give them hangar space and strongly advised them to get fuel and to continue their flight to Pittsburgh, which was fifty-five miles away.[78] Fortunately, White was able to pick up the Allegheny Airport beacon, which he followed until more good fortune found them following the tail lights of a passenger plane descending onto an approach to the runway.

They followed the big plane into the airport and onto the runway. When they exited the plane, the two pilots were told that they had violated several CAA regulations, including those that govern the distance between large passenger planes and light planes. The CAA official had White and Spencer grounded until a hearing could be arranged to decide the fate of the two Negro pilots.[79] The two pilots contacted Robert Vann, who argued their case with the CAA and Allegheny Airport officials. Due to his legal acumen and political connections, Vann was successful in getting the charges against the two pilots dismissed. The two NAAA pilots were able to keep their appointments in Pittsburgh, and were $500 richer, compliments of a donation from Robert Vann and the *Courier*.[80]

From Pittsburgh, the two men flew to New York. They also experienced minor engine problems over the Poconos but were able to repair them and proceed on to Flushing, New York. After a brief stay in New York, the NAAA pilots headed to Washington, D.C..[81]

In Washington, the two pilots met with NAAA lobbyist Edgar Brown, who took them on a whirlwind tour meeting various politicians on the Hill, including Dirksen, Illinois Sen. James Slattery, and Negro Congressman William Mitchell. In between visits, Brown spotted Sen. Harry S Truman, and introduced White and Spencer to the future president. The chance meeting proved to be a pivotal step in the movement toward full equality in the armed forces, and ultimately, integration of the armed forces. At the time of this chance encounter in 1939, Truman was a moderate from a border state that had seen its share of racism and bigotry. Truman, however, had to depend on the large block of Negro voters in Kansas City and St. Louis. Therefore, his positions on civil rights and related issues, such as antilynching bills, were considered moderate and sympathetic.[82]

More importantly, in 1939, Truman was a member of the Senate Military Affairs Committee and, in 1940-1941, he would chair the same committee. Edgar Brown knew that Senator Truman was, for politically practical reasons, a friend of the Negro. Brown explained to the senator from Missouri the nature of the NAAA mission. Truman appeared impressed, but somehow incredulous of the practice of discrimination in the Army Air Corps.[83] He may have assumed that the antidiscrimination clause of the 1939 National Defense Appropriation Bill had removed all of the barriers to African Americans seeking admittance into branches of the Armed Services. Truman asked White and Spencer whether they had applied to the Air Corps. When the two men claimed that they were discouraged from applying because of the rejection suffered by their peers, Truman told both men that they should apply.[84]

The senator from Missouri was impressed enough with the NAAA pilots, and with their argument, that he arranged a trip to look at the plane *Old Faithful*. After personally inspecting the plane and hearing of the trials and tribulations encountered by the two pilots on their trip to Washington, Truman reportedly told the pilots: "If you had the guts to fly this plane from Chicago to Washington, then I have the guts to see that you get what you ask for."[85]

The Negro press, particularly the *Defender* and the *Courier*, chronicled the exploits of the two pilots from the time they left Chicago to the time they returned. Readers of the two papers were eager to see the two adventurers. When White and Spencer returned to Chicago they were given a hero's welcome in the Negro community. To capitalize on the excitement and interest generated by the demonstration flight, Robert Vann reconstituted the select committee bird-dogging Congress on the equality of utilization issue, and renamed it the "*Courier*'s National Commission for Equality in the Army, Navy, and Air Corps."[86]

Commission members such as Dr. Emmet Scott, then the chair of the Commission, member and attorney J. Finley Wilson, and Edgar Brown appeared before the House Appropriations Committee, recommending that the committee set aside $10,000,000 of the $90,000,000 appropriated for Air Corps training for the instruction of Negro pilots. The Commission members supported their testimony by highlighting the achievements of Negro soldiers abroad and stateside during World War I, the tremendous interest among Negroes in equality of troop utilization, and the support of the editors and publishers of Negro publications, veterans, the NAAA, the Elks, and other organizations, in the quest for equality in the armed forces. The Commission's testimony was strengthened by the supportive testimony of Senator Schwartz. The senator from Wyoming insisted that the rights of his few Negro constituents and those of the 12 million other Negro citizens were the same as those that were enjoyed by other American citizens.[87]

While testifying before the same committee, Secretary of War Harry H. Woodering stated that one of the nine CAA-certified private flying schools approved and under contract with the Army Air Corps would provide training for Negro pilots, starting in July 1939. Woodering emphasized that the Negro pilots would be receiving preliminary flight training for service in the Air Corps.[88] Based on Woodering's pledge, and on testimony from other advocates of Negro participation in the Air Corps, Congressman J. Buell Snyder, (D) Pennsylvania, reported that the Appropriations Committee would support the appropriation of the Civilian Pilot Training Bill, and predicted that it would pass in the House of Representatives.[89]

It was not clear in Secretary Woodering's statement which private flying school would admit Negro pilots for preliminary flight training in preparation for military training in the Air Corps. The Air Corps had not announced any plans for utilizing Negroes as pilots and technicians in the Air Force. In fact, in June 1939, the Air Corps was still denying Negro applicants admittance to the Air Corps.[90] It appeared that the War Department was deliberately misleading Congress by making statements that would appease the Appropriations Committee members and other politicians who supported the Negro cause.

The War Department received the increased appropriation for Air Corps expansion and training without a legal mandate to admit or integrate Negro pilots into the Air Corps, and Secretary Woodering would not say anything derogatory that would uncover the War Department's intentions of circumventing, if not subverting, the Congressional intent of the antidiscrimination clause of the 1939 National Defense Appropriation Bill. In addition, the CPTP appropriation gave the Air Corps a pool of trained white civilian pilots from which to select in case of war.

During the week of 16 June 1939, H.R. 5619, the bill authorizing the Civilian Pilot Training Program, including the nondiscrimination clause, passed the Senate. The House passed the bill on 4 August 1939. Chairman of the Civil Aeronautics Authority, Robert H. Hinckley, announced that civilian pilot training could begin at Negro colleges and universities, beginning fall semester, 1939.[91] These Negro schools would apply for participation in the program along with over 200 other colleges and universities. Hinckley mentioned Howard University, Hampton Institute, Tuskegee Institute, Fisk University, and Wilberforce University as the likely candidates. Five percent of the $5.6 million allocated for the CPTP effort was to go to institutions providing flying instruction to individuals who did not have a college education. The 5 percent set aside was for flying schools such as Coffey's School of Aeronautics in Chicago.[92]

In July 1939, Secretary Woodering announced that the War Department was developing a plan to train Negro pilots. It was anticipated by the War Department that six of the nine private schools contracted by the Air Corps to provide preliminary flight instruction would admit Negro students toward the end of 1939. Upon completion of training, the students would enter advanced aviation training at Randolph and Kelly fields.[93] Secretary Woodering stopped short of announcing that the Air Corps would be accepting African Americans, because there was no plan to admit Negroes into the Air Corps. Negro civilians would receive training under the auspices of the Civil Aeronautics Authority's Civilian Pilot Training Program at selected Negro colleges, universities, and at a few private schools for individuals not in college. It appeared that the War Department was issuing press releases that were politically acceptable, to pacify advocates for equality in the armed forces and to placate the Air Corps generals, who had no intention, in 1939, of admitting African Americans to the Army Air Corps.

Young African Americans interested in military service were enthused and, consequently, misled by such statements by the War Department. Many young men, such as Roderick C. Williams, a 1939 graduate of the University of Illinois, applied to the Army Air Corps for admission to cadet training. Although he had met all of the entrance requirements, Williams was rejected on the basis of his race. In Williams's rejection letter, Maj. L. S. Smith, Adjutant General, responded, as recorded in the *Negro Yearbook, 1947*:

> The Congress has created several units of the Army exclusively for colored troops but no colored tactical units of the Air Corps have been authorized up to this time. Consequently, no provision has been made by the War Department for units to which the colored race could be assigned in the event of their completing the prescribed course of training to become military pilots. Accordingly, favorable consideration cannot be given your application for flying cadet appointment at this time. The supporting papers which contained your application are returned herewith. . . . It is suggested that you communicate with the Administrator, Civil Aeronautics, Washington, D.C., who it is understood has designated certain civilian flying schools for the training of colored pilots.[94]

The War Department was very careful not to offer any public announcements or commitment to move Negro graduates of the CPTP into the Air Corps military training program. Equivocal statements, announcements, and rejected applications produced by the War Department only added to the confusion and frustration among advocates and young Negroes interested in the Air Corps. This miscommunication would lead to misunderstanding among the men who were led to believe that successful completion of the CPTP would make them eligible to enter the Air Corps.[95] These vague proposals by the War Department served only to fuel the movement in the Negro community advocating Negro access to the Army Air Corps and other units in the armed forces.

Several Negro colleges and universities applied for CPTP funding. In September 1939, the Civil Aeronautics Authority announced that the Agricultural and Technical College at Greensboro, North Carolina, and West Virginia State College were the first Negro schools granted CPTP funding contracts.[96] They were followed by Hampton Institute, Tuskegee Institute, and the State College for Colored Students, Dover, Delaware. Howard University was the last Negro school to receive a CPTP grant in 1939. In 1940, Lincoln University (Missouri) and Wilberforce were accepted as CPTP sites.[97]

Because of its previous aviation program experience, West Virginia State was the first program to start on 1 October 1939. The institution had developed an excellent reputation for providing vocational training in their Trade and Technical Division. The Division was administered by J. C. Evans, a licensed pilot. Evans, a recipient of an M.S. degree from Massachusetts Institute of Technology, had coordinated a limited aviation program since 1934 with Wertz Field in Charlestown, West Virginia. His program already had access to airplanes, instructors, and aviation support equipment, such as navigational equipment, aerial cameras, and surveying equipment. The Division also included a model airplane construction course. Evan's program needed the least amount of adaptation to establish a training program.[98]

Howard University almost lost out on the 1939 CPTP grant award. Unlike most Negro colleges and universities, Howard was a federal institution, with financial ties to the Department of the Interior. The university's schedule for approving programs for funding required a meticulous process that relied on good timing. Unfortunately, the university's board of trustees met only twice a year—in April and October. The CAA had not released the CPTP applications in April 1939, and, therefore, the individuals at Howard interested in securing a CPTP project could only wait anxiously until October to get concurrence from the trustees to apply for the aviation program.[99]

During the interim months, the president of the university, Mordecai Johnson, contacted CAA officials and explained the university's precarious position and its intent to participate in the program. The CAA granted Howard an extension on the application period. The university then dispatched assistant professor of civil engineering Addison E. Richmond to develop a feasibility study for a CPTP project at Howard.

The dean of men, William West, assisted Richmond by introducing him to C. Alfred Anderson, who was a member of the all-Negro Washington Airmen's Club based in Arlington, Virginia. West was familiar with Anderson's skills and knew that Anderson's dedication to flying would benefit the university in its application for the CPTP grant award.[100]

Dean West and Professor Richmond found Anderson working on a road construction project and convinced him, without much difficulty, to agree to coordinate the flight school section of the program. Anderson, Richmond, and the executive secretary to the president, James R. Narbit, designed a feasibility plan and application so comprehensive that the board of trustees approved the plan without opposition. Howard University's application for a CPTP grant award was approved by the CAA. Professor Richmond was named director of Civilian Pilot Training, and Anderson was rewarded with the position of instructor and supervisor of flying.[101]

In response to mounting questions from the Negro press about the War Department's plans for graduating Negro qualifiers from the CPTP program into the Air Corps, Maj. Gen. Emery E. Adams, Adjutant General of the Army, released a statement to the press on 20 September 1939 that echoed the War Department's vague June 1939 proposal in its Congressional testimony. General Adams announced:

> the War Department was authorized to operate with the CAA by lending aircraft, aeronautical equipment and accessories as may be necessary for one school to train Negro pilots, such school may be designated by the Civil Aeronautics Authority. . . . I may state that in the authorized increases evident in the recent Presidential proclamation, it is contemplated organizing a certain number of regular Army units with Negro personnel. These units will be among the first to be organized and will constitute a part of a combat corps.[102]

The NAAA, lobbyist Edgar Brown, and the *Courier*'s National Commission for Equality in the Army Air Corps, Navy, and National Guard, speculated that General Adams's statement was an indication that the War Department was contemplating a Negro aviation unit, and training for such a unit. Brown, who had been lobbying congressmen and the CAA to authorize Chicago as a CPTP site for the 5 percent set aside, also pressed hard for the grant for advanced aviation training for Negro pilots who could form this new unit.[103]

Brown's work reaped benefits for the Chicago area. Coffey's base of operations, Harlem Airport, address of the Chicago Training Center of the Civil Aeronautics Authority, was named, on 14 October 1939, as the

Chicago recipient of a CPTP, 5 percent set aside project. In addition, the Coffey School of Aeronautics would also be one of the CAA-administered subcontractors in the Chicago School of Aeronautics, the Army Air Corps training center in the Chicago area.[104] The Air Corps training contractor, located in Glenview, Illinois, twenty miles north of Chicago, was designated to provide the experimental and advanced aviation training for Negro pilots.[105]

Edgar Brown, the NAAA, Vann's committee, and the Negro press were working with the understanding that this experiment, if deemed successful by the Air Corps and CAA, would lead to Negro admission to the Air Corps.[106]

In late November 1939, A Negro Selective Board was set up by the CAA to cooperate with the Air Corps in the design and implementation of the candidate selection process for the experimental program. Twenty Negro graduates of the CAA's CPTP course at nine CAA-designated Negro college and university training sites, including Coffey's school, would be chosen to participate in the experimental advanced training. Members of the Selective Board included Edgar Brown; Dr. J. Finley Wilson; Cornelius Coffey; Dr. F. D. Patterson, President, Tuskegee Institute; F. D. Bluford of A. and T. College, Greensboro, North Carolina; Dean Lewis K. Downing, Howard University Engineering School; and Dr. O. M. Bousfield, Chicago Board of Education. Robert Hinckley of the CAA was an ex officio member.[107]

The establishment of the Negro Selective Board was hailed as a giant step forward by the coalition of Robert Vann's Commission, the National Airmen's Association of America, the *Chicago Defender* and other prominent civil rights organizations such as the NAACP, the Urban League, and the National Bar Association. Walter White, sensing the movement, pressed the War Department to admit qualified Negro pilots into the Air Corps, and even offered to meet with War Department officials to work out a plan. The War Department did not respond.[108]

Although antilynching legislation, Negro access to state-funded colleges and universities, and voting rights were prominent issues in the NAACP campaign, full equality in the Air Corps and other branches of the service became an integral part of their 1940 agenda. The NAACP Board of Directors, as they had advocated in 1938, supported full Negro participation in the nation's mobilization planning for defense and, if necessary, war.[109] The prevailing thought in the organization, as it was among prominent African Americans in America, was that full participation in the combat arm of the military in defense of the country would make it more difficult for bigots to deny Negroes the basic rights granted to them under the Constitution. For African Americans to participate as pilots in the Air Corps would also prove to white supremacists and their sympathizers that the Negroes were just as intellectually able, emotionally courageous, and physically capable of operating complex machinery, such as airplanes, as whites were.

By 1940, the NAACP had joined the Vann coalition in using the impending threat of world conflict and presidential-election-year politics to push for full Negro participation in war mobilization in all military branches. In the minds of the civil rights advocates and change agents, military mobilization and industrialization for war were just planks in their civil rights platform, and the Negro pilots were the delegates.

The NAACP differed with the coalition in one respect. The optimum goal of the NAACP was the integration of the Negro into all aspects of American life, including the Army Air Corps. The civil rights organization would not officially or publicly endorse an all-new Negro unit or division of any kind. Consequently, the NAACP officially advocated equality in the utilization and assignment of Negro soldiers in branches of the military, but would not publicly advocate for an all-Negro training experiment administered by the Air Corps.[110] There were, however, members of the rights group who, while supporting the goal of integration within the army, disagreed with the NAACP board's means of achieving that integration. The NAACP special consul, Charles Houston, chose to support the strategy advocated by Robert Vann and the coalition.[111]

Houston, a veteran officer of World War I, knew firsthand of the extent of bigotry and racism in the army. As a field artillery expert, he had experienced the disorganized training and inappropriate placement of Negro officers in the First World War, and he knew how that improper training had affected the performance of Negro units. Houston also knew that, if properly trained, an all-Negro unit, with Negro officers, could perform brilliantly. The NAACP special counsel rationalized that, if given the opportunity, a Negro unit could, by their performance and conduct, impress the army hierarchy enough that they might seriously consider adding new Negro units, and integrating these units into existing white units, where appropriate.[112]

Fighting for the right for African Americans to serve in the army was not new for Charles Houston. In 1934, Houston, on behalf of the NAACP, requested of Gen. Douglas McArthur, then Army Chief of Staff, the status of the Negro in the armed forces, and the War Department's plans for adding Negroes to other combat units within the army, including the Air Corps.[113] Although McArthur did not respond to Houston's request for information, Houston's inquiry reflected his committment and concern regarding the utilization of the Negro in the armed forces. Attorney Houston was also instrumental in securing the NAACP's endorsement of the "Courier/Fish Bills," then under review by the House of Representatives.[114]

Due to Houston's status within the civil rights organization, the NAACP Board and Secretary Walter White respected and condoned Houston's personal association with the Vann coalition. The NAACP, however, remained, without jeopardizing their relationship with the Vann coalition, officially opposed to separate Negro divisions or units.

Notes

1. Franklin, *From Slavery to Freedom*, 425-32.
2. Ibid., 576.
3. "Our Regiments," *Pittsburgh Courier*, 12 September 1931; "Tenth Cavalry Broken Up to Make Room for Air Corps Unit which Negroes Can't Get Into," *Pittsburgh Courier*, 12 September 1931; "Reduction of Negro Army Regiments Not Due to Air Corps Expansion," *Pittsburgh Courier*, 26 September 1931; "Our Prevarications Chief of Staff," *Pittsburgh Courier*, 26 September 1931; Ulysses G. Lee, *The Employment of Negro Troops* (Washington, D.C.: Government Printing Office, 1966), 25.
4. "Let's Carry Fight Through," *Pittsburgh Courier*, 5 March 1938; Lee, *The Employment of Negro Troops*, 25.
5. Lee, *The Employment of Negro Troops*, 38.
6. Ibid., 38.
7. Ibid., 42.
8. Ibid.
9. Ibid., 45.
10. Ibid.; Alan Gropman, *The Air Force Integrates, 1945-1964* (Washington, D.C.: Office of Air Force History, U.S. Air Force, 1985), 2-5.
11. Ibid.; Ibid.; Lee, *The Employment of Negro Troops*, 45.
12. Ibid.; Ibid.; Ibid.; Alan Osur, *Blacks in the Army Air Forces During World War II*, (Washington, D.C.: Office of Air Force History, U.S. Air Force, 1977), 1-5.
13. Osur, *Blacks in the Army Air Forces*, 5.
14. Scott, *Scott's Official History of the Negro in the World War*, 16; Franklin, *From Slavery to Freedom*, 467.
15. Lee, *The Employment of Negro Troops*, 40-41.
16. Ibid.
17. Ibid., 46.
18. Franklin, *From Slavery to Freedom*, 454-57, 470, 476; DuBois, *Dusk of Dawn*, 245-48, 253-54.

19. Lee, *The Employment of Negro Troops*, 38-40, 48.
20. Ibid., 40-41.
21. Ibid., 40-41, 47.
22. Davis, *Benjamin O. Davis Jr.*, 44; Thurgood Marshall memorandum to NAACP Secretary Walter White, 30 January 1939, NAACP Papers, Library of Congress.
23. Kit C. Carter and Robert Mueller, *The Army Air Forces in World War II: Combat Chronology, 1941-1945* (Washington, D.C. Office of Air Force History, U.S. Air Force, 1973), 4-5.
24. Ibid.; "The Shortage of Fliers," *Pittsburgh Courier*, 22 January 1938; "Let's Carry Fight Through," *Pittsburgh Courier*, 5 March 1938; Louis R. Lautier, "Air Corps Could Be Increased By Black Regulars," *Pittsburgh Courier*, 21 May 1938.
25. Carter and Mueller, *The Army Air Forces in World War II*, 5-7.
26. "A Negro Division," *Pittsburgh Courier*, 19 February, 1938; "A Challenge to Ex-Soldiers, Sailors," *Pittsburgh Courier*, 26 February 1938; "20,000 Negro Jobs," *Pittsburgh Courier*, 9 April 1938.
27. "20,000 Negro Jobs," *Pittsburgh Courier*, 9 April 1938.
28. "The Shortage of Fliers," *Pittsburgh Courier*, 22 January 1938.
29. Ibid.
30. Ibid.; "A Negro Division," *Pittsburgh Courier*, 19 February 1938; Osur, *Blacks in the Army Air Forces*, 9-10.
31. Osur, *Blacks in the Army Air Forces*, 19; "A Negro Division," *Pittsburgh Courier*, 19 February 1938; R. L. Vann, "Mayors Endorse Campaign for Equality," *Pittsburgh Courier*, 11 March 1938; R. L. Vann, "Courier's Letter to Members of Congress," *Pittsburgh Courier*, 26 March 1938.
32. R. L. Vann, "Courier's Letter to Members of Congress," *Pittsburgh Courier*, 26 March 1938; "Bill Will Fight for Equalities in Army and Navy," *Pittsburgh Courier*, 9 April 1938.
33. "Bill Will Fight for Equalities in Army and Navy," *Pittsburgh Courier*, 9 April 1938.
34. "Army Bias Must Be Broken Down, Claims Houston," *Pittsburgh Courier*, 9 April 1938; "Courier Army Bills Backed by NAACP," *Pittsburgh Courier*, 30 April 1938; Marshall to White memorandum, 30 January 1939.
35. "Steering Committee Set Up to Guide Army Bills Through House, Senate," *Pittsburgh Courier*, 16 April 1938.
36. "Ten Cardinal Points in Courier's Campaign for Army and Navy Equality," *Pittsburgh Courier*, 26 March 1938.
37. "Steering Committee Set Up to Guide Army Bills Through House, Senate," *Pittsburgh Courier*, 16 April 1938.
38. Ibid.; Lautier, "Air Force Could Be Increased by Black Regulars," *Pittsburgh Courier*, 21 May 1938; Louis R. Lautier, "Reserve Corps Has Few Officers," *Pittsburgh Courier*, 25 June 1938.
39. "Fish Argues for Negro Youth at West Point," *Pittsburgh Courier*, 2 July 1938.

40. Ibid.

41. Interview with Harold Hurd.

42. Waters, *American Diary*, 204.

43. Gary R. Lewis, "Col. Robinson's National Air College Stages Gala Opening," *Chicago Defender*, 3 October 1936; Associated Negro Press, "Colonel Robinson is Names Ill. Aviation Consultant," *Chicago Defender*, 28 October 1937; Enoch P. Waters, "Black Wings Over America," *Chicago Defender*, 26 September 1942.

44. "Race Man Breaks World Record in Parachute Jump," *Pittsburgh Courier*, 3 September 1938.

45. Associated Negro Press, "Race Man Will Fly U.S. Mail," *Pittsburgh Courier*, 21 May 1938.

46. NAACP, Report on the Civilian Pilot Training Program 1939-1940, NAACP Papers, Collections of the Manuscript Division, Library of Congress, 1-7.

47. Ibid., 1-2.

48. Louis R. Lautier, "Corps Emphasized By Present Set Up," *Pittsburgh Courier*, 18 February 1939.

49. NAACP, Report on the Civilian Pilot Training Program, 2.

50. Ibid., 3-4.

51. Jesse P. Guzman, *The Negro In the Army Air Forces, Negro Yearbook, A review of Events Affecting Negro Life, 1941-1946* (Tuskegee, Alabama, 1947), 354-358. Roderick Williams participated in the Civilian Pilot Training Program at the University of Illinois in late 1938 and 1939.

52. "More Billions for Arms," *Pittsburgh Courier*, 19 November 1938; "To Increase Army, But Negroes Will Not Be Included," *Pittsburgh Courier*, 26 November 1938.

53. Associated Negro Press, "Race Conflict: A Root of War," *Pittsburgh Courier*, 26 November 1938.

54. George Schuyler, "News and Reviews," *Pittsburgh Courier*, 26 November 1938.

55. Lautier, "Corps Emphasized By Present Set-Up," *Pittsburgh Courier*, 18 February 1939.

56. Ibid.

57. Waters, *American Diary*, 204-5; "City Fliers Make Appeal to Mayor Kelly," *Chicago Defender*, 1 April 1939; Interview with Cornelius Coffey.

58. Earl W. Renfroe, "Suggests Way to Open `Closed Door' of Army," *Pittsburgh Courier*, 25 February 1939.

59. "City Fliers Make Appeal to Mayor Kelly," *Chicago Defender*, 2 April 1939; Waters, *American Diary*, 205.

60. Ibid.

61. Lautier, "Courier Fight to Gain Recognition for Race in Aviation Succeeds," *Pittsburgh Courier*, 18 March 1939.

62. Ibid.

63. Ibid.; "Contains Proviso for Race Aviators," *Pittsburgh Courier*, 1 April 1939.

64. Lautier, "Courier Fight to Gain Recognition for Race in Aviation Succeeds," *Pittsburgh Courier*, 18 March 1939; "Strike One," *Pittsburgh Courier*, 25 March 1939; "Contains Proviso for Race Aviators," *Pittsburgh Courier*, 1 April 1939.

65. "House, Senate Agree on Race Aviation School," *Pittsburgh Courier*, 25 March 1939.

66. "F.D.R. Signs Air Corps Bill at Warm Springs," *Chicago Defender*, 9 April 1939; Louis R. Lautier, "Pilot Training Bill Amended in House, 71-53," *Pittsburgh Courier*, 29 April 1939.

67. "House, Senate Agree on Race Aviation School," *Pittsburgh Courier*, 9 April 1939; "House Passes Pilot Training Bill," *New York Amsterdam News*, 29 April 1939.

68. Lautier, "Pilot Training Bill Amended in House," *Pittsburgh Courier*, 29 April 1939.

69. NAACP, Report on the Civilian Pilot Training Program, 1; Lautier, "Pilot Training Bill Amended in House," *Pittsburgh Courier*, 29 April 1939.

70. NAACP, Report on the Civilian Pilot Training Program, 1-2.

71. Waters, *American Diary*, 204-5; Interview with Cornelius Coffey; Associated Negro Press, "Chicago Pilots Plan 3,000 Mile Trip," *Pittsburgh Courier*, 6 May 1939; Chauncey Spencer, *Who Is Chauncey Spencer?* (Detroit: Broadside Press, 1975), 31.

72. Waters, *American Diary*, 205; Associated Negro Press, "Chicago Pilots Plan 3,000 Mile Trip," *Pittsburgh Courier*, 6 May 1939; Spencer, *Who is Chauncey Spencer?*, 31.

73. Waters, *American Diary*, 205.

74. Spencer, *Who is Chauncey Spencer?* 32; Waters, *American Diary*, 205; John R. Williams, "The Jones Boys of 47th Street," *Chicago Defender*, 18 December 1939.

75. Spencer, *Who is Chauncey Spencer?* 22-32.

76. "Good Will Aviators Delayed," *Pittsburgh Courier*, 13 May 1939.

77. Spencer, *Who is Chauncey Spencer?*, 32; Interview with Cornelius Coffey.

78. Peck, "Goodwill Aviators Run into Plenty of Trouble," *Pittsburgh Courier*, 20 May 1939.

79. Ibid.

80. Waters, *American Diary*, 206.

81. "Goodwill Aviators Delayed," *Pittsburgh Courier*, 13 May 1939; Interview with Cornelius Coffey.

82. Waters, *American Diary*, 206; Barton J. Bernstein, "The Ambiguous Legacy: The Truman Administration and Civil Rights," paper presented at the American Historical Association meeting in 1966, in *The Negro In Depression and War, Prelude to Revolution, 1930-1945*, edited by Dernard Sternsher (Chicago: Quadrangle Books, 1969), 269-74.

83. Spencer, *Who is Chauncey Spencer?* 34; Waters, *American Diary*, 206.

84. Ibid.; Ibid.

85. Ibid.; Ibid.

86. Spencer, *Who is Chauncey Spencer?*, 36; Waters, *American Diary*, 206; "Courier Fight to Gain Recognition Reaches New High," *Pittsburgh Courier*, 3 June 1939.

87. "War Department Plans to Include Negro Aviators," *Pittsburgh Courier*, 15 July 1939.

88. Ibid.

89. Ibid., "Courier Fight to Gain Recognition," *Pittsburgh Courier*, 3 June 1939.

90. Guzman and Workman, *Negro Yearbook, 1947*, 355. Roderick Williams was denied admission.

91. "Senate Passes Bill Providing Training for Civilian Air Corps," *Pittsburgh Courier*, 24 June 1939; "Civil Air Pilot's Bill Awaits F.D.R. Signature," *Chicago Defender*, 24 June 1939.

92. "Civil Air Pilot's Bill Awaits F.D.R. Signature," *Chicago Defender*, 24 June 1939.

93. "War Department Plans to Include Negro Aviators," *Pittsburgh Courier*, 15 July 1939.

94. Guzman and Workman, *Negro Yearbook, 1947*, 355.

95. Interview with Spann Watson, 9 March 1991, Washington, D.C.

96. "Select Two Race Colleges for Civil Aviation Course," *Pittsburgh Courier*, 16 September 1939.

97. Waters, *American Diary*, 207.

98. Monroe N. Work, *Negro Yearbook 1937-38* (Tuskegee: Negro Year Book Publishing Co., 1938), 279-82; "Air Training to Start October," *Pittsburgh Courier*, 23 September 1939.

99. "Howard Cuts Thru Red Tape to Fly," *Pittsburgh Courier*, 9 December 1939.

100. Ibid.

101. Interview with C. Alfred Anderson; "The Story of Alf Anderson," *Pittsburgh Courier*, 9 December 1939.

102. "US Army Colorline Crumbling," *Pittsburgh Courier*, 30 September 1939.

103. Ibid.; "Airport for Pilots Named," *Pittsburgh Courier*, 21 October 1939.

104. "Airport for Pilots Named," *Pittsburgh Courier*, 21 October 1939.

105. Ibid.

106. "Air School to Train Negro Military Pilots," *Pittsburgh Courier*, 2 December 1939.

107. Ibid.

108. Ted Watson, "Colored Aviation," *Pittsburgh Courier*, 13 January 1940; Morris J. MacGregor, Jr., *Integration of the Armed Forces, 1940-1965* (Washington, D.C.: Center of Military History, United States Army, Department of Defense, 1981), 14-16; Ibid.

109. McGregor, *Integration*, 14-16; "Courier Army Bills Backed by NAACP," *Pittsburgh Courier*, 30 April 1938.
110. Roy Wilkins, "Air Pilots But Segregated," *The Crisis* 48 (February 1941): 39.
111. "Army Bias Must Be Broken Down, Claims Houston," *Pittsburgh Courier*, 9 April 1938.
112. Ibid.
113. Charles Houston, Letter to General Douglas MacArthur, Chief of Staff, United States Army, War Department, Washington, D.C., regarding Attitudes of Negroes on National Defense, 9 August 1934, NAACP Papers, Collections of the Manuscript Division, Library of Congress.
114. "Courier Bills Backed by NAACP," *Pittsburgh Courier*, 30 April 1938.

Chapter 6

America Prepares for War: African Americans Not Wanted

After Germany invaded Poland in September of 1939, and World War II was declared in Europe, the Roosevelt administration knew that American involvement was a strong possibility. Although the United States's official stance was one of neutrality, its actions aligned it with England and France and pitted it against Germany. An Asian war had broken out one year prior and the neutral United States curried favor with China, which strained relations between the United States and Japan. The Roosevelt administration permitted the sale of war materials and equipment, including fighter planes, such as the Curtis Wright P-40, to England and France, in their preparation for a defense against Germany. War loans worth over $36 million were given to Denmark, Sweden, and Norway, to assist them in their defense against Germany and Russia. In addition, the United States loaned China over $50 million to protect American and British business interests from Japan.[1] China also purchased over one hundred P-40s from the United States in 1940 and accepted an American volunteer group of fighter pilots, under the command of Col. Claire Chenualt of the Army Air Corps, to assist them in their air defense against Japan.[2] The "Flying Tigers," the name given to the volunteer fighter squadron, and their activities were supported and condoned by the War Department.

While the Roosevelt administration extended credit, sold war materials and equipment and condoned American volunteer forces in France, England, China, and Scandinavian countries under attack from the countries in the Axis Pact, the United States would not allow the sale of war materials, equipment, or natural resources to Germany, Russia, and Japan.[3] This American economic boycott of the Axis powers only exacerbated the already tenuous relationships.

These geopolitical circumstances provided a scenario where a world war was inevitable.

The specter of world conflict and American involvement provided an opportunity for the Vann coalition and the NAACP. When the Roosevelt administration complained about human rights violations in Germany, the Negro press and civil rights organizations illustrated human rights violations in America. They were quick to publicly remind the Roosevelt administration that it had not offered or supported anti-lynching legislation. When the War Department became vague and unresponsive to Negro initiatives, the change agents, civil rights organizations, and the Negro press would apply the very effective "taxation without representation" and "democracy at home" strategies. The Roosevelt administration, the War Department, and Congress continued to be large targets as long as there was the possibility of America entering another world war without African Americans in the Air Corps, and especially when there were qualified and willing Negro personnel available.

The Negro coalition working toward equality of Negro utilization in the military service regarded the legislative amendments and the acceptance and involvement of the Negro schools in the CPTP as a major victory—another step toward full equality in the utilization of the Negro in the armed forces and full Negro participation in the privileges of American citizenship. The Negro coalition would increase the pressure in 1940.

The "Courier" bills introduced by Congressman Hamilton Fish in 1938 were still in committee in early 1940, and Vann's Negro coalition was determined to force some movement on the bills during the 1940 session. The National Defense Appropriation of 1939 and the activity surrounding the subsequent appropriation for the Civilian Pilot Training Program demanded attention that would otherwise have gone to the "Courier" bills. As a consequence, the "Courier" bill requiring the War Department to cease discrimination based on race in the utilization of Negroes in designated or new units was covered, in part, by Section 4 of Public Act 18 (National Defense Act). This legislation prohibited discrimination in the designation of persons to units within the armed forces based on race, and provided for the training of Negro pilots and technicians at a school designated by the CAA for the training of Air Corps enlistees. In 1940, the Vann coalition refocused on Congressional enforcement of Pubic Act 18 and its amendments.[4]

The Vann coalition suffered a major loss in February, 1940, when Robert S. Abbott, publisher of the *Chicago Defender*, died after a lengthy illness. During his tenure as the owner and publisher of the Chicago weekly, Abbott had used the *Defender* to champion the cause of civil rights for African Americans. He had kept the *Defender* in perpetual attack against lynching, poll tax, segregation in interstate travel, miscegenation laws, and discrimination against the Negro in his efforts to participate in the national defense of his country.[5]

Abbott had used the *Defender* to almost single-handedly convince thousands of Negroes to leave the South during the hard economic times during World War I and during the Depression. Chicago, Detroit, Cleveland, Indianapolis, St. Louis, and other major urban areas in the North and Midwest received thousands of African Americans who had read and heard, via the *Defender*, how much better life was in the North, compared to the oppressive South. Although the urban experience was very difficult for many of the transplants, many did succeed as laborers, entrepreneurs, and professionals. Many, for the first time, were able to vote and, in cities such as Chicago, exercised that right to the extent of Oscar DePriest, the first Negro congressman elected since. The northern migration of the Negro to urban areas, motivated, in part, by Abbott, had changed America socially and politically.[6]

By 1940, the *Defender* had developed a readership of over 1 million and was the most-read Negro newspaper in the South. Under Abbott's leadership, the *Defender* was an advocate of Negro aviation, and encouraged its editorial director, Enoch Waters, to foster Negro interest in aviation to the extent that Chicago, in the mid- to late-thirties became the national center for Negro aviation.

The *Defender*'s readership and circulation often exceeded that of the *Courier*, especially in the South and the Midwest.[7] When the two newspapers were in concert on issues and events affecting the Negroes, which was often, they were powerful shapers of Negro opinion, not to be ignored by any politician in the Northeast, Midwest, or the border states. Fortunately for Vann's coalition, Abbott's successor, John Sengstacke, continued in the same political vein as his predecessor and allowed his editorial staff, under the leadership of Enoch Waters, to remain advocates of the fight waged by the Vann coalition. Waters, himself, remained active with the National Airmen's Association of America and was instrumental in lobbying Chicago politicians for their support of Coffey's School of Aeronautics, in its application for participation in the CPTP project.

The Vann coalition learned that the Air Corps was accepting white enlistees to their cadet program and admitting the whites to its civilian training centers for preliminary flight training. Once the preliminary training was completed, whites were admitted to advanced training for the Air Corps. The coalition also learned that the "experimental" training program for African Americans at the Chicago School of Aeronautics in Glenview, Illinois, had received equipment for ground school training and was accepting Negro students. The Negro enrollees, unlike their white counterparts, were not accepted as enlistees in the Air Corps. Letters from aspiring Negro applicants to the Air Cadet program were still being rejected by the Air Corps on the basis that there was not a Negro unit to which the Negro enlistees could be assigned. As a consequence, the Negro students in the Chicago School of Aeronautics "experimental" program had to pay for their own living expenses, while white Air Corps enlistees in the same preliminary flight training program received monthly stipends of $75.[8]

The Vann coalition, citing the Glenview "experiment" and the discriminatory treatment of Negro students, accused the War Department and the Air Corps of circumvention and violation of the intent and the law specified in Public Act 18. The coalition lobbied Congress for legal remedy. Several senators, such as Sen. Styles Bridges of New Hampshire, questioned, on the floor of the Senate, the intent of the War Department in not addressing the matter of military training for Negro pilots that had supposedly been settled with Public Act 18. Senator Bridges offered proof of the War Department's intent to ignore and circumvent the law by reading into the Congressional Record a letter from the Adjutant General of the War Department, written in September 1939, to Frank S. Reed, a CPTP student and Air Corp applicant. The Adjutant General responded that the:

> War Department has taken final action on your application and that your transcript and college papers and other supporting papers have been returned to this headquarters with this statement in as much as there are no units composed of colored men in the Air Corps at the present time, the War Department can take no further action. . . .[9]

Senator Bridges asked who was responsible for the War Department's evasion of the law, and wondered what was really occurring at the Chicago School of Aeronautics training site at Glenview, Illinois.

When the War Department Military Establishment Appropriations for 1941 were presented in a bill in March 1940, discussions and testimony over the War Department's plan for Negro pilots ensued. Maj. Gen. H. H. Arnold, Chief of the Air Corps appeared before the House Appropriations Sub-Committee and explained that the Chicago School of Aeronautics was designated by the Civil Aeronautics Authority to train Negro pilots under the CAA. He added that, in keeping with the provisions of Public Act 18, the Air Corps had furnished equipment for the ground school. General Arnold also said that the CAA had initiated training for African Americans at the Glenview, Illinois site and that the Air Corps had complied to the provisions of the law by assisting the CAA in its charge to provide Negro pilots the same training provided to Air Corps personnel.[10]

General Arnold reiterated that recruitment of enlisted personnel for the Air Corps peacetime expansion was nearly complete. This statement was significant, because there was a distinction between average peacetime strength and full peacetime strength with an expansion. The War Department blurred this distinction, once confronted with the Negro utilization question, at the most convenient time. An Air Corps at full strength would have little room for new Negro units.

What the Chief of the Air Corps said revealed several dispositions that were shared by the Air Corps and the War Department, and were indicative of their policy toward African Americans in the Air Corps. First, the CAA, not the Air Corps, was responsible for training Negro pilots, including the Negro pilots involved in "experimental" advanced training at Glenview, Illinois. Second, according to the provisions of the law, in the opinion of the War Department, the Air Corps was to lend the CAA aviation equipment for the training of Negroes at one school. Third, the War Department was of the opinion that Public Act 18 did not require them to admit African Americans into the Air Corps, if there were no existing Negro units within the Air Corps.[11]

According to War Department policy, for African Americans to be admitted to the Air Corps, there must be an existent, separate, and segregated Negro unit within the Air Corps. The War Department's logic was predicated on subterfuge. The War Department stated, in private sessions, that it was planning to have Negro Air Units as soon as Negroes proved that they could fly.[12] However, the Air Corps estimated, it would take years to train pilots and mechanics. Once trained, the Negro personnel would have to be segregated from white personnel. The subterfuge was a stalling tactic, utilized by the Air Corps and the War Department to mislead Congress and to avert what they feared the most—Negro officers in command of white officers and enlisted men.[13]

Members of the Appropriation Sub-Committee, Congressmen Everett Dirksen and J. Buell Snyder, under the advisement of the Vann coalition lobbyists, made attempts to clarify the War Department's intentions for the training of Negro pilots. Dirksen asked Snyder, who was chairing the sub-committee, if the Air Corps, in his understanding, was refusing to enlist African Americans for training at the Chicago

School of Aeronautics. Chairman Snyder responded, as quoted by the *Pittsburgh Courier*, that it appeared to be the case and that there

> was no occasion to enlist them . . . when the school has trained a sufficient number of students to warrant the creation of a special unit, I am advised that the War Department will then take such steps as may be necessary looking to the utilization of this additional trained personnel.[14]

When Dirksen asked for a timetable, Snyder responded that he thought the Air Corps training would take place in the near future. Dirksen added, for the record: "The Civil Aeronautics Authority has done its duty in designating the schools. . . . It occurs to me that it is the War Department's duty to articulate that program."[15]

By April 1940, when the War Department Military Establishment Appropriations Bill for 1941 was passed by the House, the War Department's subterfuge was apparent to certain members of Congress and to the Vann coalition. In a planned reaction to the House Appropriations Sub-Committee's inquiry into the War Department plans for Negro pilots, Vann supplemented the Equality Commission with a separate committee of Negro World War I veterans, a pilot, and one of his journalists. Vann figured that a committee of veterans would be viewed with respect not shown to other members of the Vann coalition.[16] The role of this committee was to propose and lobby for two amendments to the War Department's 1941 Appropriations Bill. If ratified, the amendments would mandate that all African Americans be placed in all branches of the army.

One amendment would propose an across-the-board, 10 percent, Negro quota in all military branches. The second amendment would propose that 10 percent of the total appropriation for training Air Corps cadets, approximately $200,000, be set aside for Negro cadets and enlisted mechanics.[17]

Vann appointed fellow attorney Charles Houston and reporter Louis Lautier to co-chair the committee. Other members named to the committee were: Dr. Rayford W. Logan, professor of history at Howard University and World War I veteran officer; Col. West A. Hamilton, Officers' Reserve Corps and member of the Board of Education, Washington D.C.; Maj. C. Campbell Johnson, Infantry Reserve and executive secretary of the Twelfth Street YMCA; Ralph Mizelle, former 1st lieutenant with the 372nd Infantry; James E. Scott, 1st lieutenant 368th Infantry; Robert W. Fearing, commander of the James E. Walker Post of the American Legion; Harry Wilson, commander of the James Reese

Europe Post of the American Legion; and Henry Lincoln Johnson, Jr., president of the Elks' Civil Liberties League of the District of Columbia, president of the Washington Bar Association, and student pilot.

The first order of business included distributing letters to influential politicians and War Department officials. Committee co-chairman Houston sent a letter to Secretary of War Woodering outlining the committee's position on the utilization of Negroes in all combat units within the army. The secretary responded incredulously, although consistently with War Department press releases:

> All troops perform services of all sorts regardless of color and there are no regulations that apply especially to colored soldiers. Colored troops, individually and collectively, are subject to the same regulations as other troops. Colored units have the same proportions of grades and ratings and are accorded the same opportunities for promotion through the several grades as corresponding white units.[18]

Vann rebutted, in a 27 April 1940 *Pittsburgh Courier* editorial, that African Americans were, indeed, restricted to inactive infantry, cavalry, and the quartermaster corps, but were allowed minimum access to the medical corps serving the Negro units. Vann reiterated that the two Negro cavalry regiments were tending horses and cleaning equipment at military schools and the two infantry regiments were scattered to different parts of the country, with little or no combat equipment. Vann reminded readers that Negro officers did not command the Negro regiments, and those who qualified were assigned to teaching or ROTC duty at Negro schools, or were given commands at inactive all-Negro National Guard Units. In addition, Vann clarified that there were no African Americans in the Air, Artillery, Engineers, Signal, or Tank Corps, despite the absence of written regulations forbidding Negro participation.

The Military Committee of the Equality Commission sought, and was granted, an opportunity to testify in the 1941 Military Establishment Appropriations Hearings, held by the Senate Military Appropriations Sub-Committee. In preparation for the testimony, Houston prepared a brief summarizing the feelings of the committee. The written testimony also included a proposal for the two amendments for the sub-committee to consider. Unfortunately, due to NAACP legal obligations, Houston could not attend the hearings. Dr. Logan was selected to read Houston's brief.[19]

On 14 May 1940, Dr. Rayford Logan, on behalf of Vann's committee, appeared before the Senate Military Appropriations Sub-Committee,

chaired by Senator Elmer Thomas of Oklahoma. Dr. Logan read
Attorney Houston's brief, which contained the following key points and
proposals:

> The time was imminent for prejudice to be set aside in the interest
> of national unity and national defense. The Negro population was well
> aware of the army's treatment of the Negro soldier. . . .
>
> There was only one Negro regiment, the 25th Infantry, on Combat
> status but they were stationed in the Arizona desert and there were no
> Negro officers assigned to the 25th and, in fact, there were no Negro
> officers serving in Negro Regular Army units although there are two
> Negro combat officers in the Regular Army and several Negro officers
> in the Reserve. . . .
>
> The Army had refused Negroes applying to the Air Corps when the
> Air Corps was engaged in its largest peacetime expansion ever. . . .
>
> Negroes read and understood the requirements of Army training
> and warfare when Secretary of War Woodering exclaimed, to the House
> Committee on Military Affairs, that one can't operate war machinery
> without men. . . .
>
> Negroes read where Chief of Staff, General George C. Marshall, dur-
> ing the House hearings on the 1941 Military Establishment
> Appropriations Bill, testified that men can be trained in a matter of
> months but for the Air Corps the training of officers and skilled
> enlisted men was a more lengthy task than constructing air planes. . . .
>
> Negroes read where General Marshall testified that the provision of
> the most modern war weapons and training conditions are the most
> important elements in building morale. . . .
>
> Under the Thomason Act of 1940, Congress provided the
> Appropriation for 650 Reserve officers in various colleges and universities
> to train with units of the Regular Army and 975 Reserve officers were
> granted extended duty with the Air Corps and none were Negro. . . .
>
> The morale of the Negro citizen toward National Defense was at an
> all time low and faith in the leadership of War Department, specifically
> the Army and Navy was approaching nonexistence. . . .
>
> The government could not expect Negroes to be valiant defenders
> in time of war when the government ignores and insults them in time
> of peace. Gone are the days when the government and the Army can
> expect the Negroes to come hat in hand . . . .
>
> The Negro is willing to submit to discipline and the most rigid tests
> which the Army provides to its various branches. The Negro is willing to
> take the practical approach and accept apprenticeship in many of the
> services; and. . . .

The Negro wants assurances that we are being dealt with in good faith and that we are welcome as men in the service of our country. On 5 June 1939, Secretary Woodering testified before the House Committee on Appropriations then considering military expansion, including Air Corps expansion, that the War Department was studying ways to provide training to Negro pilots. It had been a full year since Woodering's testimony and not one Negro had been admitted to the Air Corps.[20]

Dr. Logan closed his statement by reading the following proposals for amendments requested by the committee:

We respectfully ask the Senate to write into the Appropriation Bill definite provisions for a fair and reasonable share of the appropriations to be used for the induction and training of Negroes in all branches of the Service. We ask to be incorporated in the beginning or entering grades according to our percentage of the population; we even add that justice would require our percentage of the native born and naturalized population.[21]

Dr. Logan supplemented the written statement by adding that the committee advocated an amendment to the Military Establishment Appropriations Bill, H.R. 9209, which would provide for a general 10 percent strength of Negro enlisted men and officers. The Howard professor explained that, although the committee protested and deplored the continuation of separate and segregated units forced on Negroes, the committee reluctantly accepted the separate units, with the hopes that the segregated units would be commanded by Negro officers.

On the subject of the Air Corps, Dr. Logan testified that H.R. 9209 would provide the Air Corps with $166 million, none of which would be used for the development of Negro pilots or the enlistment and training of Negro mechanics. He charged the Air Corps of ignoring the intent of Section 4 of Public Act 18 by rejecting qualified African Americans who applied for cadet training and mechanics positions, on the basis that there were no Negro units, even when the Act provided for the designation of a school to train Negro pilots and mechanics. To remedy the Air Corps' uncooperative disposition, Dr. Logan recommended that 10 percent of the $2.1 million allocated by the bill for the training of flying cadets and enlisted mechanics be earmarked for the training of Negro flying cadets and enlisted mechanics. He reiterated the point that the Negro Air Corps cadets and mechanics could be integrated into existing Air Corps units, since Public Act 18 and its discrimination clauses forbade the War Department from prohibiting qualified persons from serving in the Air Corps because of their race.[22]

Robert Vann and the committee suffered a minor setback when the Senate Appropriations Sub-Committee approved the $1.8 billion 1941 Military Establishment Appropriations Bill intact, without the Vann Military Committee amendments, and sent it to the floor for passage. The Senate passed the Bill on 27 May 1940, with a unanimous vote. The appropriation boosted the peacetime strength of the armed forces to 280,000, without new Negro units in the Air Corps. Vann and the committee members undaunted, pledged to continue the struggle for fuller participation of African Americans in the national defense program. They redirected their efforts toward influencing the president and his administration, and shaping the platform issues of the 1940 National Democratic and Republican party conventions.[23]

By June 1940, the War Department was deeply involved in developing their Protective Mobilization Plan of 1940. With the passing of the National Defense Bill in 1939, the War Department was able to factor the expansion of current units and the creation of new units into the 1940 Mobilization Plan. The War Department was organizing a national defense force of 750,000 regulars and 250,000 reserves—the largest peacetime buildup ever. The problem of Negro utilization in this expansion and buildup had yet to be addressed.[24]

Although Robert Vann, his coalition, and their political pressure had effectively challenged the status quo regarding African Americans in the Armed Services, the War Department had already supported, in theory, the 1937 proposal to utilize Negro troops at a rate equal to the Negro proportion to the total population—9.5 to 10 percent. The Department proposed the assignment of Negroes to all army units, except the Air Corps and Signal Corps, but it failed to act.[25]

In 1940, however, the War Department was forced to move beyond the theoretical and into the practical means of utilizing Negro troops in most, if not all, arms and services units. In 1940, the War Department was more cognizant of presidential election politics, and therefore, the department went about the business of planning for troop mobilization, which included several proposals on Negro utilization.[26] The Vann coalition had damaged the image of the War Department, and the Roosevelt administration more generally, in the eyes of Negro voters supportive of the push for Negro equality in national defense activity, and particularly in the Air Corps. Unlike the 1937 Plan, which was leaked to the press, the 1940 Plan would be highly classified, with the assignments carried out by fewer players, to minimize the leaks.[27]

The 1940 Mobilization Plan was primarily an updated version of the 1937 Protective Mobilization Plan. The 1940 version sought to rectify the flaws of the 1937 Plan. According, to Lee's *Employment of Negro Troops*, the War Department, in its 1940 version, made attempts to strike a balance between African Americans serving in service units and those in arms, or combat, units. In order to develop this balance in 1940, the War Department had to create new Negro combat units.[28]

Several divisions within the War Department submitted proposals on the subject. The Operations and Training Division (G-3) proposed that all of the service and combat units, including artillery, harbor defense, and antiaircraft units, be assigned a certain, but negotiable, percentage of Negroes. The Air Corps and the Signal Corps would be exempt from accepting assignments of African Americans. G-3 recommended that there be no designation of a Negro unit larger than a regiment, and that more separate battalions be created. The separate battalions would be commanded by Negro officers, who could easily be replaced by white officers if the battalions were mobilized for war. It was apparent that this particular division in the War Department did not think highly of using Negro officers. It also appeared that G-3 would not recommend the designation of a Negro division.[29]

A Negro division would require several regiments and the regiments, several battalions. All of these units would require, and the Negro community would demand, Negro officers in command positions. The War Department, in 1940, still held the opinion that a Negro officer was incompetent in many areas, and especially in leadership capability.[30] The War Department was disposed to assign white officers to the command of Negro units. The department realized, however, that in a presidential election year they could ill afford to aggravate the electorate; therefore, by not designating a Negro division they could avoid the confrontation with the Negro they would face by assigning whites to command positions in Negro units.

The War Department's position on a Negro division was confirmed in a letter from the War Department Adjutant General to Mabe Kountze, of the Associated Negro Press. In response to Kountze's 21 April 1940 letter inquiring about the possibility of the War Department organizing a Negro division from the all-Negro National Guard units, the War Department stated that it was without power to compel any state to organize a Negro National Guard unit, and that the states would be in control of these units. The Department reiterated that under the present authorized strength of the army, it was not possible to consider the organization of a Negro division and that it did not contemplate the employment of Negro National Guard

Units in any manner other than the purposes for which they had been organized.[31]

The War Plans Division of the War Department took issue with the G-3 proposal for Negro utilization. The War Plans Division reported that prohibiting the Negro from serving in the Air Corps or Signal Corps was an inefficient use of valuable manpower. The Division believed that the Air Corps and Signal Corps could use the Negro in some productive capacity. According to Lee's *Employment of Negro Troops*, the War Plans Division took the position that Negro utilization in combat services should be based on the availability of qualified personnel.[32] Therefore, the division was of the opinion that if Negro pilots qualified for and successfully completed cadet training, they should be assigned to the Air Corps as pilots.

According to Lee, the Personnel Division (G-1) also differed with the G-3 proposal. G-1 was of the opinion that each combat unit, including the Air Corps should take its 9 percent quota of Negroes, and that these Negroes should be placed in productive roles, in order to bear their proportionate share of losses on the front lines. The Personnel Division also proposed that some Negro infantry regiments be assigned to white infantry divisions.[33]

The Army Air Corps supported the Operations and Training Division (G-3) proposal. The Chief of the Air Corps, Gen. H. H. Arnold reported that African Americans could not be assigned and utilized by the Air Corps, because Negro pilots would present social problems because they could, conceivably, command white enlisted men. General Arnold explained that if Negroes were to be assigned to the Air Corps, they would be grouped in separate units, and the enlisted personnel would require years of technical training. Therefore, in the opinion of the Air Corps, African Americans could not be utilized in a productive manner. The Air Corps believed it was the responsibility of the Civil Aeronautics Authority to train Negro pilots and mechanics.[34]

By August of 1940, the War Department finally settled on a policy for the utilization of the Negro that resembled the proposal offered by the War Plans Division. The policy was almost identical to the 1937 Plan, with one exception: that Negroes would be utilized in both combat and services in all types of units for which they could qualify. The Air Corps was included in the unit designations.[35] Since it was common knowledge that the Air Corps had benefited from the army expansion in 1939, and that the Corps had grown to thirty groups, causing a shortage of pilots and technicians, the arguments against the use of African Americans in Air Corps units were not convincing.

The War Department did not have unanimous support from the commanders and chiefs of the combat units, especially the Air Corps Command.[36] This lack of consensus would be the cause of Air Corps circumvention of War Department policy regarding nondiscrimination in the use and treatment of the Negro officers in the war years that followed.

The War Department did an excellent job of keeping the Mobilization Plan for the utilization of African Americans in new combat units away from the press, the Negro civil rights groups, and the Negro public. The department did not make the final Plan official or public because of the disunity in the branches, and especially in the Air Corps.[37] Consequently, the War Department continued to reject Negro applicants to the Air Corps on the basis of the absence of Negro units. Cognizant of the rejections of Negro applicants to the Air Corps, but unaware of the War Department's plan, Negro advocates, such as the Vann coalition, continued to pressure the president, the War Department, and members of Congress.

During the interim period between the passing of the 1941 Military Establishment Bill and the National Democratic and Republican conventions, several actions, critical to the movement's drive to create equality in the utilization of Negroes in the army, occurred.

President Roosevelt reinstituted the Council of National Defense and appointed the Advisory Commission on Defense. The designation of the Council was a necessary reaction to the events in Europe and Asia. In April 1940, Germany had invaded Denmark, the Netherlands, and blitzed into France. By 22 June 1940, the Nazi power occupied Paris, and an Armistice between France and Germany was signed. On 10 July 1940, Germany mounted an air attack on Great Britain. The battle, which was to be called the Battle of Britain, was the first ever battle waged entirely in the air, with fighter planes, bombers, self-propelled rockets, and antiaircraft guns as the only weapons. Great Britain was able to repel the German attack.

This particular battle taught America that this war would require more strategic and aggressive use of the airplane. The airplane could no longer be used solely as an observation tool. The Battle of Great Britain also taught the War Department that it needed more sophisticated materials and equipment, more airplanes, and more highly skilled personnel.

The purpose of the Advisory Commission was to mobilize and coordinate a military industrial complex, in case America had to enter the war. Therefore, the Commission included representatives from the steel and automotive industries, transportation, securities and exchange, and clothing manufacturing. With the establishment of this Advisory Commission, the War Department returned to Congress seeking a supplementary appropriation to implement their Mobilization Plan.[38] The War Department also introduced proposals for military conscription. Robert Vann countered with an expanded Military Committee for Equality Commission, called the Committee on Participation of Negroes in the National Defense Programs. The committee extended membership to include professionals from the fields of education and medicine, a representative of the Alpha Kappa Alpha Sorority, and representatives from the National Urban League. The committee also consulted with vocational education specialists associated with the National Youth Administration, and with the Civilian Conservation Corps. Professor Logan remained as chair of the expanded committee.[39]

The primary purpose of the Committee on Participation of Negroes in the National Defense Programs was to serve as a watch dog organization that would monitor the activities of the President's Advisory Commission on Defense, to ensure full participation of the Negro in troop mobilization for combat, full participation of the Negro in the war industries, and full participation of the Negro in military conscription. Other key objectives included:

1. Negro officers be assigned to duty with troops of the regular army;
2. Negro units of the regular army and the National Guard be allowed to participate in training maneuvers;
3. Negro officers called to active duty be allowed to participate in training maneuvers with army troops;
4. A fair share of flying cadets and aviation mechanics in the Army Air Corps and the Navy Flying Corps;
5. A fair share of appointments to the United States Military Academy and the United States Naval Academies;
6. Appointment of Negro doctors in the Medical Corps, and nurses in the Nurses' Corps of the regular army;
7. Special regulations to be promulgated by the Office of Education to assure to Negro schools in Southern states an equitable division of Federal appropriations for vocational education of national defense workers; and
8. Appointment of a consultant in the office of Sidney Hillman, member of the National Defense Advisory Commission in charge of labor problems and labor training.[40]

With the establishment of the Committee on Negro Participation in National Defense Programs goals, Vann requested a meeting with

President Roosevelt to discuss the particulars, with hopes of persuading the president to use his executive power to increase the number of African Americans in the armed forces and to end discrimination in the assignment of African Americans to combat units such as the Air Corps. Vann also would ask the president to request that his Advisory Commission on Defense consult with the Committee on Negro Participation in National Defense Programs on defense industry issues affecting Negroes. The president's secretary, Edwin M. Watson, responded to Vann's request by writing that the president's schedule would not permit an appointment at that time. However, Mr. Watson's letter, dated 25 June 1940, reflected the War Department's public position on Negro troops. Mr. Watson's reply included the following familiar points, as they appeared in the letter printed in the 5 July 1940 issue of the *Pittsburgh Courier:*

> As you know, colored men are now serving in the Army, quite a few units being authorized for colored men exclusively. As rapidly as vacancies occur in these units new recruits are enlisted to keep up the strength of these units. A large proportion of the colored men who enlist in the Army make the service a lifetime career. For this reason there is a comparatively low turnover in colored organizations and, consequently, a comparatively small number of openings as original enlistments at any one time.

Watson continued:

> I am informed that the War Department is making definite plans for the creation of new units for colored men, should the proposed increase in the Regular Army now being considered by Congress be approved.[41]

It became clear to Vann and his supporters on the new committee that President Roosevelt was not going to lend his support to their drive for equality in the armed forces. The president, in their opinion, would not confront the bigoted administrators of the War Department, nor the senators and congressmen opposed to Negro equality, and especially not in an election year. The president's inaction led Vann to believe that President Roosevelt approved of the War Department's Jim Crow policies and practices regarding the Negro. Roosevelt's inability or unwillingness to correct the discriminatory policies of the War Department would cost him early endorsements from influential Negro publishers and editors, such as Robert Vann.[42]

In late June 1940, the Committee on Participation of Negroes in the National Defense Programs was instrumental in assisting Senator Harry H. Schwartz in his draft of an antidiscrimination amendment to H.R. 9850, a bill that would expedite and supplement the Military Establishment Appropriation passed in May 1940. Schwartz's amendment provided that no persons should be excluded from enlistment in any branch of the military establishment on account of race, creed, or color. Unfortunately, the amendment died in Conference Committee, allegedly due to strong objections from the War Department who asserted that there was no such policy excluding African Americans from any branch of service on the basis of race, and that the amendment implied that there was such a policy.[43]

The Conference Committee, led by southern senators who objected to the possibility of troop integration, offered, and the House approved, its own amendment, which provided that no Negro, because of race, should be excluded from enlistment in the army for service with the Negro military units now organized or to be organized for such service. The Committee on Participation of Negroes in the National Defense Programs responded by stating that the revised amendment was "meaningless," and that it underscored the restricted utilization of Negro troops and future enlistees on the basis of race, which was, in essence, discrimination.[44]

Publisher Vann countered the conferees' action by sending, on behalf of the *Courier* and the Committee on Participation of Negroes in the National Defense Programs, telegrams to sixty-four congressmen, soliciting their support for the Schwartz amendment, and requesting the members to ask for a roll call vote against the adoption of the conference report that included the new amendment.[45] The sixty-four congressmen represented districts in the West, Northeast, Midwest, and border states with sizable Negro and sympathetic white electorates. In addition, Vann published the telegram for his one million readers in the 22 June 1940 issue of the *Courier*.

Concurrent with Schwartz amendment debacle was the introduction of the year's first conscription bill by Senator Burke of Nebraska. This draft bill would require 40 million American men between the ages of 21 and 35 to register for military duty. If the War Department implemented the Negro quota outlined in their Mobilization Plan, approximately 4 million Negro men would be drafted. Although the Committee on Participation of Negroes in the National Defense Programs was in support of conscription, they were suspicious of the War Department's plan to use the 2 million who would probably qualify for induction.[46]

As of 1 July 1940, the War Department had not divulged Department policy toward the assignment of African Americans, other than that they expected African Americans to be assigned to existing Negro units or to new Negro units, separate from white units. The committee was not disposed to accept a segregated army that relegated Negroes to menial duty. The committee reiterated their demand for an army and navy of equality, with Negro access to all combat branches of service, and called for the elimination of any provisions that legitimized exclusion from any branch of service on the basis of race.[47]

Events such as the establishment of Vann's Committee on Participation of Negroes in the National Defense Programs, the president's response, and the Schwartz amendment debacle, provided Vann and his supporters political momentum going into the 1940 National Democratic and Republican conventions.

The Republican party, at their National Convention in Philadelphia, accepted Vann's equality and nondiscrimination planks as well as antilynching and nondiscrimination in interstate travel, among other issues in the Republican platform pushed by the eventual presidential nominee, Wendell L. Willke.[48] The Democrats at the National Convention in Chicago, however, appeared to be more interested in what Vann's political aspirations were than in his platform proposals on equality and nondiscrimination in the army, antilynching, discrimination in interstate travel and on other issues. It appeared that the Democratic party leaders were offering Vann a quid pro quo—his active participation in and endorsement of the party for their support of his equality plank in their platform. Vann did not take the offer, and was quoted as saying that he was only at the convention to seek the same equality and nondiscrimination planks that were made part of the Republican party platform, and that he would not accept an assignment in the presidential campaign in the camps of either party. The Democratic party did not endorse all of the pro-Negro resolutions in the party platform.[49]

For over a month, Vann, as he did in 1932 and 1936, withheld his endorsement of either party. Both parties waited anxiously for his answer. Vann was playing his vintage "loose leaf politics," using his newspaper and his influence over other Negro publishers and editors to cover all important political and social events of national importance affecting Negro opinion. At that time, in 1940, Robert L. Vann was arguably the most politically powerful Negro in America, with the potential to impact approximately one million Negro voters, in states with a large number of electoral college votes. During the week of 24 August, Vann announced that he was endorsing the Republican presidential ticket. The Republicans were understandably ecstatic, while the

Democrats felt betrayed, and scrambled for ways to minimize their huge political loss.

Vann cited several reasons for abandoning the Democratic party and withdrawing his (and the *Courier*'s) support for the Roosevelt administration. His primary rationale was based on the premise that the Negro vote had won the 1932 presidential election for Roosevelt, but since that time, the president had neither advocated for legislation nor issued executive orders that would have granted legal protection to millions of African Americans subjected to racial discrimination, state-supported physical intimidation and assault, and disfranchisement. Roosevelt had not repaid his debt to the Negro voters. Other reasons that factored into Vann's repudiation of the Democratic presidential ticket were:

1. Roosevelt's alleged scheme to be drafted for an unprecedented third term which included inflammatory and provocative actions and statements aimed at forcing Americans into World War II;
2. Roosevelt's stacking of the Supreme Court with politically oriented conservatives;
3. Roosevelt's unwillingness to abolish racial discrimination in the civil service, even in the Executive Branch;
4. Roosevelt's silence on racial discrimination and segregation of Negroes in the administration of New Deal programs; and
5. Roosevelt's unwillingness to prohibit discrimination and segregation in the army and navy.[50]

Summarizing his feelings, Vann editorialized in the 31 August 1940 issue of the *Courier*:

> The President has been against prejudice on everything except Negroes. . . . It may be that President Roosevelt is profoundly concerned about the plight of the colored citizen but he has never indicated such a concern for the record.[51]

Shortly after the announcement of his political preference in the 1940 presidential election, Vann became seriously ill. He remained involved in coordinating Negro involvement in the Willkie presidential campaign, however, and in providing support and advocacy for the Committee on Participation of Negroes in the National Defense Programs.

Soon after the National Democratic and Republican conventions of 1940, Congress held hearings on the supplemental appropriations requested by the War Department and the Burke Conscription Bill. The Committee on Participation of Negroes in the National Defense

Programs was planning to revive the Courier/Fish bills that had been introduced in the House of Representatives in 1938. The bills called for a representative quota of Negro cadets to be named to West Point and Annapolis, and for a prohibition on discrimination in the assignment and promotion of Negro officers and enlistees. With major Negro endorsement of the Republican presidential ticket, and with the elections less than three months away, the hearings on the War Department supplemental appropriations and on conscription gave the committee its greatest opportunity to amend or sponsor legislation on Negro participation in conscription and in defense programs.

In one of the hearings on the War Department supplemental appropriations convened in mid-August 1940 by the House Appropriations Sub-Committee, Congressman Louis Ludlow, of Indiana, asked Gen. George C. Marshall, then Chief of Staff in the War Department, whether the War Department had complied with Public Act 18, Section 4, which provided for the transfer of material to one school for the training of Negro pilots. General Marshall replied that there was no Negro aviation entity where African Americans could demonstrate their ability to fly an airplane. Marshall reiterated that the Civil Aeronautics Authority, as opposed to the Air Corps, would be the proper place to initiate training for Negro pilots. When asked by Representative Ludlow whether the War Department would consider Negro pilots trained by the CAA for Air Corps duty, Gen. George C. Marshall responded that the War Department was considering Negro pilots as he spoke.[52]

General Marshall's statement was incredible, in light of the fact that the War Department was still rejecting applications for Air Corps cadet training from qualified African Americans on the basis of race. By the time Marshall testified, there were over 250 licensed Negro pilots, several of whom qualified for Air Cadet training and had passed the primary CPTP course.[53] By 1940, there were six Negro colleges and universities with CPTP courses, and a private Negro-owned flying school, operated by African Americans with commercial pilot licenses.

An even more interesting point about General Marshall's comments was the fact that, as he was testifying, ten Negro students, graduates of the CPTP primary course, were involved in an advanced flying course at Tuskegee Institute. The advanced flight training, which began in late July 1940, was administered to the two highest rated male pilots from each Negro school active in the CPTP project. The flight training provided under the auspices of G. L. Washington, Director of the CPTP, and C. Alfred Anderson, who had been hired from Howard University's CPTP project, consisted of cross-country flight training and acrobatics. Those who successfully completed the course would be rated as instructors.

There was no commitment made by the Air Corps to admit any of the graduates of the course to the Air Corp Cadet training program.[54]

The ten Negro students enrolled in the CPTP advanced course at Tuskegee Institute were Phillip Lee and Roscoe Draper, of Hampton Institute; Erwin Lawrence, Sherman Rose, and Milton Crenshaw, of Tuskegee Institute; Elmer Jones, John Perry, and Yancey Williams, of Howard University; Graham Smith, of A. & T. College, North Carolina; and Hector Strong, of West Virginia State College.[55]

Oddly enough, the advanced course at Tuskegee Institute was the "experimental" advanced course that was supposed to have been administered by the Chicago School of Aeronautics at the Glenview, Illinois training site, as stipulated in the agreement made with the 1939 National Airmen's Association of America, the CAA, and the War Department, as provided in Public Act 18, Section 4. A Selection Board for the advanced program was appointed and was to have chosen the twenty highest-rated Negro pilots from the CPTP projects. The Negro pilots who passed the "experimental training" were to be admitted to Air Corp Cadet training.[56]

Earlier, in the spring of 1940, in preparation for the advanced training, the Chicago School of Aeronautics brought Negro instructors in the CPTP project to the Glenview airport to provide them with updated training in the instruction of acrobatics. They were to provide the flight training in the advanced program. The Negro pilot instructors involved included C. Alfred Anderson, then of Howard; Cornelius Coffey, of Harlem Airport and the Coffey School of Aeronautics; and Louis Jackson, also an instructor at Harlem Airport.[57]

While the instructor training was proceeding in Chicago, G. L. Washington, with the concurrence of Tuskegee Institute president F. D. Patterson, lobbied the CAA for the advanced CPTP project to be housed at Tuskegee. Patterson's plan was to make Tuskegee Institute the training center for advanced civilian pilot training for Negroes.[58] He was part of the Selection Board of the Chicago Aeronautical School advanced training project, and was aware of the Air Corps' intention to admit the graduates of the "experimental" program. President Patterson knew that the Institute could reap a financial harvest, if the Air Corps complied with Section 4 of Public Act 18 by loaning aviation equipment to a school, Tuskegee Institute, for the purpose of training Negro pilots.

Patterson was also astute enough to realize that if the Air Corps honored its pledge to admit Negro pilots who passed the "experimental" training, the Air Corps would bring Negroes into a segregated unit and would train them separately from whites. Therefore, the training site would be one where segregation was practiced. Tuskegee Institute was already a training site for the advanced CPTP training and, therefore, the school stood a legitimate chance of being selected as the training site for the Air Corps' Negro unit. Since the Institute hired rated flight instructors in the advanced CPTP course, it was conceivable that the Tuskegee Institute could obtain a contract from the Air Corps to provide primary flight training to the Negro cadets.

G. L. Washington was able to hire C. Alfred Anderson away from Howard University and Louis Jackson from Coffey's project at Harlem Airport, giving Tuskegee Institute two of the highest-rated Negro flight instructors in the country. With this array of instructor talent and experience in the CPTP, Tuskegee was granted funding to continue advanced CPTP flight training. Consequently, no advance training "experiment" ever occurred at the suburban Chicago site.[59] Moreover, the War Department and the Air Corps would not commit to admitting Negro graduates of the Tuskegee advanced CPTP course. The graduated pilots were told that they were simply CPTP-rated pilots who had passed the advanced course, and were not qualified applicants to the Air Corps Cadet training. Even graduates of the advanced program who applied to the Air Corps for Cadet training were rejected on the basis of race.[60] Many of the student pilots felt betrayed, and the Negro organizations, such as the Committee on Participation of Negroes in the National Defense Programs, the NAACP, and the NAAA felt that the War Department had reneged on the 1939 Chicago agreement, misled Congress, and circumvented, if not violated, Public Act 18.

In early September 1940, there were signs that the War Department was implementing parts of its 1940 Mobilization Plan pertaining to the creation of new Negro combat units. The War Department confirmed that two new Negro artillery units—the 77th and 77th Coast Artillery—had begun training in artillery at Ft. Bragg, North Carolina.[61] The War Department also worked on a proposal for selecting a higher percentage of African Americans to be drafted in the Conscription Bill being considered by Congress. In order to increase Negro troop strength to 9.5 percent of the total troop strength, the War Department would have to induct a higher percentage of Negroes at the onset of a military draft.[62] The Committee on Participation of Negroes in the National Defense Programs, unaware that the War Department had planned, in the summer of 1940, for new Negro units and an increase in Negro troop strength, claimed a minor victory in forcing the War Department to create new units and to draft more African Americans into the military.[63]

In a move that was considered partisan politics to court the Negro vote, the President's National Defense Advisory Commission made

public a protective clause providing that workers in contracted industries should not be discriminated against because of age, sex, race, or
color.[64] Other agencies associated with the President's Commission,
such as the WPA and the Office of Education responsible for vocational training, adopted the antidiscrimination clauses.

After Labor Day 1940, Congress returned to work on the Burke
Conscription Bill, which had become the Burke/Wadsworth Selective
Service Bill. The Selective Service Bill featured the following particulars:

1. It provided for registration of male citizens between the ages
   of 21 and 31 for a draft for one's year's military training;
2. It limited the draft to 900,000 men for the land forces each
   year;
3. It stipulated that the draft would take place as soon as the
   War Department could implement a system;
4. It exempted ordained ministers and divinity students from
   service, but required that they register for the draft; and
5. It stipulated that draftees would receive $21 per month, dur-
   ing their four months of training, and $30 per month for the
   remaining eight months, unless promoted to a higher
   grade.[65]

Members of the Committee on Negro Participation in National
Defense Programs, such as Dr. Rayford Logan and Dr. Emmet J. Scott,
testified before the House Military Affairs Committee, where they outlined the extent of discrimination applied to African Americans in the
armed forces, despite the stellar record of military contributions made
by Negroes before and since the existence of the United States.

Senator Robert F. Wagner, (D) New York, a long-time advocate and
sponsor of antilynching bills, authored an antidiscrimination amendment
that he thought was both responsive to the concerns of the Committee on
Participation of Negroes in the National Defense Programs and other
Negro civil rights organizations, and protective of the rights of African
Americans to enlist in the armed forces. The Wagner amendment read:

> Any person between the ages of eighteen and thirty-five regardless of
> race or color shall be afforded an opportunity to voluntarily enlist and
> be inducted into the land or naval forces, including aviation units of
> the United States for the training and service sub-section (B) if he is
> acceptable to the land or naval forces for such training and service.[66]

The bill, with the Wagner amendment, passed the Senate and was sent
to the House, where a similar bill was considered.

Although Senator Wagner specified enlistees only and did not advocate integrated units, the amendment was acclaimed by Negro Democrats, hopeful for a political advantage, as a courageous and positive step toward equality in the armed forces. Senator Wagner was, after all, a staunch supporter of the Roosevelt administration, and was, therefore, campaigning for Negro votes for the president.[67]

The Committee on Participation of Negroes in the National Defense Programs rejected the amendment, calling it inadequate, and assailed it for providing for the option of status quo discrimination in the army and navy. Members of the committee also argued, convincingly, that the amendment only provided for enlistees, and not for draftees inducted into the service. The committee convinced Congressman Fish to set aside his plans for the Courier bills and to introduce an amendment to a House bill that was almost identical to the Burke-Wadsworth Selective Service Bill. Committee members Dr. Rayford Logan, C. Campbell Johnson, Frank Coleman, and Louis Lautier prepared the language for the amendment, which became known as the Fish Amendment.[68] The Fish Amendment provided that: "In the selection and training of men, as well as the interpretation and intention of the provisions of this bill, there shall be no discrimination against any person on account of race, creed, or color."[69] The new amendment covered draftees and volunteers, and removed any options for the army and navy to discriminate in the selection of draftees and enlistees on the basis of color.

Congressman Fish presented his amendment to the House Military Affairs Committee, as a clarification and correction of the amendment in the House bill that was similar to the Wagner amendment. After limited opposition and debate from Congressman Andrew J. May, Chairman of the Military Affairs Committee over the apparent redundant language offered by Fish in his amendment, Congressman Fish was able to prevail. The House committee voted to approve the amendment and to present it to House. The House approved the Burke-Wadsworth Selective Service bill with the Fish Amendment. The Fish amendment was also approved by the House-Senate Conference responsible for the final version of the draft bill. The Burke-Wadsworth Selective Service bill, with the Fish amendment intact, passed both the House and Senate, was signed by the president on 14 September 1940, and became the Selective Service Act of 1940.[70]

The signing into law of the Selective Service Act of 1940 was considered another major victory for Robert Vann and his Committee on Participation of Negroes in the National Defense Programs, in their quest for equality in the army and navy. They knew more work had to be accomplished, however. The Army Air Corps and the navy were still rejecting applications from qualified African Americans, and the status of Negro officers in the regular army and National Guard was questionable, at best. There were new Negro combat units in artillery, coastal artillery, and antiaircraft units, but no new Negro officers were being trained to command them.[71]

On 16 September 1940, the press secretary to the president, Stephen Early, announced to the national media that 36,000 of the first 400,000 men drafted under the new Selective Service Act would be Negro, and that the War Department had initiated the development of Negro personnel for the aviation service.[72] This announcement, on the surface, was well received by the Negro community and the Negro press. Upon closer examination, however, the White House announcement was subterfuge. As late as the end of August 1940, the War Department was still rejecting applications from Negroes interested in joining the Air Corps.[73] In addition, the Negro personnel being developed for aviation service in the Air Corps were not associated with the Air Corps on 16 September 1940 and, therefore, did not exist. The War Department commented that Negro pilots were undergoing training at the Glenview, Illinois, training site, and that Negro mechanics were being trained in other NYA sites around the country. Although the Glenview site was operated by the Chicago School of Aeronautics, which had an Air Corps contract to train Air Corp Cadets, the Negro pilots in the CPTP project at Glenview were not Air Corps Cadets, or in any way connected with the Air Corps. Negro pilots in the Glenview, Illinois project, which was an integrated CPTP project, were the responsibility of the Civil Aeronautics Authority, and not the Air Corps. The White House announcement was just another political ploy to appease Negro voters.

The Committee on Participation of Negroes in the National Defense Programs recognized the announcement as subterfuge, but also viewed the news as another political advantage, and an opportunity to press the Roosevelt administration for more concessions, including an unequivocal commitment to admit and train Negro pilots and mechanics into the Air Corps, the use of more Negro officers in the Reserve and National Guard, and full training and employment of Negroes in the defense industries.

Due to the 1940 Military Establishment Appropriations and supplementary funding, the war industries were gearing up, and employment and training of whites was outpacing the employment and training of Negroes. In the early months of 1940, the employment rates for whites decreased four percentage points, from 17 to 13 percent, compared to

22 percent, for African Americans. In the states where African Americans constituted at least 20 percent of the total population, and were subjected to a segregated school system, only 6 percent of the federal funding for vocational training for defense jobs was allocated to institutions instructing Negroes. Good jobs in aircraft, iron, steel, and shipping industries were virtually closed to Negroes. By the end of 1940, there were only 240 African Americans employed in the aircraft industry.[74] Because of wholesale discrimination in the federally funded employment and training projects, the Committee on Participation of Negroes in the National Defense Programs, the NAACP, the Urban League, and other Negro organizations formed a solid coalition and sought an audience with President Roosevelt, to impress on him the urgency of their concerns and to seek executive remedy. The organizations gambled that Roosevelt would be more disposed to act with a close election quickly approaching.

Although President Roosevelt's schedule would not permit him to meet with Robert Vann in June 1940, he was ready in late September to talk to coalition members Walter White of the NAACP, A. Phillip Randolph of the Brotherhood of Sleeping Car Porters, and T. Arnold Hill of the Urban League about Negro participation in defense programs. The meeting with the president was set for 27 September 1940, and the agenda included discussing discrimination against the Negro in the armed forces and in the defense industries.[75]

Walter White had met with the president on several occasions to discuss, to no avail, antilynching legislation. White and "Negro Cabinet" members were accustomed to President Roosevelt's personable style of communication which included telling several jokes and anecdotes to lighten the seriousness of agenda items brought by the African Americans. It did not take the guests long to realize that the joking and storytelling often took most of the meeting time, and guests were often escorted out of White House with nothing accomplished.[76] This communication style worked well and was part of the president's way of evading Negro issues. The committee of three were aware of Roosevelt's capacity to steal their limited time, however, and, therefore, they reached a consensus on the issues they would discuss with the president and prepared a statement that encompassed the points that concerned the coalition.

In their 27 September 1940 meeting with the president, the three men stressed their opposition to discrimination in the armed forces and defense industries and presented the written statement to Roosevelt. The statement contained the following referendum:

1. The army should use available Negro reserve officers in the training of recruits and in other forms of active service. A policy of training additional Negro officers in all branches of service should be announced and present facilities and those to be provided in the future should be made available for such training;

2. That the president should order the army and navy to designate centers where Negroes might be trained for work in all branches of the aviation corps. In addition to pilots, navigators, bombers, gunners, radio men, and mechanics should be trained, in order to facilitate full Negro participation in the air service;

3. That the president should order the army to require the assignment of officers and enlisted personnel to existing units, and units to be established, without regard to race;

4. That the army and navy should integrate Negro physicians, dentists, pharmacists, and officers into the chemical warfare and other units, existing units and units to be established;

5. That the president should appoint Negroes to various national and local agencies engaged in the administration of the Selective Service Act of 1940;

6. That the president should order the War Department to develop effective techniques for assuring the extension of the policy of integration of positions in the navy, other than the menial services to which the Negro was restricted;

7. That the president should adopt policies for equitable participation of Negroes in employment incidental to national defense, with particular reference to army arsenals, navy yards, and industries having national defense contracts; and

8. That the president should ensure the participation of trained Negro women as army, navy, and Red Cross nurses.[77]

President Roosevelt, along with Col. Frank Knox of the Navy and Robert Patterson of the War Department, who were requested by the president to attend the meeting, accepted the referendum and pledged to eradicate, to the best of their ability, the problems of discrimination outlined in the statement. The president also promised to contact the committee of three after consulting with War Department officials and members of his cabinet.[78]

President Roosevelt, for some unknown reason, did not contact White, Hill, or Randolph with his plan for ending discrimination in the armed forces and defense industries. Instead, Roosevelt decided to present his plan to the press, an obvious attempt at grabbing headlines for the presidential campaign. The president's press secretary, Stephen Early, distributed an official statement from President Roosevelt that included the following plan:

1. The strength of the Negro personnel in the army will be maintained on the general basis of proportion of the Negro population of the country;
2. Negro organizations will be established in each major branch of the service, combat as well as noncombat;
3. Negro reserve officers eligible for active duty will be assigned to Negro units, commanded by Negro personnel;
4. When officer candidate schools are established, opportunity will be given to Negroes to qualify for Reserve commissions;
5. Negroes are being given aviation training as pilots, mechanics, and technical specialists. This training will be accelerated. Negro aviation units will be formed as soon as the necessary personnel has been trained;
6. At army arsenals and army posts, Negro civilians are provided equal opportunity for employment at work for which they are qualified by ability, education, and experience; and
7. The policy of the War Department is not to integrate Negro and white enlisted personnel in the same regimental organizations. This policy has proven satisfactory over a long period of years, and to make changes would produce situations destructive to morale and detrimental to preparation for national defense.[79]

The press statement also concluded that the War Department did not contemplate assigning Negro reserve officers, other than physicians and chaplains, to existing units in the regular army. Early added that the president's plan was developed with the assistance and concurrence of Mr. White, Mr. Hill, and Mr. Randolph.[80]

The press release of the president's plan for eliminating discrimination in the armed forces and defense industries was designed to appease southern Democrats and to placate Negro voters. The Negro press and the advocacy groups were not totally pleased with the president's response. White, Hill, and Randolph felt betrayed and "tricked" and voiced denials to the president's assertion that they concurred with the plan. To verify their denials, the three sent the referendum they had given to the president to every Negro and receptive white newspaper in the country. They also asked the president to issue a retraction of the statement that the three civil rights leaders had agreed to the president's plan.[81]

While the president's announcement may have worked with the southern Democratic leadership, and appeased southern officers in the War Department, the message received a very mixed reaction in the Negro voter community. The Negro press and the civil rights organizations accused the president of condoning and perpetuating the segregated tradition in the armed forces. The Committee on Participation of Negroes in the National Defense Programs viewed some of the items in the president's announcement regarding Negro pilots as positive. It was the first time that the War Department's plan for the utilization of African Americans in the Air Corps was made public. The president's statement verified the Air Corps plans to establish aviation units for African Americans. The committee, however, was still investigating where the Negro pilots, referred to in the president's plan, were being trained.[82]

Republican presidential candidate Wendell Willkie took full advantage of the president's support of a "Jim Crow" army, and pledged to end discrimination in the armed forces by endorsing the Negro coalition's referendum given to the president.[83] The gap between Willkie and Roosevelt in the presidential polls began to decrease and the election promised to be decided by the northern and border states with a large Negro electorate. Key Democrats in Roosevelt's administration became nervous.

One week after the infamous presidential announcement, Mr. Early was involved in an altercation with a Negro police officer in New York City. Early was arrested for allegedly kicking the officer. Mr. Early became both an embarrassment and a scapegoat of the Democratic presidential campaign. He was the messenger of the president's announcement on discrimination in the armed forces and defense industries and, therefore, took the brunt of the criticism for attempting to co-opt the White, Hill, and Randolph committee. His unfortunate encounter with the Negro policeman only served to further anger Negroes and officials of the Democratic party, and consequently, forced Roosevelt to order Early to retract all statements tying the White, Hill, and Randolph committee to the president's plan for ending discrimination in the armed forces and defense industries.[84]

As the 1940 election drew near, the Democratic party searched for opportunities to restore the lagging Negro support. During this period, the Negro press offered the Democrats several options to exercise. When one hundred white colonels were promoted to general by the War Department in October 1940, the Negro press called for an explanation for the exclusion of Col. B. O. Davis, Sr. from the promotion list.[85] At that time, Colonel Davis was the only Negro colonel in the regular army with combat status. The Committee on Participation of Negroes in the National Defense Programs renewed their request for a special assistant to the secretary of war to serve as an advisor on Negro affairs in the armed forces and defense industries. This individual would serve in the same capacity as Dr. Emmet Scott in World War I. As early as 1938, Robert Vann and his Committee on Equality in the armed forces had lobbied the War Department and Congress for the appointment of a special assistant on Negro affairs to the War Department. At that time, Vann and his committee recommended Lt. Benjamin O. Davis, Jr. for the special assistant position.[86]

The Roosevelt administration and Democratic party leaders, apparently fearful of alienating the southern Democratic voting block, did not respond immediately to the suggestions to promote Colonel Davis and to assign a special assistant to the War Department.

Senator Wagner offered what he thought was another solution. The Senator from New York introduced a resolution, entitled Resolution 75, that would provide for a special Senate committee to investigate discrimination in employment in defense industries, vocational training the army, navy, Air Corps, Medical Corps, and in the operation of the Selective Service Act and local draft boards.[87] Members of the Senate from the South successfully argued that the Senate Committee to Investigate the National Defense Program, chaired by Senator Harry Truman, could provide the same results and, therefore, the resolution died in committee. When Walter White tried to put himself on the agenda of Truman's committee, he was told by Truman that the committee schedule would not allow it to hear testimony from members of the Committee on Participation of Negroes in the National Defense until spring 1941. It became clear, at that point, that the Committee on Participation of Negroes in the National Defense Programs would need an executive order from the president in order to achieve their goal.[88]

With the Wagner Resolution dead, Democratic party leaders and Roosevelt's advisors investigated other opportunities to assuage Negro press influence on the Negro voters. Their greatest opportunity came on 24 October 1940, when Robert Vann died, after a lengthy illness.[89] President Roosevelt acted very quickly in taking advantage of the great political lost to the Negro community and the Republican party, by announcing on the following day the appointments of Col. B. O. Davis, Sr. to brigadier general and Judge William Hastie to special assistant to the secretary of war. In addition, C. Campbell Johnson was appointed special assistant to the director of selective service.[90]

The executive appointments were well received by the Negro press, civil rights organizations, and the Committee on Participation of

Negroes in the National Defense Programs. Although the Republican party leaders described the appointments as a desperate political ploy by Roosevelt to capture the Negro vote, it was difficult for Negro advocacy groups to publicly criticize the appointments, especially Davis, Sr.'s promotion, which made him the first Negro general in American history. What made Davis's promotion interesting was that he was one year away from the mandatory retirement age of sixty-four and the fact that he was not promoted earlier in October 1940 with the other one hundred colonels. In addition, it was widely known in the Negro civil rights and press community that Davis, Sr. was mustered out of the army as a lieutenant in 1899, reenlisted as a private, and worked his way back up the chain of command. Davis, Sr., however, was denied combat command assignments in the regular army and for thirty-five years, Davis, Sr. was shuttled back and forth to teaching positions at Negro colleges and universities such as Wilberforce University and Tuskegee Institute.

Between his teaching assignments, where he taught military science and instructed Reserve Officer Training Corps students, Davis, Sr. was the coordinator of the Gold Star voyages to France for mothers and widows of Negro soldiers slain in World War I. He also served as the instructor of the 372nd Ohio National Guard and the instructor and commanding officer of the 369th Infantry, New York National Guard. Shortly after the 369th became an artillery and antiaircraft unit, Davis, Sr. was appointed to brigadier general. Two months after his appointment to brigadier general, he was assigned the command of a brigade within the Second Cavalry Division, a Negro unit located at Ft. Riley, Kansas, that was classified as inactive in the 1940 War Department Mobilization Plans. Six months later, in June 1941, Davis was assigned, at retirement age, to the War Department as a special assistant to the inspector general.[91] It was as if the Roosevelt administration and the War Department had assured the southern senators and the army commanders and chiefs that Davis would not command an active unit within the regular army, and that his promotion and function was purely symbolic.

Judge Hastie's appointment, however, appeared to be politically inconsistent with Roosevelt's policy toward civil rights. For Hastie, the former federal judge of the Virgin Islands, and, in 1940, dean of Howard University's law school, was a renowned civil rights lawyer associated with the NAACP legal defense team. In addition, Judge Hastie was an integrationist, and viewed segregation as a form of discrimination. Hastie's social and political philosophies were antithetical to the opinions and philosophies shared in the War Department.[92] The Hastie appointment, even if it were meant to be symbolic, was an advantage to the NAACP and the Committee on Participation of Negroes in the

National Defense Programs in their quest for equality in the armed forces. However, the incompatibility of the theoretical and philosophical positions on discrimination in the armed services, and especially in the Air Corps, between commanders and chiefs in the War Department and Hastie would lead to friction in the early stages of the war.

Although American history does not recognize the significance of the human rights and political contributions made by Robert Vann, it appears that the timing of Vann's death and the resultant appointments of Hastie, Davis, and Johnson, contributed to the retention of Negro support for President Roosevelt in his reelection bid. Roosevelt was elected to an unprecedented third term.

The Committee on Participation of Negroes in the National Defense Programs did not cease activity with Robert Vann's death. The committee continued in the struggle that Vann had initiated. One month after Vann's death, the committee met at Hampton Institute to map out their agenda for 1941. At the Hampton Conference on the Participation of Negroes in National Defense, more than 2,000 businessmen, educators, and politicians caucused and gave unanimous support to the committee as it renewed its pledge to fight against discrimination and segregation in the army and navy and in defense contracts. Consequently, full participation in the Air Corps became the group's immediate focus.[93]

When the president issued an announcement of the new Air Corps commitment to admit and train Negro pilots, members of the Committee on Participation of Negroes in the National Defense Programs were interested in where the training for the Negro pilots and technical personnel would take place. In October of 1940, the War Department, Air Corps, and the Civil Aeronautics Authority were preparing proposals for aviation training sites for pilots and technical specialists. The proposal preparation required site visits and meetings with directors and flight instructors at the Negro schools with CPTP projects. Rumors spread regarding the Air Corps, and CAA's interest in placing an Air Corps training school for Negro pilots, mechanics, and other technical support personnel, at the Tuskegee CPTP site. It was no secret that G. L. Washington, director of the Tuskegee CPTP project, wanted the Air Corps training contract.[94]

National Airmen's Association of America members working with the CPTP project at Harlem Airport in Chicago and at the Glenview, Illinois training site, heard the Tuskegee rumors and protested even the possibility of the Glenview site being passed over in favor of a segregated training program offered at Tuskegee. The Chicago Urban League and Enoch Waters, of the *Chicago Defender*, on behalf of the

National Airmen's Association, vigorously protested to the NAACP, citing the Chicago experience as being recognized as the premier flight training center for African Americans in the country. The assistant secretary of the NAACP, Roy Wilkins, sent the letter to Judge Hastie at the War Department, asserting that the NAACP had no knowledge of such a plan of the Air Corps and CAA to centralize Negro pilot and technical training at Tuskegee. Wilkins added that the NAACP did not wish to enter any feud between the NAAA in Chicago and the Tuskegee Institute, but if forced to support the Alabama site or none at all, Wilkins revealed that he would choose Tuskegee. Wilkins told Hastie that he felt that the civil rights organization would not get "very far objecting to the location."[95]

Actually, according to Lee's *Employment of Negro Troops*, the Air Corps, as early as September 1940, was considering three training sites for Negro pilots and technical crews. The Glenview site of the Chicago School of Aeronautics, the Aeronautical University in Chicago, at Chanute Field in Rantoul, Illinois, and Tuskegee Institute. The Air Corps also analyzed a plan for the assignment of one squadron that was to make up a combat unit within the Air Corps.[96]

The Air Corps was in a period of expansion and experienced a pilot shortage. There was little logic to the Air Corps' persistence and stubbornness in its refusal to utilize as many qualified Negro pilots as possible, in as many flying units as necessary. In addition, the Air Corps had established a goal of producing 25,000 planes by 1942 and needed at least 36,000 pilots to fly them. The Air Corps 1941 quota for pilots was set at 25,000, but in 1940, the Corps was graduating only 475 pilots per month. At the 1940 graduation rate, the Air Corps would, conceivably, have 11,400 pilots to fly 36,000 planes in 1942.[97]

By October 1940, eighteen civilian flying schools were under contract to provide primary training to cadets and only four military basic and advanced flight schools were administered by the Air Corps. Two of the military flight training schools, Maxwell Field in Montgomery, Alabama, and Moffet Field in Sunnyvale, California, were just a few months old.[98] By the middle of October 1940 the Air Corps was seriously considering Tuskegee as the training site for the Negro squadron because of the weather conditions, less air traffic, its proximity to the Maxwell Field training site in Montgomery, and, more importantly, its tradition as a segregated environment, therefore, relieving the Air Corps of its "social problem."[99] The Air Corps realized that once the Negro cadets completed their flight training, they would be officers. The primary fear of the Air Corps was to have Negro officers at an airfield where white enlisted men were assigned for duty.

Due to the lack of resources for Air Corps mechanical training at Tuskegee Institute, and the existence of other established Air Corps technical schools, the Air Corps decided that technical training of mechanics and other specialists would take place at Chanute Field. The Chanute facility was in an isolated area of Illinois and, therefore, ideal for social isolation of Negro troops. The Air Corps kept their site selections of Tuskegee Institute and Chanute Field classified until they made their formal announcement in January 1941.[100]

During the planning period between October and the end of December 1940, the Air Corps decided to designate the Negro flying unit as a pursuit squadron.[101] Many experts believed that pursuit flying was the most difficult form of flying requiring skills in navigation, gunnery, and acrobatic flying. With the announcement of the designation of a Negro pursuit squadron, Negro civil rights groups and Negro aviators argued the wisdom and the merit of the Air Corps decision.[102] The African American advocates argued that the Air Corps could have assigned the unit bombardier duty, observation duty, transport duty, or coastal patrol. Consequently, the Negro community accepted the dangerous designation as another tough struggle to overcome, especially when they had no other options.

The Air Corps also decided during the planning period to place the administrative command of the Negro unit under white officers. After the unit's successful completion of flight training and on-the-job experience, Negro officers would take over the administrative duties of the unit.[103]

Negro applications for the Air Corps continued to come into the War Department, but between September and November 1940, Negro applicants were still being rejected on the basis of race. By the end of November, however, a few Negro applicants received letters indicating that their applications had been received and referred to the appropriate Personnel unit and filed until trained personnel was available.[104] A few Negro applicants were allowed to take the Air Corps written entrance exam and the physical examination. In late November 1940, George Roberts of West Virginia was the first Negro known to take and successfully complete the entrance exam.[105]

A few African Americans whose applications were rejected during the fall of 1940, contemplated, with the assistance and urging of the NAACP, suing the War Department and the Air Corps. The NAACP was looking for a test case prior to the president's announcement of the Air Corps plan to accept and train Negroes.[106] Professor Richman, of Howard University, had contacted two of his mechanical engineering students, Yancey Williams and Spann Watson, who had completed the

University's CPTP, to encourage them to sue the War Department, the army, and the Air Corps over their discriminatory admissions policy. Both students agreed to file suit. Yancey Williams was to have been the principle plaintiff in the suit, and Spann Watson would have been the alternate. Williams was to have been the plaintiff because he had received a rejection letter although he had passed the CPTP advanced course and had a pilot instructor's rating. Yancey Williams was, therefore, eminently qualified to be considered for the Air Corps. Mr. Watson agreed to participate in the suit because he had received one of the rejection letters from the War Department. The filing of Williams's lawsuit was postponed after the president's announcement of the planned inclusion of Negroes in the Air Corps.[107]

Optimistic over President Roosevelt's appointments of Hastie, Davis, and Johnson, yet very suspicious of the president's new policies for equal utilization of Negroes in national defense, especially in the Air Corps and defense industries, the Committee on Participation of Negroes in the National Defense Programs and the NAACP chose to serve as observers of President Roosevelt's commitment to action.

As early as December 1940, the Air Corps had selected Tuskegee Institute as the training site for the new Negro Air Corps unit. For no apparent reason, other than those pertaining to the national security, the Air Corps chose to keep confidential the fact that Negro civilian and regular army personnel were recruited and selected to provide administrative and training duty within the Air Corps' new Negro squadron. William M. Womack, who had completed his graduate work at The University of Michigan, was recruited in December 1940 by Ernest Smith, then the director of Physical Training at the Army Air Corps Southeastern Training Command, for the position of Director of Physical Training for the Negro squadron. Womack had worked with Smith while in graduate school. Womack accepted the position and reported to Tuskegee Institute in February 1941.[108] Hayden Johnson, a Negro reserve officer, was called into active duty in July 1941 as the first administrative officer of the new Negro squadron. Johnson's brother, Maurice Johnson, was selected as the unit's first medical officer.[109]

Candidates for cadet training were to be chosen from the pilots who successfully completed the CAA's advanced course. By January 1941, there were approximately twenty Negro pilots who had completed the advanced course and, therefore, would qualify for Air Corps Cadet training. Consequently, there were hundreds of African Americans of proper age with pilot's licenses prior to the CPTP project, and at least two pilots of proper age with combat experience, who could not be considered for the Air Corps. The pilots who could not be considered included James Peck, who flew combat missions for the Loyalists in the Spanish Civil War, and Earl Vann Wong, who, in 1938, flew fighter planes in China's Royal Pursuit Squadron.[110] The technical personnel were to be chosen from enlisted men in the regular army and from new enlistees. Chanute Field would be the training site for the Negro enlisted personnel assigned to the Air Corps.[111]

Although he did not live to see the full effect of his fight for the elimination of discrimination in the armed forces and national defense programs, Robert Vann, through his entrepreneurial skills, political acumen, and leadership, provided the Negro community with invaluable and effective strategies to utilize in the struggle for civil rights in the America of the immediate future. Now, with Negro participation in the Air Corps about to become a reality, these strategies would become even more important during the impending war years.

Notes

1. "American Un-neutrality," *Pittsburgh Courier*, 20 April 1940; Franklin, *From Slavery to Freedom*, 574-76.
2. Enzo Angelucci and Peter Bowers, *The American Fighter: The Definitive Guide to American Fighter Aircraft from 1917 to the Present* (New York: Orion Books, 1985), 162-63.
3. "American Un-neutrality," *Pittsburgh Courier*, 20 April 1940.
4. "Want Race Troops Used in Every Branch of Service," *Pittsburgh Courier*, 25 May 1940; "Senate Group to Hear Logan," *Pittsburgh Courier*, 15 May 1940.
5. "Abbott Is Buried in Chicago," *Pittsburgh Courier*, 9 March 1940.
6. Waters, *American Diary*, 114-18, 140.
7. Ibid., 206.
8. Ibid., 134, 136-38; Harold L. Gould, Director Department of Industrial Relations and Research, Chicago Urban League, letter to Walter White regarding Chicago Urban League's concern for Jim Crow training of pilots at Tuskegee Institute, 15 November 1940, NAACP Papers, Collections of the Manuscript Division, Library of Congress; Roy Wilkins letter to William Hastie regarding Enoch P. Water's concern regarding Jim Crow training of Negro pilots in CDAA Training at Tuskegee Institute, 15 November 1940, NAACP Papers, Collections of the Manuscript Division, Library of Congress.
9. "US Army Ignores Law for Training of Colored Pilots," *Pittsburgh Courier*, 10 February 1940.
10. "Training of Race Pilots for Army Air Corps Being Given Wide Detour," *Pittsburgh Courier*, 13 April 1940.
11. Ibid.
12. Ibid.

13. Osur, *Blacks in the Army Air Forces*, 21-22.
14. "Ban Against Negroes in Air Corps Discussed," *Pittsburgh Courier*, 20 April 1940.
15. Ibid.
16. "Lautier, Houston on Delegation to Have Bill Amended," *Pittsburgh Courier*, 27 April 1940; "Courier Board Is Chosen By Vann," *Pittsburgh Courier*, 4 May 1940.
17. Ibid.; Ibid.; Lee, *The Employment of Negro Troops*, 47.
18. "Senate Group to Hear Logan," *Pittsburgh Courier*, 11 May 1940.
19. Ibid.
20. "Courier's Appeal to U.S. Senate," *Pittsburgh Courier*, 18 May 1940.
21. Ibid.
22. Ibid.
23. Lautier, "Houston on Delegation To Have Bill Amended," *Pittsburgh Courier*, 27 April 1940; "Senate Committee Turns Deaf Ear to Army Plan," *Pittsburgh Courier*, 1 June 1940.
24. "Want Race Troops Used in Every Branch of Service," *Pittsburgh Courier*, 25 May 1940.
25. Lee, *The Employment of Negro Troops*, 46.
26. Ibid., 46-48.
27. Ibid., 48.
28. Ibid., 46.
29. Ibid., 46, 48.
30. Ibid., 45, 46, 47; Osur, *Blacks in the Army Air Forces*, 1-6.
31. Mabe Kountze, "War Department Not Figuring on Negro Division," *Pittsburgh Courier*, 1 June 1940.
32. Lee, *The Employment of Negro Troops*, 46-47.
33. Ibid., 47.
34. Ibid., 47.
35. Ibid., 49-50; Osur, *Blacks in the Army Air Forces*, 24.
36. Lee, *The Employment of Negro Troops*, 47, 50; Osur, *Blacks in the Army Air Forces*, 22-23.
37. Lee, *The Employment of Negro Troops*, 48-49.
38. Osur, *Blacks in the Army Air Forces*, 24; "Courier War Committee to Act as `Watchdog' for Race," *Pittsburgh Courier*, 8 June 1940.
39. "Courier War Committee to Act as `Watchdog' for Race," *Pittsburgh Courier*, 8 June 1940.
40. "What Courier Army Committee Seeks," *Pittsburgh Courier*, 5 July 1940.
41. "White House Awaits Action of Congress," *Pittsburgh Courier*, 25 June 1940.
42. Robert L. Vann, "Van Breaks Political Silence—We Are For Wilkie," *Pittsburgh Courier*, 24 August 1940.
43. "Army, Navy, Air Jim-Crow Amendment Is Rejected," *Pittsburgh Courier*, 22 June 1940.
44. "Negro Youths May Not Be Kept Out of Colored Army Units,"

Pittsburgh Courier, 29 June 1940.

45. Robert L. Vann, "64 U.S. Congressmen Get Wire from Courier Editor; Asked to Act," *Pittsburgh Courier*, 22 June 1940.
46. "Conscription," *Pittsburgh Courier*, 29 June 1940.
47. Ibid.; "What Courier Army Committee Seeks," *Pittsburgh Courier*, 6 July 1940.
48. "G.O.P. May Fight Army, Navy, Ban," *Pittsburgh Courier*, 20 July 1940; "Courier Editor Seeks Army, Navy Democratic Plank," *Pittsburgh Courier*, 20 July 1940.
49. "Courier Editor Seeks Army, Navy Democratic Plank," *Pittsburgh Courier*, 20 July 1940; Vann, "Vann Breaks Political Silence," *Pittsburgh Courier*, 24 August 1940.
50. Vann, "Van Breaks Political Silence," *Pittsburgh Courier*, 24 August 1940.
51. "The President and Precedent," *Pittsburgh Courier*, 31 August 1940.
52. "Implies Race Men Are Not Capable of Being Army Pilots," *Pittsburgh Courier*, 17 August 1940.
53. William Lane Austin, *Negro Aviators*, Negro Statistical Bulletin No. 3, Washington, D.C.: Department of Commerce, Bureau of the Census, 1940, 1-21.
54. "Cream of Crop of Young C.A.A. Pilots at Tuskegee," *Pittsburgh Courier*, 31 August 1940; "Air School to Train Negro Military Pilots," *Pittsburgh Courier*, 2 December 1939.
55. "Cream of Crop of Young C.A.A. Pilots at Tuskegee," *Pittsburgh Courier*, 31 August 1940
56. "Air School to Train Negro Military Pilots," *Pittsburgh Courier*, 2 December 1939.
57. Gould letter to White.
58. Ibid.
59. Ibid.
60. Interview with Phillip Lee, 8 August 1990, Los Angeles, California.
61. Wendell Smith, "Artillery Unit Being Trained at Fort Bragg I, N.C.," *Pittsburgh Courier*, 7 September 1940.
62. "Draft 36,000 Negroes," *Pittsburgh Courier*, 21 September 1990; Lee, *The Employment of Negro Troops*, 49.
63. Ibid.
64. "'Open Door' Policy," *Pittsburgh Courier*, 7 September 1940.
65. "Here Are Differences Between Senate and House Draft Bills," *Pittsburgh Courier*, 14 September 1940.
66. "That Wagner Amendment," *Pittsburgh Courier*, 7 September 1940; MacGregor, *Integration of the Armed Forces*, 11-12.
67. "That Wagner Amendment," *Pittsburgh Courier*, 7 September 1940.
68. "Fish Amendment Covers Draftees and Volunteers," *Pittsburgh Courier*, 14 September 1940.
69. Ibid.

70. MacGregor, *Integration of the Armed Forces*, 12-13.
71. "We Tip Our Hat of Thanks," *Pittsburgh Courier*, 28 September 1940.
72. "Draft 36,000 Negroes," *Pittsburgh Courier*, 21 September 1940.
73. Interview with Spann Watson; Spann Watson letter to Captain C.R. Landon, Headquarters, Second Corps Area, Office of the Corps Area Commander, 16 November 1940, Application to Army Air Corps, 16 November 1940, NAACP Papers, Collections of the Manuscript Division, Library of Congress.
74. Neil Wynn, *The Afro-American and the Second World War* (New York: Holes & Meior Publishers, 1976), 41.
75. White, *A Man Called White*, 186.
76. Ibid., 169.
77. Ibid., 186-87; "Here's What the Committee Asked For," *Pittsburgh Courier*, 19 October 1940.
78. White, *A Man Called White*, 187.
79. Ibid.; "Trio of Leaders Deny Approving Segregated Army," *Pittsburgh Courier*, 19 October 1940.
80. "Charge White House Trickery, And Here Is What They Were Given," *Pittsburgh Courier*, 19 October 1940.
81. "Here is What Committee Asked For," *Pittsburgh Courier*, 19 October 1940.
82. "When Will Negroes Fly for U.S.?" *Pittsburgh Courier*, 26 October 1940.
83. White, *A Man Called White*, 187.
84. Ibid.
85. "No More 1917-18," *Pittsburgh Courier*, 12 October; "Davis Overlooked As Army Promotes White Colonels," *Pittsburgh Courier*, 12 October 1940.
86. Associated Negro Press, "Ask Negro Advisor In War Department," *Pittsburgh Courier*, 3 August 1938.
87. White, *A Man Called White*, 189.
88. Ibid., 189.
89. "Vann Dies," *Pittsburgh Courier*, 2 November 1940; James H. Brewer, "Robert Lee Vann, 100-3.
90. "Race Men to Defense Posts," *Pittsburgh Courier*, 2 November 1940; White, *A Man Called White*, 188.
91. "Race Men to Defense Posts," *Pittsburgh Courier*, 2 November 1940; "No More 1917-18," *Pittsburgh Courier*, 12 October 1940.
92. Franklin, *From Slavery to Freedom*, 577; "Race Men to Defense Posts," *Pittsburgh Courier*, 2 November 1940.
93. P. L. Prattis, "National Leaders Converse on Hampton," *Pittsburgh Courier*, 30 November 1940.
94. Lee, *Employment of Negro Troops*, 116-18; Roy Wilkins letter to William H. Hastie regarding Enoch Waters over aviation training at Tuskegee Institute, 15 November 1940; Harold D. Gould letter to Walter White regarding Negroes and the Army Air Corps, 15 November 1940.

95. Roy Wilkins letter to William H. Hastie regarding Enoch Waters over aviation training at Tuskegee Institute, 15 November 1940.
96. Lee, *Employment of Negro Troops*, 116-19.
97. "Running Short of Fliers," *Pittsburgh Courier*, 21 December 1940; "Army—The Problem, Air Pilots," *Time*, 28 October 1940.
98. "Army—The Problem, Air Pilots," *Time*, 28 October 1940.
99. Lee, *Employment of Negro Troops*, 118-19.
100. Ibid., 117.
101. Ibid.
102. James Peck, "When Do We Fly," *The Crisis* 47 (December 1940): 376-78.
103. Lee, *Employment of Negro Troops*, 117.
104. Interview with Spann Watson.
105. "Passes Preliminary Tests for Admission to Army Air Corps," *Pittsburgh Courier*, 30 November 1940.
106. "Action In Court Is Hinted," *Pittsburgh Courier*, 5 October 1940.
107. Interview with Spann Watson.
108. Interview with William M. Womack, 1 March 1990, Detroit, Michigan.
109. Haydon Johnson, *The Fighting 99th Air Squadron, 1941-45* (New York: Vantage Press, Inc., 1987), 1-2.
110. Huang Wei Yen, "Chinese Air 'Act' Born In Georgia," *Pittsburgh Courier*, 2 September 1938.
111. Lee, *Employment of Negro Troops*, 117.

Chapter 7

The Experiment:
The "Smoke Screen"

In late 1940, after several months as civilian aide to the secretary of war, Judge Hastie had the opportunity to review the Army Air Corps National Defense Plan and its employment of Negro troops. Initially, Hastie objected to the utilization of racial segregation in the Air Corps plan for the employment of Negroes in aviation squadrons. Hastie viewed the Tuskegee training site as a wasteful and an expensive use of limited human and economic resources that were already available at existing air bases and training centers. In addition, Hastie reported that higher morale could be established if Negroes and whites were trained together at the three Air Corps training centers then in service.[1]

Judge Hastie's stand was consistent with his and the NAACP's integrationist philosophy. The former judge assumed that his responsibility was to ensure a fair and equal integration of the Negro into the national defense plans submitted by all branches of the armed forces. Hastie considered his objective possible, with the support of undersecretary of war and fellow judge, Robert Patterson. It was Patterson who received most of Hastie's communication and who offered an open mind to Hastie on issues of integration and discrimination in the armed forces.

In early January 1941, Judge Hastie withdrew his opposition to the Air Corps plans. He felt that the inclusion of African Americans in military aviation, even as a separated squadron, was a positive action, and a situation that could be manipulated, over time. Judge Hastie warned the secretary of war in December 1940, however, that the Negro press and the public would be very critical of the Air Corps' plans for a separate Negro air squadron at Tuskegee.[2]

On 16 January 1941, the War Department announced its plans for the employment of an all-Negro pursuit squadron to be trained at

Tuskegee. This squadron would consist of thirty-three pilots and a ground crew of two hundred and fifty men. A contract of approximately $2 million was given to the Negro firms of Hilyard Robinson, architect, and McCissack and McCissack, contractors.[3]

The press and the public, especially the NAACP, launched an attack on the War Department and the Air Corps. The attacks from the Negro press were aimed at Washington's alleged hypocrisy in advocating unified national defense and outrage at the fascism and racism practiced by the Axis members, while ignoring America's own racism perpetuated by War Department and the Army Air Corps. The NAACP accused the War Department in an editorial in *The Crisis* magazine, of maintaining the old army pattern of segregation, and said that the custom of segregation "was the cause of most of the trouble experienced by African Americans in civilian as well as military life. Until segregation as a procedure is overthrown, the race will be hobbled in all its endeavors in every field."[4]

As if they were taking a cue from Judge Hastie, the NAACP took advantage of the War Department opening by testing the sincerity of the War Department. The civil rights group supported the suit filed by Yancey Williams on 17 January 1941, to force the War Department to reconsider his application for flying cadet training. The civil rights organization assigned Special Counsel Thurgood Marshall, W. Robert Ming, Jr., and Leon Ransom of the National Legal Committee, to assist Williams's attorney, Wendell L. McConnel, of Washington D.C., in the preparation and filing of the case. Williams, a senior at Howard and a graduate of the CAA primary and secondary training courses, had applied and was rejected in 1940. At that time, the Air Corps replied in a letter that stated:

> Receipt is acknowledged of your application for appointment as flying cadet. The Commanding General directs you to be informed that appropriate Air Corps units are not available at this time, at which colored applicants can be given flying cadet training.
>
> Your interest in flying is appreciated, and your application has been recorded for future consideration in the event facilities become available for training of colored flying cadet applicants.[5]

While waiting for his answer, Williams was inducted into the infantry where he remained until late 1943, when he was accepted and transferred into the cadet program.

The NAACP and the Negro press continued the attack on the War Department. In an April 1941 editorial in the *The Crisis*, Roy Wilkins

The first graduating class of flying cadets: from left to right, Lt. Mac Ross, Maj. Benjamin O. Davis, Jr., Flight Instructor, Lt. Charles DeBow, Lt. George S. Roberts, and Lt. Lemuel Custis.

Cadets receiving wings and officers' commissions at Tuskegee.

Obstacle Course at Tuskegee built by William Womack.

Colonel Benjamin O. Davis, Jr. with Trainer.

A 477th Bombardment Group briefing. Lt. Daniel "Chappie" James is second from the right.

Members of the 99th Pursuit Squadron: Lts. James Wiley, Willie Ashley, Herbert Carter, Spann Watson, and P. Smith.

Dale White, Enoch Waters, and Chauncey Spencer.

Members of the National Airmen's Association Conference—Chicago, August 1939. Willa Brown with the white hat in the front row.

Cornelius Coffey (center) shaking hands with Dale White with Chauncey Spencer looking on before cross-country flight to Washington.

Mechanics install a fuel tank on the wing of a P-51.

Pfc. John Fields, Armorer with the 332d Fighter Group in Italy, 1944.

Lt. Clarence "Lucky" Lester with Crewchief Sgt. Conige C. Mormon of the 332nd Fighter Group

Pilot in P-39 taking off.

Heavyweight Champion Joe Louis holding Junior in Italy, 1944.

Capt. William Campbell, Lt. Col. George Roberts, Capt. Henry Perry, and Lt. Herman Lawson of the 99th Fighter Squadron in Italy, 1944.

General Henry Strothers and Colonel Benjamin O. Davis, Jr., reviewing pilots and troops in Italy.

618th Bomber Squadron, 477th Medium Bombardment Group.

333nd fighter pilots.

Lena Horne with colonel Noel Parrish at Tuskegee Army Air Field.

General Benjamin O. Davis, Sr. (far left) and Colonel Robert L. Selway in receiving line at Selfridge Field, 1943.

Colonel Benjamin O. Davis, Jr., in Italy, 1944.

Lt. Lemuel Custis of the 99th Pursuit Squadron in sicily, 1943.

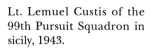

Capt. William Womack on terrace of Rest Camp in Naples, Italy.

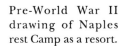

Pre-World War II drawing of Naples rest Camp as a resort.

332nd Fighter Group officers on R and R at the Rest Camp in Naples, Italy

Lt. Herbert Carter, 99th Pursuit Squadron.

Capt. William Campbell, 332nd Fighter Group, pilot with the original 99th Pursuit Squadron and the 99th Fighter Squadron.

Briefing before mission, 99th Pursuit Squadron.

Cornelius Coffey (far right) to the rescue of Goodwill Flight in Ohio, 1939.
Courtesy of Richard Macon.

Dr. F. Patterson, President,
Tuskegee Institute

Gen. Nathaniel Twining,
Col. Benjamin O. Davis, Jr.,
and Capt. Robert Tresville
in Ramitelli, Italy, 1944

A-24 Officers in the 332nd Fighter Group: Capts. William Ellsbery, Edward Gleed, William Womack, and Felix Kirkpatrick.

A-19 Lt. Coleman Young (3rd from right) at Freeman Field.

Three (3) AT-6s in formation over Tuskegee.

Pilot in the P-51.

called the official announcements from the War Department relating to the recruitment and training of Negro pilots an Army Air Corps "smoke screen" to confuse and placate the Negro public while doing little training of Negro pilots. Wilkins complained that, although the army claimed a shortage in pilots and had pledged training for 30,000 pilots, only one-tenth of 1 percent—thirty-three—would be Negro pilots, and they would be "trained off in a corner by themselves for a squadron of twenty-seven planes."[6] The Negro press, especially the *Chicago Defender*, and other advocates, such as the Chicago-based National Airmen's Association, demanded explanations from the War Department for the establishment of segregated training centers for African-American pilots in the South, when there were better facilities already in use in the Chicago area.[7]

The Airmen's Association also questioned the Air Corps' choice of pursuit flying for the new Negro squadron. The association maintained that pursuit flying, unlike other forms of flying, required the single pilot to master flying, navigation, and gunnery skills, therefore making pursuit flying the most difficult form to learn. Judge Hastie agreed with the Airmen's Association, viewing pursuit flying as the most dangerous and difficult form of air combat.[8] The Army Air Corps rationalized that pursuit flying was the most basic form of flying, and once the pilots mastered pursuit flying, they could handle other complex aircraft. The other "complex aircraft" included small-, medium-, and long-range bombers, which required several crewmen, with specialties in navigation, bombardment, meteorology, and large-caliber gunnery. The Air Corps could not allow racially integrated training, which would have been required if they chose bomber pilot and crew training for African Americans.[9] Because of the lack of new training facilities for Negroes, the Air Corps would have been forced to utilize existing training facilities that had been set aside for whites. Establishing a separate pursuit squadron was the least expensive option that the Air Corps could accept in accordance with their policy of segregation at all costs.

The press and the NAACP both questioned the rationale and the War Department's intent in setting up a separate training center for Negro pilots and ground crews at a facility that had not yet been built. They complained that the start of military training for Negro pilots would not begin until the airfield at Tuskegee was completed in October of 1941.[10]

The War Department, and especially the Chief of Army Air Corps, Gen. Henry "Hap" Arnold, were surprised and somewhat perturbed at the outcome of and the feedback received from the announcement of the plans for a Negro pilot program and the designation of a pursuit squadron. General Arnold, in particular, made remarks in a May 1941 memorandum to Chief of Staff General George C. Marshall that inferred that the segregated Negro pilot training program was a great opportunity for African Americans, but that they were ungrateful for the opportunity, and could alienate the Army Air Corps and risk losing the entire program by demanding integrated pilot training.[11]

Sensing that the War Department, and especially the Army Air Corps, might be setting up smoke screens instead of progressing with the development of aviation squadrons and pilot training, the NAACP increased the pressure on the War Department to follow through with its commitment, unattractive as it was, to provide a Negro pursuit squadron. In February 1941, NAACP Secretary Walter White issued letters to all of the Negro colleges that were participating in the CAA Civilian Pilot Training Program, asking them to send him a mailing list of all graduates of their respective CAA programs.[12] Mr. White also requested from the Commerce Department a listing of all licensed Negro pilots in the United States. The NAACP mailed letters to all licensed Negro pilots and graduates of the CAA program, inquiring of their interest in applying to the Army Air Corps. By the end of March, the NAACP had received responses from 150 individuals interested in flying cadet training in the Army Air Corps. Mr. White sent the list of names to Judge Hastie, who referred them to the War Department's G-3 (Training).[13] The NAACP responded to all of the letters and referred the prospects to the local army recruiting stations for applications, telling them that if they experienced any problems they should notify their local NAACP office.

Immediately after the War Department announced its plans to develop Negro aviation squadrons, and especially after the announcement of the planned pursuit squadron, the Army Air Corps became the most popular branch of service for men already in the regular army, and for those men who planned on enlisting.[14] To these young Negro men, even a segregated Air Corps offered new opportunities for those seeking more exiting and rewarding careers than were available to them in the regular military.

Concurrent with the announcement of the activation of the 99th Pursuit Squadron on 19 March 1941, the army instituted the Army General Classification Test (AGCT). This assessment tool was to measure a soldier's learning ability.[15] With the results of the AGCT, the army could classify its troops into five categorical levels of ability, with Category I reflecting the highest ability and Category V reflecting the lowest level of ability. With the identification of individuals by ability, the army, in its planning for national defense and mobilization, could select officers, enlisted men with specializations, or enlisted men best suited for less complex military tasks. Since the AGCT was biased in favor of those with more education, usually indicative of better economic backgrounds, a greater percentage of whites had scores high enough to place them in categories reflective of higher ability, while a greater percentage of African Americans had scores that placed them in categories reflecting lower ability.[16]

All of the armed forces had a quota for Negro troops, and the army received the bulk of the Negro enlistments, since the other branches, namely the navy and marines, would not accept the War Department quota. Therefore, the Air Corps received several thousand enlisted Negro men with low AGCT scores. Since the Air Corps had historically rejected Negro applicants for cadet and technical training on the grounds that aviation was a specialized occupation requiring special technical skills, the preponderance of Negro enlistees with low AGCT scores provided them with the rationale for assigning the majority of their quota of nine Negro aviation squadrons of 250 men each to air base defense units, quartermaster battalions, ordinance companies, transportation, and other non-aviation areas.[17]

The majority of the Negro enlistees in the Air Corps in 1941 were assigned to housekeeping, maintenance, and labor chores. There were, however, several thousand Negro enlistees with high AGCT scores who were not allowed into the Air Corps because of the Air Corps' Negro quota and its policy of not inducting more Negro specialists than there were spaces available for them in the new specialized units.[18] With the 99th Pursuit Squadron being, at the time, the only specialty squadron for Negroes in the Air Corps, many eligible and qualified enlistees were either inducted into other, less attractive branches of the army where their skills were wasted, or they were put into one of the "housekeeping, maintenance, or transportation units" that made up the nine aviation squadrons.[19]

The Air Corps already had tough eligibility requirements, and the corps was confident that Negro soldiers would not have the qualifications to be members of the 99th Pursuit Squadron. To the surprise of the Air Corps, 278 of the Negro quota of 2,500 enlistees passed the examination for Air Corps Technical School and, therefore, met all of the Army Air Corps' standards for training.[20] Subsequently, the men who entered nonflying technical training for the 99th Pursuit Squadron were among the best qualified, regardless of race. Most, if not all, of the enlistees were high school graduates; some possessed college degrees, and one held a Ph.D. None of these men, however, were selected to be officers.[21]

Technical training for the 99th Pursuit nonflying personnel was conducted at Chanute Air Field in Rantoul, Illinois, primarily because construction of the Air Field at Tuskegee was not completed, and there were no facilities at Tuskegee, at that time, for operating a technical training school. The training was divided into three specialty areas: armament, airplane mechanics, and communications. Even though Chanute housed other white enlisted personnel undergoing the same training, the training of the 99th personnel was conducted separately. All housing, recreational, and educational facilities were segregated.[22]

The squadron unit needed officers and, therefore, the corps selected five enlistees to serve as cadets. Beginning in early June 1941, the five cadets received specialized, but segregated and separate, training in armament, aircraft maintenance, and communications at Chanute Field.[23] The Air Corps plan included providing the cadets with on-the-job training for ninety days at an air base. After that time, the "90-day wonders" would be commissioned as 2nd lieutenants.[24]

The Air Corps postponed military training for Negro pilots for as long as it was militarily and politically possible. The provision of such training lagged considerably behind the training of ground personnel, due to construction delay at Tuskegee and the Air Corps' insistence on segregated training. The Yancey Williams suit and the public protest had forced the hand of the War Department and the Air Corps, and by June 1941, the corps had less support from the War Department in its adamant stance against African-American pilots.[25] In addition to the list of prospective applicants provided by the NAACP, the Air Corps had an extensive list of qualified African-American applicants dating back to 1939. Included in the list of applicants were college graduates, licensed pilots from the Civilian Pilots Training Program, and at least twenty certified pilots from the Advanced CPTP training provided at Tuskegee in 1940. Since Tuskegee had the only military pilot training for African Americans, applicants to the cadet program would have to wait up to two years to enter pilot training. During the interim period, draft deferments of many applicants expired and many prospective Negro pilots were drafted into the army or became ineligible for the cadet training because of age.[26]

By June 1941, the Corps had selected thirty-five men, all college graduates, and one West Point man, from the pool of applicants.[27] In addition to the educational qualifications for eligibility, cadets could not be over 26 years of age, married, over 6 feet tall, or weigh more than 170 pounds.[28] From a battery of physical exams and psychological tests, the group of thirty-five was pared to thirteen.[29] It is interesting to note that among the thirteen there was only one cadet with the advanced CPTP training, and there was one West Point man who was an officer in the regular army, with no pilot training. The West Pointer, Capt. Benjamin O. Davis Jr., was also 29 years of age, 6'1" tall, and married. In Davis's case, the marriage prohibition that applied to cadets was waived, due to the fact that Davis was married before the activation of the squadron. Davis was made commandant of the cadets.[30]

The cadet with the advanced civilian pilot training, George "Spanky" Roberts, was appointed commandant of the cadets during basic and advanced flight training. Yancey Williams, Phillip Lee, Spann Watson, Roscoe Draper, Elmer Jones, and the other CPTP advanced students who went through the specialized course at Tuskegee were not selected for the first class of cadets.[31]

Captain Davis, the first Negro West Point graduate of the twentieth century, class of 1936, was the son of the armed forces' only other ranking African-American field officer and only African-American general, Benjamin O. Davis, Sr. The junior Davis successfully survived the West Point racially motivated silent treatment and demerit system for four years, an unprecedented and unimaginable feat by any cadet, to finish within the top forty in his class. Davis had applied for admission into the Air Corps Cadet program in 1935. He, like all other African Americans at that time, was told that there were no Negro Air Corps squadrons and that there were no plans to institute one and, therefore, the segregated Air Corps had no place for him.[32] Clearly, if the army would not admit the son of its only ranking African-American officer and a West Point graduate, the corps was closed to all African Americans.

After West Point, Davis, Jr. was sent to the 24th Infantry at Ft. Benning, Georgia, and shortly thereafter to infantry school. Captain Davis was assigned to Negro colleges to teach military science and to command Junior ROTC units. His tour of duty included infantry school at Ft. Benning, 1937-1938; Tuskegee Institute, 1938-1941; and Ft. Riley, Kansas, 1941, where Davis was assigned for the first time under his father, who was promoted to brigadier general. It appeared that the army had consigned Davis, Jr., like his father, to a teaching or nonessential role, in segregated settings where opportunities for advancement would be limited. In March of 1941, the senior Davis received a letter from the Air Corps requesting the transfer of his son to the Air Corps for the new, all-Negro 99th Pursuit Squadron cadet program. Finally, in June 1941, Davis received his orders to report to Tuskegee for flight training.[33]

The inaugural class of thirteen flying cadets of the 99th Pursuit Squadron began its training at Tuskegee Institute on 19 July 1941. All of the men, who were dubbed the "Lonely Eagles" by the Negro press, resided in a bath house on the Tuskegee campus. Their training consisted of four levels: preflight, or ground school; primary flight training; basic military flight training; and advanced military flight training. All of the instruction was provided by military personnel except the physical education activity and some of the primary flight training which was conducted by Tuskegee Institute Flying School chief, C. Alfred Anderson. Preflight training was provided in a dormitory on the Tuskegee campus. Primary flight training took place at Moton Field, an airfield owned by the institute. Basic and advanced flight training was to occur at the new army field, once it was completed.[34] If the cadets successfully completed the four phases to the satisfaction of all of the instructors, they would receive their pilot's wings and a commission as an officer in the Army Air Corps. Captain Davis was working with the understanding that, if he won his wings, he would command the pursuit squadron.[35]

The highlight of the year was Eleanor Roosevelt's visit to Tuskegee. A trustee of Tuskegee Institute, Mrs. Roosevelt was on campus to visit the Infant Paralysis Clinic. She had an interest in Tuskegee Institute's Flying School. The First Lady allegedly made the comment that she had always heard that African Americans could not fly airplanes. She arranged for her Secret Service men to get her a ride on one of the planes used for instruction. Chief Alfred Anderson took her up in his Piper Cub for an exhilarating flight. After the flight, she posed with Anderson in the plane, and the photo was printed in all of the major white and Negro papers. Mrs. Roosevelt's flight with Anderson all but eliminated America's perception that the Negro did not possess the skills to negotiate an airplane.[36]

The technical specialists of the 99th training at Chanute Field, completed their training in October 1941 and on 7 November 1941 were to be transferred to active air bases for practical experience. Proficiency tests scores show that the men of the 99th were not only competent, but the most talented specialists to graduate from the Chanute training program.[37] The Air Corps opted to continue their policy of segregation by assigning the men to two bases in the South. The men were sent to Maxwell Air Base in Montgomery, Alabama. As space and provisions became available, the men were to be assigned to the Tuskegee Army Air Field, then under construction. At Maxwell, the men of the 99th were not allowed to apply skills that would give them the experience needed to acquire rank and commission. These soldiers were assigned to housekeeping detail and were even found in the city of Montgomery manicuring state property. Since many of the members of the 99th were from the North, they had many problems with the local folks and the segregated environment of Montgomery, Alabama. The morale problem was considerable. By the end of 1941, it appeared that the corps had no intention of using the 99th for any meaningful task, other than cleaning military bases.[38]

Judge Hastie suspected the Air Corps' "smoke screen" and the tenacity of certain branches of the armed forces, in their maintenance of segregated and discriminatory situations for Negro soldiers in the South. The civilian aide still felt that the War Department and the Air Corps would act with reason and responsibility, once presented with the facts and suggestions for remedy.

In late September 1941, Judge Hastie submitted to Judge Robert Patterson a study assessing the employment of Negro soldiers in the National Defense Program. The study, entitled "Survey and Recommendations Concerning the Integration of the Negro Soldier into the Army," charged the War Department with not using the Negro soldier in a productive and dignified manner. In the report, Hastie called the utilization of the southern approach and philosophy of segregation in the employment of the Negro troops a system that "retards the training of the Negro soldiers." The report included an indictment that only 5 percent of the 1.5 million enlisted men were Negro and that most of the Negro enlisted men were "disproportionately concentrated in the Corps of Engineers, the Quartermaster Corps, and Overhead Installations . . . performing duties of unskilled and menial character." He went on to say that the War Department's insistence on new separate and segregated units created a backlog of talented Negroes in the Selective Service System, waiting to be inducted, while whites were being inducted at a faster rate because of the availability of existing units. Hastie called the policy of separating Negro and white soldiers, while insisting the preservation of democracy worldwide, hypocritical.[39]

In his report, Judge Hastie offered four recommendations that the War Department could use as a remedy to the situation:

1. New organizations must be developed to relieve the excess of Negro selectees;
2. Negro combat regiments should be incorporated into divisions, and single companies and detachments should be eliminated;
3. Isolated small Negro units who are the only Negroes on the station should be transferred to other stations. This would preclude the need to establish duplicative recreational and housing facilities; and
4. A beginning should be made for the employment of soldiers without racial separation.[40]

Judge Hastie also took his message to the public. In late September 1941, in a speech at the dedication ceremonies for the Anacostia Leave Camp, the civilian aide challenged southern state and local civilian law enforcement officials, veteran associations, and state and local press organizations, to protect the rights of the man in uniform. He charged them with the responsibility of blunting the humiliation suffered by Negro soldiers at the hands of white civilians located near southern camps and bases. He implored the War Department to train military police to protect and respect the Negro in uniform and, where possible, to expand the deployment of Negro military police as part of the military police force. Hastie warned that the attacks against Negro soldiers must be dealt with in a militant manner and that America "cannot be a united and effective nation in the face of a foreign foe so long as any substantial number of us condone and appease un-American attitudes and practices at home."[41]

In a speech on morale for national defense given to the National Executive Board of the National Lawyers Guild on 4 October 1941 in Washington D.C., Judge Hastie examined the emotional paradox of a Negro in America, defending his country against fascism and imperialism. Hastie explained:

> There are millions of other Americans who must be made to feel their own lives and in their daily experiences some significant movement toward of professed ideals. Men will not struggle unto death on the basis of any rationalization that they may become worse off that they are now. They must have an affirmative sense of present well being and the optimism which attends a consciousness of progress now being experienced.[42]

Hastie continued:

> I speak with great conviction because I know the perplexity of the American Negro, the most disadvantaged group in America today. The Negro, whether he be soldier or civilian, finds it difficult to concentrate on the horrors of a Germany without civil liberties, when his immediate attention is continually diverted to proscriptions at home. So long as he is treated as an inferior, something less that a full citizen here, he finds it difficult to become excited over a worse status in a Nazi world. That is not logic, but is human nature. . . . In my view the spirit of the Army is made of the same stuff as the spirit of the nation. Morale cannot be imposed. Both the danger to American life from without and the promise of American life from within must be made real to all of us.[43]

When the War Department responded to Judge Hastie's study and recommendation, it did not accept or agree, primarily because of his recommendation of racial integration. The chief of staff, General Marshall, in his 1 December 1941 memorandum on the study and recommendations, stated:

> The Army should not be charged with accomplishing a solution to solving a social problem that has perplexed the American people throughout the history of this nation. . . . The War Department cannot ignore the social relationships between Negroes and whites which have been established by the American people through custom and habit . . . that either through lack of educational opportunities or other causes the level of intelligence and occupational skill of the negro population is considerably below that of white and . . . that experiments within the Army in the solution of social problems are fraught with danger to efficiency, discipline, and morale.[44]

The individuals in the War Department who were weary of Hastie's role, were now certain that he was a representative of the NAACP working in the War Department. After Hastie's report was issued in the War Department, communication coming from the War Department, usually routed to Hastie's office, was confiscated or diverted to the adjutant general's office or the office of the administrative assistant. Judge Hastie was also not consulted on matters pertaining to new developments in training and employment of Negro troops.[45]

One of Judge Hastie's goals, prior to the dissemination of the study and recommendations was the development of mutually beneficial relationships between the Negro press and the War Department. Hastie, in cooperation with the Bureau of Public Relations, scheduled a conference on 8 December 1941 for black editors and publishers. As fate would have it, the "Editors Conference" convened the day after the Japanese invasion of Pearl Harbor and the day before the president appeared before Congress to declare war on the Japanese and the Axis powers.

The conference agenda was full, and featured Chief of Staff Gen. George C. Marshall and representatives from the Adjutant General's Department; the Bureau of Public Relations; the Inspector General's office; and other relevant divisions within the War Department. The purpose of the conference was to orient Negro newspersons to the mechanics of the War Department. The department rationalized that if the editors and publishers were acquainted with the different functions of the department divisions, they would have a better understanding of the logic behind the decision-making relative to the military.[46]

The shocking events at Pearl Harbor only served to pique the interest of the editors and publishers, who viewed the conference as a rare opportunity to get the "scoop" on the Negro soldier's position in the War Department mobilization plans. Anticipating, but uncertain, the representatives of the War Department were both tentative and defensive. General Marshall spoke of much progress made in the area of training and deployment, and said that the War Department expected more positive changes. He also stated that he was personally dissatisfied with the progress. In addition, General Marshall announced the establishment of an all-Negro division. The other representatives presented noncontroversial and glib orientations of their respective division responsibility. The representative from the Adjutant General's Department, Col. E. R. Householder, however, did create some controversy. Colonel Householder argued in his presentation that the army did not create the problem of discrimination and that the army

> cannot be made the means of engendering conflict among the mass of the people because of a stand with respect to Negroes which is not compatible with the position attained by the Negro in civilian life. . . . The Army is not a sociological laboratory; to be effective it must be organized and trained according to the principles which will insure success. Experiments to meet the wishes and demands of the champions of every race and creed for the solution of their problems are a danger to efficiency, discipline and morale and would result in ultimate defeat.[47]

Initially the editors and publishers were confused with the divergent messages sent by General Marshall and Colonel Householder. Most of the newspapermen chose to react to the positive bent in General Marshall's announcement of the new division, his personal feelings about discrimination in the military training and troop deployment, and his announcement of a new Negro division. A few newsmen, especially those associated with the *Pittsburgh Courier,* took issue with Householder's statements, and expressed empathy with Judge Hastie in his seemingly impossible task of changing War Department attitudes. The *Courier* editorialized that Householder's "quibbling" could "jeopardize national unity."[48] The Negro participants of the conference were unaware of General Marshall's 1 December 1941 response to Hastie's recommendations for Negro troop integration and how closely the two presentations approximated in content and intent. Few, if any, editors and publishers who participated in the conference knew that Colonel Householder's presentation reflected the true feelings, intent, and policy of the War Department regarding racial segregation and discrimination.

Immediately after the Japanese attack on Pearl Harbor, on 7 December 1941, the Air Corps transferred the mechanics and specialists from Maxwell to the airfield in Tuskegee and gave them rank, and the five nonflying cadets received commissions. The men joined the flying cadets at Tuskegee in the mud, in what they called "Tent City." Segregated housing in Tuskegee limited their housing options to tents on the airfield. The "Tent City" crew literally watched the airfield and attached barracks take shape.[49]

Of the original thirteen members of the first class of flying cadets, eight "washed out" or failed in one of the levels before basic flight training. They could not handle the psychological stress tests administered in advanced training by the military instructors.[50] During this particular period, the cadets had white and mostly southern flight instructors in all phases of flight training. Those cadets who were not oriented to military discipline would experience difficulty with the intensive style of military drilling. Cadets from the North would most assuredly have had difficulty with southern officers using abusive and racially insensitive language. One cadet, Fredrick "Jimmy" Moore, "washed out" the day before graduation.[51]

Only five cadets graduated from the training in March 1942 (42 C). The five cadets were Capt. Benjamin O. Davis Jr., George S. Roberts, Lemuel Custis, Charles DeBow, and Mac Ross. Besides Davis, Roberts, Debow, and Ross had had training in military protocol as junior ROTC students while in college, and Cadet Custis had had quasi-military training as a policeman in Hartford, Connecticut. Captain Davis and Cadet Custis had to work very hard on their flying skills to keep up with the others, who had much more experience gained from the CPTP program. Tenacity and a tremendous will to succeed paid off, as both Davis and Custis were proficient enough to pass all phases of the flight training.[52]

From the graduation of the first class in March 1942 to the class of September 1942 (42 J), thirty-three pilots received their wings, and the 99th Pursuit Squadron now had enough pilots and trained ground, administrative, and medical crews to be deployed as a combat unit. In March 1942, shortly before Davis's graduation from cadet training, the Army Air Corps, then called the Army Air Forces, promoted Davis two grades, to lieutenant colonel. Davis's promotion to lieutenant colonel was consistent with the promotion schedule of the West Point Class of 1936. His promotion to major, however, was overdue. Later in March 1942, Lt. Colonel Davis was assigned the command of the 99th Pursuit Squadron.[53]

Several talented men passed through cadet training during the period after the inauguration of the first class. The Air Corps quota was thirty-three pilots for the 99th, but the corps was assigning ten to fifteen cadets every five weeks to Tuskegee. Most of the cadets "washed out." It was not uncommon for the Army Air Force to wash out 50 to 65 percent of its cadet classes. The second class of cadets at Tuskegee graduated three. The Air Force and its training command felt that the tough regimen forced out the weak and accentuated the strong pilots.[54] In this regard, however, the wash out rate at Tuskegee Army Air Field was significantly higher than that of other training command bases. According to statements made by William Hastic later in 1943, 58 percent of Negro pilot trainees washed out compared to 41 percent of white pilots who failed the training. The wash out rate would have a disproportionately negative impact on the 99th. Since there was only one squadron in which to place Negro pilots, even an average wash out rate would severely limit the number of pilots available for duty. As a result of the wash out rate, the number of replacement pilots for an all Negro squadron would be adversely affected. Consequently, the pilots of the 99th would have to fly more consecutive combat missions without rest than a comparable white fighter squadron.[55]

Between 1941, when the cadet training began, and March 1943, African-American pilots who washed out had few options available. They could be reassigned to artillery, quartermaster corps, or engineering battalions, or be discharged out of the army and therefore become eligible for the draft.[56] From 1941 to late 1943, the only flying option available to African Americans in the United States was pursuit flying, considered the most complex and dangerous type of flying. There were a few African Americans who chose to cross the border to Canada to participate in the Canadian Royal Air Force. Fred Hutchinson, of the Coffey School of Aeronautics, volunteered in the Canadian Royal Air Force and flew successful bombing missions in Europe in 1942.[57]

White cadets, however, had a wide range of options even if they washed out of pursuit flight training. Flight training in medium- and long-range bombers, reconnaissance, and navigation were available to white cadets. In addition, white cadets could receive training at several air bases within a training command, all over the country. White fighter groups and squadrons did not have a pilot replacement problem.[58]

Many of the cadets in the 99th pilot training washed out in the primary phase of the training. After the first class of cadets, the succeeding classes were taught, in the primary phase, by African-American civilian pilots. C. Alfred (Chief) Anderson was the supervisor of this phase of flight training at the Institute's Moton Field. Chief had a reputation for providing as much assistance as needed to get a cadet through the primary level. Chief also had a reputation for spotting talent and for being honest. Chief was known to give random precheck flights to cadets who were weak in some areas, in order to prepare them for the official check ride that would be their final evaluation, and possibly their last ride as a cadet. If Chief gave a cadet a check ride, the cadet knew that Chief was going to give an honest appraisal.[59]

If a cadet washed out in the basic or advanced phases of flight training, the reasons were based on personalities, politics, or other arbitrary criteria. During these two levels of instruction, the training personnel were military, white, and southern. These instructors applied as much verbal and psychological abuse as possible to upset the cadet. If the cadet succumbed to the abuse, as many did, they could not perform to the best of their ability and were, subsequently, "washed out."[60] The instructors knew how many cadets were going to graduate, so they set out with the intent to eliminate a prescribed number of cadets. One flight instructor by the name of McGoon had such a reputation for eliminating cadets during check rides that the cadets feared that if they were chosen for a check ride by McGoon, they were finished. The cadets even had a saying whenever McGoon was giving check rides: "McGoon is going to get him a coon."[61]

Adding to the stress of flight training was the limited social life on the Tuskegee Army Air Field and the danger of southern segregated life in the city of Tuskegee. The base was a self-contained town within a town. Since it was an all Negro base, African-American personnel had complete access to its theater, mess halls, Px, and officers' club. The base post exchange restaurant and the lavatories in the base administrative offices had "white" and "colored" sections, which served as reminder that segregation was the manner of the day.[62] Most of the white officers lived in the town, and therefore the friction normally associated with segregation was kept at a minimum. The initial base commander, Maj. James Ellison, was supportive of the segregation at Tuskegee and did not encourage any socialization of the races, on or off the base. It was Ellison's job to develop the airfield and set up the administrative infrastructure. Major Ellison supported his officers, regardless of color, while on duty. He even placed an African-American officer, Capt. Hayden Johnson, in charge of airfield headquarters, commanding a group of several white noncommissioned personnel. Early in the deployment of the 99th, Capt. Johnson and this group guarded the initial supply depot until additional army personnel arrived.[63]

Major Ellison did not endear himself to the local white folks in the town of Tuskegee and Macon County. He was an army man and did what he could to carry out the duties assigned to him as the base commander. On one occasion, Ellison had to resort to a show of force in

Tuskegee when the sheriff, Pat Evans, disarmed one of Ellison's black military policemen. Sheriff Evans, like most southern law enforcement officers, was intolerant of , if not intimidated by, any black military man bearing arms. Major Ellison not only retrieved the weapon but unequivocally warned Evans about interfering in army matters.[64]

Tuskegee Institute was a traditional school, with conservative values regarding their coed students. Strict curfews for the young ladies limited the opportunities for contact and, therefore, the men often had to travel off campus for entertainment. As soon as they would reach the Tuskegee town limits, they would have difficulty with Mr. Evans for jaywalking or driving five miles over the speed limit. Sheriff Evans showed no respect for the African-American officer in uniform, even if that officer was about to give his life for Mr. Evans's freedom and security. Evans would, invariably, address the officers as "boy," regardless of the officers' age or rank.[65]

Tuskegee was in Macon County. This county was a "dry" county. The officers and black instructors who had a need for alcoholic beverages stronger than 2 percent beer would cross into another county, or even into Georgia to purchase liquor. The men would transport the whiskey and wine by car and, if necessary, even by plane. If the men used their automobiles, they were subject to being apprehended by Sheriff Evans, and the liquor would be confiscated. It seemed that Mr. Evans had informants all over eastern Alabama and western Georgia. By the time the officers and other smugglers arrived in Tuskegee, they would be pounced on by Evans for alleged speeding. Evans, operating on a tip from the seller, would have reasonable suspicion to search the vehicles. Evans usually kept the liquor that he found. Some airmen even resorted to buying homemade, distilled liquor from local black entrepreneurs. The production and distribution of the spirits were located so deep in the forests of eastern Alabama that Evans did not know where to search. The drink that was bought was triple digit proof and was known to take the "color out of Coca Cola."[66]

If the officers, cadets, and other base personnel attempted to travel long distances, they did so under segregated and inhospitable conditions. The train depot for Tuskegee was in a little town called Chehaw. The depot at Chehaw was also segregated. Officers of the Army Air Corps were forced to ride in overcrowded coaches and, at times, baggage cars. Because of local laws, customs, and traditions, they were not allowed to travel first class or coach in the less-crowded "white" train cars, even if they were empty. Even federal laws barring discrimination interstate commerce and travel were ignored. Many railroad companies operating in several states did not offer equal facilities for blacks. Even when black officers traveled first class by train via interstate routes, they were not exempt from being ordered out of "white" Pullman coaches and into substandard "colored" coaches by overzealous railroad conductors.[67] Army officers traveling interstate should not have been affected by state or local laws. The officers should have been protected by federal law governing interstate travel. When these acts of discrimination were reported to the War Department, it reluctantly petitioned the American Railroad Association. Subsequently, a few railroad companies were persuaded to provide space to black military passengers with Pullman passes whenever space was available.[68]

After the declaration of war and the subsequent mobilization effort, the Negro press and civil rights organizations, still confused about Negro troop status, continued to monitor the activities, policies, and practices of the War Department regarding the treatment and deployment of African Americans in World War II. For the first time since 1917, when President Wilson requested Congress to declare war on Germany, several members of the Negro press and several civil rights organizations questioned America's response and the appropriate response of its Negro citizens. While advocating Negro participation in the selective service process in 1940, the NAACP and the Negro press kept an accounting of human rights violations perpetrated against African Americans and took a proactive role in relating the Roosevelt administration's view of the war to the civil rights ideals of the American Negro. Clearly, the NAACP and other civil rights organizations and the Negro press, as in World War I, saw World War II as an opportunity for civil rights gains. The success of the drive to amend the Selective Service Act and the pressure on the War Department that led to the establishment of pilot training, and the success of the March on Washington movement, which led to the establishment of the Fair Employment Practices Commission, were victories that only served to increase their appetite.

The War Department's equivocality on the status of the deployment of the Negro soldier in the aftermath of the Editor's Conference, and the subsequent mobilization for war, simply fueled the fire. In January 1942, Walter White, of the NAACP, wrote a letter to General Marshall requesting the general to expand on his personal feelings that the War Department had not done enough in the way of using Negro soldiers in an equitable and productive fashion. Mr. White also volunteered to assist the War Department in doing a better job in its deployment of Negro troops. In his letter, Mr. White suggested the establishment of new integrated units within the army, up to the division level.[69] Mr. White and the NAACP were rebuffed by the War Department in a glib and terse letter reiterating the War Department position that it was not a social laboratory and that they must proceed with the mobilization and utilization of all troops in a manner that would ensure high morale and efficiency.

During the early part of 1942, the Negro press kept a vigilance on the level of Negro participation in the War mobilization plans. A February 1942, editorial in *The Crisis* on the "Negro in the United States Army" accused the Army Air Corps of restricting the number of Negro cadets taking training when the Air Corps had already announced a shortage of pilots and of restricting Negro doctors and nurses to Negro soldiers.[70] In its 14 February 1942 issue, the *Pittsburgh Courier,* blamed the Air Corps for depriving their own country of needed airmen. The article went on to indict the Air Corps with keeping eligible pilot candidates in a bottleneck, vulnerable to the draft, and for ignoring African Americans with commercial and cross-country licenses who had applied for instructor status. The *Courier* called the Air Corps policy of restricting African Americans to one unit demoralizing and a waste of public funds, when only a small part of the Tuskegee Institute was in use.[71] Emmet J. Scott, Judge Hastie's predecessor during World War I, wrote in the *Courier* that America was waging a fight on two fronts for justice— one against the "destructive forces of terrorism, force and aggression; on the other, for a New Order, based on justice and morality, peace and progress and complete liberty." Scott called for the Roosevelt administration to correct wasteful spending, overlapping agencies, and duplication of effort.[72]

The Negro press and civil rights organizations kept close watch on reported incidents of violence and discrimination against Negro soldiers. In 1942, the Negro press reported several stories per week about white civilian or white military police brutality, including fatal assaults on Negro soldiers. At many army and Air Corps camps and bases, Negro troops were restricted from mess, theaters, and postal exchanges, and from buses used by white troops. Reports of racial incidents emanating from southern white officers were frequently printed. The press reported on the low morale among Negro soldiers, especially those who were from the North and stationed in the South who were uncertain who the real enemy in the war was. In a 1942 editorial, *The Crisis* claimed that Negro troops and civilians discovered "that the United States Army the Mightiest force in the land, meekly surrendered control over its Negro troops to any white constable, sheriff, or mayor in Dixie who wanted to take over."[73] In reacting to the War Department's remark that the army was not a social laboratory, *The Crisis* added "these must be rooted out whether they reside in the *Mein Kampf* of a Hitler, or in a memorandum in the adjutant general's office in the American Army."[74]

Tuskegee was not exempt from the white-on-Negro violence and discrimination. The "experiment," as the Air Corps Command called it, was under close scrutiny by the press and civil rights intelligentsia, who only tolerated the project as a rare opportunity for African Americans to fly for the Air Corps. In 1942, there were two events involving Tuskegee personnel that almost escalated into race riots. First, in April 1942, a soldier was arrested in the town of Tuskegee and was being taken to jail by the town sheriff. A Negro military policeman, accompanied by a small band of M.P.s from the Tuskegee base, intercepted the sheriff and took the soldier, at gunpoint, from the sheriff. As the Negro M.P.s proceeded to escort their prisoner back to the base stockade, they were ambushed, disarmed, and beaten by the sheriff, who was joined by his deputies, the Alabama state police, and several white civilians armed with shotguns and pistols. Negro soldiers who witnessed the event called other Negro soldiers on the base, who gathered up weapons and headed to town to confront the white law enforcement officials and civilians. White officers, who resided in the town, were ordered by the base commander to find and order the enlisted men, still in the town, back to the base. The armed soldiers, who were on their way to protect the base and their fellow soldiers, were stopped by the base commander and ordered back to the base. The arrested Negro soldier was returned to the base.[75]

The second incident happened in Montgomery, but involved a nurse stationed at Tuskegee. In the fall of 1942, nurse Nora Green boarded a bus in Montgomery after shopping. It was an ordinary bus and Ms. Green assumed that it was a public vehicle. The white driver of the bus informed her that it was a bus for whites and ordered her to leave the bus. Nurse Green refused and was assaulted by the driver. Not only was she beaten, she was also arrested and held overnight in a Montgomery jail. When she returned to Tuskegee, word of her ordeal reached the officers and enlisted men on the Tuskegee Field. The men, enraged over the endless oppression and humiliation, acquired weapons and were headed for Montgomery when they were met at the gate by the military police and the base commander, who ordered them to return to quarters. The NAACP complained to the War Department and the Department of Justice but were stymied because Ms. Green decided not to press charges. She was, allegedly, ordered not to discuss the incident.[76]

The Negro press and the NAACP were so relentless and effective in their reporting and coverage of the Negro soldier in segregated training and in segregated circumstances in the South that the War Department, G-2 (Intelligence) had its Bureau of Public Relations, News Division, canvas all of the Negro papers and articles on the military. The news division rated the articles as unfavorable, favorable, or neutral.[77] The news division found so many articles "unfavorable" that the War Department pressured the Justice Department and the president to contemplate indictments against the editors and publishers of some of the Negro newspapers for sedition and interference with the war effort. In December 1942, President Roosevelt warned Walter White that the evidence against some of the editors was, in his opinion, weak, but that "some men high in government believed that convictions could be secured." Mr. White advised the president that to "abolish segregation in the armed services and to end discrimination in government-financed war industries would transform these papers from critics of the war effort into enthusiastic supporters."[78] White also suggested that the president integrate his press conferences and have more personal conferences with the Negro editors. Shortly after White's conference with the president, the Justice Department shelved their investigation of the editors. There was a temporary shortage of newsprint for certain Negro newspapers, however.[79]

In January 1943, the NAACP convened a conference with the editors of the twenty-four largest Negro newspapers. In that conference, it was decided that, in light of the close calls with the Justice Department, codependency and cooperation were necessary. The NAACP offered their Washington branch office as an information center and liaison office to the War Department that could be utilized on a cooperative basis by the newspapers. Shortly thereafter, the Negro Newspaper Publishers Association was formed and the Special Interest Section for the Negro press was staffed with Negro officers in the Public Relations Bureau.[80]

There was ample evidence to support the notion that the Negro press was disposed toward patriotism, and not sedition. In 1942, most Negro newspapers condemned the Nazi and Axis powers and had done so since 1936. The editors of the weekly papers published editorials and encouraged readers to send letters in support of the American and Allied war effort. In the 31 January 1942 issue of the *Pittsburgh Courier*, a letter to the editor from James C. Thompson of Wichita, Kansas, was featured. The editor of the *Courier* was so inspired by the letter that he featured it prominently a second time in the 11 April 1942 issue.[81] In his letter, Mr. Thompson presented rhetorical questions on the theme of self-sacrifice in the war effort in order to live like only half an American. Mr. Thompson answered that "While we keep defense and victory in the forefront that we don't lose site of our fight for true democracy at home." He went on to say that if the Allied countries have the 'VV' for Victory" sign to rally them to fight for victory over aggression, slavery, and tyranny, then the Negro should have "double VV" for double victory. The fist V was for victory over the enemies without and the second V was for victory over the enemies within. The *Courier* adopted Mr. Thompson's concept and coined it "Double V" for "Double Victory." The *Courier* staff artist, Wilbert L. Holloway, designed a graphic that was used as the "Double V" logo for the remainder of the war.[82]

The "Double V" concept and slogan was adopted by all of the Negro press and civil rights organizations and advocates. Its supporters also included Eleanor Roosevelt, Emmet J. Scott, Wendell Willke, several U.S. senators and representatives, and future presidential candidate Thomas E. Dewey. There was a promotional campaign that included bumper stickers, lapel buttons, sweaters, recordings, and beauty pageants. The "Double V" campaign was one of the most extensive patriotic drives in the country during the war.

With the antagonistic Negro press and the NAACP, the War Department scrambled for alternatives and answers to the Negro problem in a military system with a significant number of southern officers dedicated to maintaining racially segregated armed forces. By 1942 it was clear that Judge Hastie was not going to be an accomodationist in the mold of Emmett Scott. Judge Hastie, in the minds of the department heads in the War Department, was a liability and an agent of the NAACP, rather than an asset to the War Department's plan for a segregated armed forces in World War II. More and more communication and activity relating to the training and deployment of Negro soldiers was routed around or kept away from Hastie's office.

Rather than dealing with Judge Hastie, Secretary of War Henry Stimson, at the suggestion of G-1 (Personnel Department), appointed an advisory committee on Negro troop policies on 27 August 1942.[83] According to G-1, the committee would evaluate racial incidents, propose social reforms, and handle concerns regarding the training and deployment of Negro soldiers. Initially, the War Department was interested in awarding the chairmanship of the committee to a white man who was president of one of the Negro colleges, namely the president of Hampton Institute. However, General Marshall allegedly wanted a small committee of War Department insiders that could be, if not trusted, at least controlled. Secretary Stimson, at the suggestion of General Marshall, appointed Assistant Secretary of War John J. McCloy as chairman of the committee. The committee was called the McCloy Committee.[84]

The McCloy Committee membership consisted of representatives from the various departments within the War Department. Included on the committee was Gen. Benjamin O. Davis, Sr., representing the Inspector General's Office, and the ranking black officer in the armed forces. Not only was Judge Hastie not invited to join the committee, he was not even officially informed of its existence. Hastie reportedly learned of the committee from his assistant, Truman Gibson, who was also a family friend of the Davis's and relatively close to General Davis, Sr. Undersecretary of War Judge Patterson was also not aware of the assignment of the committee. Judge Patterson had to persuade Hastie not to resign. Judge Hastie was allowed to attend the committee meetings but was not assigned membership.[85]

Assistant Secretary McCloy shared the War Department's position on the status of the Negro in the armed forces. McCloy felt that Negroes should subordinate their concerns regarding segregation and discrimination to the goal of winning the war. He felt that there were forces within the country, namely the Negro press and the NAACP, misleading the Negro.[86] As a consequence, the McCloy Committee did not act on or accomplish anything of substance in 1942, including a proposal submitted by General Davis, Sr. that sought to eliminate the obvious "Jim Crow" practices and customs on military bases. He proposed orientation courses for white soldiers, and recommended that all officers in the army refrain from using the epithet "nigger."[87] Action on this proposal and others was deferred until late 1943 and 1944.

An experienced military man and an insider with personal knowledge of many of the War Department personalities, General Davis, Sr. chose the strategy of breaking down obvious and humiliating aspects of segregation and discrimination. He attacked racial epithets and segregated toilets, buses, and theaters, as opposed to changing, all at once, the social system of segregation to integration. This microapproach by General Davis, Sr. would prove effective in 1944 and 1945, the later war years.

Judge Hastie continued to work through Judge Patterson's office on issues related to Negro troops that were referred to his office. Hastie also assisted the McCloy Committee in the identification of issues covered in General Davis's proposal and other proposals on similar subjects.

The pilots and technical specialists of the 99th Pursuit Squadron concentrated on training and preparation for war. By October 1942, the pursuit squadron was at full strength and ready for combat deployment, despite the turmoil surrounding their separate existence. In February 1942, the Air Corps was graduating enough Negro pilots to start another squadron. The 100th Fighter Squadron was activated, on paper, primarily to serve as a separate unit that could be deployed for combat somewhere overseas, and as a unit that could supply replacement pilots for the 99th Pursuit Squadron. By the summer of 1942, the Army Air Force, formerly the Air Corps, decided to form a Negro fighter group. In October 1942, the 332nd Fighter Group was activated at Tuskegee Army Air Field. Lt. William Womack was the first officer assigned to the new all-Negro group as the adjutant officer. This group included three separate fighter squadrons: the 100th, 301st, and the 302d. The 99th was kept separate, as an unattached unit, so that it could prove itself in combat.[88]

Benjamin O. Davis, Jr., a lieutenant colonel by October 1942, was the commanding officer of the 99th. During the latter part of 1942, Colonel Davis asserted himself as the leader in all respects of the pursuit squadron. Colonel Davis developed respect among the men and a reputation as a serious disciplinarian and no-nonsense administrator. Davis was known to give spot inspections, looking for unpolished shoes and dirty fingernails, while cadets and officers where still living in the mud in "Tent City."[89] In a speech to the Cadet Class of 42G in July 1942, Colonel Davis stressed to the new officers that their success in the in the Army Air Force would depend on how they built on their background. He emphasized the importance of adequate sleep, exercise, recreation, and saving. He demanded punctuality and competence in every job.[90] There would be no Joe Spratmos in Davis's squadron.

As Colonel Davis received his promotions, and as more officers received their commissions at Tuskegee Army Air Field, Judge Hastie began to question the War Department and the Air Corps' commitment to turning over the administration of the Air Field to Negro officers, as proposed in the original National Defense Plans of the Air Corps. Colonel Davis did serve, for a short time, as the executive of troops, until he assumed command of the 99th. Davis was not replaced, for his position was created especially for him.[91] Negro officers served only in the assistant capacity. Hastie monitored the progress promotion system at Tuskegee and was well aware of the segregation and discrimination that existed on the base under the command of Col. Frederick Kimble. Colonel Kimble, who had replaced Major Ellison in January of 1942, administered a Negro airfield with only one Negro promoted, at Kimble's request, over the rank of captain, and this officer was in the medical corps.[92]

The Air Force referred Hastie's complaint about the lack of Negro administrators at Tuskegee to the Southeastern Army Air Force Training Command in Montgomery, Alabama, who proceeded to inform Hastie that the Army Air Corps National Defense Plans for the deployment of African Americans at Tuskegee were designed during peacetime and therefore, did not apply to a wartime situation that called for efficiency and competency, not social experimentation.[93]

Judge Hastie was also aware that activation of the 100th Fighter Squadron and 332nd Fighter Group would necessitate additional technical training and officer candidates for Negroes. Hastie noted that training schools were also added to the Tuskegee site, and he suspected that the Air Force was intent on amassing all of its Negro flying and ground personnel at Tuskegee. Chanute Field was no longer training Negro technicians, because the Air Force rationalized that it was more efficient to train technicians where their flying units were stationed. In addition, the Air Force was, for the first time, providing its own basic training to enlistees. The Air Force, because of its policy of segregating soldiers by race, was disposed to consider Tuskegee as the site for basic training, technical school, Officer Candidate School, flight training, and combat training for African Americans in the Army Air Force.[94]

Hastie learned, through the Negro press, of the War Department and Air Force feasibility study of designating Tuskegee as the site for all-purpose Negro enlistee and officer training in the Air Force. When Judge Hastie inquired into the validity of the plan, the War Department and the Air Force Command both expressed no knowledge of such a plan or feasibility study. When Hastie read another announcement of the Air Force's plan to assign all training for enlisted men and officers to Tuskegee, Judge Hastie offered his resignation, effective 30 January 1943, to Secretary of War Stimson. Stimson accepted Hastie's resignation.[95]

In his resignation, Judge Hastie pledged to go public with his charges against the War Department and the Army Air Forces. For two successive months, the major Negro newspapers, who were supportive and empathetic, printed a series of articles authored by Hastie. In the articles, the former civilian aide accused the War Department and Army Air Forces of discrimination, which led to wasteful federal spending of millions, waste of qualified manpower, risking the national security, and low morale among thousands of patriotic citizens. The NAACP even published a twenty-six page article by Judge Hastie entitled "On Clipped Wings."[96] With Judge Hastie's resignation and subsequent writings, the Negro press refocused on Tuskegee Army Air Field and all its negatives. Negro newspapers, such as the *Pittsburgh Courier, Chicago Defender,* and the *Baltimore Afro-American,* printed in-depth, investigative series on the status of the Negro soldier-in-training at the Tuskegee base.[97] The Negro press, in 1941 and 1942, questioned the War Department's rationale for activating a segregated and separate squadron in the Air Corps. With the 99th a reality in late 1942 and early

1943, the Negro press redirected the questioning to the War Department's plans for deploying the squadron for combat. The NAACP continued to lobby the War Department for a racially integrated squadron.[98]

Against the backdrop of an antagonistic Negro press, the skeptical NAACP, the resignation and subsequent attacks from Judge Hastie, and poor morale as the result of the Tuskegee environment, the men of the 99th and 332nd continued to train at intense levels. Most of the men believed life in the Army Air Corps was a better life than in the infantry. Most of the men were aware of the importance of their success, and they believed that success would bring them civil rights gains after the war.

The 99th had been prepared for deployment since March 1942, when the War Department and Army Air Forces tentatively assigned them to the Liberia Task Force. According to the War Department data, the 99th would patrol the coast of Liberia, protecting the country against raids by the German, Italian, and French German sympathizers and opportunists, also known as the Vichy French. The War Department and the Army Air Forces had found a comfortable and relatively safe assignment for the 99th—a Negro Air Force protecting a U.S.-sponsored Negro protectorate in Africa. The 99th trained diligently but was never called.[99]

The 99th remained on call for the Liberia Task Force for ten months. By that time (January 1943), however, the Axis threat to the Northwest and the Mediterranean coasts of Africa was no longer serious. The War Department also considered sending the 99th to China to join Gen. Claire Chenault's "China Air Task Force." The Operations Division of the Africa-Middle East Theatre Group thought the China assignment was too dangerous for inexperienced squadrons. The War Department probably rationalized that the China assignment could cause enough fatalities to fuel the conspiracy theory that the War Department sent the 99th to be eliminated and, therefore, the China assignment was viewed as politically dangerous.[100]

The 99th, while waiting for the War Department to find a suitable combat assignment, continued to train. Since they would have been using P-40s in Liberia, the Air Force sent them old war-fatigued P-40s from the China campaign. The planes still had the "Flying Tiger" markings on them.[101] Due to the changes in dates of embarkation, the pilots of the 99th repeatedly practiced formation flying, gunnery, dive bombing, and strafing. Several pilots had logged more than two hundred hours in the P-40s. White pilots of pursuit squadrons were being sent into combat with an average log time of fifty hours. Ground crew members of the 99th became proficient, with repetition. They mastered the breaking down and rebuilding of old P-40 engines. Accidents at Tuskegee Air Field due to engine failure were almost nonexistent.[102]

Some men of the 99th found it difficult, however, to deal with the anxiety of endless anticipation for combat, while stationed in the South. There were two accidents of note due to stress related to the anxiety. One pilot, named Dawson, was killed trying to double loop a railroad bridge. Another pilot was killed when his propeller caught the water while he was skimming low over Lake Martin, near Tuskegee.[103]

The departure of Colonel Kimble in January 1943 and the promotion of Col. Noel F. Parrish from director of flight training to base commander made the social life a little more bearable. Even though Parrish was southern-born, he was disposed to treating Negro soldiers in his command with a modicum of respect. He had spent time in Chicago in the late thirties as the Air Corps supervisor with the CAA Civilian Pilot Training Program (CPTP) at the Chicago School of Aeronautics. Colonel Parrish was very familiar with Cornelius Coffey and his School of Aeronautics. Parrish was helpful in providing the Coffey School with an A-6 Trainer engine. He also assisted the Coffey School in their successful application for a training contract in the CPTP. The Chicago experience had convinced Parrish that African Americans could not only fly, but could build and repair airplanes as well.[104]

Although he did not change the segregation policy on the base or in Tuskegee, Colonel Parrish on occasion visited the base officers' club, which in 1943, was a de facto Negro officers' club. He consulted prominent African Americans on complex issues, and he kept in contact with Gen. Benjamin O. Davis, Sr., who had a personal and professional interest in the Tuskegee "Experiment." Parrish's thoughtful and straightforward personality and administrative style won the respect of the Negro officers and enlisted men.[105]

Although many of the men of the 99th were unaware of his advocacy, Gen. Benjamin O. Davis, Sr. worked diligently inside the War Department to ensure the development and deployment of the 99th. As a representative of the Inspector General's Office, Davis, Sr. made several visits to the Tuskegee Base, at crucial times. He was there when the first class of cadets started flight training in August 1941; in April 1942, shortly after the first cadet class graduated; and in March 1943, right before the 99th was deployed for combat.[106] As a member of the McCloy Committee, Davis, Sr. formally and privately pushed for the deployment of the 99th to combat in April 1943. It appeared, through his quiet, behind-the-scenes advocacy, that Davis, Sr. was supportive of the civil rights push of Judge Hastie and the civil rights agencies.

However, General Davis's style reflected tight discipline and patience in attacking the obvious barriers.[107] The Davis protest over segregation would be waged in the boardroom in the War Department and over the skies of North Africa and Italy. He was, first, a soldier, second, a supportive father to the only other ranking Negro officer in the armed forces, and third, a civil rights advocate.

After studying several assignments to combat theatres that could accommodate a separate and segregated pursuit squadron, the War Department concurred with the Army Air Corps decision to send the 99th to the North African theatre of operations.[108]

In March 1943, Colonel Parrish gave a farewell speech worthy of note. Parrish told the men:

> I must face you with the fact that you, as Negroes, have not been particularly encouraged to be heroic in the past. You have been more often taught to be patient and to endure misfortune. Those are excellent abilities and I hope you can continue to cultivate them and keep them. But there is a time to keep quiet and a time to fight and the time for you to fight is soon. Not to fight for me, for the Air Corps, for Negroes, or even for yourselves. I hope you will think of yourselves as fighting, first of all, for this nation, not because its a perfect nation, from your standpoint, but it is our nation, and an improving nation, and the best nation of all. . . . I can only remind you in the midst of these problems of race that seem so serious now . . . that we must not forget the human race, to which we all belong, and which is the major problem after all. . . . You are, first of all, all men. No one can ask more than that you acquit yourselves like men. Each of you, and all of us, must prove first of all that we are capable of the dignity and nobility of manhood; that we can when the occasion calls for it, fight and die for a cause that is greater than any one life, or any one man, or any one group of men.[109]

The speech was well received, as excerpts of the speech were printed by most of the major Negro newspapers, including the March 1943 issue of *The Crisis* magazine.

On 15 April 1943, the 99th Pursuit Squadron boarded a luxury liner docked near Camp Shanks, New York and headed to North Africa. They arrived in Morocco on April 24th and the next day were sent to their first camp site, in QuedN'ja, near Fez, Morocco. In Fez, the social life was enhanced by the visits of Josephine Baker, who was in self-imposed exile and working for the French Resistance. Ms. Baker introduced the men to all the important families in Fez, making the social life pleasant, as well as safe. While they were stationed near Fez, they adopted a

Moroccan boy they called Junior. Junior served as the squadron transla-
tor and chief barterer when the squadron members went to the
market.[110]

While they were at QuedN'ja, the 99th undertook their introduction
to combat training. The 99th received twenty-seven new P-40s, which, in
1943, were obsolete. The German Bf 109, Fw 190 and the Italian
Maachi 205 fighter planes were faster and could climb higher than the
P-40. The P-40, however, was durable and very maneuverable in the
hands of the pilots of the 99th.[111]

The pilots were instructed in air combat maneuvers by Col. Phillip
Cochran, Maj. Ralph Keyes, and Maj. Robert Fackler. All three instructors were air combat veterans of the England and North African theatre
campaigns.[112]

It was not unusual for a new squadron to receive an orientation to
combat, but it was highly unusual for the Air Forces to send a pursuit
unit into combat with a commander with no combat experience. This
fact was not lost among the pilots of the 99th. Although they were eager
to engage the enemy in combat, they harbored reservations and experienced anxiety over the knowledge that they would be led in combat by
someone with no combat experience.[113] Some of these reservations
were relieved by the training at QuedN'ja.

The 99th moved to Cape Bon on the Tunisian Peninsula, and set up
for the final phase of training and introduction to combat. They were
attached to the 33rd Fighter Group, a veteran unit in the North African
theatre commanded by Col. William Momyer. The 33rd was assigned to
the 12th Air Force, which was involved in tactical missions against the
Axis powers. It was understood that the 33rd, also equipped with P-40s,
would be assigned missions of opportunity. The 99th would be involved
in strafing tanks, trains, trucks, bridges, and troops. It would, on occasion, fly escort for medium-range bombers.[114]

Colonel Momyer retained the segregation and separation policy of
the Army Air Forces. The 99th's camp was in a dry lake bed near an
olive grove, five miles away from the nearest squadron within the group.
Although the 99th received daily briefings on the combat activity of the
33rd Fighter Group and the 12th Air Force, they were not told, at times,
about certain briefing sessions. Since there was such a distance between
the 99th camp and the Group Operations Headquarters, the 99th officers would sometimes arrive at the end of the briefings, only to be told
to follow the lead of the squadron providing the training. There were
times when the white operations officer would fly to the 99th camp,
brief the 99th, and fly back to group headquarters, just to avoid having
integrated briefing sessions.[115]

The final phase of the training was, in actuality, introduction to combat. Colonel Davis selected four of his pilots to accompany a veteran squadron on a combat mission to Pantelleria. The training of the four Negro pilots consisted of flying wingman for an experienced pilot. Lts. William Campbell, Charles Hall, Clarence Jamision, and James Wiley flew wing in combat for the first time on 2 June 1943. Flying as wingmen for one mission was all of the combat training that the 99th pilots received. This treatment was also unusual. Fortunately, there were very few enemy fighters sighted on these training missions.[116]

On 9 June 1943, a flight led by Lt. Charles Dryden was headed for a strafing mission on Pantelleria when they were attacked by German aircraft. This attack was the first contact that the 99th had had with the enemy. After the initial shock of being attacked for the first time, the pilots regrouped and engaged the enemy pilots in "dog fights." The pilots of the 99th eventually drove the German aircraft away without losing any planes. In this skirmish, Lt. Willie Ashley was the first pilot of the 99th to be credited with disabling an enemy plane.[117] Unfortunately for the German pilots, the pilots of the 99th were very familiar with the P-40, and very adept at flying the airplane. Two days later, Pantelleria surrendered to Allied forces. The 99th had participated in the air assault over Pantelleria and when they learned that, for the first time in history, a battle had been won with air power alone, the men of the 99th gained confidence. The pilots were eager to engage the Germans in combat.[118]

The engineering officer, Lt. Herbert Carter, and the ground crew mechanics also had to deal with a new element—sand. In the dry season, sand was everywhere and it would get into the engine parts and cause the engine to break down. P-40 engines had to be disassembled and parts cleaned every twenty-five hours of service. Heat also caused a problem. With the heat, and the fact that the engines were liquid-cooled, engines would easily overheat.[119]

Engine parts and cleaning agents were a problem as well. If these components were not brought with them from America, procuring them was next to impossible. The ground crew mechanics had to exercise some ingenuity in keeping the planes in the air in the Mediterranean climate. One such ingenious idea came when the 99th found out that they did not have spark plug cleaning fluid or new spark plugs. A 99th mechanic, P. C. Corbin developed a spark plug cleaner by filling a drum with some sand, drilling a hole for the spark plug, inserting the spark plug, and using an air pressure gun to blast the spark plug with sand crystals. While planes from other squadrons were disabled with faulty plugs, mechanics were curious to know what kept the planes of the 99th in the air. Once the 99th ground crew shared their secret, they gained a reputation as one of the best ground crews in the North African theatre.[120]

Another fact unique to 99th was that they were not integrated into the other squadrons. Usually a fighter group has three squadrons. However, due to the War Department and Air Forces segregation policy, the 99th was attached to the 33rd Fighter Group as a fourth squadron. With the 99th placed in the corner, several miles away from another sister squadron, the unit was vulnerable to being bombed out of existence by the German Luftwaffe in their nightly bombing raids. When the Germans bombed in the area of the 99th they seldom caused very much damage. This was quite remarkable, considering that the German Intelligence was well aware of the 99th and their location.[121]

After Pantelleria, Sicily became the next target for the Allies. The 99th was ordered to move to El Haouria, on the far eastern tip of Cape Bon. On 30 June 1943, they were attached to the 324th Fighter Group, already involved in the invasion of Sicily. During the following week, the 99th pilots were engaged in escorting medium-range bombers to Sicily. On 2 July, while escorting the bombers from a target in Sicily, the pilots of the 99th encountered a German fighter squadron attacking the bombers. Lt. Charles Hall saw two German planes following one of the bombers headed for the space between the fighter planes and the bomber, and he turned his P-40 inside of the German fighters. Lieutenant Hall fired his guns and saw his tracers hit the second German plane. The aircraft suddenly fell off and headed straight to the ground, raising a black cloud of smoke. Hall became the first member of the 99th to have a confirmed kill. When the squadron returned to the base, they were personally congratulated by Gen. Dwight Eisenhower and three other generals in the Mediterranean theatre of operations.[122]

It appeared that the experiment was over, and that the 99th had proven that they could fly and maintain fighter planes, as well as fly and maintain them under combat conditions. The men were not concerned with simply proving the experiment successful as much as they were concerned with the manner in which they proved the experiment successful. They knew that their progress, as well as their conduct, would be monitored very closely. They were aware that the future of African Americans in the Army Air Forces hinged on their performance and conduct. More importantly, they knew that their performance would determine their civil rights status and the status of other Negroes in America after the war.[123]

Hall's victories were tempered by the loss of two pilots of the 99th. Even with the losses, the pilots and ground crew members were hungry for aerial victories. The 99th spent the next three weeks dive-bombing and strafing enemy strongholds in Sicily. It appeared to the pilots of the 99th that the German pilots had no interest in defending Sicily, and were not eager to pursue them or defend the island.[124] The Negro pilots were unaware that the German army and air force were pulling back to defend Italy. The 99th pilots were as eager as ever to engage the German pilots in combat. They became anxious and annoyed when German fighters would not engage them or when German planes were not sighted on bombing and staff missions in Sicily. Even the ground crew resorted to placing stickers on the windshields of the planes. The stickers read: "Do you want to live forever?"[125]

Toward the end of July 1943, the 99th moved to Licata, Sicily, and welcomed their first replacement pilots. From that time to the middle of August 1943, the 99th participated in the strafing and dive-bombing of strategic positions in Sicily, until the island was captured near the end of August.

The men of the 99th passed the first test. Of the twenty-eight pilots, including Colonel Davis, three were killed, two in airfield-related accidents. The men of the squadron flew over 800 sorties and averaged, individually, more consecutive combat hours than pilots in other fully manned squadrons. Other squadrons averaged thirty-five men when the 99th had twenty-seven, minus the commanding officer. The men could not enjoy recreation and relaxation because of the pressure of carrying the fate of Negro American every time they took off. They also had no rest camp available to them in a segregated theatre of operations.[126]

Colonel Davis had done an admirable job of commanding the 99th. He exhibited skills in administering and disciplining the men to the point where he got the ultimate performance out of all of them. Unfortunately, he had to put some emotional distance between himself and his men. He felt that he had to be very serious, businesslike, and a disciplinarian, in order for them to respect him and get the job done.[127] This must have been very difficult, since Colonel Davis was not the natural leader of the 99th. He was chosen by the military establishment over others in his group with more flying experience. He knew that the men were aware of this, and that some may not have had confidence in him.

The Army Air Forces put Davis in the unusual and precarious position of commanding a pursuit squadron when he had no combat experience.[128] Segregationist policies of the Air Forces forbade any social interaction between Davis and his officer contemporaries in combat. Therefore, he could not seek assistance from fellow officers with combat experience, when confronted with complex problems. Colonel Davis and the squadron survived and Davis earned the respect of his men.

On 2 September 1943, Davis received a new assignment to command the 332nd Fighter Group.

Notes

1. Lee, *The Employment of Negro Troops*, 118.
2. Ibid., 118-19.
3. Ibid., 119; Osur, *Blacks in the Army Air Forces*, 24.
4. Roy Wilkins, "Air Pilots But Segregated," *The Crisis* 48 (February 1941): 39.
5. "Councils Back Suit of Yancey Williams to Enter Army Air Corps," *The Crisis* 48 (March 1941): 87-88.
6. Roy Wilkins, "Army Air Corps Smoke Screen," *The Crisis* 48 (April 1941): 103.
7. Howard D. Gould letter to Walter White; Cornelius R. Coffey letter to editor of *Louisville Leader*, 22 February 1941.
8. James Peck, "When Do We Fly," 376-78; Osur, *Blacks in the Army Air Forces*, 25.
9. Osur, *Blacks in the Army Air Forces*, 25.
10. Wilkins, "Army Air Corps Smoke Screen," 63.
11. Lee, *The Employment of Negro Troops*, 118.
12. Walter White letter to all Negro graduates of CPTP, 21 February 1941, NAACP Papers, Collection of the Manuscript Division, Library of Congress.
13. William Hastie letter to Thurgood Marshall regarding Negro Licenced Pilots, 25 February 1941, NAACP Papers, Collections of the Manuscript Division, Library of Congress.
14. Morris MacGregor Jr., *Integration of the Armed Forces*, 28; Osur, *Blacks in the Army Air Forces*, 227.
15. MacGregor, *Integration of the Armed Forces*, 24-25; Osur, *Blacks in the Army Air Forces*, 26.
16. Ibid., 24; Osur, *Blacks in the Army Air Forces*, 26.
17. Lee, *The Employment of Negro Troops*, 137; MacGregor, *Integration of the Armed Forces*, 28, Osur, 25-26.
18. Lee, *The Employment of Negro Troops*, 137-38.
19. Ibid.; Osur, *Blacks in the Army Air Forces*, 27-28.
20. Charles E. Francis, *The Tuskegee Airmen: The Men Who Changed a Nation* (Boston: Brandon Publishing Company, 1988), 19; Interview with Harry Sheppard, 9 August 1990, Los Angeles, California.
21. Interview with Harry Sheppard; Lee, *The Employment of Negro Troops*, 252.

22. Lee, *The Employment of Negro Troops*, 117; Francis, *The Tuskegee Airmen*, 19-20; Interview with Omar P. Blair, 8 August 1990, Los Angeles, California; Interview with Harry Sheppard; Tuskegee Airmen, Inc., East Coast Chapter, *The Tuskegee Airman Story* (Washington, D.C.: O'Dennis Associates, 1988), 4.

23. Tuskegee Airmen, Inc., *The Tuskegee Airmen Story*, 4; Special Order of 99th Technical Crew and Cadets to Tuskegee Army Air Field Southeast Training Command, Army Air Force, 9 December 1941.

24. Interview with William Thompson, 10 October 1990, Chicago, Illinois; Lee, *The Employment of Negro Troops*, 148; Osur, *Blacks in the Army Air Forces*, 35; MacGregor, *Integration of the Armed Forces*, 30.

25. MacGregor, *Integration of the Armed Forces*, 28.

26. Osur, *Blacks in the Army Air Forces*, 28-29; Francis, *The Tuskegee Airmen*, 15.

27. Davis, *Benjamin O. Davis, Jr.*, 83.

28. William Hastie letter to Thurgood Marshall regarding Eligibility for Aviation Cadets, 13 February 1941, Eligibility for Aviation Cadet, NAACP Papers, Collections of the Manuscript Division, Library of Congress.

29. Tuskegee Airmen, Inc., *The Tuskegee Airman Story*, 4; Interview with Lemuel Custis, 10 August 1991, Detroit, Michigan.

30. Davis, *An Autobiography*, 83; Interview with Lemuel Custis; "99th," *Time* 38 (15 September 1941): 32.

31. "99th," *Time* 38 (15 September 1941): 32; Interview with Spann Watson; Interview with Phillip Lee.

32. Davis, *An Autobiography*, 27-48.

33. Ibid., 63-70.

34. Lee, *The Employment of Negro Troops*, 118; Interview with Lemuel Custis; Interview with William Womack; Davis, *An Autobiography*, 63; Robert A. Rose, *Lonely Eagles: The Story of American Black Air Force in World War II* (Los Angeles: Tuskegee Airman, Inc., Los Angeles Chapter, 1976), 14-15.

35. Davis, *An Autobiography*, 69.

36. Interview with C. Alfred Anderson.

37. Interview with Harry Sheppard; Interview with Omar P. Blair; Tuskegee Airmen, Inc., *The Tuskegee Airman Story*, 5; Rose, *Lonely Eagles*, 16.

38. Rose, *Lonely Eagles*, 16; Interview with Harry Shepard; Interview with Milton Henry, 16 March 1991; Francis, *The Tuskegee Airmen*, 20.

39. Lee, *The Employment of Negro Troops*, 136-39.

40. Ibid., 138-39.

41. Assistant Secretary of War (ASW), McCloy Files, 20 September 1941, National Archives.

42. ASW, McCloy Files, 4 October 1941, National Archives.

43. Ibid.

44. Lee, *The Employment of Negro Troops,* 140; MacGregor, *Integration of the Armed Forces,* 21-22.
45. Lee, *The Employment of Negro Troops,* 146.
46. Ibid., 141; MacGregor, *Integration of the Armed Forces,* 22-23.
47. ASW McCloy Files, 8 December 1941, National Archives; MacGregor, *Integration of the Armed Forces,* 22-23; Lee, *The Employment of Negro Troops,* 142.
48. "No Time for Quibbles," *Pittsburg Courier,* 20 December 1941.
49. Interview with William M. Womack; Johnson, *The Fighting 99th,* 2; Interview with Jenny Washington, 10 May 1990, Lansing, Michigan; Interview with C. Alfred Anderson.
50. Interview with C. Alfred Anderson; Interview with Lemuel Custis.
51. Interview with William M. Womack; Interview with Lemuel Custis.
52. Interview with C. Alfred Anderson; Interview with Lemuel Custis.
53. Davis, *An Autobiography,* 88; Johnson, *The Fighting 99th,* 6.
54. Interview with C. Alfred Anderson; Osur, *Blacks in the Army Air Forces,* 28-29.
55. Interview with Herbert Carter, 10 June 1990, Tuskegee, Alabama; William H. Hastie, "Color Restricts Army Pilots to 100 When 1,000 Can Be Trained," *Baltimore Afro American,* 20 February 1943.
56. Osur, *Blacks in the Army Air Forces,* 42; MacGregor, *Integration of the Armed Forces,* 29; "Color Restricts Army Pilots to 200," *Baltimore Afro American,* 20 February 1943.
57. "Canadian Aviation Captain First Negro to Fly Atlantic," *Pittsburgh Courier,* 16 May 1942.
58. Osur, *Blacks in the Army Air Forces,* 29; MacGregor, *Integration of the Armed Forces,* 29.
59. Interview with C. Alfred Anderson; Interview with Richard Macon, 2 February 1990, Detroit, Michigan; Interview with Alexander Jefferson, 19 April 1990, Detroit, Michigan; Interview with Charles Dryden, 18 April 1991, Atlanta, Georgia.
60. Interview with Phillip Lee; Interview with Gilbert Cargill, 10 April 1990, Detroit, Michigan.
61. Interview with Alexander Jefferson.
62. Interview with William M. Womack; Richard M. Dalfiume, *Desegregation of the United States Armed Forces* (Columbia: University of Missouri Press, 1966), 184; Gropman, *The Air Force Integrates,* 10.
63. Johnson, *The Fighting 99th,* 2.
64. Francis, *The Tuskegee Airmen,* 20; Interview with William M. Womack; Interview with C. Alfred Anderson.
65. Interview with C. Alfred Anderson; Interview with Spann Watson; Interview with John Whitehead, 8 August 1990, Los Angeles, California; Interview with Omar Blair.
66. Interview with Omar Blair; Interview with Fred Hutchins, 8-9 August 1990, Los Angeles, California.

67. Interview with William M. Womack; Interview with Leroy Gillead, 7-9 August 1990, Los Angeles, California.
68. Interview with Richard Macon; MacGregor, *Integration of the Armed Forces*, 45.
69. Lee, *The Employment of Negro Troops*, 143; White, *A Man Called White*, 222.
70. Roy Wilkins, "The Negro in the United States Army," *The Crisis* 49 (February 1942): 47.
71. "Claim Air Corps Bias Depriving U.S. of Airmen," *Pittsburgh Courier*, 14 February 1942.
72. Emmett J. Scott, "America Now Waging Fight on Two Fronts for Justice," *Pittsburgh Courier*, 2 May 1942.
73. Wilkins, "The Negro in the United States Army," 47.
74. Ibid.
75. Davis, *An Autobiography* 77; Lee, *The Employment of Negro Troops*, 356; Interview with Robert Pitts, 1 March 1990, Detroit, Michigan; Interview with William M. Womack; Interview with C. Alfred Anderson.
76. White, *A Man Called White*, 222-23; Interview with Robert Pitts.
77. Lee, *The Employment of Negro Troops*, 383.
78. White, *A Man Called White*, 207-8.
79. Ibid., 208.
80. Ibid., 208-9; Lee, *The Employment of Negro Troops*, 307.
81. "These Men Developed the `Double V' Idea," *Pittsburgh Courier*, 11 April 1942.
82. Ibid.
83. Lee, *The Employment of Negro Troops*, 157. MacGregor, *Integration of the Armed Forces*, 34-35; Dailfume, *Desegregation*, 82.
84. Lee, *The Employment of Negro Troops*, 157-58.
85. Ibid., 157.
86. Ibid., 158-59; Dailfume, *Desegregation*, 83.
87. Lee, *The Employment of Negro Troops*, 160-61; Dalifume, *Desegregation*, 86-87.
88. Francis, *The Tuskegee Airmen*, 75-76; Lee, *The Employment of Negro Troops*, 119; Interview with William M. Womack.
89. Interview with Lemuel Custis; Interview with William Thompson.
90. "Commencement Ceremonies for Class of 42G," *Hawk's Cry*, 16 July 1942.
91. Lee, *The Employment of Negro Troops*, 163; Davis, *An Autobiography*, 88.
92. Special Correspondent, "Blame Command for Low Morale at Tuskegee Base," *Pittsburgh Courier*, 20 February 1943.
93. Lee, *The Employment of Negro Troops*, 163-64.
94. Ibid., 164-65; Osur, *Blacks in the Army Air Forces*, 41-42; Dailfume, *Desegregation*, 84.
95. Dalifume, *Desegregation*, 84-85; Lee, *The Employment of Negro Troops*, 170.
96. William H. Hastie, "Hastie Raps Army," *Pittsburgh Courier*, 27 February

1943; "Segregated Air Training Unfeasible, Hastie Says," *Pittsburgh Courier*, 20 February 1943; William H. Hastie, "Color Restricts Army Pilots to 200," *Baltimore Afro-American*, 20 February 1943; Lee, *The Employment of Negro Troops*, 175; William H. Hastie, *On Clipped Wings; The Story of Jim Crow in the Army Air Corps*, NAACP Crisis Pamplet, New York, 1943.

97. Roger Didier, "Dent May Succeed Hastie," *Pittsburgh Courier*, 30 January 1943; John Jasper, "Discrimination in Air Forces Causes Dr. Hastie to Resign from War Dept.," *Baltimore Afro-American*, 6 February 1943; "Hastie Will Get Spingard Award," *Pittsburgh Courier*, 20 March 1943.

98. Roy Wilkins, "Hastie Resigns," *The Crisis* 50 (February 1943): 41.

99. Lee, *The Employment of Negro Troops*, 451; Francis, *The Tuskegee Airmen*, 23-24.

100. Lee, *The Employment of Negro Troops*, 452; Davis, *An Autobiography*, 90.

101. Interview with Herbert Carter; Interview with Spann Watson; Davis, *An Autobiography*, 88.

102. Interview with Herbert Carter; Interview with Clarence Jamison, 11 May 1991, Columbus, Ohio; Davis, *An Autobiography*, 91.

103. Interview with C. Alfred Anderson; Interview with Spann Watson.

104. Interview with Cornelius Coffey; Osur, *Blacks in the Army Air Forces*, 44-45; Interview with Spann Watson; Interview with Clarence Jamison.

105. Special Correspondent, "Blame Command for Low Morale at Tuskegee Base," *Pittsburgh Courier*, 20 February 1943; Osur, *Blacks in the Army Air Forces*, 45.

106. "Gen. Davis Sr. Visits TAAF," *Hawk's Cry*, 16 February 1943; Johnson, *The Fighting 99th*, 7.

107. Lee, *The Employment of Negro Troops*, 450; Osur, *Blacks in the Army Air Forces*, 87-88; MacGregor, *Integration of the Armed Forces*, 37, 39.

108. Lee, *The Employment of Negro Troops*, 452; Johnson, *The Fighting 99th*, 10-11; Davis, *An Autobiography*, 94.

109. Roy Wilkins, "Farewell Speech to Our Pilots," *The Crisis* 50 (March 1943): 72.

110. Francis, *The Tuskegee Airmen*, 27-29; Johnson, *The Fighting 99th*, 11; Interview with William Thompson.

111. Enzo Angelucci and Peter Bowers, *The American Fighter: The Definitive Guide to American Fighter Aircraft from 1917 to the Present* (New York: Orion Books, 1985), 167. Barry C. Wheeler, *Military Aircraft Markings and Profiles* (New York: Gallery Books, 1990), 54, 78, 92; Davis, *An Autobiography*, 96.

112. Davis, *An Autobiography*, 97; Francis, *The Tuskegee Airmen*, 30.

113. Johnson, *The Fighting 99th*, 6; Lee, *The Employment of Negro Troops*, 458-59; Interview with Spann Watson; Interview with Clarence Jamison; Interview with Lemuel Custis.

114. Mauer Mauer, *Air Force Combat Units of World War II* (Washington, D.C.: Office of Air Force History, 1983); Davis, *An Autobiography* 98-99.

115. Interview with Herbert Carter; Interview with William Thompson; Interview with Clarence Jamison.

116. Interview with Clarence Jamison; Francis, *The Tuskegee Airmen*, 34.

117. Interview with Charles Dryden; Interview with Clarence Jamison; Francis, *The Tuskegee Airmen*, 34-36; Rose, *Lonely Eagles*, 57.

118. Rose, *Lonely Eagles*, 57-58; Francis, *The Tuskegee Airmen*, 36.

119. Interview with Herbert Carter.

120. Interview with Rufus Mitchell, 7 August 1990, Los Angeles, California.

121. Interview with Herbert Carter; Interview with William Thompson.

122. Rose, *Lonely Eagles*, 58; Francis, *The Tuskegee Airmen*, 40; Davis, *An Autobiography*, 100.

123. Interview with William Thompson; Interview with Herbert Carter.

124. Interview with John Rogers, 2 February 1991, Chicago; Interview with Clarence Jamison.

125. Interview with William Thompson.

126. "Col. Davis Tells Story of the 99th Pursuit Squadron's Part in the War," *Baltimore Afro-American*, 18 September 1943; Interview with William Thompson; Interview with Herbert Carter; Interview with John W. Rogers.

128. Interview with Spann Watson.

Chapter 8

War on Two Fronts

An unsuspecting Colonel Davis received orders on 2 September 1943 to return to the United States to train and command the all-black 332nd Fighter Group stationed at Selfridge Air Base, near Detroit. Davis had harbored no illusions about commanding a fighter group. He was painfully aware of his role, and that of his men, as subjects in an experiment, closely scrutinized by the Army Air Force, War Department, and black America. He and his men knew of the potential impact of the evaluation of the experiment. From the outset, the 332nd was commanded by white officers. Colonel Davis and his men assumed that the 332nd would be deployed with a white command structure.[1] Colonel Davis left Capt. George Roberts, a very capable pilot and administrator, in charge of the 99th.

Shortly after arriving in the states, Colonel Davis, on 10 September 1943, held a press conference to report the status of the 99th. The press conference, held at the Pentagon, was attended by his father, Gen. Benjamin O. Davis, special advisor to the secretary of war, Truman Gibson, and several members of the black press.[2] Colonel Davis's presentation covered several points for the record, including the history of the 99th, the responsibilities, the training overseas, and the combat experience. Davis stated that he and the members of the 99th were well aware that their squadron was an experiment, and that knowing this placed great pressure on the men to succeed. He and his men were burdened with the knowledge that success or failure would reflect on the entire race, in general, and the future of the race in the Army Air Force, in particular. This burden provided little time for pleasure and recreation. He reiterated that the 99th was well trained in the P-40 fighter plane and had an average flight time of 250 hours per pilot. Even though the P-40 was slower than the enemy fighter planes, the P-40 could outmaneuver the Axis planes. He also stated that, more importantly, the squadron received and completed one fourth of the missions given to the 33rd Fighter Group, led by Colonel Momyer. Therefore, in Colonel Davis's opinion, the 99th proved that they could fly combat planes as well as any other squadron.[3]

Davis's presentation was a carefully worded report on the combat experiences of the 99th. Davis did not report any discriminatory or segregated treatment given by Colonel Momyer and others in the North African theatre. Davis even went so far as to state that "there was not a single circumstance or incident which could be regarded as discriminatory by the most rabid race leader."[4] Davis also stated that when Colonel Momyer allocated missions, he treated the 99th as one of his own squadrons.[5] It was as if General Davis, Sr. and Truman Gibson, Hastie's interim replacement, had orchestrated the report and the press conference in a manner that would placate the black public, but not offend the president, the secretary of war, or the Army Air Force command. They sensed, instinctively, trying times ahead.

Davis and Gibson expected the 99th to be closely scrutinized, but they expected fair play. They suspected, but were unaware of, the Army Air Force command's attempts to discredit the 99th. As soon as the 99th was involved in combat in North Africa, the campaign to discredit the squadron started, with negative reports emanating from Colonel Momyer, commanding officer of the 33rd Fighter Group, to which the 99th was attached. In early September 1943, concurrent with Colonel Davis's reassignment, a compilation of these reports was sent to Momyer's superior officer Gen. Edwin J. House, commander of XII Air Support Headquarters.[6] In his report, Momyer accused the men of the 99th of having less than satisfactory air discipline and of failing to show any ability to work and fight together as a team. Momyer indicted the 99th for leaving their flying formation when attacked by enemy air craft. Momyer also stated that the squadron "lacked aggressive spirit that is necessary for a well organized fighter squadron."[7] He accused the squadron of passing up dangerous primary targets for undefended secondary targets and of turning back from a mission because of weather, while another squadron completed the mission. Momyer berated Colonel Davis by reporting that Davis had requested, during their battle of Sicily, that his men be given three days of rest after 28 sorties because of combat fatigue, while white squadrons continued to fly with an average of 70 sorties.[8] Momyer, clearly, portrayed the 99th as undisciplined, cowardly, and lazy.

Colonel Momyer's intent was most obvious in his most deadly criticism at the end of the report. He charged that the 99th Fighter Squadron was, in his opinion, "not of the fighting caliber of any squadron in this group. They have failed to display any aggressiveness and desire for combat that are necessary to a first class fighting organization."[9] On 16 September 1943, General House endorsed Momyer's report on the 99th Fighter Squadron's performance and sent the report, with a cover letter, up the chain of command of the Army Air Force. Included in House's cover letter, was the charge that the consensus of the officers under his command, including medical staff, was that "negroes did not possess the proper reflexes to make a first class fighter pilot."[10] Since the Air Force was unwilling to replace the 99th command structure with whites, citing sociological problems, General House recommended that the 99th be assigned to the Coastal Air Force in Northwest Africa and that "if and when a Negro Group was formed in the United States, it be kept there for defense command duties."[11]

General House's report and recommendations were endorsed by Gen. John H. Cannon, Deputy Commander of the Northwest African Tactical Air Force. General Cannon delivered the recommendations to General Spaatz, commanding officer of the Twelfth Air Force in North Africa. On the same day, 16 September 1943, the 20 September issue of *Time* magazine hit the newsstands with an article entitled "Experiment Proved?" The story contained highlights presented at Colonel Davis's press conference. The article also included, interestingly enough, an "unofficial report" from an army "source" in the Mediterranean theatre that the theatre command was unhappy with the combat performance of the 99th Fighter Squadron and that "there was a plan a few weeks ago to attach it to the Coastal Air Command, in which it would be assigned to routine convoy cover."[12] The "unofficial report" revealed classified information on the wartime deployment plans for a squadron within the Army Air Force. This was highly unusual. Apparently there was a leak in the Army Air Force public relations staff. The author concluded that the lack of information and the limited combat experience made it difficult to answer the question posed in the title of the article. The author did state that black pilots would continue to train in a segregated manner, but that black cadets would be trained together with whites in medium bomber training.[13]

On 19 September 1943, General Spaatz endorsed the recommendations from General Cannon and added that the 99th had more than the required training for combat, were processed into combat slowly, and that "no squadron had been introduced to this theatre with a better background for training."[14] The compilation of reports and recommendations emanating from the commanding officer of the 33rd Fighter Group was processed rapidly through the chain of command of the Twelfth Air Force in North Africa and was forwarded to the Chief of the Commander of Army Air Forces, Gen. Henry Hap Arnold. By the end of September 1943, General Arnold and the Army Air Force had been convinced of the 99th Fighter Squadron's supposed ineffectiveness and lack of competence in combat. The Air Force Command even resorted to using the squadron's training schedule against them, charging that the 99th had the advantage of training for eight months, instead of the usual three months given to white squadrons, and that, therefore, the 99th should have been more successful than their record indicated.

It appeared that the Army Air Force Command chose not to admit that their inability and unwillingness to deploy the 99th in a combat theatre commanded by bigoted generals was a contributing factor to the extended training. The 99th was ready for deployment in October 1942, and, therefore, until their deployment to Africa the following April, the pilots of the 99th had nothing to do, other than train and practice flying in formation. Ironically, the extended training enhanced the pilots' familiarity with the P-40. Their mastery of this fighter plane may have saved many of their lives.[15]

On 4 October 1943, General Arnold forwarded the performance reports and recommendations to Gen. George Marshall, Chief of Staff. Included in the reports were the recommendation to move the 99th and the 332nd to the rear defense area and the recommendation to abandon the activation and training of the all-Negro 477th Medium Bombardment Group. Also included in the package of recommendations pertaining to the 99th was a letter, drafted for President Roosevelt's signature, of approval for implementation.[16]

General Marshall, by the nature of his position, had to be more cognizant of the political fallout for reassigning the 99th and curtailing the activation and training of the 332nd and medium bombardment group. The *Time* article had raised a lot of question from the black press and the black community at large. Marshall was aware of the power of the black press and issued a communiqué to the Office of War Information to issue denials to any questions regarding plans to reassign the 99th and the Fighter Group to rear defense areas. Army Air Force Public Relations staff continued to announce that black cadets would train with white cadets in the new medium bomber group.[17] The army was catching the ire of the black community regarding the utilization of black troops on the ground and in the air. In April of 1943, only 79,000 of 500,000 black troops were activated overseas; two-thirds of the troops seas; two-thirds of the troops were in service areas—engineering, quartermaster, and transportation units.[18] The black press and the black community, in support of the Double V campaign, demanded black participation on the war front, not as cooks and construction workers, but as combat soldiers. Even the Advisory Committee on Negro Troop Policies—the McCloy Committee—proposed that a black combat unit be sent to the front immediately.[19]

General Marshall had to find a way to appease his generals in the Air Force, but he also could not afford to further weaken either the patriotism of any American population during wartime or the morale of his white troops. In light of the Air Force recommendations, General Marshall ordered G-3, his Operations and Training Division, to analyze the entire Negro combat situation, ground as well as air.[20]

On 8 October 1943, G-3 reported to General Marshall that, after analyzing the employment of blacks in all of the combat theatres, it found that blacks had not been involved in combat to the extent that one could evaluate, conclusively, their effectiveness. G-3 reported that it had not arrived at any conclusion to justify any fundamental change in policy affecting the employment of black troops overseas. Further, G-3 recommended that the Army Air Force send the 332nd Fighter Group to a combat situation in the Mediterranean theatre, where the value of the units could be adequately assessed.[21]

On 13 October 1943, the McCloy Committee met to discuss the efficiency report and recommendations regarding the 99th. Committee members Truman Gibson and General Davis, Sr., advocates for the 99th, sparred with supporters of the army's recommendations. In defense of the 99th, General Davis maintained that performance in a single combat campaign did not merit the removal of an entire squadron. He argued for continuing the deployment of the 99th and 332nd for combat. Truman Gibson reminded committee members that other white squadrons also did not perform well in their introduction into combat. Gibson also highlighted the fact that the 99th was introduced to combat without combat-experienced flight leaders. To avoid an impasse on racial issues, McCloy recommended that committee members hold their opinions until they interviewed Colonel Davis.[22]

Gibson and General Davis were well aware of the ramifications of the McCloy Committee discussion and its prospective impact on the ability of black citizens to participate in the war effort. They both knew that limited involvement in the war effort by blacks would delay the march toward the acquisition of civil rights. General Davis, Sr., the father of the ranking black officer in the Army Air Force, must have felt that the military careers of his son and many others were at stake. The future of blacks in the military and, to a certain extent, the future of the civil rights movement, hinged on the testimony of Colonel Davis.

The McCloy Committee, representing the secretary of war, was faced with three sets of recommendations on what to do with the 99th. G-3 of General Marshall's staff wanted to retain the 99th and deploy the 332 Fighter Group, to give the experiment a stern test. The Operations Division of the Army Air Force wanted the 99th and the 332nd assigned to a rear defense area, for coastal patrol. Operations also wanted the activation and training of the black medium bombardier group terminated. General Arnold, Chief Commander of the Army Air Force concurred with Operations. However, he wanted the recommendations to be approved by President Roosevelt.

Before the meeting with Colonel Davis, McCloy negotiated a consensus among the commanding officers of the Air Force, the G-3 Chief of Staff; and the Operations Division of the Air Force. McCloy recommended that they seek input from Eisenhower's Chief of Staff, Gen. Walter B. Smith. General Smith, however, referred the problem to the theatre command.[23] For the Air Force, the theatre command was under General Spaatz, who endorsed the original Air Force recommendation to move the 99th and the 332nd to the rear defense area and to disband training of the 477th Medium Bombardment Group.

At the request of the McCloy Committee, Colonel Davis appeared for testimony on 16 October 1943, at the Pentagon. Colonel Davis was well prepared for the presentation. He was aware of the *Time* magazine article and was, by the time of the testimony, familiar with the Momyer letter. Colonel Davis was also burdened by the enormity of his task. Whatever anger that was felt toward Momyer and the Air Force had to be submerged. Davis dealt with the specific charges leveled in the Momyer report.

To the charge that the squadron lacked air discipline, Colonel Davis reported that any mistakes made by the squadron were made on the first missions and were due to the inexperience of the command and squadron. He reiterated that on the first mission the squadron, in its first encounter with the enemy, broke from a flight formation of sixes to twos. In response to the charge of avoiding primary targets in favor of less dangerous secondary targets, Davis rebutted that when his squadron was assigned to a mission they completed it, and that on the mission in question, the weather, which could be documented, was a factor. No secondary target was involved. In rebuttal to the charge that he requested leave for his men after twenty-eight sorties, Colonel Davis stated that his squadron of twenty-six men operated continuously for two months without having the luxury of replacement pilots that the whites had. Therefore, his pilots had to fly up to six missions per day, without relief. The other squadrons he asserted, consisted of thirty to thirty-five men. In response to the charge that his men lacked aggression, Colonel Davis reported that when his squadron was given a bombing mission, they bombed the target. Davis added that every man in the 99th was aware that the success of the 99th would impact the status of blacks in the Army Air Force and the army as a whole and that each man performed his job as if the race depended on him.[24]

It was difficult to gauge whether Colonel Davis's performance in front of the McCloy Committee was the sole determining factor in delaying the implementation of the Army Air Forces plans to reassign the 99th, place the 332nd on coastal patrol, and disband the medium bombardier group. When the army was queried by the black press about its redeployment plans for the 99th, the official word from the army was that it was continuing its plans to leave the 99th in the Mediterranean theatre, and that it would deploy the 332 there, as well. The army also continued to announce its plans to activate the medium bombardier squadron. The manner of Colonel Davis's presentation was a factor. His West Point bearing and his intimate knowledge of military protocol during stressful presentations served him and, ultimately, Negro airmen well. On 27 October 1943, General Arnold gave the order to proceed with the bombardment group, and training continued for the replacements for the 99th and 332.[25] Colonel Davis focused on his new assignment, which was to get the 332nd, stationed at Selfridge Air Base, trained, disciplined, and combat-ready.

When Colonel Davis arrived at Selfridge in September 1943, he inherited a less than enviable situation. For the men of the 332nd Fighter Group and related service groups, 1943 was a tragic and tumultuous year. The majority of the men in the 332nd were overjoyed to leave the segregated and dehumanizing South for the promised land of the North. The men were shocked and disappointed to find that segregation extended beyond the geographical boundaries of the South. Their new base, Selfridge, located near Detroit, was also racially segregated. Although Michigan had a civil rights law barring discrimination on the basis of race, and army regulations forbade discrimination in the use of base facilities, the base PX, theater, cafeterias, and recreational areas were segregated by race. Housing on base for the officers of the 332nd was nonexistent. Many of the officers had to find residence with willing black families in Detroit. The segregation policy at Selfridge was implemented by the base commander, Col. William Colman, and sanctioned by the commander of the First Air Force, Gen. Frank O. Hunter.[26]

A Georgia-born World War I combat veteran, General Hunter preferred Jim Crow policies to integrated facilities. He felt Jim Crow was best for Army Air Force morale.[27] The presence of a unit of white Women's Army Corps, WACS, at Selfridge strengthened the base command's resolve to segregate the races. After the arrival of the 332nd in March 1943, the WACS were forbidden to converse with men of the 332nd and were escorted to and from duty by white military police. The WACS were not allowed to work the control tower if members of the 332nd were on duty in the tower.[28]

Certain squadrons and service units within the 332nd were stationed 250 miles north of Selfridge at the affiliate base in Oscoda, Michigan. The Oscoda base was used primarily for gunnery practice and was also segregated. The white residents of Iosco and Oscoda counties were not pleased with the presence of a group of black men flying armed P-40s and P-39s over their property. Initially, recreational activities such as the theater, bowling alley, motels, and restaurants in Oscoda were not available to the members of the 332nd. The men had to resort to arranging busloads of women from Saginaw, Flint, and Detroit area churches and Double V Clubs for social events.[29] To make matters worse, Colonel Colman was given a cottage, by an area businessman, near the Oscoda base. Colman intended to use the cottage as a white officer's club. The Colonel had the cottage renovated and stocked with a refrigerator, generator, and cots.[30]

Members of the 332nd stationed at Selfridge were more fortunate to have Detroit less than thirty miles from the base. Officers who had access to Detroit, enjoyed a rich nightlife in Detroit, especially in Paradise Valley. The "Valley" featured several nightclubs where the big name entertainment acts played and beautiful women strayed. Easy access to Detroit probably delayed an explosive situation at Selfridge Field over the officer's club at Lufberry Hall. Black officers who chose to reside on base resided in segregated quarters. Their club was located in the back room of one of the officers' barracks. When all officers had to pay dues for the use of the officer's club at Lufberry Hall, where they were denied membership because of race, friction among races at Selfridge increased. Lufberry Hall became more of an issue when the men were confined to base. During this confinement, when the men tried unsuccessfully to enter the officer's club, protest groups among the officers and enlisted men became organized.[31]

On 5 May 1943, an inebriated Colonel Colman shot and seriously wounded his driver, a black enlisted man named Willie McCrae. The shooting incident attracted enough attention to warrant an investigation by a Michigan congressman, Paul Shafer, a member of the House

Military Affairs Committee. Congressman Shafer divulged that Colonel Colman and others at Selfridge Field had been under investigation for their connection with permanent assignment of military personnel to Selfridge in exchange for money. Shafer was convinced that Colman shot McCrae with the intent to cover up and impede any investigation into the assignment for pay scheme.[32] Colman was immediately arrested, taken into custody, and placed under psychiatric care. McCrae was hospitalized in critical condition and was unavailable for comment. A key witness, Sgt. Myron Collins, was also placed under arrest. Shafer believed that the army was "whitewashing an unsavory mess."[33] Further investigation uncovered two Detroit civilians who were charged in Federal Court in Detroit for conspiracy to take money from draftees with intent to obtain permanent assignment at Selfridge. Congressman Shafer claimed to have information linking the two civilians with Colman, and he requested the House committee to investigate.[34]

Tensions among the black airmen ran high regarding the shooting, to the extent that, the next night, a black sentry shot a white civilian attempting to enter the base illegally. The army responded immediately by sending War Department investigators to the scene. Julius Amberg, legal aide to Robert Patterson, Undersecretary of War, was sent to Selfridge for the duration of the investigation. Col. Franklin Babcock, of the Inspector General's Office, and several assistants were also dispatched to the base to investigate the McCrae shooting.[35] After a brief investigation, the First Air Force Command decided to court-martial Colonel Colman. The trial was scheduled for September 1943.[36]

Shortly after the McCrae shooting, tragedy struck the 332nd. In May and June 1943, Lts. Wilmeth Sidat Singh, Jerome Edwards, Nathaniel Hill, and Luther L. Blakeney were lost to plane accidents due to a combination of weather over Lake Huron and, allegedly, faulty equipment. Lieutenant Singh allegedly flew a P-40 that was used by the American Volunteer Flying Tiger Squadron in China in 1940. These planes were fatigued and had a tendency to overheat and stall. The 332nd had several of the old P-40s to train in at Tuskegee and at Selfridge, until they received P-39s later in the summer of 1943.[37] Some of the planes had been known to have logged over a hundred missions before they were sent to the states to be used as trainers. Col. Samuel Westbrook admitted, after Singh's death, that the men had complained about the condition of the trainers and that he had requested, to no avail, new equipment from Army Air Force supplies. Colonel Westbrook was relieved of duty shortly after the death of Sidat Singh.[38]

On 20 June 1943, violence broke out in nearby Detroit. The nation experienced the year's worse race riot. Tensions between the races in

Detroit had been strained for several years, dating back to the time when a black physician, Oswan Sweet, had shot into a white mob while defending his home in a white neighborhood. As late as 1943, blacks and whites were migrating en masse to Detroit, competing for jobs in the war industry. Between 1940 and 1943, as many as 50,000 blacks, along with 300,000 whites, migrated to Detroit from the South.[39] The whites brought with them their racist concepts and indoctrinations. With real housing shortages in Detroit, competition for housing among the newcomers was fierce. To exacerbate the problem, the city of Detroit built federal housing projects that had only limited slots for black families. As blacks struggled with housing discrimination, patience and order wore thin. Early in 1943, violence broke out at a federally funded housing project called the Sojourner Truth Housing Project.[40] It was only a matter of time before violence would engulf the Motor City.

The riot came during a hot night on 20 June 1943, at Belle Isle, an island park on the east side of Detroit. Although no one has ever reported, with complete accuracy, the incident which ignited the riot, there were rumors ranging from an altercation between a white and a black, after a traffic accident, that escalated, allegedly, into a fist fight between young gangs of whites and blacks, to a black boy chased by fifty whites, to a baby being thrown into the Detroit River. It was substantiated, however, that white and black mobs fought hand-to-hand. Innocent persons, both white and black, were attacked. During the evening of June 20th, white mobs converged on Black Bottom, the black section of town, and assaulted blacks at random, burning and turning over cars and buses. When the blacks fought back, the Detroit police, who were unwilling or incapable of stopping whites from invading the black community, used excessive force against them. There were eyewitness reports of police officers returning several thousand rounds of gunfire and tear gas into a building that housed several black families after one of the occupants allegedly fired a shot at the white mob who were throwing bricks at the windows of the building. According to the witnesses, when the residents were force out by the tear gas and the gunfire, they were beaten by the officers and placed under arrested.[41]

By 22 June 1943, President Roosevelt had ordered 1,200 federal troops into Detroit to restore order. By the time the soldiers arrived, 25 persons were dead, 600 injured, and 1,300 arrested. Eighteen of the 25 persons killed were black; the majority, reportedly, killed by police, who were heavily concentrated in the black community.[42]

The base command at Selfridge was prepared for the reaction of the men to the riots. Col. William Boyd, the new base commander, and Col.

Robert Selway, new commander of the 332nd, ordered the black airmen at Selfridge and Oscoda confined to base.[43] They knew the airmen were aware of the riot and were anxious to do something. The thought of black pilots buzzing over Detroit with armed P-39s, in defense of blacks, was disturbing, if not frightening. A group of black men from the quartermaster unit at Ft. Custer in Battle Creek acquired some guns and ammunition and headed to Detroit to help out their families. They were apprehended by the State police.[44] White sentries were brought from Ft. Custer to surround the quarters of the 332nd and service units at Selfridge Field Air Base. The Selfridge Field Command was afraid that black fighter pilots were too close to sympathetic ears in Detroit.[45]

After the riots, in the late summer of 1943, Selway instituted a rigorous training schedule for the 332nd. His motto, "Get to your damn guns," was posted all over the base. The group pilots, according to Selway's interview in the press, were averaging a total of 500 hours per month. When Selway took command, the hours increased to 600 hours per month.[46] The increase in training time meant more time on base and less time in Detroit. With more time on base, access to the officer's club and other facilities at Selfridge Field came into focus, and organized protest was revived. The men attempted to relieve their anxieties about the riots, their confinement, and the officer's club, by participating in daredevil flights during training. Some of the adventures included looping the Ambassador Bridge in Detroit, flying under the Blue Water Bridge in Port Huron, buzzing chicken farms in Mt. Clemens and mink farms in Oscoda, and flying circles around the tops of tall buildings in downtown Detroit.[47]

By the time Colonel Davis had arrived at Selfridge Field, in September 1943, several assertive, aggressive, and talented men had joined the 332nd Fighter Group. These young men, fresh from Tuskegee, were not as reticent as the original members of the 99th to express their displeasure with the segregation. These individuals led several futile attempts in vain to desegregate the officer's club, base theater, mess, PX, and other base facilities. In the theater, the seats for blacks and whites were designated by a white line in the center of the theater. Once seated, the men would employ what they called the "checkerboard" move. When the lights went out blacks and cooperative whites changed seats, so that they would be sitting together. When the lights came on, the manager of the theater would be surprised to find blacks and whites sitting together.[48]

A few of the young officers of the 332nd had reputations that preceded them. Lt. Milton R. Henry, from Philadelphia, was, at the time, one of only a few black men in the South who had gotten away with assaulting a white public transportation officer and lived to talk about it. In Montgomery, Alabama, in the spring of 1942, Henry, traumatized and intolerant of the physical and psychological oppression of blacks in the South, boarded a bus, only to later be told to move to the rear in favor of white passengers. Henry, a soldier preparing to fight for his country, had reached his limit of accommodating Alabama's system of segregation. He found himself walking up to the driver and demanding his nickel back and adding, for emphasis, that he should punch the driver in the mouth, which he then proceeded to do. To the shock of no one, the driver pulled out a .45 caliber handgun, but before he could fire, Henry grabbed his hand and wrestled with him until they fell through the door of the bus and out onto the street. Fortunately for Henry, British cadets in training at Maxwell Field, who were on the bus, rescued Henry from the bus driver and the local police, and remained with him until the military police came to bring him back to Maxwell, where he spent a short time in the stockade. He was then sent to Signal Corps Officer Candidate School in Ft. Monmouth, New Jersey, and arrived at Tuskegee as an officer in October 1942. Lieutenant Henry was a key factor in organizing airmen for the purpose of protesting segregation at Selfridge Field in 1943 and 1944.[49]

Concurrent to Colonel Davis's arrival at Selfridge was the court-martial trial of Colonel Colman. Colonel Colman was being tried on twenty-eight charges, including shooting Pvt. William McCrae, being drunk four times on duty, misappropriating military equipment, accepting the use of a vacation lodge from a contractor, using army employees for private work, and committing fraud by transferring and promoting men to and at Selfridge.[50] Prior to the court-martial trial, rumors were planted that Colman disliked and distrusted blacks and did not want them as drivers. The story was that he shot McCrae while in a drunken rage over seeing a black man as his driver. This story was picked up by the black press, who publicized the upcoming trial with hopes that justice would prevail.[51]

The Colman trial illuminated marital difficulties between Colman and his wife. There were reports that Colman's regular driver, a white enlisted man, was having an affair with Colman's wife. Testimony in the trial corroborated a dispute between Colman and his wife on the night of the McCrae shooting. On that particular night, according to eyewitness testimony, Colman and his wife argued and his wife left him to call the driver. She instructed the driver to pick up her son and drop him by Colman's quarters. For some reason, maybe fear of retribution, the regular driver sent McCrae instead. Reportedly, McCrae was shot as he was about to remove Colman's son from the command vehicle to Colman's personal car. There was testimony to the fact that Colman was drunk and incoherent.[52] In addition, there was testimony from physicians and psychiatrists that Colman had been under psychiatric care in the past, and that alcohol may have exacerbated Colman's erratic behavior. Colman testified that he did not remember shooting McCrae or the details of that evening. Colman was convicted on five of the twenty-eight charges: careless discharge of a firearm and drunk and disorderly conduct on four occasions. He was found not guilty of violating the 93rd Article of War for assault and battery with intent to do bodily harm upon Private McCrae. Colman was sentenced to a demotion to the permanent rank of captain, and banned from the promotion list for three years. Colonel Colman left the service a short time later.[53]

The national press, black and white, charged gross injustice. Several newspapers carried editorials slamming the verdict, contrasting the Colman case with other harsh verdicts given black servicemen for lesser crimes. The *Baltimore Afro-American* related the case of black soldiers who were given up to fifteen years for firing shots in a town in Mississippi where no one was even hurt. The *Chicago Sun* editorialized "the court-martial has done a grievous injury to the good name of the armed services to the cause of interracial harmony, and simple justice."[54] The light sentence only strengthened the resolve of the men of the 332nd to protest segregation and discrimination at Selfridge Field. They were pleased with the assignment of Colonel Davis to the command and they hoped he could bring about some change for the better.

On 17 October 1943, three weeks after the court-martial of Colonel Colman, General Hunter addressed the officers of the 332nd, stressing the need for discipline and competent performance in preparation for the war. Hunter announced that the Army Air Force was not a social laboratory for integration purposes for civilian appeasement, and that any protest of the army's segregation policy was a problem that affected overall military readiness. General Hunter pledged that his command would do everything necessary to prepare the 332nd for combat.[55]

In the week prior to General Hunter's visit, General Davis, Sr., representing the Inspector General's Office, and Truman Gibson, representing the McCloy Committee, visited Selfridge to review the status of training, preparedness, and condition of morale. Although General Davis heard complaints from Lieutenant Henry and others about the segregated conditions at Selfridge Field and the base and group commanders' unwillingness to adhere to army regulations banning discrimination in the use of base facilities by officers, General Davis reported that there was no discrimination at Selfridge Air Base. General Davis also reported, incredibly, that blacks of the 332nd and whites of the 403rd trained together and that there was no discrimination in the dining room, PX, or the theater.[56] What General Davis and Truman Gibson participated in was an integrated dinner given in their honor. It would have been embarrassing for the army to refuse to allow the ranking black officer, first black general, and a representative of the secretary of war to dine with the all-white base command. What General Davis and Mr. Gibson saw was a segregated theater, with blacks on one side and whites on the other. The white and black officers did not share dining room accommodations. The dining rooms were in separate buildings. The officer's club at Lufberry Hall was temporarily integrated for the visit of the Washington dignitaries.

Technically, General Davis's report to the Inspector General was accurate. There was no discrimination viewed by him or Gibson on that particular visit. In 1943, equal access to segregated facilities of equal quality was considered legal and consistent with the separate but equal doctrine, and in step with War Department philosophy and custom, as specified in the War Department Pamphlet 20-6, "Command of Negro Troops."[57] The men of the 332nd had equal access to segregated and equal facilities, therefore, there was no discrimination.

It was apparent that General Davis, Sr. and Mr. Gibson were weary of the week's events. The fate of the 99th and 332nd still hung on a string of uncertainty. There was still a slight chance of sending an all-black fighter group to the Mediterranean theatre under the command of a West Point man, a black man, the son of the first and only black general in the armed forces. The segregated conditions at Selfridge Field had to be viewed with delicate caution. A negative report from General Davis could have rankled General Hunter and the rest of the Army Air Force Command, who, at that time, were still willing to assign the 99th and the 332nd to coastal patrol in a rear defense area. Such an assignment would effectively negate the contribution of black airmen in the war effort, and the careers of Colonel Davis and other black officers in the army. It appeared that, in the minds of General Davis and Truman Gibson, the war against segregation and discrimination would be best fought on the battlefield, where black officers could prove, unequivocally, that they were competent and patriotic, and deserving of equal rights.

Upon Colonel Davis's arrival at Selfridge Field, the white command structure of the 332nd was converted to a black command.[58] From October to 20 December 1943, Colonel Davis, along with several veterans of the 99th who returned with him in September, including Lts. Charles Dryden, Louis Purnell, Lee Rayford, Walter Lawson, and

Graham Smith, and those who arrived shortly thereafter: Capt. William Campbell and Lt. Spann Watson, shaped the three squadrons of the 332nd Fighter Group into a tight and efficient unit. Several members of the group tried to enter the officer's club, however, and were ordered out. Eventually, without the active support of the new Group Command, and with Detroit nearby, the officer's club and the desegregation of other facilities on the base became a secondary issue to combat preparedness.[59]

On 24 December 1943, the 332nd left for the Mediterranean theatre. When they reached Camp Patrick Henry, the embarkation point in Newport News, Virginia, the men discovered that they were to sit in the segregated section of the movie house. The men objected. Expecting to fight and possibly die for their country, they felt that they were entitled to sit where they pleased. The proprietor of the theater demanded that the soldiers obey the laws and customs of the establishment. The men, who were issued .45 caliber hand guns, threatened to take their seats and desegregate the theater by force. A call was made to Colonel Davis, who impressed upon the proprietor the wisdom of relaxing his segregated policy. The men of the 332nd desegregated the movie house at Camp Patrick Henry.[60] The 332nd left Camp Patrick Henry for Italy on 31 December 1943.

Shortly before the 332nd was deployed for combat in Italy, another all-black fighter squadron, the 553rd, was activated to provide replacement pilots for the 99th Pursuit Squadron and the 332nd Fighter Group. Lts. Dryden and Watson were chosen to remain as instructors for the new squadron. The men of the 553rd squadron and the bomber pilots of the newly activated 477th Medium Bombardment Group remained at Selfridge Field. The issue of the officer's club and segregated facilities at Selfridge Field resurfaced. This time, the young officers who had led the protest earlier in the year were joined by veterans of the 99th, who had experienced combat and were not about to accept separate facilities on an army air base.[61] 1944 was to be a pivotal year for the nonviolent protest movement generated at Selfridge Field.

On New Year's Day 1944, the officers of the 553rd and the 477th implemented the first phase of their strategy for desegregating the officers' club at Selfridge Field. The plan was to send a group of three officers, at different time intervals, to gain admittance to the club. The men were familiar with the Articles of War and the penalty for violating them. They knew that if they approached the club in a large group, all of them could be court-martialed for inciting a dispute or riot, or even worse—mutiny. If they approached the club in groups of threes, at different time intervals, their actions would appear incidental. The objective of the first group was to go as far as they could in gaining admittance to the club without being arrested and court-martialed. They were to report their progress, or lack thereof, to the group, upon their return from the club. The first group, which included Milton Henry and Lloyd Hathcott, gained admittance, were seated, and were about to order when the base commander, Colonel Boyd, approached them and, with very offensive language, ordered them out of the club. The three men returned to their quarters to report the incident to the group. The group proceeded to implement phase two.[62]

The next day, 2 January 1944, the men were ready to enact phase two when Col. Charles Gayle, the commanding officer of the 553rd Squadron, met with all of the officers of the squadron and told them that if they set foot into the officer's club, he would court-martial them for inciting a riot. Since the officers of the group did not consider this a direct or legal order not to attend the club, they sent the second group of three officers to the officer's club later that night. This group, which included Charles Dryden, Robert O'Neal, and W. H. Johnson, was met inside the door of the club by Colonel Gayle, who immediately issued a direct order to leave the club. The officers complied with the order and returned to the group, and it was decided that phase three was to be deployed as soon as possible.[63]

About a week later, the week of 6 January 1944, Lieutenant Henry took leave to visit Philadelphia. While there, Henry took an excursion to Mitchell Field in New York, headquarters of the First Air Force Command, to file a complaint about the racial discrimination and the unfair treatment the black officers were receiving at Selfridge Field. After meeting with the Judge Advocate and the inspector general, Lieutenant Henry, unsatisfied with the response he received, traveled to Washington, where he called on the secretary of war's office, who referred him to one of the undersecretaries, Robert Patterson.[64] Concurrently, the other officers in the protest group contacted the black press to lodge complaints of racism and discrimination at Selfridge Field. These reports were well received by the press, who were disposed to distrust the Army Office of Information staff.

It was during his visit to the office of the secretary of war that Lieutenant Henry must have made an impression. Three weeks later, the Army Inspector General's office dispatched General Davis and Col. Harvey Shoemaker to Selfridge Field to review the conditions and charges of racism and discrimination perpetrated against the black officers.[65]

❂   ❂   ❂

About one month had passed since Colonel Davis had left the 99th in Sicily. The Squadron moved to Italy and was commanded by Maj. George "Spanky" Roberts, a natural and capable leader and an excellent pilot. The 99th was attached to the 79th Fighter Group in Foggia, under the command of Col. Robert Bates. It was most ironic that, while the men of the black airmen were fighting for freedom from racism on the home front, the men of the 99th were, unlike their previous segregated experiences with the 33rd and the 324th fighter groups, welcomed as an equal squadron, along with the 79th. The men of the four squadrons ate together, flew missions together, attended briefings together in the cold and the mud in Foggia, and later in Madna. The 99th benefited from the combat experience of the 79th Fighter Group and acquired confidence in their own capabilities. Although the 99th lacked the experience gained by other squadrons of the 79th, they soon proved to be as effective and contributed as much as the other squadrons to the war effort.[66] On 30 November 1943, the 79th flew a record twenty-six missions in one day. The pilots and ground crew of the 99th participated in nine of the twenty-six. On that impressive day the ground crew of the 99th worked around the clock in cold, wet, and muddy weather, repairing P-40 fighter planes, their props, engines, guns, and instruments.[67]

The 99th, operating as a part of the 79th, developed expertise as dive bombers, and started to receive complements for proficiency, along with the other squadrons of the 79th. By the time the 99th moved with the 79th to Capodichino, near Naples, to prepare for the Allied ground invasion of Anzio in January 1944, General Spaatz, commander of the 12th Air Force, was impressed enough with their performance that he asked General Arnold to send two more fighter squadrons to join with the 99th, to form a fighter group.[68] Arnold's Air Staff commander, General Craig, informed Arnold on 11 January that the 332nd was on their way to join the Twelfth Air Force. On that day, all the proposals for the reassignment of the 99th and the 332nd to rear defense areas and the termination of the activation of the 477th Medium Bombardment Group were canceled by the War Department, but not by the Army Air Force.[69]

In early January 1944, Walter White, of the NAACP, made his sojourn to Europe to investigate the complaints and condition of black soldiers, including those of the 99th, on the war front. While in Europe, White was discouraged by the harsh and unfair treatment given the black soldier for minor wartime offenses, compared to whites who committed more serious crimes. While visiting Naples, the civil rights activist was appalled when he saw posters on billboards that, when translated, stated that

> Italian women must not associate with Negro soldiers because the Negro is an inferior human being and must live in America only among his own and the machine gun will cut down the prostitute who sells her honor of her race, and the people will seek revenge upon her and her black son when this crime has been brought to life.[70]

White brought this to the attention of the Italian authorities, who denied any association with the posters. The chief of staff of the Mediterranean theatre ordered an investigation. The insidious work was attributed to a colonel and two enlisted men who, according to the general, were court-martialed. Mr. White also found public notices in hotels stating that blacks were not welcome. These, also, were the work of racist American soldiers. The Italians denied knowledge of any such bigoted policies.[71] Members of the 99th were aware of these conditions, and many chose to forgo rest and relaxation assignments off base until they were stateside or until a rest camp was established by the 332 Fighter Group, on their arrival in February and March of 1944.[72]

When White caught up with 99th, he was pleased to see the squadron integrated into the combat and social activities of the 79th. When the 79th celebrated the anniversary of their combat deployment with a party in Naples, the NAACP secretary was heartened as he witnessed the whites of the 79th disobey, with impunity, an order by the theatre commander, Gen. Jacob Devers, prohibiting blacks and whites from socializing where there was dancing.[73] Mr. White was so moved by the success of the 99th in an integrated fighter group that he recommended in his report and recommendations to General Eisenhower and the War Department on the status of black troops in Europe, that the 99th continue with the 79th and that another integrated unit be established under the command of Colonel Davis. In the same report, White did not support the establishment of an all-black fighter group.[74]

Mr. White happened to visit the 99th during the Anzio invasion. The Anzio mission was a critical but dangerous mission for the Allies. In order to free Rome, the Allies had to go through Anzio, and the best way to Anzio was by surprise. The Allies faked an invasion to southern France, then swung around toward Anzio. The Axis forces were forced to entrench in the mountain ranges surrounding and overlooking the beachheads and valleys eight miles outside of Anzio.

When the allied troops landed, on 22 January 1944, they discovered that the beachhead, itself, was small and flat, making any troop movements easily detectable and within range of all of the Axis defensive fire power.[75] The German and other Axis troops were determined not to lose this position. From their defensive positions, some encamped in monasteries and connecting tunnels, they bombed the beachhead continuously, making it difficult for ground troops to advance. The 79th and other fighter groups of the 12th Air Force were assigned missions to support the ground troops by strafing and divebombing railyards, troops, gunnery placements, bridges, and communication centers, with the intention of isolating the battle to a confined area, and strangling off reinforcements and supplies.

For five days the 99th patrolled the beachheads to protect convoys of men, supplies, and equipment. They encountered few enemy aircraft until 27 January 1944. On that day, Capt. Clarence Jamison led a flight of twelve planes on a patrol mission, when they sighted about twenty-four enemy planes and, in their eagerness for action, jumped on them. They fought furiously for about five minutes and, in that amount of time, five enemy aircraft were destroyed. All twelve planes in Jamison's flight returned to a celebration.[76] Later on the same day, a patrol flight led by Lt. James Wiley spotted enemy aircraft and engaged them in a quick but deadly air battle that cost the Axis at least three aircraft. The squadron lost Lt. Samuel Bruce during the dogfight.[77]

Despite the loss of Bruce, the men of the 99th Pursuit Squadron were ecstatic and full of confidence over their success, after going almost six months without destroying an enemy aircraft. The next day, 28 January 1944, while on beachfront patrol, a mission led by Capt. Charles Hall ended with four German planes being shot down.[78] Captain Hall was given credit for destroying two, thus becoming the first black American pilot in the war to down three enemy planes. The success of the 79th Fighter Group, in general, and the success of the 99th during the Anzio missions of 27 and 28 January 1944 brought General Cannon, commander of the North African Training Command to the base at Capodichino to congratulate the members of the 99th.[79] The success of Anzio gave the men of the 99th confidence in themselves and each other. General Cannon's congratulatory visit was the Army Air Force's grudging acknowledgment that black fighter pilots and maintenance men could contribute effectively to the war effort.

In late January 1944, General Davis and Colonel Shoemaker completed their report on the charges of racial discrimination at Selfridge. General Davis took this opportunity to disclose racial discrimination against black officers by charging that the base commander denied black officers access to the officer's club, a violation of army regulation and War Department instructions. General Davis also added that the base commander used "insulting language in conveying his views on the subject of Negro officers."[80] In addition, the report mentioned Colonel Gayle's threat to court-martial men under his command for inciting a riot if they entered the officer's club. The Inspector General accepted the report and turned it over to the War Department, which, in turn, distributed the report to the Army Air Force Command for their review and recommendation.

The Army Air Force issued a report by its Inspector General stating that "definite directions that recreational and social activities on each base, whereupon colored and white troops are stationed jointly, should be provided and handled so as to avoid charges of discrimination or prejudice towards members of either race."[81] The statement meant that the base commander at Selfridge had circumvented War Department policy by maintaining separate but equal recreational and social activities on the base to ward off charges of discrimination. The report also said that construction of a new gym, service club, and officer's club for black airmen had begun. The War Department viewed the Air Force's response as inadequate, in light of the 1940 Army Regulation 210-10 that outlawed segregation and discrimination at officer's clubs.[82]

In February of 1944, the War Department asked for a follow-up review. The Air Force responded that the officer's club, the site of contention, had been closed and, therefore, there was no longer a problem. The Air Force report concluded that the proximity of Detroit, with its "communists and racial agitators among the negroes" was the problem, and that members of the black press were exploiting the racial issues to precipitate racial riots.[83] The report recommended a change in location, such as the Caribbean, where the press and local agitators could not distract the men from training. The report recommended a relocation study be implemented, including analyzing sites within the states that would be conducive to training without interference.[84]

The War Department was under much pressure from civil rights groups and the press to act; 1944 was an election year and the Democrat incumbent administration could not afford to insult a major minority population. Much to General Hunter's chagrin, the War Department ordered the Air Force Command to issue a reprimand to Colonel Boyd, with General Hunter's endorsement.[85]

During the same time period, the War Department, under the advisement of attorney Truman Gibson and Gen. B.O. Davis, Sr. of the McCloy Committee, the War Department distributed a morale-building film entitled "The Negro Soldier." The film, produced in 1943 by Frank

Capra, featured hard working and patriotic black soldiers making their contributions to the war effort. The film depicted civilian blacks as churchgoing, pious, and patriotic, not as lawless rioters. The War Department marketed the film to the general public to project the positive image of the black soldier and family, and to the black population to confirm the War Department's intent to use the black soldier in a productive fashion.[86]

The War Department appeared to be moving toward equal treatment of Negro officers. The Army Air Force, however, was intent on circumventing and obstructing vague War Department policy regarding the use of officers clubs and recreational facilities. Consequently, the Boyd reprimand did not sit well with General Hunter. Hunter believed that he had the support of the Air Force Command when he supported Colonel Boyd's officer's club membership policy that excluded black officers. Hunter was told by high-ranking Army Air Force officers, including Chief of Air Staff, Gen. Barney Giles, that he had their "backing 100 percent."[87] Even General Arnold, chief of the Air Force, according to Giles, approved what Hunter called "his order" for the officer's club. General Hunter tried to soften the reprimand by adding that Boyd was acting on orders from his commanding officer and that the commanding officer should also receive a reprimand. The Air Force Command rejected Hunter's plea for a lesser reprimand for Colonel Boyd. In early March 1944, Colonel Boyd was forced to resign and Colonel Gayle was reassigned.[88]

It was apparent that Colonel Boyd would be the public sacrifice for the army's racist policies, which he only obeyed. It was also apparent that in 1944, the Air Force had no inclination to enforce, in all Air Force commands and theatres, the army regulation regarding discrimination and segregation in officer's clubs, unless they were forced to by outside pressure. The War Department was selective, if not indecisive and vague, in its enforcement of the army regulation forbidding segregation and discrimination in the use of officer's clubs in the states and overseas. General Hunter felt that he had the tacit, if not philosophical, support of the Air Force Command Headquarters in continuing his policy of encouraging segregated officer's clubs. Hunter was free to focus his attention on getting rid of the "negro agitators" in his command.[89]

Lt. Milton Henry became a target of General Hunter's First Air Force, and of the U.S. Army Air Force, as soon as he lodged his complaint with the War Department. Lieutenant Henry's every move was monitored by his commanding officer and other officers of the 553rd, and a colonel of the First Air Force Command was even dispatched to Selfridge to assist with an inspection tour in order to spy on Lieutenant Henry.[90]

The case against Lieutenant Henry was initiated on 15 February 1944, when Henry had a heated discussion with a sergeant who neglected to pick Lieutenant Henry up from a designated point at a designated time, as Henry had ordered. Col. Arthur R. DeBolt, First Command Headquarters, overheard the conversation and interrupted, telling Lieutenant Henry, "Joe, go ahead and sell your papers," and then reported the incident to Colonel Gayle, Lieutenant Henry's commanding officer. Colonel Gayle summoned Lieutenant Henry to his office and asked what had happened.[91] As Lieutenant Henry was explaining the incident, Colonel Gayle interrupted Henry to remind him that at a recent staff meeting officers were told that they would walk, due to a shortage in transportation. Gayle continue by asking Henry how he expected to get promotions and remain in the army with his attitude. Lieutenant Henry, fighting to maintain his composure, retorted that he had gotten his promotion through initiative and integrity, and that the white officers present could not say that. Colonel Gayle then asked DeBolt's opinion of the situation. DeBolt felt that the matter should be dropped, but that Lieutenant Henry should exercise more discretion if he wanted a career in the Army Air Force. DeBolt described the Air Force as a small organization, expanding fast, where promotions could be had fast because of the Air Force's status as a minority force. DeBolt added that if Henry could not change his attitude, he should leave the army. To this, Lieutenant Henry responded that the Russian and French revolutions were initiated by minorities and that he, too, would some day be in a position to dictate. Colonel Gayle dismissed Lieutenant Henry by saying that he did not see how Henry could receive further promotions or remain in the army, with his attitude.[92]

It was highly unusual for a commanding officer to summon and question a subordinate officer's handling of a disagreement with a sergeant without hearing the subordinate officer's complaint. While Lieutenant Henry's discourse with Colonel Gayle and Colonel DeBolt was not directed in anger, the episode proved incriminating. Gayle and DeBolt considered Lieutenant Henry's response to their questioning disrespectful to a superior officer which was a court-martial offense.[93] The Army Air Force had a wartime conduct violation they could use in establishing a case against Milton Henry.

Unfortunately, a recurrence of a chronic illness that had put Lieutenant Henry in the hospital for part of 1942, late 1943, and as recently as February 1944, struck during the time that the Army Air Force was building its case. Lieutenant Henry suffered from what was then called Boecks Sarcoidosis, a disease that enlarges the lymph nodes in large glands in the body, such as the chest and the neck. Symptoms associated with sarcoidosis were loss of weight, pain, and numbness in extremities after exertion, tightness in the chest, shortness of breath, chronic fatigue, a cough, and difficulty with vision. In his visits to hospitals, Lieutenant Henry complained of most of these symptoms. Because of these bouts of recurring symptoms, the medical examining board of the most recent treating hospital, Percy Jones Hospital in Battle Creek, Michigan, ruled that Lieutenant Henry could not be assigned full duty as a fighter pilot.[94] With his flying status limited, Henry was assigned the position of assistant communications officer responsible for radio maintenance, homing stations, and equipment in the runway control tower.[95]

Lieutenant Henry had confided to his fellow officers in the barracks that he was not well and had difficulty waking up in the morning, and asked them to wake him. When those wake-up attempts proved futile, Lieutenant Henry appeared late for duty. During one two-week period in mid-March, Lieutenant Henry was reported absent from duty at his post and absent without leave seven times.[96] When questioned about his tardiness and absenteeism, Lieutenant Henry replied in an irritable manner, often attributable to the illness. This irritability was misconstrued by his superior officers as disrespect. The new squadron commander who replaced Colonel Gayle, Col. Sam Triffy, assumed the same role as his predecessor in building a case against Lieutenant Henry. Colonel Triffy, on one occasion on 9 March 1944, asked Col. W. R. Morgan, Chief of Staff, First Fighter Command, to listen in on a phone conversation between Maj. Joseph E. Price of the 553rd and an "impudent" Lieutenant Henry. Major Price was attempting to find out why Lieutenant Henry had been absent from duty.[97]

As a consequence of his "disrespect to superior officers" and the seven days of tardiness and absenteeism from duty, on 21 March 1944, Lieutenant Henry was charged with violating the 61st, 63rd, and 96th Articles of War. On 22 March 1944, he was placed under administrative restriction to Selfridge Field to await court-martial. By the command of General Hunter, on 10 April 1944, the Henry case was referred to Capt. James W. Redden, Trial Judge Advocate, for court-martial.[98]

The court-martial of Lt. Milton R. Henry convened on 24 April 1944, at Selfridge Field. Lieutenant Henry was represented by civilian counsel, Elvin L. Davenport and Francis M. Dent. Henry retained military counsel, Lt. Edward K. Nichols, Jr.[99] The counsel for Lieutenant Henry challenged the presence of Capt. James Pughsley on the court for cause. Lieutenant Henry felt that Captain Pughsley, an older black man, could not be impartial since he and Pughsley had argued on several occasions.

The court voted to retain Pughsley. Henry's counsel peremptorily challenged Pughsley, and he was excused from the court.[100] Trial Judge Advocate Redden peremptorily challenged Maj. James Ramsey, a medical officer and one of the few blacks on the court. Major Ramsey was excused.[101]

Lieutenant Henry pleaded not guilty to all of the charges. Throughout the trial, Lieutenant Henry's counsel argued that Lieutenant Henry was not totally responsible for his chronic absenteeism during the period in question. His counsel cited his illness as a key factor in Henry's inability to report for duty. The counsel produced physicians who stated, in their opinion, that Lieutenant Henry, with his illness, probably should not have be inducted into the army. Two physicians who treated Lieutenant Henry at Percy Jones Hospital recommended that Lieutenant Henry be assigned to limited duty, and one psychologist from Percy Jones Hospital testified that Lieutenant Henry should not be in the army in his current state of mind and recommended that Lieutenant Henry be retired from the army.[102] Radiology experts, medical internists, and physicians experienced in treating sarcoidosis, agreed that x-rays illustrated no improvement in Lieutenant Henry's condition from September 1943 to February 1944. All of the physicians who testified agreed that chronic fatigue was a common symptom of sarcoidosis.[103] In addition, three officers who had known and resided in the officer barracks with Henry prior to and during the period in question testified that Henry had requested that they wake him because he had difficulty getting up and getting to duty on time. The three officers stated under oath that they had made attempts, to no avail, to wake Henry.[104]

The counsel for Lieutenant Henry challenged the charge of being disrespectful to a superior officer by countering that Lieutenant Henry's demeanor during the conversation in question was not disrespectful and that what he had actually said was taken out of context. The counsel made an attempt to depict Lieutenant Henry as a talented young black officer, frustrated with his illness and the army's attempts at racial discrimination and unable to control his physical and emotional response to his predicament.[105]

The prosecution set out to depict Lieutenant Henry as "impudent, disrespectful," and arrogant, to the point of being derelict in his duty to the army. The prosecution acknowledged Lieutenant Henry's illness, but contended that the disease did not render Lieutenant Henry incapacitated to the point of being absent from his station. The prosecution presented several witnesses, including Colonel Gayle, Colonel DeBolt, and Colonel Triffy to corroborate their contention that Lieutenant

Henry represented himself in a disrespectful manner when questioned by superior officers.[106] The trial Judge Advocate sought to establish proof of Lieutenant Henry's unexcused absenteeism by examining several witnesses who testified to Lieutenant Henry's whereabouts during the period in question.[107]

In rebuttal to expert medical witnesses for the defense, the prosecution brought forth the 553rd flight surgeon and a medical officer, an internist from Connecticut, who both testified that Lieutenant Henry's illness was not severe enough to keep him from reporting for duty in a punctual manner.[108] The internist from Connecticut based his medical opinion on his examination of Lieutenant Henry on 22 April 1944, two days before the start of the court-martial. The internist also admitted that x-rays shown to him of Lieutenant Henry's sarcoid condition, from September 1943 to February 1944, indicated no appreciable change in the prevalence of the condition.[109]

Nevertheless, Lt. Milton R. Henry was found guilty of all charges and was discharged from the army on 10 August 1944, upon the signature of President Roosevelt.[110]

General Hunter appeared at Selfridge shortly after the trial ended. All of the black officers of the fighter squadrons, bombardment group, and attached service units stationed at Selfridge were ordered to the base theater. Hunter wanted his message to the black officers to be unequivocal. In his address, General Hunter warned the men, in an arrogant, very callous, and insensitive manner,

> this country is not ready or willing to accept a colored officer as the equal of a white one. You are not in the Army to advance your race. Your prime purpose should be in taking your training and fighting for your country. As for racial agitators, they will be weeded out and dealt with.[111]

It was obvious that Milton Henry was one of the agitators weeded out. The black officers were enraged and insulted, and vowed to step up the officer's club protest, but General Hunter was a step ahead of them. The officer's club remained closed, and the men were temporarily grounded and ordered confined to Selfridge Field for about a week. On 5 May 1944, without prior orders or notice, under darkness of night, the men of the 553rd boarded a train headed east and the men of the 477th boarded a train headed south.[112]

The 553rd officers were elated to learn the train was headed east through Canada toward New York. The officers relaxed by playing card games and sipping whiskey smuggled aboard the train. Some officers even prepared telegrams to be sent to relatives, informing them of the good news—no more segregation. Their elation was short-lived, however, when they discovered the train had switched tracks and was heading south. To their disappointment, the train proceeded south until it reached Walterborro, South Carolina. As the train neared the depot, the men noticed that on both sides of the train there were white armed sentries in full battle dress every twenty feet.[113]

The black officers of the 477th were taken south by train to Louisville, Kentucky, and Ft. Knox, and then to a tiny air base inside Ft. Knox called Godman Field.[114] Godman was four to five times smaller than Selfridge Field, with runways too short for bombers. Godman Field was also surrounded by Ft. Knox. The Air Force's public rationale for the two moves was predicated on poor flying conditions, winter weather, smoke from industrial centers, and other hazards and interruptions.[115] The rationale gleaned from research shows that the Air Force accomplished what it had wished for in the 1943 Air Inspector recommendations included in its study of War Department charges of racial discrimination at Selfridge—complete isolation of black airmen from local agitators and the press, and the placement of the men in a local environment with a disposition to control and contain blacks through state and local segregation laws.[116]

When the 553rd settled on the base in Walterboro, they found a completely segregated officer's barracks, gym, mess, PX, and theater. They also discovered that they had an officer's club to themselves, compliments of the white officers, who rented a private club off-base in town, rather than desegregate their club at Walterboro.[117]

The men of 477th were segregated at Godman in the same manner. The officer's club at Godman was not a major issue because the white officers of the 477th accepted the offer of the other white officers at Ft. Knox to join their private officer's club.[118] Fortunately for the black officers of the 477th, Louisville was in close proximity and provided social outlets in a manner similar to Detroit. Louisville, however, was segregated in every way. Housing for black officers and their wives was a serious issue at Godman. There were only four housing units on Godman Field, and they were occupied by civilian base employees. The married couples were limited to Louisville, thirty-five miles away. White officers and their wives, however, had access to housing in Ft. Knox, which surrounded Godman Field.[119]

In Walterboro, there were few social outlets in a segregated town for the airmen of the 553rd. Restaurants, buses, and theaters were segregated. General Hunter and the Air Force made sure the men of the 477th and the 553 had no distractions in their preparation for war.

The situation in Walterboro was unbearable for most of the black officers in the 553rd. As the year wore on and the training became more and more monotonous, local friction was inevitable. At Godman, black officers in the 477th, especially those with combat experience, found themselves on the promotion treadmill, being passed up and supervised by young whites. Whenever a white officer was promoted to another assignment, Colonel Selway, supported by the Air Force Command, would get another white officer in his place.[120] This promotion lockout would be the seed of discontent in the following year.

✪　　✪　　✪

The 332nd Fighter Group landed in Italy on 3 February 1944 and found that they were assigned coastal patrol with the 62nd Fighter Wing of the 12th Air Force. The 332nd Fighter Group consisted of three squadrons, the 100th, the 301st, and the 302d. The 100th, under the command of West Point graduate Capt. Robert Tresville, was operational on 5 February 1944 and flying convoy missions out of Montecorvino near Naples. The other two squadrons, the 301st, led by Capt. Charles Debow (and later Capt. Lee Rayford), and the 302nd, led by Lt. Melvin "Red" Jackson, were operational by 15 February at the Montecorvino base.[121] Colonel Davis, still weary from his close call at the Pentagon, viewed the assignment as an insult and the result of recommendations from the Mediterranean Air Force theatre command, adamantly opposed to giving black fighter pilots an opportunity to participate, productively, in the war. The coastal patrol and protection of supply and equipment convoys headed to Anzio, however, were vitally important to the planned offensive on Monte Cassino.[122]

The attack on Cassino was designed to choke off the supply routes of the Germans and Axis allies to this part of Italy. The rationale was based on the strategy that, if the Axis members were cut off from reinforcements, a massive ground and air offensive could push the Germans northward, where they could be squeezed by Allied troops pushing from the east and the north. In addition, the fall of Cassino would facilitate the fall of Rome, a great psychological and strategic loss for the Axis powers. The offensive on Cassino was called, appropriately, "Operation Strangle."[123]

By 6 March, the squadrons of the 332nd were operating out of the Montecorvino base, flying coastal patrols and escorting convoys in used P-39s, in a support role for Operation Strangle. The P-39s were old planes given to the 12th Air Force Command by the British, who were dissatisfied with the planes' performance. For a short time, the 100th

Fighter Squadron flew brand new P-39Qs, with more firepower. According to 332nd pilots, the P-39 had a problem with stability, due to the engine sitting behind the pilot which caused a problem in the center of gravity. If you crash-landed in the P-39, there was a fear that the engine would push through and crush the pilot, or, because of the rounded belly, it would rock forward and crush the forward cannon. If the plane was loaded with ammunition, it was too light in the nose and too heavy in the tail. The plane responded dangerously to tight turns, and would often stall and spin. It was also considered unstable at slow speeds. Eventually, the Air Force grounded the planes and gave them to the Russian Air Force.[124] Fortunately, during this short period, the 332nd did not encounter many enemy aircraft.

The men of the 99th, however, were in the middle of Operation Strangle. The 99th, along with other fighter and bomber squadrons in the 12th Air Force, bombarded Cassino with over five hundred planes. The air attack was recorded as the most concentrated bombing of a limited area in the history of warfare. Everything was leveled, including the Blessed Monastery, on the top of Mount Cassino.[125] Up until Operation Strangle, the bombing of the Monastery was forbidden. When intelligence reportedly confirmed beliefs that the monastery was an Axis storage facility, with underground tunnels, the 79th Fighter Group, including members of the 99th, blew up the religious landmark.

With the train lines destroyed and only limited air transport capability, the Axis powers resorted to trucking supplies into Rome and other battlefronts south of Rome. Since the roads were full of bomb craters, daylight travel was the only option available for the Axis machine. The supply trucks were easy targets and the fighter pilots of the 99th developed a reputation for being among the most accurate dive bombers and strafing experts in the Mediterranean theatre.[126]

During the first week in April 1944, the 99th was reassigned and attached to the 324th Fighter Group in Cerola, Italy. The men of the 99th were disappointed with their new assignment. They had been able to build relationships with members of the 79th that forged the group into the most effective fighter group in the Mediterranean theatre.[127] The experience also proved, much to the chagrin of the Army Air Force, that white and black pilots and crewmen working together could be effective. The 99th was, for the third time, attached as a separate and segregated squadron in a fighter group. It was clear that the War Department had no intentions of implementing Walter White's recommendation of an integrated fighter group under the command of Colonel Davis. Nevertheless, the squadron, then under the command of Capt. Erwin Lawrence, continued its dive-bombing and strafing missions in Cassino, in preparation for the invasion of Rome.

The 99th developed such a reputation for accuracy, that General Eaker, commander, Mediterranean Allied Air Force, along with Colonel Davis, visited the 99th on 20 April 1944 and told them that, because of their "magnificent showing since coming to the Mediterranean theatre, especially in the Anzio beached operation, you have not only won the plaudits of the Air Force, but you have earned the opportunity to apply your talent to much more advanced work than was at one time planned for you."[128] This was what Colonel Davis wanted to hear. He felt that the men deserved more challenging and productive missions, commensurate with their experience and expertise. Earlier in the month of March, General Eaker had informed Davis of his preliminary plans to use the black fighter group for bomber escort on the Air Force's strategic strikes into German held territories in Eastern Europe and into Germany, itself.[129] About one month after Eaker's visit with the 99th, the 332nd was transferred to the 15th Strategic Air Force, under the command of Gen. Dean Strother. They were placed under the 15th Fighter Command, which consisted of long-range bombers, B-17s and B-24s, and fighter planes, such as the P-47 and P-51.[130]

Unlike the 12th Air Force, which utilized tactical missions aimed at supporting ground troops and knocking out enemy supply lines in the locally affected area, the 15th Fighter Command concentrated on striking and destroying the German war machine, including its military industrial complex, its energy reserves, and its transportation systems. The strategy necessitated long and dangerous flights into the heart of Axis territory. This offensive strategy proved costly. Hundreds of bombers were lost to German fighter planes and defensive ground fire in their retreat from affected targets.[131] The fact was that General Eaker needed as many experienced fighter pilots to fly escort for the bombers as possible. The 332nd was placed on the Adriatic coast of Italy, in Ramitelli, and equipped with used, high mileage P-47s. The switch to the P-47s enabled the pilots of the 332nd to fly limited range escort missions. The "jug," as it was called, could fly faster and perform more efficiently at high altitudes than the P-39s that were previously assigned to the group. The fighter pilots of the 332nd could now compete favorably with the German pilots, who flew planes, such as the Bf 109 and the Fw 190, that were superior to the American P-40 and P-39.[132]

The 332nd was pressed into service almost immediately. Since they had veterans from the 99th with combat experience and officers with over 150 hours of flight time in P-39s and significant time towing targets in the P-47 during training, the transition to the P-47 did not take long. On their first significant escort mission on 9 June 1944, to Munich, Germany, pilots in the 302d Fighter Squadron shot down five enemy aircraft.[133] This was an important test in that it proved that the young black pilots could handle themselves in dogfights. Prior to the first escort mission, Colonel Davis briefed the men on the 15th Air Force Command's (and his) meaning of escort. During the Mediterranean campaign, the 15th Air Force had lost too many bombers to enemy fighters. In General Strother's view, many pilots were looking for kills instead of protecting the bombers.[134] The German pilots had developed a strategy for attacking the bombers. A flight of German fighter planes would act as a decoy to lure kill-happy Allied pilots away from the bombers. Left unprotected, the bombers would be bushwhacked by another flight of previously undetected Germans. Experience taught the Air Force that the German fighters were not disposed to attack a formation of bombers if the fighter escorts remained in close support or in a top and bottom cover formation. Colonel Davis informed his men, in no uncertain terms, that they must stay with and protect the bombers.[135]

Tragedy struck the group on 24 June 1944. While leading a very low-flying flight, to escape coastal radar, on a dive bombing mission near Corsica in treacherous weather, Captain Tresville, reportedly glancing at a map, lost control of his P-47 and hit the water, never to be seen again.[136] On that same flight, the 332nd lost three pilots to the Tyrrhenian Sea. The 332nd experienced glory the next day. On its way to strafe supply routes and troop concentrations in Yugoslavia, the flight, led by Capt. Joseph Elsberry, found themselves in the Triesti Harbor, where they flew into some flak from an enemy destroyer patrolling the harbor. The pilots elected to attack the ship with their machine guns. They attacked in pairs with Lt. Wendell Pruit and Lt. Gwynn Pierson making direct hits, causing the ship to explode. Up to this point in the war, according to published accounts of the mission, no other fighter aircraft had ever sunk a destroyer with machine gun fire.[137]

The 332nd may have been gaining the respect of their white counter-parts in the Mediterranean theatre as competent pilots, but they continued to be segregated militarily and socially from other fighter groups in the theatre. When white officers secured rest and relaxation passes, they had luxurious clubs all over Europe at their disposal, and especially the rest camp at the Isle of Capri. The Isle of Capri rest camp was segregated and officers of the 332nd resented it. A few black officers even resorted to "buzzing" the rest camp sending sand, towels, food, and people flying in every direction.[138]

The 332nd had a beautiful, well-run rest camp of their own, nestled in the mountain overlooking the Bay of Naples in view of Mt. Vesuvius. The view was breathtaking. The rest camp was expertly run by Capt. William Womack, and served as a refuge from the exhaustive efforts of dive bombing, strafing, and escorting bombers. Captain Womack was able to hire personnel from the city of Naples who served as chefs, waitresses, barbers, and entertainers for the men of the 332nd. Captain Womack made sure that the rest camp had the latest tunes from the jazz artists and vocalists of the times. The rest camp was also well stocked with the finest liquor. As beautiful and well run as the 332nd rest camp was, however, it was not equal to the beachfront rest camp for white officers.[139]

The 99th was closer to the rest camp than the 332nd. For the first time, the 99th could enjoy decent rest and relaxation periods. The 99th, however, still operated separately from the 332nd. The 99th, remained on the west coast of Italy, to participate in the liberation of Rome. Their dive bombing and strafing expertise in the P-40s was evident in the invasion, as the pilots of the 99th strafed armed vehicles and troop concentrations in the area. The squadron also blew up a key bridge, used by the Germans to move troops.[140] After the Rome objective, the Allied ground and air forces pushed the Germans northward. It was during this period that the 99th was reassigned and attached to another fighter group—the 86th. For the remainder of June 1944, the 99th moved northward with the 86th, dive bombing railroads in northern Italy. On one of its last missions as a separate squadron, the 99th took out approximately five hundred railroad cars carrying supplies in the Po Valley.[141] On 3 July 1944, the 99th Pursuit Squadron joined the 332nd at Ramitelli, where it became the 99th Fighter Squadron.[142] It was at this time that the group received used P-51 fighter aircraft, that would enable them to fly long-range escort missions. The transition to the P-51 was, for the most part, smooth.

The 332nd Fighter Group contained four squadrons, which was unusual for the Air Force.[143] Segregation established many precedents. Officers of the 332nd feared that the more experienced pilots of the 99th would assume all the leadership rolls. Conversely, officers in the 99th felt that they would have to report to inexperienced pilots.[144] An example of this predicament was Capt. Mac Ross. Captain Ross was in the first graduating class with Colonel Davis at Tuskegee. Instead of being selected as one of the pilots to go to North Africa in 1943, Ross was assigned the command of the 100th Fighter Squadron, then being formed at Tuskegee. When the 332nd Fighter Group was activated and sent to Selfridge, Ross remained commander of the 100th, until

Colonel Davis returned to Selfridge from Sicily. Colonel Davis reassigned Ross to group operations officer and gave Captain Tresville the command of the 100th.[145] When the 332nd reached Italy, Ross was given the assignment of flying the 332nd transport plane. In July 1944, the 99th joined the 332nd, forming a four squadron group. Colonel Davis opted to go with an operations officer with combat experience and relieved Captain Ross in favor of Lt. Alonzo Davis, a veteran of the 99th. In his transition training in the P-51, Ross was killed on 11 July 1944.[146]

Many in the 332nd felt that Captain Ross was despondent over his reassignment and had committed suicide. After investigating the crash scene, others believed that Captain Ross may have had trouble handling the used P-51. They attributed the accident to Ross's lack of experience in flying combat aircraft.[147] Fortunately, Colonel Davis's administrative skills and leadership, in addition to the preponderance of war activity, precluded intergroup friction and potential for mutiny over personnel issues, such as the reassignment and subsequent death of Captain Ross.[148]

On 12 July 1944, the 332nd, flying one of its first escort missions as a four-squadron group in P-51s, provided protection for B-17s on a bombing mission to southern France. On this mission, the group shot down five German aircraft. Capt. Joseph Elsberry destroyed three of the five enemy planes.[149] The 332nd continued to experience success, including shooting down eleven planes on one mission on 18 July 1944.[150] They soon developed a reputation among the bomber groups for not abandoning them when enemy fighters were sighted, and for their proficiency at repelling the fighters, once they attacked the bombers.[151]

It was strafing and dive bombing that cost the group the most men. Considered the most dangerous type of combat flying because low altitude flying rendered a plane vulnerable to ground fire of all types, dive bombing and strafing became the most undesired of missions. The attack modes were necessary, however, for ground troop support, disruption of enemy supply mechanisms, and the destruction of communication and radar systems.[152] In preparation for the invasion of southern France in August of 1944, the squadrons of the 332nd were directed to strafe and destroy the radar sites on the southern coast of France. The 332nd Intelligence informed the men that if they were successful in knocking out the radar sites on the coastlines, the invading Allied armies could go in unimpeded. Intelligence had discovered that the German army did not have enough technicians to repair the damage in time to stop the invasion. The 332nd sent pilots from all four squadrons to different parts of the southern coast of France, to take out radar installations. The squadrons attacked in flights of two, and as the pilots swooped into the beachheads at 400 mph, firing .50 caliber machine guns, the German antiaircraft guns had an unobstructed view and clear shots. If the American planes were not hit coming in, they were hit coming out, after their pass at the radar positions. The 332nd lost six men that day to gunfire on the beachhead. Five of the six men were captured by German troops and held as prisoners of war until May 1945.[153]

The 332nd spent the rest of 1944 concentrating on disrupting the production and supply of oil in the German oil centers. Their bomber escort missions took them to Ploeiste oil fields in Romania and other German oil fields in Austria, Czechoslovakia, and Germany, itself.[154] Their reputation as preeminent bomber escorts remained intact. The bombers soon referred to the 332nd as "redtails," a name taken from the colors of the rear tails of the P-51s flown by the 332nd pilots. Up to this point, the pilots of the 332nd had not lost a bomber to enemy aircraft attack.[155]

Feeling the effects of an energy shortage and persistent bombing in German industrial areas, Hitler and his military hierarchy made a decision about the tactical use of revolutionary aircraft that could prove to be the ultimate interceptor aircraft.[156]

❂   ❂   ❂

The 553rd, stationed at Walterboro, were subjected to second-class treatment both on and off the base. In June 1944, the Army Air Force had no reason to be concerned about outside agitators, in the form of the NAACP or the press, in Walterboro, South Carolina. With social outlets limited, the men of the 553rd were anxious to find ways of relieving the stress of a segregated world. The men attempted to desegregate the base theater by using the checkerboard tactic used at Selfridge Field. This time they did not find whites who were as cooperative as those at Selfridge. As a result, the men were ordered out of the theater.[157] The men decided to devise a creative response to the undignified treatment. During the next practice flight, the men, led by Charles Dryden and Captain Clark, two veterans of the 99th, flew a simulated low-altitude, high-speed attack on a water tower next to the house of the mayor of Walterboro. This "buzzing" of the tower caused severe vibrations that shook the mayor's house, and every house in the neighborhood, bringing almost everything in the house crashing to the floor. Later on in the flight, Dryden led the men in a "buzzing" of the control tower at the Walterborro base. For this incident, Dryden was court-martialed.[158]

Shortly before Dryden's court-martial trial, General Hunter paid a visit to Walterboro. The men of the 553rd, both white and black, were summoned to the base theater and told that segregation on that base was going to remain and that was the way it was going to be and that if any soldier had a problem, he was to raise his hand. Captain Dryden raised his hand. He was acknowledged by Hunter, who asked if Dryden was the officer being court-martialed. Dryden answered in the affirmative and General Hunter then retorted that he did not want to speak to Dryden.[159] Dryden was later convicted of violating the 96th Article of War—for buzzing the base. The sentence was dismissal from the service. Dryden was shocked and felt betrayed. He had felt sure of an acquittal, since four of the nine court-martial board member were black, and were combat veterans who had flown with Dryden in North Africa and Sicily. Dryden knew that acquittal or conviction required two-thirds of the votes. He therefore knew that one black had voted to convict him.[160]

Once his trial record was sent up the chain of command of the Army Air Corps, Judge Advocate General's purview, it was found that a flaw in the challenge of the court process precluded certain rights and options allowed to Dryden. The Judge Advocate General ruled that Dryden was denied the right to challenge a court member's presence on the court. With that discrepancy, the Judge Advocate General ordered a new trial for Captain Dryden. Dryden had a second trial and was convicted, but given a lighter sentence—fined three months pay, confined to base for three months, and suspended from promotion for one year. Another agitator was "weeded" out.[161]

Those who were veterans of combat campaigns with the 99th, and who were married, were especially agitated by their treatment at the hands of whites in the town. Their wives were forced to used segregated and inadequate laundry facilities. Housing was also virtually nonexistent as many wives resided with black families in larger towns nearby. The stores in Walterboro, would not offer full service to the wives. Many would travel to Atlanta to shop at department stores that treated them as respected customers. The wives, usually very sophisticated and well dressed compared to most women in Walterboro, black or white, were sexually harassed by the white civilians and airmen. The veteran officers suffered through this and many other indignities, even while attempting to secure basic services.[162] On two such occasions, Capt. Spann Watson could no longer control his anger and decorum.

Captain Watson's wife was very attractive, well educated, and presented herself in a dignified manner. When Mrs. Watson attempted to go shopping, white gentlemen would always harass her and try to "pick her up." An exasperated Captain Watson suggested that she secure the license plate numbers of the men the next time she went to the store. He then asked if the offenders were military people, and his wife answered in the affirmative. The next day the harassment continued and Mrs. Watson was successful in getting the license plate numbers, which she reported to her husband. Captain Watson traced the car tags and found the car parked outside the white enlisted mens' barracks at Walterborro. Watson went into the barracks and asked who had the New Jersey tags. A young man stood up and said that the car was his. Watson told him that he was from Hakensack, New Jersey, and in one quick decisive move put a .45 pistol to the temple of the young man and threatened that if he wanted to see the sun set tomorrow, he had better not try to pick up his wife again. Watson told the young man that he had a choice. The man chose to leave Watson's wife alone.[163]

Not long after the sexual harassment incident, Captain Watson was involved in another incident in Walterboro, at an automobile repair shop. Watson had a tire that needed to be fixed and had been promised several appointments by the black mechanic on duty. Watson took advantage of the offer and left his tire to be repaired. When he returned later in the day he had found that the tire had not been repaired. When Watson asked why his tire was not fixed, a white man interrupted and told the repairman to continue working on his other project—the white man's vehicle. When Watson objected, the white customer slapped him. A veil of rage swept over Captain Watson. He dropped the tire he was inspecting and punched the white man, who happened to be the mayor of the city, in the face, taking him to the floor. Before Captain Watson knew, he was surrounded by the white mechanics and customers in the garage. One of the white mechanics swung a water hose at him narrowly missing his head. He retaliated by pushing the man into the group of mechanics, who rushed at him. He started swinging at anyone who came near him, striking some and scaring others. When Captain Watson noticed one of the men leaving the fight to get what Watson instinctively knew was a firearm, the soldier ran from the garage. Watson ran as fast as he could toward the nearest military police station. When he reached it he found that it was manned with two white M.P.s. Captain Watson told them that he was being chased by white townspeople and that the M.P.s had better get their guns ready and call the base for backup. Captain Watson knew that he was in grave danger, and he explained to the M.P.s that if they did not want to use their weapons, they should give him a handgun, so that he could protect himself until support arrived from the base. Watson felt that if he were to die, he would die honorably, and would take a few with him.[164]

Within minutes, a mob, led by the mayor of Walterboro, showed up at the military police station and asked that Captain Watson be handed over to them. The two M.P.s who had drawn their guns warned the mayor and other local law enforcement officers who had joined the mob that Captain Watson was under the jurisdiction of the army and that if he broke any laws, the army would handle it. The crowd was not too happy about the response, and was growing angrier. Captain Watson was not sure how much longer the two armed M.P.s could serve as a deterrent to the lynching that the crowd was after. Fortunately for Captain Watson and the M.P.s, the base commander, Colonel Prince, arrived at the station with a couple of jeep-loads of military officers armed with Thompson submachine guns. Prince asked the townspeople what had happened, then met with Captain Watson and told him that he believed him and that he should get back to the base as soon as possible. Colonel Prince tried to diffuse the explosive situation by telling the mayor and his police officers that the army would prosecute Captain Watson and that he would take their official complaints. When Captain Watson got back to the base, he was ordered to leave Walterboro that evening. Under the darkness of night, Captain Watson left Walterboro, picked up his wife in a nearby town, and headed for Godman Field, Kentucky, to join the 477th.[165]

The 477th Medium Bombardment Group continued their training at Godman Field without the distraction of the officer's club issue. Since its activation, in the spring of 1943, the development of the 477th was retarded by indecision on the part of the Army Air Force as to whether to terminate deployment of black airmen to combat situations. The 477th was actually deactivated in the late summer of 1943.[166] When the Air Force Command decided to defer any decisions on the deployment of black airmen, the 477th was reactivated in January 1944, under the command of Colonel Selway. The group was to have four squadrons, including 176 pilots and 128 navigators, bombardiers, and ground crew.[167]

With the deployment of the 332nd Fighter Group, there was an acute need for replacements for fighter pilots, so the training for bomber pilots was secondary to the training of fighter pilot replacements for the 332nd. With the uncertain status of the 477th, training of navigators and bombardiers was sporadic and disjointed.[168] By October 1944, only ninety bomber pilots were trained. Only twenty-three navigators and bombardiers were at Godman. Since there were no full combat crews, the pilots flew several thousand hours worth of training exercises. They became so proficient that they had only one accident in 14,000 hours of flying. Even General Hunter admitted that their accident rate was exceptionally low. The skills of the pilots were honed on a flying field with less acreage and shorter runways than Selfridge. The 14,000 hours included gunnery practice, which had to take place at Walterborro because Godman Field had no gunnery range.[169]

The various units which made up the bombardier squadron were not trained together in the same location until late 1944. By February 1945, the 477th had about 150 pilots, and over 100 bombardiers and navigators, enough to start combat training with four squadrons—the 616th, 617th, 618th, and 619th. Included in the 477th were veteran fighter pilots from the original 99th Pursuit Squadron. These pilots were to be used as instructors for the Replacement Training Unit and the Overseas Training Unit that were part of the group. The 477th flew over 3,000 hours of combat crew training, with only one accident.[170]

Though the officer's club was a secondary issue at Godman Field, the lack of promotion opportunities among the black officers was a primary issue. The 477th and its Table of Organization became a promotion mill for young white officers. The tenure of service for white officers in squadron command positions was four months. When a white officer in the command was reassigned elsewhere, a white officer would replace him.[171]

The designation of white officers as base supervisory and instructor personnel made it easier for white officers to move from one assignment to another. For example, a white officer would serve, on a temporary basis, in a squadron position that would require a higher grade. When a promotion to the higher grade became available, the white officer would get the promotion, based on experience, and move elsewhere. The supervisory experience gained would give them an advantage over black officers competing for the same promotions.[172]

There were situations where there were black officers and experienced fighter pilots, with more combat hours than the whites in command positions.[173] The black officers were stuck at the grade of captain for several years. Several of the officers, frustrated at the lack of opportunity, knowingly risked their lives by volunteering for second combat tours as fighter pilots in the 332nd.[174] Other officers, such as Maj. Arthur B. Hayes, were reassigned or transferred, to accommodate white officers. Major Hayes was executive officer of one of the squadrons at Selfridge Field. When the white officers complained about serving with a black officer, Hayes was reassigned to adjutant. Less than a month later, he was transferred to Godman and given the assignment of mess officer, a duty reserved for a 1st lieutenant. His previous positions were given to white officers.[175] The black officers were determined to solve this dilemma.

In early March 1945, the 477th was moved to Freeman Field, in Seymour, Indiana. The rationale for the move was based on the larger runways, hangar space, and better weather conditions for flying.[176] Seymour, Indiana, unlike Louisville, did not have a large black population base with which the black officers and enlisted men could socialize. General Hunter and Colonel Selway were faced with a new dilemma. The War Department had issued a memorandum on 8 July 1944 which forbade discrimination in admission to base recreational facilities based on race. This memorandum was to serve as a reminder to all Air Force Command that the army intended to enforce army regulations regarding racial discrimination on base facilities.[177] General Hunter preferred a training base that was isolated from a sizable black population and the press. Freeman Field gave Hunter the isolation, but the War Department memorandum did not provide him with the legal support to segregate his officers by race. Even as late as December 1944, General Hunter strongly felt that racial friction would occur between white and blacks if they trained together and that priority ought to be given to producing maximum efficiency in white combat training crews, rather than to lowing the quality of combat training by integrating white units, just to appease agitators.[178] Selway, acting on his understanding of General Hunters feeling, informed the men shortly before leaving Godman that there would be two equal officer's clubs, one for trainees and one for supervisors.[179] The stage was set by General Hunter and Colonel Selway for confrontation with the black officers and the War Department.

✪   ✪   ✪

In the early months of 1945, the 15th Air Force pounded away at the German War production machine. Bombing raids were flown to places as far away as Poland and Germany, itself, including cities as large as Munich and Berlin. Attacks were made on oil refineries, tank arsenals, and jet fighter production centers. Squeezed from the east and west and being driven northward toward Berlin, the Hitler regime released the ultimate fighter plane for combat deployment on a large scale. The Messerschmitt 262 jet fighter, introduced into combat in the summer of 1944 but first used as part of a jet fighter group in March 1945, was nearly 100 mph faster, and much more devastating, than any fighter plane the Allies possessed, including the P-51 Mustangs flown by the American forces.[180] The Me 262 was truly the state of the art fighter plane. Its purpose was to intercept the bombers, which were leveling factories, towns, and the German war infrastructure at an alarming rate.

The debut of the ME 262 Fighter Group was both successful and frightening. On 19 March 1945, a group of 37 jet fighters were sent to intercept 120 American bombers of the 8th Air Force on a mission to destroy jet aircraft plants and military vehicle production centers in Neuburg and Baumenheim, Germany. The jets destroyed fifteen bombers, with thirteen kills and two probables, while losing only three of their planes.[181] The victory translated into 195 American men dead and $3.8 million dollars worth of military hardware lost. The success of the Me 262s received the immediate attention of all of the air forces in the Mediterranean theatre. The 15th Air Force Bomber Groups immediately stepped up bombing runs on all of Germany's jet production factories, while fighter groups of the 15th Air Force grappled with a strategy for stopping the jets in the air.[182]

Fortunately, the Allies were wining the war against time. Hitler's and the German Air Force's indecision on the combat role of the Me 262 during 1941-1943 impeded mass production of the jet fighter until November 1944. The jet, designed by Prof. Willy Messerschmitt in 1938, was developed to overtake the Allied fighters, primarily the British Hurricane and Spitfire planes, which were piston-driven machines.[183] The jets could outfly the Allied forces' best fighter planes and shoot down the slow-moving bombers that were knocking out German-held positions. The jet prototype was completed by the summer of 1941, however, the Luftwaffe, although very interested, was leery about spending limited resources on a developmental fighter plane.[184] The Bf 109 and the Fw 190, the current German fighters, had proven capable through 1941.

By 1942, the prototype was successfully test flown and prepared for testing by the Luftwaffe. In April and May 1943, the prototype was flown by the Luftwaffe's best pilot at the time—General Adolf Galland. The German ace was impressed with the plane and recommended to the Luftwaffe that production of an updated version of the Me 109 be scrapped in favor of the Me 262.[185] The Luftwaffe was still cautious about appropriating expenditures for production of the Me 262, so, at General Galland's urging, they enlisted Hitler's opinion. Hitler was interested in a superspeed bomber and requested, much to the Luftwaffe's chagrin, that if the Me 262 were to go into production, it be fitted with 550-pound bombs. Hitler was bent on avenging the bombing of German industrial and civilian targets by dive bombing Allied targets on the English coast and getting away before the Allied fighter aircraft could pursue. The Fuhrer ordered the production of the Me 262 as a fighter bomber to be ready for use in combat by April 1944.[186]

The Messerschmitt contractor could not meet the production deadline for the fighter bomber debut. Hitler was furious when he was told that the jet was being produced as a fighter. He directed the Luftwaffe to order the contractor to build the Me 262 to his specifications.[187] By June of 1944, Hitler was painfully aware of the error in his decision to build the jet fighter as a bomber. German energy resources needed protection from the onslaught of Allied bombers over German-held territories. By September 1944, Hitler had approved a production schedule that would allow every twentieth Me 262 built to be constructed as a fighter. By November 1944, Hitler finally gave permission to start mass production of the Me 262 as a fighter plane. However, he ordered that every plane be equipped to carry a 550-pound bomb, in case of emergency.[188]

As soon as Allied Intelligence speculated that most were aware of the new emphasis on the jet and its production as a fighter, bombing raids were ordered to disrupt if not destroy, Germany's capability for mass producing the plane. The 332nd Fighter Group knew that they would get the call to escort some of the B-24s and B-17s on the raids over Germany. They also knew that a confrontation with the Me 262 was inevitable. They had an opportunity to view the jet fighter up close in December 1944, when the jets made a pass at them while the 332nd were escorting bombers in a bombing raid.[189] The group intelligence and engineering officers were briefed on the capabilities and weaknesses of the jet fighter. This information was passed on to the squadron commanders and pilots. Intelligence had gathered data that indicated the Me 262s, even with the 550-pound bombs, were considerably faster that the P-51s flown by the 332nd. Without the bombs, the jet's speed would make it difficult to see and track. The pilots were instructed to do everything in the plane twice as fast as they would do when encountering conventional Luftwaffe fighters. Sighting the jet first was the prime objective. The speed of the jet made it mandatory that the pilot see it before the jet pilot spotted them. Turns would have to be executed faster and more precisely and shooting would have to be very accurate.[190]

Fortunately for the 332nd, the Me 262 was engineered with two glaring weaknesses. Intelligence revealed that the jet engine consumed so much fuel, compared to the more fuel efficient piston engine, that the jet had fuel-capacity for only forty-five minute flights. Clearly the military objective for the jets was to strike quickly, intercept the bombers, and escape enemy fighter planes. With such limited flying range, the Me 262 could be followed by a P-51 until the jet exhausted its fuel, and then shot down as it slowed to land. The second disadvantage attributable to Me 262 engineering was its maneuverability. The jet was built for speed, not for agility. This agility factor gave the P-51 pilots a much needed advantage in that the Mustang could out turn the Me 262. The

332nd pilots would let the jet get within firing range, then turn or roll sharply, letting the jet fly by, and then hit the jet with a deflection shot.[191] Another factor which gave the 332nd pilots a chance against the jet fighter was that, by this juncture in the war, Allied intelligence indicated that the best German fighter pilots had already been killed and that young, inexperienced fighter pilots were being sent up against combat veterans.[192]

The 332nd was given a mission to escort long-range bombers to Berlin, to attack jet and tank production plants. The mission was to take place on 24 March 1945. The 332nd would participate in the escort mission with other 15th Air Force Command Fighter Groups. The "Redtails," a name given to the 332nd by white bomber groups, were instructed to relieve a P-38 fighter group over Brux and then to escort the bombers to the edge of Berlin, where the 332nd would be relieved by another P-51 group.[193]

The Berlin mission was to be a 1,600-mile round-trip undertaking. Most of the P-51s assigned to the 332nd were fitted with extra-sized, 110-gallon fuel tanks. However, Capt. Edward Gleed, group operations officer, learned from one of the flight leaders, Lt. Woodrow Crockett, that there were approximately twelve planes in the 100th Fighter Squadron that were not fitted with the extra-sized tanks. The Berlin mission required all of the P-51s of the group, therefore, all of the planes had to be fitted with the large tanks.[194]

Captain Gleed enlisted the services of Capt. Omar Blair, armorer from the 96th Service Unit attached to the 332nd. Captain Blair was asked by Gleed to locate the large tanks, procure them, and deliver them to the line that night for installation.[195] Blair went to the supply depot to order and pick up the tanks, but found that there were none in stock. The supply officer informed Captain Blair that a shipment of extra-sized tanks, requisitioned for another fighter group, were coming in by train from Naples. That was what Captain Blair wanted to hear. Later that evening, Captain Blair and a few enlisted men, armed with submachine guns, commandeered six flatbed trucks and intercepted the train about forty miles outside of Ramitelli. Blair had a truck driven across the track, blocking the train, and ordered, with machine gun aimed, the shocked white staff sergeants operating the train to show them where the tanks were located. Blair's men loaded the tanks onto the trucks, Blair thanked the conductor for his generosity, and they headed back to Rametilli. They drove the trucks back to the base at Rametilli and unloaded them at the repair line. The next morning, 24 March 1945, all of the P-51s in the 100th Fighter Squadron were fitted with extra-sized fuel tanks.[196]

On the Berlin mission the morning of 24 March 1945, the 332nd pilots relieved the P-37 Group over Brux and took the bombers to the rendezvous point, where another P-51 group would escort the bombers over their targets in Berlin. For some unknown reason, the other group did not arrive on time and the 332nd was ordered to escort the bombers into Berlin, over the target.[197] Captain Gleed's concerns were prophetic, and Captain Blair's train robbery made it possible for the pilots to undertake, with confidence, the long flight to Berlin.

The pilots of the 332nd encountered twenty German jets over Berlin. In a frenzied fight that took place in about five minutes, the 332nd shot down three jets, disabled two, and did not lose a bomber to the jets. The jets were destroyed in a situation studied by the pilots prior to the mission. The Me 262s were shot down with deflection shots, catching them as they were in a vertical climb, flying through the bomber formations. They were also downed by pilots using the quick turn maneuver and following the jet as it sped past. For this mission the, 332nd received the Distinguished Unit Citation.[198]

Only 1,300 Me 262s were built, and many never got off of the ground, due to Allied bombing runs.[199] If Hitler and the Luftwaffe had been fully behind the development of the ME 262 in 1941, and if the engine technology could have been mastered before 1943, they could have discouraged Allied bombing raids of war production centers and oil reserves. They could have established air cover for most of Europe, thus prolonging the war or perhaps changing the course of the war.[200]

The 332nd Fighter Group had a very successful March and April in 1945. On 31 March 1945, the group shot down thirteen fighter planes during a strafing mission in Linz, Germany. On 1 April 1945, during a bomber escort mission to St. Polten, the group fought with German fighters and destroyed twelve.[201] When Germany surrendered on 8 May 1945, the 332nd had clearly established a fighting record beyond reproach. Up to this point in the war, they had not lost a single bomber to fighter aircraft, including the Me 262.[202] The 332nd had prospered and prevailed despite racism and segregation. While the 332nd experienced success overseas, however, the men of the 477th were to engage in another form of combat for freedom.

The officers of the 477th were transferred to Freeman Field on 5 March 1945. Those officers and enlisted men of the "E" and "C" squadrons and service units who were part of the transition team experienced immediate local opposition to their presence in Seymour, Indiana. The married officers settled into the Ridgeview public housing projects, which were close to the base. Restaurants, laundry facilities and other social and basic service facilities were closed to the families of the officers.[203] Freeman Field became the place of work and social life for the black officer and his family.

As soon as the officers and enlisted men arrived, they noticed that the Club #1, used by the noncommissioned officers, was assigned to the Overseas Training Unit (OTU) and Replacement Training Unit (RTU) officer personnel on base. They also noticed that the regular Officer's Club #2 was designated for the base supervisory, instructor, or command personnel. It just so happened that all of the blacks on the base, including Flight Surgeon Maj. James Ramsey, Group Supply Officer Lt. Walter Nicholson, Special Services Officer Lt. Joseph Echols, and Lt. Arthur Hayes, the mess officer, who were part of the command personnel, were considered training personnel and barred from membership in Club #2.[204]

There was a marked difference between the two clubs. Club #2, used by the white officers, had a large fireplace and a game room with billiard tables, table tennis, and card tables. The officer's mess hall was attached to the building and a guest house was situated next to the mess. Club #1, to be used by the black officers, had a large room heated by two large coal stoves, a faded wooden bar, and card tables. The club did not contain billiard tables, table tennis facilities, a guest house, or a mess hall.[205] The Negro Officers' Mess Council and the Officers' Club Governor's Board, the all-black officers' group that administered the Godman Field Club, met before the move and voted to recommend to Colonel Selway that all of the furniture and fixtures in Club #1 be given to the noncommissioned men, since they had no club assigned to them. Selway later vetoed the recommendation.[206]

The Officers' Mess Council and the Officers' Club Governor's Board began to plot a strategy, and planned their first series of protests over the use of Club #2. The older and experienced black officers plotted to use the club protest for integration as a strategy for forcing the white officers to seek transfers and assignments to other bases, thus freeing up command positions for themselves. The younger officers were supportive, but more interested in desegregating the officers' club to assuage their feelings of equality. As more bombardiers, navigators, and pilots from the OTU arrived, the planning group expanded beyond the Officers' Mess Council and the Officers' Club Governor's Board. A few of the incoming personnel assumed coordinating roles in the planning group.[207]

The officers selected 8 March 1945 as the day to attempt to test the segregation policy of Officers' Club #2. As in the case of the Selfridge Field protest, the officers were well aware of their limits under the

Articles of War. They would not disobey direct orders to vacate the club.
Their intent was to peaceably gain admittance to Club #2, or be given
an unequivocal explanation of why the base commander, Col. Selway,
insisted on violating army regulations pertaining to officer access to
recreational facilities.

The strategy was to approach the officers' club in groups of threes,
sixty to one hundred yards apart. This was done to give the impression
that black officer interest in the club was on an individualized and incidental basis. This strategy would make it more difficult for Colonel
Selway to charge them with inciting a riot. Once in the club, the officers
would fan out and sit at the bar, play billiards, table tennis, or a game of
poker.[208]

On 8 March 1945, the first group of officers, including combat veterans of the 99th and 332nd, Capts. James T. Wiley, Clarence Jamison,
and John W. Rogers, were successful in gaining admittance to Club #2.
Once they sat down and requested service, however, Maj. A. W. White,
the officer in charge of the club and affiliate mess hall, ordered them
out of the club. When the black officers questioned his authority, and
the legality of his order, Major White stated that, by orders of Colonel
Selway, no colored officers would be allowed to use the club facilities.
Upon hearing this, the black officers left the club and reported the incident to the rest of the group.[209]

The nest night, 9 March 1945, Lt. William Parks, of the Service
Group attached to the 477th, went to Officers' Club #2 and met Major
White at the door. According to the Army Clerk of the Court documents and transcripts of the Freeman Field trials, the following dialogue occurred between Lieutenant Parks and Major White:

> "Negro officers are not allowed in this officers' club"
> "Why?" asked Lieutenant Parks.
> "Well it's by the order of the man," offered the Major.
> "Who is the man?" asked Parks.
> "Colonel Selway," the major retorted.

With that information, Lieutenant Parks left and reported to the
group.[210]

The group, after hearing the report, decided that the next route
would be a written request to Colonel Selway, asking him to clarify the
membership policy at Club #2. The group assisted Lieutenant Parks in
the composition of a letter, sent to Colonel Selway on 10 March 1945,
requesting further clarification of policies on the use of the Officers'
Club #2 facilities. The letter must have had an impact, for Colonel
Selway called General Hunter for advice.

"General, I think I need to close the club here at Freeman until we get some word that what we are doing is legal," advised Selway, according to the Army Clerk of Court documents and government documents documenting the conversation.

"What club?" Hunter asked sardonically.

"The one that belongs to white officers," offered Selway.

"Oh no, I wouldn't do that. As far as I'm concerned you've gotten out orders assigning one club to the OTU Group and one club to the permanent party personnel, and don't say anything about color, race or creed. You've complied with my orders. I'd be delighted for them to commit enough actions that way so I can court-martial some of them." advised Hunter.[211]

Colonel Selway had support for his discriminatory policies. Selway also felt comfortable with the knowledge that a few of the black officers were reporting the actions and plans of the protest group.[212] Selway directed Col. John B. Patterson, deputy commander of the 477th, to meet with the black officers offering resistance to his policy and to warn Lieutenant Parks that his letter could negate its intended purpose. Colonel Patterson directed Col. Thomas Keach, executive officer of the 477th, to meet with Lieutenant Parks.[213]

Later that day, Colonel Keach held a meeting in the base theater to discuss Selway's policy. Just prior to the meeting, Keach met with Lieutenant Parks and warned him that his letter and black officer objections to the officers' club membership policy, would only bring trouble for Lieutenant Parks and the others and could jeopardize the existence of the 477th Medium Bombardment Group.[214] The group heard of the threat and were eager to meet with Colonel Keach. When Keach convened the meeting, Col. John B. Patterson, Deputy Commander, presided. Colonel Patterson read Selway's policy and dealt directly with the questions that the group had about the officers' club policy. When the black officers reminded Colonel Patterson of the army regulations 210-10 forbidding discrimination based on race in the use of base recreational facilities, Colonel Patterson replied the army regulations did not apply to a training facility, such as Freeman Field. Supposedly under the instruction of Colonel Selway, Patterson read a letter, reportedly from General Hunter, that designated all supervisory, command, and instructional personnel by title at Freeman.[215] The group took note and complained that none of the titles mentioned were held by black men. Colonel Patterson then read what was considered a warning from Hunter to the black officers. Patterson read that any OTU officer who set foot in Club #2 would be tried for insubordination. This threat caused considerable concern among black officers, who knew that all of the OTU officers were black. They also knew that a court-martial for insubordination could end a military career and, in wartime, could result in death by firing squad. The threat, however, was only effective in slowing the protest momentum temporarily.[216]

The Mess Council, Officers' Club Governor's Board, and other members of the protest group kept other officers of the 477th, stationed on other bases practicing combat maneuvers or preparing for their transition to Freeman Field, appraised of the situation. Most of the officers at these locations pledged to support and participate in the officers' club protest. Between 1 April and 5 April 1945, officers of the OTU and RTU units remaining at affiliate air bases reported to Freeman.[217] Both units had experienced and young officers serving together. The RTU consisted of experienced fighter pilots, who were assigned to bomber pilot training, and bomber pilots with several hundred hours of B-25 flight training. Their responsibility was the training of replacement pilots, bombardiers, and navigators for the group. The OTU included bomber pilots, navigators, bombardiers, and service units in training for overseas duty.[218]

Included in the RTU were combat veterans of the 99th Pursuit Squadron and the 332nd Fighter Group. These officers, such as Spann Watson, Clarence Jamison, James Wiley, John Rogers, and Robert O'Neal, were very intolerant of any discrimination pertaining to the officers' club or the promotion system based on race.[219] Officers of the OTU, such as William Ellis, Elmore Kennedy (president of the Officers Club Association), E. E. Richardson, Marsden Thompson, Coleman Young, Daniel "Chappie" James, and Shirley Clinton, had hundreds of hours of training as B-25 pilots, bombardiers, and navigators, and several years as officers in the Army Air Corps. These men were tired of, and insulted by, the segregationist policies of the 477th command.[220]

By 5 April 1945, most of the officers from the RTU and the OTU units had arrived at Freeman Field. Upon their arrival, the men arranged a meeting consisting of the Mess Council, Officers' Club Governors' Board, and interested officers, to discuss and implement protest strategy.[221] Lt. Coleman Young was instrumental in formulating strategy on the protest tactics used for the officers' club. Lieutenant Young relied on his experience gained in the successful protest of the discriminatory officers' club and mess policy the year before at Midland, Texas. The base command at the Midland base had determined that the black bombardier/navigators would be treated as cadets and not as officers. As cadets, they were not to use the facilities set aside for supervisory and base personnel, who were all white. The base commander had an officers' club constructed in the back of the black officers' barracks. A letter was drafted and signed by the twenty-nine black officers in the squadron, including Lieutenant Young, and sent to the Inspector General in the War Department. The letter included a threat of the resignation of twenty-nine commissions. For some reason, the base commander was certain that Lieutenant Young had authored the letter. The inspector general sent a review committee to Midland, and their recommendations led to the reassignment of the base commander and the removal of the discriminatory base policies.[222]

Marsden Thompson was the Billeting and Mess Officer at Godman Field. He was also the president of the Officers' Mess Council. Lieutenant Thompson had been stationed at Selfridge during the officers' club contention and the court-martial of Lt. Milton Henry. He was also, at one time, executive officer of the 618th Bomber Squadron. He knew firsthand the racial discrimination of the promotion system. As more white officers came to the 477th command, Lieutenant Thompson was reassigned to Mess Officer of the Group.[223] He knew the particulars of the white officers in command of the 477th and gave the black officers invaluable consultation on what to expect from the 477th command. Lt. William Ellis, who was also stationed at Selfridge, participated in the officers' club protest, along with Lieutenant Henry. Lieutenant Ellis played a key role in recruiting the young and veteran officers to participate in the Freeman Field demonstration.[224]

The black officers decided to initiate their demonstration at 8:00 P.M. on the evening of 5 April 1945. Lt. William Coleman, a law student, tutored the men on the proper and legal responses to orders and directives from the military police or the mess officer in charge of the club. The men were told that if they were denied entrance by the M.P., they were to ask for the commanding officer, to get an explanation as to why they could not enter. It was important to send the men who had never heard or been presented with the base policy regarding Officers' Club #2 to the club. By using this strategy, the new arrivals, if denied entrance to the club, could not be charged for disobeying the 10 March 1945 order from the 477th deputy commander not to attempt to enter the club. The black officers were also told to state that they were base personnel, not trainee personnel. Lieutenant Coleman and the others rationalized that the officers were members of several base units and, therefore, base personnel. The plan also included sending as many combat veterans and squadron and unit officers as possible. This plan would make it difficult for the commanding officer to identify them as trainees.[225]

The men lined up in groups of three to go to Club #2. They proceeded to the club in sixty-yard intervals, so that their arrivals would not appear coordinated. Lt. Robert Payton, Lt. Clifford Garrett, and Flight Officer Markus Clarkson were the first to reach the doors of the Officers' Club #2. As they approached the building, they were stopped by a Provost Marshall. It became obvious to the three officers that the Military Police were expecting them. Clearly, Colonel Selway had a spy in the group.[226]

According to the Army Clerk of the Court documents and the Freeman Field trial transcripts, the following dialogue took place:

"I'm sorry, only base personnel allowed in this club," the M.P. ordered.

"I have just arrived on the Field and I'm base personnel," replied Lieutenant Payton.

The M.P. retorted, "I have an order that gives me permission to keep out officers who are not base personnel. I'll get Major White to verify my order."

The M.P. returned to the door with Major White, the mess commander, who drawled.

"Only base personnel are allowed in this club."

"But I'm base personnel. I just arrived on the Field," repeated Lieutenant Payton.

"Lets be frank with one another. The truth of the matter is that colored officers aren't allowed in this club whether you are base personnel or not," stated Major White.[227]

After hearing the real reason, the black officers turned and left the building. On their way back to the officers quarters, the officers met with the second group and explained what has transpired. The second group, consisting of Lt. Marsden Thompson, Lt. Shirley Clinton, and Lt. Coleman Young, approached the door of the club. Lieutenant Thompson opened the door and was immediately met by the M.P.

"You can't be admitted to this club," the M.P. ordered.

"Why?" answered Lieutenant Thompson.

"If you step outside, I will tell you," replied the M.P.

Lieutenant Thompson stepped back outside the door, followed by the M.P.

"This club is not for your use."

"Why?"

"This club is for use of the base personnel."

"I'm base personnel, why can't I use the club?" interrupted Lieutenant Clinton.

"I can't answer that question" answered a perturbed M.P.

At that point, Lieutenant Thompson, who was standing to the left of the M.P., walked into the club. The M.P. grabbed Lieutenant Thompson and pushed him.

"Get your hands off me" demanded Thompson.[228]

Lieutenant Clinton slipped past the M.P. on the right side and entered the club. The M.P. whirled around and pushed Lieutenant Clinton. By this time, all of the men who were headed to the club, including, Lieutenant Payton, Lieutenant Garrett, and Flight Officer Clarkson, who had returned, were poised in the entrance. About eighteen officers entered the club. The M.P., frustrated, walked to the back of the club to get Major White.[229]

The men fanned out over different parts of the club. Lieutenant Young sat at the bar and ordered a drink. The bartender refused to serve him because he was ordered "not to serve colored officers."[230] Lieutenant Thompson went to play pinball, as others sat at card tables. The men were in the club for about five minutes when Major White motioned for them to meet with him.

"If you men refuse to leave the club, I will have to place you under arrest" threatened Major White.

"Major, sir, we are not refusing to leave, but we would like to know why we must leave?" replied Thompson.

"I have orders. Please give me your names." White ignored Thompson's inquiry.[231]

While Major White was taking the names, Captain Chiappe, Combat Crew Training Squadron commanding officer, came over and told the men that he wanted to see them after Major White had finished taking names.

"You are placed in arrest in quarters," White pronounced.

Captain Chiappe assembled the men.

"As your commanding officer, any difficulties you were having you should have brought them to my attention," advised Chiappe.

"You are not to question the order of any officer in charge of acting under the order of Colonel Selway."

"Is this a white officers' club?" asked one of the black officers.

"No" blurted Chiappe. "This club is for supervisor and base personnel and the club you are supposed to use is T-885. We'll meet tomorrow morning to discuss this. Now go to your barracks and remain in arrest as you were informed by Major White."[232]

The black officers obeyed Chiappe's order and returned to the barracks.

About 10:15 P.M. that evening, three more black officers, including
Lt. James Kennedy, Lt. Roger Terry, and a Flight Officer named
Goodman, left for the club and met the M.P., who was barring the
door.

"Just a minute, Lieutenant. Are you OTU personnel?"

"No we ain't," answered Lieutenant Terry.

"Lieutenant, this is a private club for base and supervisory personnel."

"We are base officers because we are in a base unit," countered
Terry.[233]

Lieutenant Terry then reached for the screen door used to enter the
club. He pulled the screen door out to the point where it brushed up
against the M.P.

"If you go in you will be put under arrest," warned the M.P.

The other two black officers followed Lieutenant Terry into the club.
Major White approached the black officers immediately.

"What is your name Lieutenant?" White addressed Lieutenant Terry.

"Lieutenant Roger Terry."

"What are your names," demanded White of the other two black officers.

"Lieutenant Kennedy, sir." "Flight Officer Goodman, sir."

"You officers are under arrest. I want you to return to your quarters"
ordered White.

"Why are we under arrest?" inquired Lieutenant Kennedy.

"I don't have to answer that," said Major White.

The three officers left the club for their barracks.[234]

A total of thirty-six black officers entered the club that evening and
thirty-six were told to report to their quarters and remain there under
arrest.[235]

The men were eager to meet with Captain Chiappe the next morning to state their grievances. Captain Chiappe, however, brought the
club legal officer, Captain Ochs, and read a base order, dated 1 April
1945, from Colonel Selway designating the buildings and areas to be
used by OTU personnel.[236] Selway's order was an extension of previous
base commander Colonel Bradford's policy on cadet use of base facilities, issued prior to the arrival of the 477th at Freeman Field.[237] After
questioning Chiappe and Ochs, the protest group was disappointed and
knew they would have to carry out the demonstration as planned.

The unprecedented arrest of the thirty-six black officers for entering the officers' club, went unnoticed by the press. The arrested officers, concerned about a possible news blackout, quickly designed ways to get the communication out about their plight. All of the officers who had access to telephones gave messages to friends and relatives. Capt. Watson and Lt. Ellis arranged for their wives to drive up to the barracks, pick up the mail, and drive it to the Seymour Post Office. The wives also drove around to the club, to see if it were open. When the wives drove back to the barracks and notified the men that the club was open, the second wave of black officers was sent to integrate Officers' Club #2.[238]

That afternoon, 6 April 1945, twenty-four different officers tried to gain entrance into the club. They were also were placed under arrest. The number of officers arrested over the two-day period totaled sixty. Of the sixty black officers arrested, two were combat veterans—Spann Watson and Robert O'Neal. Lt. William Ellis was also among the sixty officers arrested.[239] Later that evening, Colonel Selway ordered the club closed.

That evening, Colonel Patterson, with instruction from Colonel Selway, met with the sixty men and warned them that a memorandum had been issued that day on the subject of disciplinary action, formally ordering the arrest of the sixty men for violating the 69th Article of War. Patterson advised the men not to attempt to enter the club and that the base command was expecting a ruling from the Advocate General of the Army Air Force on the legality and validity of the 1 April 1945 order designating use of base facilities.[240]

The following day, 7 April 1945, the Advocate General ruled that Selway's policy was weak and that he should release the sixty officers, but keep the first three officers who maneuvered their way into the club, specifically, Lieutenant Thompson, Lieutenant Clinton, and Lieutenant Terry.[241] The next day, 8 April 1945, General Haines, Commanding General, First Bomber Command under General Hunter, arrived at Freeman Field to discuss the problem with Colonel Selway. Selway informed Haines that two of the five combat veterans of the 99th and 332nd had been arrested. Officers Jamison, Rogers, and Wiley, also attempted to enter the officers club earlier in March. They were ordered out of the club, but not arrested. Clearly, they were not trainees. If these officers continued to support the arrested officers, the situation could prove embarrassing on a international level. To alleviate this potential problem, Colonel Selway requested that the five officers be transferred from Freeman Field. Gaines accommodated Selway's request and, later in April 1945, Jamison, Rogers, and Wiley were temporarily assigned off base. On the following day, 9 April 1945, fifty-seven men, including Spann Watson and Robert O'Neal, were released.[242]

General Hunter, who remained undeterred in his goal of segregating officers in his command, sought advice from Army Air Force Headquarters. Colonel Selway, through Hunter, was advised by the Judge Advocate's Office to strengthen his base housing and mess hall regulations by designating facilities for certain squadrons without reference to race.[243] On 9 April 1945, Colonel Selway issued a new Base Regulation 85-2 which was entitled "Assignment of Housing." Base Regulation 85-2 designated mess and recreational facilities for officers, flight officers, and warrant officers. The regulation effectively limited the access of all black officers in Combat Command Training Squadrons, including the two housekeeping squadrons, "E" and "C," respectively, by classifying officers of these squadrons as trainees. The base regulation specified what latrines, mess halls, clubs, and tennis courts were available for base supervisory, instructor, and command personnel, and those facilities available to personnel undergoing OTU, combat crew, ground and air replacement training, and squadrons "E" and "C."[244] There were a chaplain, a flight surgeon, and twenty black officers in "E" and "C" squadrons. These officers were not part of the Combat Command Training Squadrons. Technically, if they were exempt from the order, the officers, who were not part of the RTU or the OTU, could use any base facility, including Officers' Club #2.[245]

The new base order also did not affect the white officers of the all-black 387th Service Group, which was attached to the 477th. The officers of this group were not base supervisory, instructional, or command personnel, but had access to housing and recreational facilities available to base supervisory, instructional, and command personnel.[246]

The first section of Base Regulation 85-2 outlined the army's standards governing the control and implementation of curfews and assignment of housing and recreational facilities of personnel undergoing training, as differentiated from standards governing permanent party, base, supervisory, instructor, and command personnel. General Hunter felt that he had the legal and political support of the Army Air Force and Colonel Selway felt secure only with the Army Air Force and General Hunter's direction.[247]

This new regulation was posted on the base bulletin boards on 9 April, and all officers of the 477th were ordered to read and sign, to verify that they read and understood the order. The majority of the black officers, especially those who were arrested, expected something from Washington. Instinctively, they were skeptical of any new development such as a new base regulation on assignment of housing and recreational facilities. Many of the black officers would not sign the order.[248]

Colonel Selway directed Maj. Joseph Murphy to call a conference with all the black officers on 10 April, with the intention of ordering all of the black officers in the 477th to endorse the new regulation. Over one hundred officers either refused to endorse the regulation, on advice from Lieutenant Coleman, declined to sign, stating that it was not possible to sign the order because it was in complete conflict with Army Regulation 210-10 and that they did not understand the definitions of command, supervisory and instructional personnel.[249] Lieutenant Coleman sent a letter to Colonel Selway, requesting the army standards mentioned in the Base Regulation 85-2, a definition of command, supervisory, and instructor personnel, and a reason why the officers of the 387th Service Group were not excluded from Officers' Club #2. Lieutenant Coleman also stated in the letter that the base regulation appeared to be in direct conflict with Army Regulation 210-10.[250] In addition, some officers, hoping not to be viewed as disobeying an order, scratched out the words "fully understand" and signed the regulation.[251]

Colonel Selway still had not extracted what he wanted from the black officers—a complete endorsement of a base regulation that would virtually segregate the black officers from the whites at Freeman Field.

On 11 and 12 April 1945, Selway established and instructed a board of officers, consisting of Colonel Patterson, Colonel Keach, Capts. James Pughsley, Ochs, and Chiappe, and Lieutenant Rogers, along with a civilian stenographer, to order approximately one hundred officers to appear, on an individual basis, before the Board to endorse the base regulation.[252] Each man was asked to give name, rank, serial, and whether they had read the base regulation. At this point, some of the officers replied "no statement," utilizing the 24th Article of War. Some officers claimed that they did not understand the regulation. The regulation was read to each officer. The officers were then asked to sign. The men again refused, either by invoking the 24th Article of War, "no statement," or stating that they did not understand. Colonel Patterson then read the 64th Article of War which pertains to disobeying a direct order from a superior officer during wartime. He then ordered Captain Chiappe, Commanding Officer of the Squadrons, to give a direct order.

According to the NAACP Report of the Freeman Field incident and letters pertaining to the incident in the NAACP Files, Library of Congress, the following dialogue occurred:

"I now order you to sign the endorsement," Chiappe ordered.

"No" replied some of the men. "No statement," replied most of the men.

"You are under arrest. Go back to your quarters" ordered Chiappe.[253]

One-hundred-one officers were arrested.[254] The 101 officers included about 40 of the 60 officers arrested on April 5th and 6th. On 13 April 1945, the 101 black officers were placed under arrest and secretly flown to Godman Field, under the guise of ninety-day temporary duty, and kept in barracks surrounded by barbed wire fences and guarded by sentries. Under arrest in barracks, the officers contemplated who benefited more in a democracy during wartime—they, themselves, or the German prisoners, roaming relatively free around the Godman Base.[255]

On 13 April 1945, the NAACP sent Washington D.C. chapter president Leslie Perry to investigate what had happened at Freeman Field. In a two-day period, Mr. Perry privately interviewed over fifty men, including Lieutenants Thompson, Clinton, and Terry. Perry was told of the discriminatory actions in the promotion system and in the use of base recreational outlets, including the officers' club.[256] Colonel Selway provided Perry with an interview, in which he contended that it was standard procedure for the Air Force to separate officer trainees in recreational clubs and that such standards referred to in the Base Regulation 85-2 were approved by the commanding general for purposes of efficiency. Selway claimed that "everything he has done with the respect to the separation of military personnel has had the complete approval of General Hunter, his superior. In fact, General Hunter directed that the order in question be written and issued as it then stood."[257] When asked why he issued a direct order under the 64th Article of War, the violation of which could lead to capital punishment, Selway answered that General Hunter wanted the order given under the 64th Article of War, so that no one would misunderstand it.[258] During the interview, Perry also asked permission to officially interview the three officers under arrest. Selway denied the request, stating that the officers had not been formally charge because the commanding general—Hunter—had not approved the charges.[259]

While Perry was at Freeman, almost all of the black officers still on base took several rides to the officers' club to gain entrance. Colonel Selway, forewarned by a group spy, kept the club closed. When the men approached the club, Colonel Patterson would ask who the spokesperson for the group was, and all of the members would respond, "no one."[260] Perry filed his investigative report on 16 April 1945.

As the pressure began to mount on the War Department from the NAACP, the Urban League, the press, congressmen, and political organizations, Gen. George Marshall, Chief of Staff, Armed Forces, became nervous, and on 19 April 1945, he ordered the 101 men released with administrative reprimands. On 20 April 1945, General Hunter received the order to release the 101 officers from arrest with reprimands. The three under arrest for allegedly "jostling" the M.P. while entering the club, were to be court-martialed, however.[261] Hunter felt that his command responsibility had been stripped from him for a second time. His intent was to court-martial all 101 men, with the approval of General Arnold and the Air Force Command. The men were released on 25 April 1945. All were given administrative reprimands. Once given an administrative reprimand, an officer's career in the Army Air Force was irreparably damaged. Administrative reprimands had to be fully endorsed and, therefore, the men drafted an endorsement for all of the 101 officers to use, in answer to the administrative reprimand. Spann Watson drove and hand-carried the draft to Judge William Hastie for final drafting. All but four of the officers used the Hastie endorsement.[262]

The War Department's McCloy Committee became involved in the case in early May, 1945. By 5 May 1945, they had received, from the Army Air Force, a review of the Freeman Field, arrests, and the circumstances leading up to the arrests. The review from the Air Force included a recommendation from the Inspector General that stated that Base Regulation 85-2 was consistent with War Department policy, as stipulated in the War Department's Pamphlet 20-6 on the Command of Negro Troops, and the law of separate but equal accommodations.[263] The McCloy Committee, and especially Truman Gibson, was not impressed with the Air Force's review or the Inspector General's recommendation. Gibson went on the record to describe the review as "a fabric of deception and subterfuge."[264] As a result, the McCloy Committee conducted its own investigation of the Freeman Field incident, and on 18 May 1945, reported that Selway's actions violated Army Regulation 210-10 and recommended that the War Department amend its Pamphlet 20-6 by stating its objections to segregation. The committee also recommended that Selway's violation of the army regulation be brought to the attention of General Arnold, chief of Army Air Forces.[265] The report, however, stated that Selway was within his administrative purview when he had the officers arrested. The report did not respond to the plight of the three officers still being held under arrest, though they had not been formally charged. The committee appeared to have believed the sworn statements of the M.P.s, who reported that all three officers under arrest had "jostled an M.P." after receiving a direct order.[266]

The Air Force Command did not appreciate the McCloy Committee report and recommendations. The Air Force appealed directly to McCloy, and stressed the intent of Pamphlet 20-6 that segregation should be utilized when white and black officers were together on the base. This policy, they maintained, was consistent with customs of the country.[267] The War Department, however, could not withdraw the McCloy Committee recommendations especially in light of their ruling in the Selfridge Field Officers' Club situation.[268]

The pressure from civil rights organizations and the press intensified, with continuous requests for information about the War Department and Air Force Inspector General reports and what action the War Department intended to take against Colonel Selway and General Hunter.[269] In addition, the black press carried stories and editorials weekly, asking for justice on the behalf of the 101 men and the 3 officers still under arrest. George Schuyler of the *Pittsburgh Courier*, commented:

> Everytime a Negro willingly accepts second class status, a piece of his soul vanishes never to return. No man with a shadow of self respect can remain a man while accepting the status of a slave yet we have too many Negroes who not only accept it, but actually defend it on the ground of expediency which some "leaders" call "racial statesmanship." It is impossible for any man to be a first class officer if constantly forced into a second class position. . . . It is a pleasure to note that the War Department has had the good sense to release these young men to duty, and it is to be hoped that the High Command will take steps to see that there is no recurrence of such incidents. The regulations are quite clear and it is doubtful that if any appreciable percentage of the American population wants to see Army officers humiliated, no matter what their color or "race". . . . All praise to these 101 young men who have set an example for all Negroes to follow."[270]

The War Department issued press releases indicating that an investigation of the Freeman Field incident was being conducted and that they would have a statement for the press and the public as soon as their probe was completed.[271] The press, however, discovered that the 477th had been secretly moved to Godman Field shortly after the 101 had been released, and that Selway would be relieved of command.[272] The press also learned from the black officers at Godman that the officers had requested the War Department to remove Selway from command. The officers based their request on a confiscated secret "official" letter addressed to Selway, dated 27 April 1945, which stated that, after the move to Godman, the squadrons would be commanded by white officers. The officers reported that the letter directed Selway to place no white officer below the rank of Major and no black officer above the rank of major, precluding black officers from the command of the group or squadrons. The officers of the 477th also offered two other demands: that the three officers under arrest be released; and that the War Department eliminate discrimination.[273]

From all appearances, the War Department was procrastinating, in search of the best political route out of the Freeman Field predicament. According to War Department documents, the assistant Judge Advocate General felt that no action should be taken against the officers under arrest. He, and other members of the Judge Advocate General's office, were also of the opinion that the officers should not be tried for general court-martial, but rather that disciplinary action should be taken against them under the 104th Article of War, which would be no worse than an administrative reprimand.[274] The Judge Advocate's office felt that trying the officers on violation of the 64th Article of War could result in a sentence of capital punishment, something the army could not politically afford. They recommended that the officers be transferred to another station.[275]

The McCloy Committee recommended an expedition of the trial for the three officers under arrest. The committee, however, did not recommend trial by any specific court, or an opinion on which Article of War violation the three officers should be charged. The secretary of war approved the committee recommendations.[276]

The recommendations of the Judge Advocate General in Charge of Military Justice were sent to the Commanding General, Army Air Forces, through the Air Judge Advocate. However, General Hunter clearly wanted to make an example of the three officers. He was able to convince the Air Force Command and the Air Judge Advocate to reject the War Department recommendations and eventually approve the court-martial charges of violations of the 64th Article of War.[277]

As of 2 June 1945, the War Department still had not issued its McCloy Committee report and recommendations on the Freeman Field situation to the public, nor had the War Department advised the press on what would become of Colonel Selway. The press reminded the War Department of its own policy of removing from command a superior officer who had lost the respect of his command. When the War Department was asked what their plans were for Selway, who was still in command of the 477th, Undersecretary of War Patterson responded: "You will just have to be patient with us."[278]

The NAACP had become very impatient with the War Department. On 14 June 1945, Secretary of the NAACP Walter White sent Secretary of War Stimson a wire, reminding Stimson that the NAACP had informed the War Department, on 19 April 1945, that Colonel Selway's base regulation was in violation of army regulations. Mr. White used this opportunity to inform Stimson that Lts. Clinton, Terry, and Thompson were still being detained without being formally charged. White reminded Secretary Stimson that the incarceration of the three officers without the issuance of formal charges was in direct violation of Army Regulation 600-355, which stated that any person subject to military law placed in arrest or confinement must be tried immediately or the charges must be dismissed and the person released.[279]

Mr. White also complained of Selway's status as commander, and of the support he had received from General Hunter, even when Selway had violated department regulations. The NAACP urged the release of the three lieutenants and urged corrective action be expedited for the "underlying conditions" in the 477th, before they were sent overseas.[280] It appears, given the last sentence of the wire, that the NAACP secretary was aware of the Army Air Force's plans to use the 477th overseas, and may have been aware that a change in command was to take place.

While in Italy, in late May 1945, Colonel Davis had received orders to select some of his crack pilots and ground crewmen to return with him to prepare the 477th for combat deployment in the Pacific theatre. The command structure of the 477th was to change from white to black. Davis took command of the 477th on 21 June 1945 and became the first black airbase commander on 1 July 1945.[281] The 477th Bombardment Group became the 477th Composite Group. Two of the bomber squadrons were eliminated and a fighter squadron, the 99th, was added to the group. Colonel Selway was relieved of his duty as commanding officer of the 477th and Godman Field.[282]

On 14 June 1945, on the same day that the NAACP wire arrived, by the order of Secretary Stimson, the War Department amended Pamphlet 20-6 to read:

> Where conditions make it desirable, War Department instructions permit the local commander to provide separate recreational facilities, such as army exchanges, theaters, or sections of theaters, for the use of particular military units. However, it is the basic policy of the War Department that the provision of such separate facility does not permit the exclusion, on the basis of race or color, of any member of the military service from using any and all facilities established in public buildings. Paragraph 19, AR 210-20, is explicit in defining the application of

this policy to membership in officers clubs, messes, or similar social organizations.[283]

The order was given to all commanding generals overseas and in the states. This order was perceived as a positive step in civil rights statesmanship. The reality, however, was that Godman Field and the 477th Composite Group would be an all-Negro and completely separated unit. Even the officers of the all-Negro 387th Service Group were moved out, and black officers, selected by Colonel Davis, moved in.

Colonel Davis inherited an immediate problem in the Freeman Field Three, the name given the officers under arrest. He knew something had to be done quickly. The three officers had been held under arrest for a precedent-setting eighty days at Freeman Field and now Godman without being formally charged for court-martial and a total of eighty-seven days under arrest without a trial.[284] Not only were they confined to quarters, they were not allowed to perform their duties as officers in the Army Air Force. Lieutenant Clinton was even denied private counsel by Colonel Selway, because the 477th commanding officer had not received court-martial charges from the First Air Force Command.[285] This gross violation of Army Regulations would prove very embarrassing to Colonel Davis, especially when the Negro press was reporting that he would be the Air Force's first Negro general.[286] When asked by the Negro press what he planned to do, Colonel Davis remarked that he intended to try the men as soon as possible and get on with combat training for the Pacific conflict.[287]

The men were served formal charges on 24 June 1945, and were to stand trial, beginning on 2 July 1945.[288] The NAACP volunteered to represent the three officers. Theodore Berry, of the Cincinnati NAACP chapter, and a long-time confidant of NAACP lawyer Thurgood Marshall, was retained, at the request of Judge William Hastie, as defense counsel. There were to be two separate trials, one for Lts. Clinton and Thompson and one for Lieutenant Terry.[289]

The Clinton and Thompson trial convened on 2 July 1945, with an all-black court-martial court. Officers detailed for the court were Col. Benjamin O. Davis, president of the Court; Capts. George L. Knox, James T. Wiley, John H. Duren, Charles R. Stanton, William T. Yates, Elmore M. Kennedy, Fitzroy Newsom; Lt. William R. Ming, Jr., Judge Advocate General's Department, Law Member; and Lt. James Y. Carter. Prosecuting attornies were Capt. James W. Redden, Trial Judge Advocate, and Lt. Charles R. Hall, Asst. Trial Judge Advocate. The defense team consisted of Capt. Cassius A. Harris, III; Defense Counsel and Lt. William T. Coleman, Jr., Asst. Defense Counsel. Both Clinton and Thompson declined the services of Lieutenant Harris, and stated that they desired to retain attorneys Theodore M. Berry and Harold Tyler of Chicago, Illinois, as defense counsel and Lieutenant Coleman and Lt. Edward K. Nichols, of the 387th Group, as special counsel.[290]

Prior to the trial, a few of the detailed court members allegedly met surreptitiously with the defense counsel for the three accused and advised them to challenge, peremptorily, Colonel Davis's seat on the court. The officers who gave the advice feared that Colonel Davis, being a West Point man and an officer aspiring to be the first black general in the Air Force, might be disposed to find the accused guilty as charged, to save his career. The officers who disagreed with Col. Davis's position felt that their careers would be in jeopardy. Those court members who owed their command responsibilities to Colonel Davis feared that a favorable decision made by the court toward the three accused could cost Colonel Davis his career, as well as theirs.[291] Either way, the officers felt that they could not afford to have Colonel Davis on the court.

When the court convened on 2 July 1945, the defense counsel for Clinton and Thompson peremptorily challenged Colonel Davis. Colonel Davis was excused from the court. The prosecution peremptorily challenged Captain Stanton, who they feared was disposed to rule in favor of the accused officers. He was also excused from the court.[292]

Lieutenant Clinton and Lieutenant Thompson were both charged with violating the 64th Article of War, and three specifications therein, and the 68th Article of War with one specification. The violations of the 64th Article of War were defined by the officers' alleged willful disobedience of a direct and lawful order given by an M.P. (the mess officer of Club #2), and the offer of violence against the M.P., a superior officer. The possible sentence was capital punishment. The violation of the 68th Article of War was defined by the officers' apparent involvement in a disorder, after they refused to obey a direct order from a superior officer.[293]

The prosecution presented several witnesses, including the M.P., the mess officer, and other M.P.s, to establish the case that Clinton and Thompson disobeyed a direct order and offered violence against a superior officer. The prosecution was unable, however, to establish that the order given by the M.P. was a lawful order, or that the M.P. actually gave the order not to enter the club.[294] The prosecution was also unsuccessful in proving, beyond doubt that the accused officers touched the M.P. while entering the club. Since the prosecution could not establish the fact that Clinton and Thompson came to the club in a large group with intentions to cause a disturbance, the charge of violating the 68th Article of War was weak.[295]

The defense counsel, led by Berry, was able, in his cross-examination of witnesses for the prosecution, to establish some doubt that the Clinton and Thompson received a direct order not to enter the club. Berry was able to verify, in the cross-examination of the mess officer, that the M.P. was given orders not to let any colored officers into the club, whether they were base personnel or not.[296] This acknowledgment cast doubt on the legality of the 1 April 1945 order from which the Provost Marshall gave his instruction to the M.P.s. Any such order would be in violation of army regulations. Attorney Berry's questioning of Colonel Selway uncovered the fact that Selway did not intend for the 1 April base order to exclude all officers from the club. That part of Selway's testimony also gave credence to the theory that the order given by the M.P. could have been illegal.[297]

Colonel Selway appeared insolent, to the members of the court. When he was called as a witness, he saluted the flag instead of the court.[298] When questioned by the defense counsel about base orders of 10 March and 1 April 1945, Selway was evasive and vague. He did, however, state that the March order was given to his deputy orally and was predicated on the base order of the previous Freeman Field commander.[299] He gave his most illuminating testimony when he stated that he had received telephone instructions from General Hunter on numerous occasions, concerning assignment and use of facilities at Freeman Field, but had no written order from him.[300] This portion of the testimony insinuated that he was acting on verbal orders from General Hunter and not of his own volition. Selway also attempted to disassociate himself from the command of Freeman Field on 10 March 1945 and, therefore, disassociate himself from the responsibility for issuing an illegal order. Attorney Berry was successful in establishing the fact that Freeman Field, in March, 1945, was a sub-base of Godman Field and, therefore, under the command of Colonel Selway.[301] At this point in his testimony, Selway stated that he objected to the questioning as objectionable, irrelevant, and immaterial. The court overruled his objections.[302]

The defense counsel offered several eyewitnesses who testified that the accused officers did not touch the M.P. while entering the club and that the only jostling was by the M.P., who grabbed Thompson's shoulder and pushed him into the club. The witnesses also testified that they heard no order from the M.P. not to enter the officers' club and that the accused did not come with a group of officers with intent to cause a disturbance. Attorney Berry also produced a witness, Lieutenant Payton, who testified that the mess officer had informed him on 5 April 1945 that he could not enter the club because no colored officers were to be admitted.[303] Lts.

Thompson and Clinton both maintained their composure when cross-examined by the prosecution, and maintained their contention that they did not receive an order not to enter the club.[304]

There were no closing arguments by the prosecution or the defense. The court was closed and, after secret ballot, the accused officers where found not guilty of all specifications and charges.[305]

The Terry court-martial trial began the next morning, 3 July 1945. The same officers were detailed to the court and the same prosecution and defense counsel retained. The prosecution requested, and received, a continuance of the case until 1:00 P.M., in order to take up the matter of the case with command headquarters.[306]

When the court convened, the prosecution peremptorily challenged Captain Stanton and the defense counsel peremptorily challenged Colonel Davis. Both were excused.[307] The accused was charged with violation of the 64th Article of War and two specifications therein, namely, Lieutenant Terry willfully disobeyed a lawful order from a superior officer and offered violence to a superior officer when given an order. Possible sentence, if convicted, was capital punishment. Lieutenant Terry pleaded not guilty to the charges.[308]

Before Lieutenant Terry pleaded, Attorney Berry entered a special plea of motion to discharge or dismiss Specification 1 of the charge, due to the fact that the alleged order given to Terry was in violation of Army Regulation 210-10, Paragraph 19 and, therefore, on its face, an illegal order. The law member, acting on behalf of the court, denied the motion to dismiss the charge.[309]

The prosecution produced several witnesses, including the M.P., who testified that to Lieutenant Terry and the other two officers who accompanied him were given a direct order not to enter the officers' club. The witnesses also testified that Lieutenant Terry ignored the order, pushed the M.P. out of the way, and entered the club. The M.P. stated that Terry pushed him away from the door, opened the door and pushed him further to the side of the door.[310]

The defense counsel attempted to discredit the M.P. and other witnesses, who claimed they knew which officers were trainees and which officers were members of the club. The M.P. confessed that he did not stop any white officers from entering the club because that was what he was ordered to do. He testified that all of the officers he stopped were black.[311] Colonel Selway was also called as a witness for the defense. Selway, as in the previous Thompson/Clinton trial, was evasive and vague and when challenged by Berry, he would object to every question on the grounds that it was irrelevant and immaterial. The law member reminded Selway that the witness had no right to object to questions.

Berry succeeded in getting Selway to admit that the order given to the M.P.s to bar certain officers from the officers' club was not a negative order and that it did not restrict anyone from the use of any facility due to color.[312] Berry produced a witness, Lt. Clarence Jarret, who established the fact that the mess officer told him and the other officers who attempted to enter the club earlier on the night of 5 April 1945, that he had orders not to allow any colored personnel to enter the club.[313] This testimony cast doubt on the legality and intent of the order given to Lieutenant Terry by the M.P.

Lieutenant Terry took the stand and testified, in his own defense, that he did not push the M.P. from the door.[314] He testified that he was not sure whether he was a member of the 477th Group, but he knew he was a member of the Replacement Training Unit.[315] The prosecution attempted to take advantage of Terry's alleged vulnerability and uncertainty. They established, with Terry's testimony, that Lieutenant Terry considered himself a trainee and had some knowledge of which buildings were accessible. Terry, fighting back his anger, testified that he had no understanding that he was prohibited from the building, even after being warned by the M.P. that if he entered the building he would be arrested. The law member of the court then asked Lieutenant Terry whether it was his understanding that he was to enter only under penalty. Terry answered no. Terry added that he did not know the officer in front of the door was an M.P. He claimed that he was already headed into the club when he heard the order.[316] It appeared that Lieutenant Terry's anger, albeit justified, and equivocality might have cost him.

The court, by secret ballot, found Lieutenant Terry not guilty of violating the 64th Article of War, Specification 1, as defined by the willful disobedience of a legal order charge. Surprisingly, Lieutenant Terry was found guilty of violating the 64th Article of War, Specification 2, offering violence to a superior officer when given an order. Lieutenant Terry was sentenced to forfeit $150 in pay. The fine was to be secured in three monthly allotments.[317] This sentence baffled even the Judge Advocate General of the First Air Force. In his review of the case and verdict, the Judge Advocate wrote that " unless the acquittal of Specification 1 was upon the ground that the M.P.'s order was illegal, the findings are inconsistent."[318] The Judge Advocate was of the opinion that the court must have considered the M.P.'s order in violation of Army Regulation 210-10, Paragraph 19, and, therefore, illegal. It appeared that the activity that stuck in the minds of the court members was the assertiveness exhibited by Lieutenant Terry while entering the club, and his uncertainty regarding his status on the base.

The Judge Advocate General commented that, regardless of the illegality of the M.P.'s order, Lieutenant Terry was found guilty of offering violence against a superior officer while disobeying an order and, therefore, should have been given a sentence "commensurate with the gravity of the offense."[319] A conviction for violation of the 64th Article of War could result in death for the perpetrator. The Judge Advocate opined that the sentence of forfeiture of $50 per month for three months, was "grossly inadequate."[320] He recommended, however, that the sentence be approved.

General Hunter was angered and frustrated over the sentence given to Lieutenant Terry and the acquittal of Lts. Clinton and Thompson. He reluctantly accepted the opinion of his Judge Advocate General, complaining that the sentences were "grossly inadequate."[321] Hunter's hands were now tied. He no longer had the legal support of the War Department or the Air Force Judge Advocate General. The foundation for the integration of a federal institution was constructed. The legal support for racist and discriminatory policies no longer existed. The 477th Composite Group, however, was still relegated to separate and unequal facilities at Godman Field.

Notes

1. Davis, *Benjamin O. Davis, Jr. American: An Autobiography*, 102; Interview with William M. Womack.
2. "Colonel Davis Tells Story of 99th," *Baltimore Afro-American*, 18 September 1943; Lee, *The Employment of Negro Troops*, 454.
3. "Colonel Davis Tells Story of 99th," *Baltimore Afro-American*, 18 September 1943.
4. Ibid.
5. Ibid.
6. Lee, *The Employment of Negro Troops*, 453.
7. Ibid., 453-54; Osur, *Blacks in the Army Air Forces*, 45-49.
8. Lee, *The Employment of Negro Troops*, 454.
9. Ibid.
10. Ibid., 455; Osur, *Blacks in the Army Air Forces*, 49.
11. Lee, *The Employment of Negro Troops*, 49.
12. "Experiment Proved?" *Time* (20 September 1943): 66-68.
13. Ibid.
14. Lee, *The Employment of Negro Troops*, 455.
15. "Colonel Davis Tells Story of 99th," *Baltimore Afro-American*, 18 September 1943; Lee, *The Employment of Negro Troops*, 455.
16. Lee, *The Employment of Negro Troops*, 455.
17. Francis, *The Tuskegee Airmen*, 52; "Experiment Proved?" *Time* (20

September 1943): 68; "Segregation Banned as Air Corps Plans Bombing Unit," *Baltimore Afro-American*, 30 September 1943; Gropman, *The Air Force Integrates, 1945-1964*, 13.

18. MacGregor, *Integration of the Armed Forces*, 38; Lee, *The Employment of Negro Troops*, 450; Ernest E. Johnson, "Negro Fliers Seen Victims of General's Planned Segregation," *Pittsburgh Courier*, 2 June 1945.

19. Lee, *The Employment of Negro Troops*, 450.

20. Gropman, *The Air Force Integrates*, 14; Lee, *The Employment of Negro Troops*, 456.

21. Lee, *The Employment of Negro Troops*, 458.

22. Ibid.; Osur, *Blacks in the Army Air Forces*, 50.

23. Lee, *The The Employment of Negro Troops*, 458-60; Osur, *Blacks in the Army Air Forces*, 52.

24. Osur, *Blacks in the Army Air Forces*, 50; Lee, *The Employment of Negro Troops*, 459-60.

25. Osur, *Blacks in the Army Air Forces*, 52; Lee, *The Employment of Negro Troops*, 461, 463, 467.

26. Interview with William M. Womack; Davis, *An Autobiography*, 110-11; Osur, *Blacks in the Army Air Forces*, 53.

27. Gropman, *The Air Force Integrates*, 18-19; Johnson, "Negro Fliers Seen Victims of General's Planned Segregation," *Pittsburgh Courier*, 2 June 1945.

28. Interview with William M. Womack; McGovern, *Black Eagles*, 42-43.

29. Interview with Omar P. Blair; Davis, *An Autobiography*, 11.

30. Memorandum, HQDA, Third Air Force, Office of the Staff Judge Advocate to Commanding General Third Air Force, 11 October 1943, 4, 7, 11; General Court Martial Order Number 596, 20 October 1943.

31. Interview with William M. Womack; Interview with Alexander Jefferson; Interview with Milton Henry.

32. "Allege Bribery in Death at Air Field," *Baltimore Afro-American*, 15 May 1943.

33. Ibid.

34. Ibid.

35. Ibid.

36. Ibid.; Ralph Mathews, "Jealousy Not Hate Caused Camp Shooting," *Baltimore Afro-American*, 22 May 1943; "Public Court-Martial," *Baltimore Afro-American*, 11 September 1943.

37. "Air Crashes Kill 3," *Baltimore Afro-American*, 15 May 1943; Ralph Mathews, "Pilot Still Missing, Army Officially Assumes Flyer Dead," *Baltimore Afro-American*, 22 May 1943; Interview with Alexander Jefferson.

38. Ralph Mathews, "Pilot Still Missing, Army Officially Assumes Flyer Dead," *Baltimore Afro-American*, 22 May 1943.

39. Franklin, *From Slavery to Freedom*, 597.

40. Interview with William M. Womack; White, *A Man Called White*, 224.

41. White, *A Man Called White*, 225-30; T. John Wood, "Detroit Riot Toll 25, FDR Orders Military to Take City," *Baltimore Afro-American*, 26 June 1943.

42. Wood, "Detroit Riot Toll 25, FDR Orders Military to Take City," *Baltimore Afro-American*, 26 June 1943.

43. Interview with William M. Womack; Interview with Omar Blair; Interview with Alexander Jefferson.

44. Levi Jolley, "Soldiers Trying to Reach Riot," *Baltimore Afro-American*, 26 June 1943.

45. Interview with William M. Womack; Interview with Alexander Jefferson; Interview with Omar Blair.

46. "Flyers Have No-Accident Record, but Keep It Quiet," *Baltimore Afro-American*, 9 October 1943.

47. Interview with Alexander Jefferson; Interview with Omar Blair; Douglas Hall, "Flyer at Selfridge Field Tells of Close Calls in Air," *Baltimore Afro-American*, 16 October 1943; Interview with Walter Downs, 27 January 1990, Detroit, Michigan.

48. Interview with Milton Henry; Interview with Alexander Jefferson; McGovern, *Black Eagles*, 43.

49. Interview with Milton Henry.

50. "Public Court Martial," *Baltimore Afro-American*, 11 September 1943; General Court Martial, Number 596, William Colman, 20 October 1943, 2-6.

51. Ralph Mathews, "Jealousy, Not Hate, Caused Camp Shooting," *Baltimore Afro-American*, 22 May 1943.

52. Ibid.; Associated Negro Press, Col. Colman's Light Sentence Under Criticism," *Baltimore Afro-American*, 25 September 1943; Memorandum to Commanding General, Third Air Force from Officer of the Staff Judge Advocate, Re: Review of Stuff Judge Advocate, United States vs. Colman, William T, Colonel, Air Corps, 11 October 1943.

53. General Court Martial Order No. 596, 30 October 1943, William Colman; Associated Negro Press, "Col. Colman's Light Sentence Under Criticism," *Baltimore Afro-American*, 25 September 1943.

54. Associated Negro Press, "Col. Colman's Light Sentence Under Criticism," *Baltimore Afro-American*, 25 September 1943, quoted in *The Chicago Sun*.

55. Davis, *An Autobiography*, 114; Gropman, *The Air Force Integrates*, 18; Interview with William M. Womack.

56. Staff Correspondent, "Races Train Together at Selfridge Field," *Baltimore Afro-American*, 16 October 1943; Osur, *Blacks in the Army Air Forces*, 55.

57. "Command of Negro Troops" highlighted problems white officers would have commanding Negro troops. The pamphlet also directed base commanders to make black facilities equal to white.

58. Interview with William M. Womack. Mr. Womack was the first Negro

officer assigned to the 332nd, in May 1943; Robert A. Rose, *Lonely Eagles: The Story of American Black Air Force in World War II* (Los Angeles: Tuskegee Airmen, Inc., Los Angeles Chapter, 1976), 67; Francis, *The Tuskegee Airmen*, 78.

59. Interview with Milton Henry.

60. Interview with Walter Downs; Davis, *An Autobiography*, 114.

61. Interview with Charles Dryden; Interview with Spann Watson; Interview with Milton Henry.

62. Interview with Milton Henry; Interview with Charles Dryden; Osur, *Blacks in the Army Air Forces*, 55.

63. Interview with Charles Dryden; Osur, *Blacks in the Army Air Forces*, 55.

64. Interview with Milton Henry; General Court Martial Records, 10 August 1944.

65. "Oust Colonel at Selfridge Field," *Pittsburgh Courier*, 18 March 1944; Ernest E. Johnson, "Negro Fliers Seen Victims of General's Planned Segregation, *Pittsburgh Courier*, 2 June 1945; Osur, *Blacks in the Army Air Forces*, 55; Interview with Milton Henry.

66. Francis, *The Tuskegee Airmen*, 64-65.

67. Ibid.; Interview with Clarence Jamison; Interview with John W. Rogers; Interview with Herbert Carter.

68. Interview with Herbert Carter; Francis, *The Tuskegee Airmen*, 56-57; Lee, *The Employment of Negro Troops*, 466.

69. Lee, *The Employment of Negro Troops*, 467.

70. White, *A Man Called White*, 237.

71. Ibid.

72. Interview with Herbert Carter.

73. Walter White memorandum to War Department, regarding "Observations in North African and Middle Eastern Theatres of Operation," 22 April 1944, NAACP Files, Collection of the Manuscript Division, Library of Congress.

74. Ibid.

75. Francis, *The Tuskegee Airmen*, 58; Interview with Clarence Jamison; Interview with Herbert Carter.

76. Interview with Clarence Jamison; Francis, *The Tuskegee Airmen*, 59-60.

77. Francis, *The Tuskegee Airmen*, 60.

78. Ibid., 62.

79. Interview with Clarence Jamison; Francis, *The Tuskegee Airmen*, 61.

80. Gropman, *The Air Force Integrates*, 18; Osur, *Blacks in the Army Air Forces*, 55.

81. Osur, *Blacks in the Army Air Forces*, 55-56.

82. Gropman, *The Air Force Integrates*, 18-19.

83. Osur, *Blacks in the Army Air Forces*, 56.

84. Ibid.

85. Gropman, *The Air Force Integrates*, 18-19; Osur, *Blacks in the Army Air Forces*, 57.

86. Osur, *Blacks in the Army Air Forces*, 79; Lee, *The Employment of Negro Troops*, 387.

87. Gropman, *The Air Force Integrates*, 18-20; Osur, *Blacks in the Army Air Forces*, 57-58.

88. Gropman, *The Air Force Integrates*, 18; Osur, *Blacks in the Army Air Forces*, 57-58.

89. Osur, *Blacks in the Army Air Forces*, 59. Gropman, *The Air Force Integrates*, 17; Johnson, "Negro Fliers Seen Victims of General's Planned Segregation," *Pittsburgh Courier*, 2 June 1945.

90. Department of the Army, U.S. Army Court of Military Review, Office of the Clerk. Court Martial Record, Milton R. Henry, 8 May 1944, sworn statement from Lt. Col. Charles A. Gayle, 30 March 1944.

91. Ibid.; Charles Wartman, "Find Selfridge Pilot Guilty, Trial Lasted 2 Days Appeal May be Asked," *Michigan Chronicle*, 28 April 1944.

92. Court Martial Record, Milton R. Henry and Statement from Lt. Col. Charles A. Gayle; Charles Wartman, "Find Selfridge Pilot guilty, Trial Lasted 2 Days Appeal May Be Asked," *Michigan Chronicle*, 1 May 1944; Interview with Milton Henry.

93. Ibid., sworn statement, Lt. Col. Arthur DeBolt, 22 March 1944; Court Martial Record, Milton R. Henry, 5 May 1944; Testimony of Col. DeBolt, 19-22; Testimony of Col. Gayle, 13-18.

94. Charles Wartman, "Find Selfridge Pilot Guilty, Trial Lasted 2 Days Appeal May be Asked," *Michigan Chronicle*, 28 April 1944; Court Martial Record, Milton R. Henry, 5 May 1944, Testimony of Dr. Lt. Col. Charles M. Caravati, Medical Corps, Chief of Medicine, Percy Jones Hospital, Battle Creek Michigan, 69, 77.

95. Court Martial Record, Milton R. Henry, 5 May 1944, Testimony of Col. Sam P. Triffy, Commanding Officer, 553rd Fighter Squadron, Selfridge Field, Michigan.

96. Ibid., Testimony of Lt. Rice L. Carothers, HDQ, 553rd Fighter Squadron, 99-101, Testimony of Lt. Maurice L. Johnson, HDQ 553rd. Fighter Squadron, Selfridge Field, Michigan, 101-4.

97. Ibid., Testimony of Lt. Col. Sam P. Trilby, 54-55; Memorandum to Commanding General I Fighter Command, Mitchell Field, New York from Commanding Officer AAB, Selfridge Field, Michigan, 21 March 1944; Testimony of Major Joseph B. Price, 553rd. Fighter Group Selfridge Field, Michigan, 21 March 1944; Testimony of Major Joseph B. Price, 553rd. Fighter Group, Selfridge Field, Michigan, 60-61.

98. Court Martial Record, Milton R. Henry, 8 May 1944; Charge Sheet, 21 March 1944. Administrative Registration Memorandum to Lt. Milton Henry from Lt. Col. Triffy, 21 March 1944; Charge Sheet, 11 April 1944.

99. Court Martial Record, Milton R. Henry, 5 May 1944, Proceedings of a General Court Martial, Special Order Number 101, Organization of the Court.

100. Ibid.
101. Ibid.
102. Ibid., Testimony of Lt. Charles Caravati, 71-71, 77, 80, 85, Testimony Lt. Col. Paul A. Petric, Medical Corps, Perry Jones Hospital, Battle Creek, Michigan, 91-92.
103. Ibid., Testimony of Captain William J. Cosgrove, Medical Corps, 115th Army Air Forces Base Unit, Section B, Regional Station Hospital, Selfridge Field, Michigan, 88-89; Testimony Dr. Maureen Waver, Herman Klefer Hospital, Detroit, Michigan, 95-98.
104. Ibid., Testimony, Lt. Rice L. Carothers, 533rd Fighter Squadron, 99-100; Lt. Maurie L. Johnson, 533rd Fighter Squadron, 103, 104; Lt. Charles E. Anderson, 553rd Fighter Squadron, 105.
105. Ibid., Defense Cross Examination of Testimony given by Col. Charles A. Gayle, 15-18; Defense Cross examination of Testimony given by Col. Arthur DeBolt, 23-26.
106. Ibid., Testimony of Lt. Col. Charles Gayle, 10-13, 18; Lt. Col. Arthur DeBolt, 19-22, 26; Lt. Col. Sam P. Driffy, 52-55.
107. Ibid., Testimony of Major Joseph B. Price, 553rd Fighter Squadron, 56-62; Lt. Hayward Burns, 553rd Fighter Squadron, 45-47.
108. Ibid., Testimony of Captain Lambert J. Agin, Medical Corps, 553rd Fighter Squadron, 106; Lt. Col. Harry C. Kroon, Medical Corps, Bradley Field, Conn., 109-11.
109. Ibid., Testimony of Lt. Col. Harry C. Kroon, 109, 114.
110. General Court Martial Trial Record, Lt. Milton R. Henry, 5 May 1944, General Court Martial Orders. No. 441, War Department, 16 August 1944.
111. Johnson, "Negro Fliers Seen Victims of General's Planned Segregation," *Pittsburgh Courier*, 2 June 1945; Interview with Alexander Jefferson; Interview with Richard Macon; McGovern, *Black Eagles*, 43-44.
112. Interview with Richard Macon; Interview with Alexander Jefferson; Interview with Charles Dryden; Osur, *Blacks in the Army Air Forces*, 59, Johnson, "Negro Fliers Seen Victims of General's Planned Segregation," *Pittsburgh Courier*, 2 June 1945.
113. Interview with Richard Macon; Interview with Charles Dryden; Interview with Alexander Jefferson.
114. Osur, *Blacks in the Army Air Forces*, 59; Gropman, *The Air Force Integrates*, 16.
115. Gropman, *The Air Force Integrates*, 16; Osur, *Blacks in the Army Air Forces*, 59; Interview with Elmore Kennedy, 5 June 1990, Detroit, Michigan.
116. Osur, *Blacks in the Army Air Forces*, 56, 60; Gropman, *The Air Force Integrates*, 16.
117. Interview with Spann Watson; Johnson, "Negro Fliers Seen Victims of General's Planned Segregation," *Pittsburgh Courier*, 2 June 1945; Osur, *Blacks in the Army Air Forces*, 60; Interview with Alexander Jefferson.

118. Interview with Elmore Kennedy; Davis, *An Autobiography*, 141-42.
119. Interview with Elmore Kennedy; Davis, *An Autobiography*, 149.
120. Gropman, *The Air Force Integrates*, 25; Leslie S. Perry, "Report to Walter White on the Investigation of Freeman Field, Indiana (477th Medium Bomb Group), 13-14 April 1945," NAACP Papers, Collections of the Manuscript Division, Library of Congress.
121. Interview with William M. Womack; Interview with Walter Downs; Francis, *The Tuskegee Airmen*, 81-82. Rose, *Lonely Eagles*, 67.
122. Francis, *The Tuskegee Airmen*, 67-68, 81.
123. Ibid.
124. Interview with Walter Downs; Interview with Alexander Jefferson; Interview with Richard Macon; Interview with Fred Hutchins.
125. Francis, *The Tuskegee Airmen*, 67; Davis, *An Autobiography*, 119.
126. Davis, *An Autobiography*, 119; Interview with Herbert Carter.
127. Interview with Herbert Carter; Francis, *The Tuskegee Airmen*, 68.
128. Francis, *The Tuskegee Airmen*, 69; Interview with Herbert Carter; Davis, *An Autobiography*, 119.
129. Davis, *An Autobiography*, 118; Francis, *The Tuskegee Airmen*, 86.
130. Ibid.
131. Interview with Herbert Carter; Francis, *The Tuskegee Airmen*, 85; Carter and Mueller, *The Army Air Forces in World War II*, 213, 470.
132. Interview with Herbert Carter.
133. Francis, *The Tuskegee Airmen*, 92.
134. Ibid., 85-86; Interview with Herbert Carter.
135. Francis, *The Tuskegee Airmen*, 86; Interview with Walter Downs; Interview with Fred Hutchins.
136. Interview with Walter Downs; Interview with Woodrow Crockett, 9 August 1990, Los Angeles, California; Francis, *The Tuskegee Airmen*, 95. Rose, *Lonely Eagles*, 68-69.
137. Interview with William Holliman, 5 May 1990, Detroit, Michigan; Francis, *The Tuskegee Airmen*, 96-97; Rose, *Lonely Eagles*, 69.
138. Interview with William M. Womack; Interview with Richard Macon.
139. Interview with William M. Womack; Interview with William Holliman; Davis, *An Autobiography*, 137.
140. Francis, *The Tuskegee Airmen*, 72-73, 101.
141. Ibid.
142. Ibid., 73; Carter and Mueller, The Army Air Forces, 213.
143. Fighter Squadrons as a rule contained only three squadrons (Carter and Mueller, *The Army Air Forces*, 213).
144. Interview with Herbert Carter; Interview with Fred Hutchins; Interview with William Holliman.
145. Interview with William M. Womack; Francis, *The Tuskegee Airmen*, 75, 102-3.
146. Interview with Charles Dryden; Interview with Walter Downs.
147. Francis, *The Tuskegee Airmen*, 103; Interview with William M. Womack;

Interview with William Holliman; Interview with Woodrow Crockett; Interview with Fred Hutchins.

148. Interview with Herbert Carter; Interview with Woodcrow Crockett.
149. Rose, *Lonely Eagles*, 70; Francis, *The Tuskegee Airmen*, 103-5.
150. Francis, *The Tuskegee Airmen*, 106; Rose, *Lonely Eagles*, 71.
151. Interview with Herbert Carter; Interview with Walter Downs; Interview with Fred Hutchins.
152. Interview with Richard Macon; Interview with Alexander Jefferson; Interview with Fred Hutchins.
153. Interview with Richard Macon; Interview with Alexander Jefferson; Interview with Walter Downs; Interview with Woodrow Crockett; Francis, *The Tuskegee Airmen*, 123-25.
154. Carter and Mueller, *The Army Air Forces*, 213, 470; Francis, *The Tuskegee Airmen*, 129-34.
155. Interview with Woodrow Crockett; Interview with Walter Downs; Interview with Fred Hutchins; Rose, *Lonely Eagles*, 69, 73.
156. Richard Suchenwirth, *The German Air Force in WWII: Historical Turning Points in the German Air Force War Effort* (New York: U.S. Air Force Historical Studies, U.S. Air Force Historical Division, Arno Press, 1968), 125.
157. Interview with Charles Dryden.
158. Ibid., Mary Penick Motley, *The Invisible Soldier: the Experience of the Black Soldier, World War II* (Detroit: Wayne State University Press, 1975), 219; Interview with Alexander Jefferson.
159. Interview with Charles Dryden; Interview with Richard Macon.
160. Interview with Charles Dryden.
161. Interview with Charles Dryden; Johnson, "Negro Fliers Victims of General's Planned Segregation," *Pittsburgh Courier*, 2 June 1945.
162. Interview with Spann Watson.
163. Ibid.
164. Ibid.
165. Ibid.
166. Carter and Mueller, *The Army Air Forces*, 349; Lee, *The Employment of Negro Troops*, 455.
167. Carter and Mueller, *The Army Air Forces*, 350; Lee, *The Employment of Negro Troops*, 462-463.
168. Lee, *The Employment of Negro Troops*, 464.
169. Gropman, *The Air Force Integrates*, 16; Osur, *Blacks in the Army Air Forces*, 109.
170. Gropman, *The Air Force Integrates, 1943-1964*, 20; Osur, *Blacks in the Army Air Forces*, 109-10.
171. Gropman, *The Air Force Integrates, 1943-1964*, 20.; Osur, *Blacks in the Army Air Forces*, 112; Perry, "Investigation of Freeman Field," Report to Walter White on the Investigation of Freeman Field, Indiana (477th Medium Bomb Group), 13-14 April 1945.

172. Perry, "Investigation of Freeman Field."

173. Osur, *Blacks in the Army Air Forces,* 112

174. Interview with Spann Watson.

175. Perry, "Investigation of Freeman Field."

176. Gropman, *The Air Force Integrates,* 16; Interview with Wardell Polk, 18 February 1990, Detroit, Michigan; Interview with Elmore Kennedy.

177. Memorandum from Adjutant General's Office, War Department, to Commanding General's Army Air Forces, All service Commands Military Districts Washington, Subject: Recreational Facilities, 8 July 1944.

178. Gropman, *The Air Force Integrates,* 17; Osur, *Blacks in the Army Air Forces,* 112.

179. Interview with Wardell Polk; Interview with Elmore Kennedy; Gropman, *The Air Force Integrates,* 20; Osur, *Blacks in the Army Air Forces,* 114.

180. Suchenwirth, *The German Air Force,* 119; Interview with Walter Downs.

181. Edward Jablonski, *Wings of Fire, Air War Volume IV* (Garden City, New York: Doubleday, 1972), 115; Carter and Mueller, *The Army Air Forces,* 602; Suchenwirth, *The German Air Force,* 118.

182. Francis, *The Tuskegee Airmen,* 155-56.

183. Suchenwirth, *The German Air Force,* 122.

184. Ibid., 120-21.

185. Ibid.,

186. Ibid., 121, 123-24.

187. Ibid., 123.

188. Ibid., 125.

189. Interview with Walter Downs; Davis, *An Autobiography,* 131.

190. Interview with Walter Downs; Interview with Herbert Carter.

191. Interview with Walter Downs; Interview with Herbert Carter; Interview John Whitehead.

192. Interview with Walter Downs; Interview with Herbert Carter; Interview John Whitehead.

193. Interview with Walter Downs; Davis, *An Autobiography,* 133; Francis, *The Tuskegee Airmen,* 158; Interview with Fred Hutchins.

194. Interview with Woodrow Crockett.

195. Interview with Omar Blair.

196. Ibid.; Interview with Woodrow Crockett; George Watson Sr., *Memorable Memoirs* (New York: Carlton Press, Inc., 1987), 98.

197. Interview with Woodrow Crockett; Interview with Walter Downs; Interview with Omar Blair; Interview with Fred Hutchins.

198. Interview with Walter Downs; Rose, *Lonely Eagles,* 73; Francis, *The Tuskegee Airmen,* 158-60; Davis, *An Autobiography,* 133.

199. Suchenwirth, *The German Air Force,* 126.

200. Interview with Walter Downs; Davis, *An Autobiography,* 131; Suchenwirth, *The German Air Force,* 118, 126.

201. Francis, *The Tuskegee Airmen*, 160-61; Carter and Mueller, *The Army Air Forces*, 614-15.
202. Davis, *An Autobiography*, 137.
203. Gropman, *The Air Force Integrates*, 16; Perry, "Investigation of Freeman Field."
204. Perry, "Investigation of Freeman Field."
205. Ibid.
206. Interview with Elmore Kennedy; Perry, "Investigation of Freeman Field."
207. Perry, "Investigation of Freeman Field."; Interview with E. E. Richardson, 9 August 1990, Los Angeles, California; Interview with Leroy Gillead.
208. Interview with Wardell Polk.
209. Interview with Clarence Jamison; Interview with John W. Rogers; Perry, "Investigation of Freeman Field."
210. Testimony of Lt. William Parks, Court Martial Record of Trial, Marsdon A. Thompson, Shirley R. Clinton, HQDA (JAAJ-CC), 26 July 1945, 40.
211. Ibid., Testimony of Col. Robert R. Selway, 49; Gropman, *The Air Force Integrates*, 21; Osur, *Blacks in the Army Air Forces*, 114; Perry, "Investigation of Freeman Field."
212. Interview with Wardell Polk; Interview with Elmore Kennedy; Gropman, *The Air Force Integrates*, 21.
213. General Court Martial Record of Trial, Marsden Thompson, Shirley R. Clinton, HQDA (JAAJ-CC), 26 July 1945, Testimony of Col. John B. Patterson, Deputy Commander 477th, 45; Perry, "Investigation of Freeman Field."
214. Perry, "Investigation of Freeman Field."
215. Ibid.; General Court Martial Record of Trial, Shirley Clinton, Marsdon Thompson, HQDA (JAAJ-CC), 26 July 1945, Testimony of Lt. William J. Parks, 41-42.
216. Ibid.; Interview with Leroy Gillead; letter from Leroy Gillead to Louis Zollar, 19 April 1945.
217. Interview with Wardell Polk; Perry, "Investigation of Freeman Field."
218. Interview with Leroy Gillead; Interview with Elmore Kennedy.
219. Perry, "Investigation of Freeman Field."; Interview with Clarence Jamison; Interview with Spann Watson.
220. Interview with Elmore Kennedy; Interview with Spann Watson.
221. Interview with Wardell Polk; Perry, "Investigation of Freeman Field."
222. Interview with Wardell Polk; Interview with Leroy Gillead; Motley, *The Invisible Soldier*, 70-71.
223. General Court Martial Record of Trial, Marsden Thompson, Shirley Clinton, HQDA (JAAJ-CC), 26 July 1945, Chronological Record of Military Experience Lt. Marsden Thompson, 7 April 1945.

224. Interview with Wardell Polk; Interview with Spann Watson; Interview with Milton Henry.

225. Interview with Wardell Polk; Interview with Spann Watson; Interview with Leroy Gillead; Perry, "Investigation of Freeman Field"; General Court Martial Record of Trial, Marsdon Thompson, Shirley Clinton, HQDA (JAAJ-CC), 26 July 1945; General Court Martial Record, Marsden Thompson, Shirley Clinton, HQDA (JAAJ-CC), 26 July 1945, Testimony of Lt. Robert Payton, 61; General Court Martial Record, Marsden Thompson, Shirley Clinton, HQDA (JAAJ-CC), 26 July 1945, Testimony of Lt. Coleman Young, 65; General Court Martial Record, Marsden Thompson, Shirley Clinton, HQDA (JAAJ-CC), 26 July 1945, Testimony of Lt. Clarence Garrot, 74.

226. General Court Martial Record, Marsden Thompson, Shirley Clinton, HQDA (JAAJ-CC), 26 July 1945, Testimony of Lt. Robert Payton, 60-61; General Court Martial Record, Marsden Thompson, Shirley Clinton, HQDA (JAAJ-CC), 26 July 1945, Testimony of Lt. Clarence Jarrett, 74; General Court Martial Record, Marsden Thompson, Shirley Clinton, HQDA (JAAJ-CC), 26 July 1945, Testimony of, Lt. Coleman Young, 64; Interview with Spann Watson.

227. Court Martial Record, Marsden Thompson, Shirley Clinton, HQDA (JAAJ-CC), 26 July 1945, Testimony of Lt. Robert Payton, 61.

228. General Court Martial Record, Marsden Thompson, Shirley Clinton, HQDA (JAAJ-CC), 26 July 1945, Testimony of Lt. Coleman Young, 64-65.

229. General Court Martial Record, Marsden Thompson, Shirley Clinton, HQDA (JAAJ-CC), 26 July 1945, Testimony F/O Howard Story Squadron E, 81; General Court Martial Record, Marsden Thompson, Shirley Clinton, HQDA (JAAJ-CC), 26 July 1945, Testimony of Lt. Joseph Rogers, Service Unit, HDQ Section, 15.

230. General Court Martial Record, Marsden Thompson, Shirley Clinton, HQDA (JAAJ-CC), 26 July 1945, Testimony of Lt. Joseph Rogers, 15-16; General Court Martial Record, Marsden Thompson, Shirley Clinton, HQDA (JAAJ-CC), 26 July 1945, Testimony of Lt. Coleman Young, 65.

231. General Court Martial Record, Marsden Thompson, Shirley Clinton, HQDA (JAAJ-CC), 26 July 1945, Testimony of Lt. Coleman Young, 65.

232. General Court Martial Record, Marsden Thompson, Shirley Clinton, HQDA (JAAJ-CC), 26 July 1945, Testimony of Marsdon Thompson, 98; General Court Martial Record, Marsden Thompson, Shirley Clinton, HQDA (JAAJ-CC), 26 July 1945, Testimony of Lt. Coleman Young, 64-67.

233. General Court Martial Record, Marsden Thompson, Shirley Clinton, HQDA (JAAJ-CC), 26 July 1945, Testimony of Captain Anthony N. Chiappe, 123rd, Base Unit, 25, 32; General Court Martial Record, Marsden Thompson, Shirley Clinton, HQDA (JAAJ-CC), 26 July 1945, Testimony of Major Andrew M. White, Wakeman General Hospital, 22.

234. General Court Martial Record of Trial, Roger Terry, 5 August 1945, Testimony of James B. Kennedy, 46.
235. Interview with Wardell Polk; Perry, "Investigation of Freeman Field."
236. Perry, "Investigation of Freeman Field."
237. Ibid.; General Court Martial Record of Trial, Marsden Thompson, Shirley Clinton, HQDA (JAAJ-CC), 26 July 1945, Testimony of Col. Robert L. Selway, 48.
238. Interview with Spann Watson; Interview with E. E. Anderson.
239. Perry, "Investigation of Freeman Field."
240. Ibid.
241. Osur, *Blacks in the Army Air Forces*, 115; Gropman, *The Air Force Integrates*, 22.
242. Perry, "Investigation of Freeman Field."; Interview with Clarence Jamison; Interview with Spann Watson.
243. Osur, *Blacks in the Army Air Forces*, 116-17; Gropman, *The Air Force Integrates*, 22-24.
244. Perry, "Investigation of Freeman Field"; Headquarters Freeman Field, Seymour, Indiana, Base Regulations, Number 85-2 Assignment of Housing, 9 April 1945.
245. Osur, *Blacks in the Army Air Forces*, 116; Gropman, *The Air Force Integrates*, 23.
246. Perry, "Investigation of Freeman Field"; Attachment Letter to Commanding Officer, Freeman Field from Lt. William, T. Coleman, Jr., 118th AAF Base Unit, C Squadron, 10 April 1945.
247. Osur, *Blacks in the Army Air Forces*, 115-16; Gropman, *The Air Force Integrates*, 24.
248. Interview with Wardell Polk; Gropman, *The Air Force Integrates*, 23.
249. Perry, "Investigation of Freeman Field"; Interview with Spann Watson; Interview Leroy Gilliard.
250. Perry, "Investigation of Freeman Field"; attachment letter to Commanding Officer, Freeman Field, from Lt. William T. Coleman Jr., 188th AAF Base Unit, C Squadron, 10 April 1945.
251. Interview with Spann Watson; Interview with Wardell Polk; Interview with Leroy Gillead.
252. Letter from Leroy Gillead to Louis Zollar, 19 April 1945; Perry, "Investigation of Freeman Field."
253. Ibid.; Ibid.
254. Perry, "Investigation of Freeman Field"; Gropman, *The Air Force Integrates*, 23.
255. Interview with Wardell Polk; Interview with Leroy Gillead; Charles Davis, "Pilots Arrested," *Pittsburgh Courier*, 14 April 1945.
256. Perry, "Investigation of Freeman Field."
257. Ibid.
258. Ibid.
259. Ibid.

259. Ibid.

260. Ibid.

261. Osur, *Blacks in the Army Air Forces*, 118; Gropman, *The Air Force Integrates*, 25-26.

262. Interview with Spann Watson; Interview with Leroy Gillead.

263. Gropman, *The Air Force Integrates*, 27; Osur, *Blacks in the Army Air Forces*, 120.

264. Gropman, *The Air Force Integrates*, 27.

265. Osur, *Blacks in the Army Air Forces*, 120-21; Gropman, *The Air Force Integrates*, 28.

266. General Court Martial Record, Marsdon Thompson, Shirley Clinton, HQDA (JAAJ-CC), 26 July 1945, sworn statements from Lt. Joseph Rogers, Lt. Stacey Brower, and Lt. James Rice; General Court Martial Record, Roger Terry, 5 August 1945, sworn statement from, Lt. James M. Rice, Lt. Robert O. Harrison, and Lt. Stacey Brewer.

267. Osur, *Blacks in the Army Air Forces*, 120; Gropman, *The Air Force Integrates*, 28.

268. Osur, *Blacks in the Army Air Forces*, 121; Gropman, *The Air Force Integrates*, 29.

269. "Army May Move Colonel Selway," *Pittsburgh Courier*, 28 April 1945; "Secrecy Covers Transfer of 101 Officers of 4775h," *Pittsburgh Courier*, 5 May 1945; "477th Wants Selway Removed, New Order Limits Promotions," *Pittsburgh Courier*, 2 June 1945.

270. George S. Schuyler, "Views and Review," *Pittsburgh Courier*, 5 May 1945.

271. "Army May Move Colonel Selway," *Pittsburgh Courier*, 28 April 1945.

272. "Officers Transferred, Continued to Await Probe, Group Sent to Kentucky," *Pittsburgh Courier*, 21 April 1945.

273. Ibid..

274. General Court Martial Record, Marsden Thompson, Shirley Clinton HQDA (JAAJ-CC), 26 July 1945; letter from the Judge Advocate General, Maj. Gen. Myron C. Cramer, the Air Judge Advocate to Commanding General, AAF, ATT, Deputy Chief of Air Staff, 11 June 1945; John H. Young, "No Bickering Over 477th—Patterson, Denies News Suppressed," *Pittsburgh Courier*, 26 May 1945.

275. General Court Martial Record, Marsden Thompson, Shirley Clinton, HQDA, JAAJ-CC, 26 July 1945, memorandum for the Judge Advocate General from Col. R. F. Kunkel, Judge Advocate General Dept. Chief, Military Justice Division.

276. General Court Martial Record, Marsden Thompson, Shirley Clinton, HQDA, JAAJ-CC, 26 July 1945, memorandum for the Judge Advocate General, Subject: Court Martial Charges Against Second Lieutenants Robert L. Terry, Marden A. Thompson, and Shirley R. Clinton, 14 May 1945.

277. General Court Martial Records, Marsdon Thompson, Shirley Clinton, HQDA (JAAJ-CC), 26 July 1945, Recommendation of Col. Henry

Harmelling; Judge Advocate, Report of staff Judge Advocate to Convening Authority on Court Martial charges, 11 April 1945, 4; letter to the Judge Advocate General, Att: Chief Military Justice Division, from Col. H. G. Culton, Deputy Chief Air Staff, HQ, AAF, 21 June 1945.

278. "What of Col. Selway-Courier? Be Patient with Us!" *Pittsburgh Courier*, 2 June 1945.

279. Walter White straight wire to Henry J. Stimson, War Department, 14 June 1945.

280. Ibid.

281. "Col. Davis to be General, Will Assume Command of 477th Bomber Group," *Baltimore Afro-American*, 23 June 1945.

282. R. M. Phillips, "Orders 477th Group to Pacific. Slated to Leave in Late Summer or Fall," *Baltimore Afro-American*, 30 June 1945.

283. Memorandum No. 600-45, Command of Negro Troops, by Order of the Secretary of War and Chief of Staff, 14 June 1945.

284. General Court Martial Record, Marsden Thompson, Shirley Clinton, HQDA (JAAJ-CC), 26 July 1945; Roger Terry, 5 August 1945, Court Martial Charge Sheet formally signed 24 June 1945, Charge Sheet initiated 9 April 1945.

285. Ibid., Memorandum to the Judge Advocate General, Judge Advocate General's Department, Washington D.C., through Commanding Officer, 477th Bombardment Group, Godman Field, Kentucky, 19 May 1945, Subject: Clarification of Arrest -Marsden A. Thompson.

286. "Col. Davis to be General, Will Assume Command of 477th Bomber Group," *Baltimore Afro-American*, 23 June 1945.

287. Davis, *An Autobiography*, 143; "Col. Davis to be General, Will Assume Command of 477th Bomber Group," *Baltimore Afro-American*, 23 June 1945.

288. NAACP Press Service Release, "NAACP to Represent 477th Officers in Trial"; General Court Martial Record, Marsden Thompson, Shirley Clinton, HQDA (JAAJ-CC), 26 July 1945, Roger Terry, 5 August 1945, Charge Sheet, 24 June 1945.

289. Press Service of the NAACP, "NAACP to represent 477th Officers in Trial," 28 June 1945.

290. General Court Martial Record, Marsdon Thompson, Shirley Clinton, HQDA (JAAJ-CC), 26 July 1945, Detail for the Court, 27 June 1965, Organization of the Court, 2 July 1945, 3.

291. Interview with Elmore Kennedy.

292. General Court Martial Record, Marsden Thompson, Shirley Clinton, 26 July 1945, Organization of the Court, 2 July 1945, 3; telephone interview, Theodore Berry, 12 October 1990.

293. General Court Martial Record of Trial, Marsden Thompson, Shirley Clinton, 24 July 1945, Arraignment, 4-5.

294. Ibid., Testimony and Cross Examination of Lt. Joseph Rogers 8-11, 16; Major Andrew White, 21-23; Lt. Robert Dayton, 59-62; Lt. Coleman A. Young, 63-68; Flight Officer Howard Story, 78-84, 85-86.

295. Ibid., Testimony and Cross Examination of Lt. Shirley Clinton and Lt. Marsden Thompson, 87-84, 95-100.

296. Ibid., Testimony and Cross Examination of Major Andrew White, 21-23; Lt. Joseph Rogers, 8-11, 16; and Lt. William Parks, Jr., 40.

297. Ibid., Testimony of Col. Robert L. Selway, 51.

298. Interview with Elmore Kennedy.

299. General Court Martial Record of Trial, Marsden Thompson, Shirley Clinton, 26 July 1945, Testimony of Col. Robert L. Selway, 47-48.

300. Ibid., 47-48, 51-53.

301. Ibid., 52.

302. Ibid., Testimony of Lt. Coleman A. Young, 63-68; Flight Officer Howard Story, 78-84; and Lt. Clifton Garret, 73.

303. Ibid., Testimony of Lt. Robert Payton, 60.

304. Ibid., Testimony of Lt. Marsdsen Thompson, 95-100; Lt. Shirley Clinton, 87-92, 94.

305. Ibid., Findings, 102.

306. Court Martial Record, Lt. Roger Terry (JAAJ-CC), 3 August 1945, 3.

307. Ibid., 4-5.

308. Ibid., Arraignment, 6, 8.

309. Ibid., 8

310. Ibid., Testimony of Lt. Joseph Rogers, 10; Lt. James Rice, 17-18; Lt. Robert Harrison, 23, 26.

311. Ibid., Testimony of Lt. Joseph Rogers, 14.

312. Ibid., Testimony of Col. Robert L. Selway, 36-37.

313. Ibid., 38, 40, Lt. Clarence Jarret, 44.

314. Interview with Elmore Kennedy.

315. General Court Martial Record, Lt. Roger Terry (JAAJ-CC), 5 August 1945, Testimony of Lt. Roger Terry, 53.

316. Ibid., 58-60.

317. Ibid., Findings, 53.

318. Ibid., Review of the Staff Judge Advocate on Record of Trial by General Court Martial; 28 July 1945, 3.

319. Ibid.

320. Ibid.

321. Ibid., HDQ First Air Force, Mitchell Field New York, General Court Martial Orders, Number 209, 30 July 1945.

Chapter 9

Beyond the Call of Duty

Several men of the 332nd Fighter Group were involved in heroic actions. A few of these men served beyond the call of duty, in self-sacrificing deeds, even to the extent of losing the limited personal freedom allowed a Negro in the Army Air Corps.

During the preparation for the invasion of southern France, in August 1944, the four squadrons were ordered to strafe the coastal radar sites that the Germans would use to detect invading aircraft. The 332nd Intelligence knew that if the radar installation were destroyed, allied armies and air force units could attack with little or no opposition from the German troops.[1] The squadrons attacked in flights of two, and as they settled the planes into the strafing positions, they realized that German antiaircraft gun operators had a clear shot at them from their beachhead entrenchments. The P-51s were hit hard as they came in to strafe and as they pulled out into evasive maneuvers. Six planes were shot down.[2]

One of the pilots hit was Lt. Richard Macon, of the 99th Fighter Squadron, from Birmingham, Alabama. The plane ahead of him, piloted by Lt. Joseph Gordon, was hit by a barrage of antiaircraft rounds and blew up. The bullets from the antiaircraft guns that destroyed Lieutenant Gordon's plane also damaged Lieutenant Macon's fighter. The bullets tore through the canopy and, suddenly, Macon's plane flipped over on its back. Macon tried to maneuver the plane upright but the steering mechanism would not respond. Lieutenant Macon knew that his control mechanisms were shot out. Macon's P-51 was only 200 feet from the ground, flying at a 400 mph. He went through all of the emergency procedures to evacuate the plane and then, suddenly, everything in the cockpit, according to

Macon, went red, and he lost consciousness. Macon later learned from his wingman on the mission that when his plane flipped over, upside down, creating negative gravity, Macon had a "red out," instead of a "black out." He fell against his stick and somehow his canopy opened, Macon bailed out of the airplane, and his parachute opened. His plane continued a short distance, however, and crashed into a warehouse, killing several German troops.[3]

When Lieutenant Macon regained consciousness, he was on the ground. He was startled by what he determined was a group of legs that belonged to Frenchmen. In his state of confusion, he thought he had made it back to France. He attempted to get up, but could not, and lost consciousness again. When he regained consciousness, the people were still present. When he tried to rise to his feet, he fell again. He could not understand why the Frenchmen would not help him. He understood when he saw the German troops standing above him. They commanded him, in German, to get up. He could not, and two German soldiers grabbed the Negro pilot, forcing him to his feet, at which point Macon lost consciousness again. He found out later that he had fractured his neck, and his lower body, below his waist, was paralyzed. He could not walk, so the German soldiers carried him to a coal-burning squad car.[4]

They took Lieutenant Macon to a makeshift field hospital in a school. Macon had heard all types of horror stories about German torture of war prisoners, and those stories were on his mind when the soldiers carried him into the hospital. As soon as Lieutenant Macon arrived, two doctors approached him and applied a cloth with ether to his nose, rendering him unconscious. Because of his condition, Macon could not fight back or attempt to escape, but he tried. In an attempt to control the Negro lieutenant, the German doctors strapped his arms and legs to a long table. The doctors then treated his neck injury.

When Macon regained consciousness, he was on a cot, and the first thing he did was to check to see if his privates were still intact. He was somewhat relieved to find them there. They had put what Macon thought was a French prisoner in the room to act as Macon's caretaker. When news spread through the French village that the Germans had captured the American pilot whose plane had destroyed the warehouse, the affected German crew came over to execute Lieutenant Macon for his deed. When they arrived in Macon's room, they ordered him to get up. When the French prisoner rose to assist Macon, the German guards kicked him in an attempt to discourage him from helping Macon. When the guards went to force Macon up, the Negro flyer blacked out. The German jailers realized that he was seriously injured. That night they transferred Macon to a farm with walls surrounding it that would make it difficult for the allies or the French Resistance to rescue the American pilot.[5]

The next morning, they blindfolded him and took him to the firing squad. Since he was still paralyzed they propped him up against a wall to give themselves a steady target. Lieutenant Macon, in a sense, felt relieved that he was going to be shot instead of tortured to death. The execution officer said, in German, "ready," "aim," and just before he said "fire," Macon heard someone yell "attention." All of the troops pulled their weapons down. Macon then heard someone yell "Lt. Richard Macon." The execution officer pointed a German captain from the area command unit toward Lieutenant Macon. The officer had him transferred to a schoolhouse where he was to be interrogated.[6]

They interrogated Macon for several hours. They wanted to know why the Allies were strafing southern France when all the fighting was in the north, Macon, however, told them nothing. He was later taken to the north, toward the Rhine Valley, and when they arrived at another farm, he was put in an animal barn and placed in a feeding trough filled with hay. Later that day, he heard someone else enter the barn. A German guard had a lantern and was issuing orders to someone else in the barn with him. When the guard made his way to Lieutenant Macon, the pilot heard someone say: "Hey, its a spook."[7] Immediately, Lieutenant Macon knew it was a member from his squadron. The person with the voice turn out to be Lt. Alexander Jefferson, who had been shot down on the same mission and later captured. Another squadron member, Lieutenant Daniels, was also shot down and captured. From that point on, they kept the three Negro prisoners together until they arrived at the designated prison camp.[8]

The prisoners were taken into Frankfort, Germany, to prisoner-of-war camps. The three Negro officers were separated. Lieutenant Macon was placed in an interrogation room with a small window and a cement slab for a bed. On the naked cement were body lice and other insects. Macon was forced to sleep on the cement slab. For breakfast, Macon was served only a slice of bread with margarine. Later in the morning, he was interrogated by a German officer who was fluent in English. Macon gave them only his name and serial number. The interrogation officer told Macon that he was not sure he was who he claimed he was. Ironically, all of the pilots on the mission to southern France were given foreign identification papers, in case they were lost or captured. Lieutenant Macon's alias was that of a Moroccan who was mute and was a good worker around airports. The German interrogators had confiscated his foreign papers and, therefore, wanted to make sure that he was, indeed, Lieutenant Macon.[9]

The German interrogator queried Lieutenant Macon about his background, his training, and facts about the mission that brought him to France. The Negro pilot was impressed with what the German intelligence knew about Negroes in America and, particularly, what they knew about Tuskegee. The interrogator pulled out a huge file titled "The 332nd." He had Macon's high school class picture, a picture of him from the *Pittsburgh Courier* leaving Birmingham for Tuskegee, and even a picture of Macon and his graduating class at Tuskegee, with Macon's face circled with an "x" across it. He even knew the code name given to Macon whenever he flew. When Macon gave him half of the code, he was convinced that Macon was, indeed, Lieutenant Macon. However, Lieutenant Macon pleaded ignorance to pointed questions and gave the interrogator nothing. The interrogator resorted to threats of Gestapo torture if Macon did not cooperate. Macon asked him about another pilot, Willie Griffin, who was shot down. The German officer told him that Lieutenant Griffin had been captured and sent to a prison camp in northern Germany, near Denmark. Lieutenant Macon was told that Griffin had cooperated and was sent to a German country club with golf courses and tennis courts. Macon was told the same amenities would be his, if he cooperated.[10]

The interrogator tried another tactic. The German officer told the lieutenant that he lived in the United States for ten years, five in California and five in New York. The German said he saw how the Americans treated the Negro and could not understand why African Americans could allow themselves to be treated in such a manner. He could not understand how Negroes would come over to Europe to fight for a country that treated them in such a cruel manner. Lieutenant Macon responded that the German officer was right, but that African Americans understood that, in a comparison of the two countries, the German government could take away all of their liberties and they would have no legal recourse. In America, Lieutenant Macon continued, African Americans, at least had access to legal redress. Macon also told the German officer that when he returned to America, he would continue the struggle to exercise those rights. The German officer told the American pilot that he could fight for Germany, and offered him a P-51. Macon declined.[11]

The Germans marched their prisoners of war further north in Germany to prison camps in Nuremberg and, eventually, Muesburg and Munich, where the prisoners feared they would be burned in the mass ovens. These marches were called atrocity marches, because they included several men in groups numbering 144, marching hundreds of miles in snow and vulnerable to air attacks from Allied planes shooting at the German trucks and tanks leading and trailing the march. During one of the marches, a native German teenager staring at Lieutenant Macon, who was probably the first Negro he had ever seen, spat on the ground and called Lieutenant Macon "Naegger," which in the German language translates to "Negro." The way it was pronounced gave Lieutenant Macon the impression the teen was calling him a nigger. Lieutenant Macon grabbed the boy by the neck and choked him, until his fellow prisoners and the guards rescued the boy.[12]

While incarcerated in a camp at Muesburg, called Stalag Luft 3, men in the group to which Macon was assigned continually attempted to escape. The prisoners had organizations for various assignments, under the designation of S-1, S-2, S-3, S-4, etc. One group took care of supplies, one photography, another intelligence. If a prisoner wanted to escape, he had to have his plans approved by the S-2 organization. S-2 would review and analyze the escape plan thoroughly before it gave its approval. Often it would not approve an escape plan that was poorly designed. Macon was part of S-2. Since there were no Negroes in the areas where the prison camps were located, the African-American soldiers could not attempt any escapes. They spent their time assisting other allied prisoners in their escape attempts. The prison camp always employed spies to monitor the activities of the prisoners. Final escape plans were always conducted within a closed circle of organization members.[13]

There were several tunnels built by Macon's organization. The tunnels were called Tom, Dick, and Harry. In Lieutenant Macon's barracks, the tunnel was built under the barracks' stove. Most tunnels were built under a stove, because there was usually a hole in the floor where the stove was installed. When the digging took place, the stove was usually left in place, while prisoners played poker near it. When a digger wanted to come up, or if there was danger, certain tapping sounds were used as a form of communication.

Lieutenant Macon's building was fifty yards from the woods. Therefore, a large tunnel had to be built and something had to been done with the tons of dirt that would be dug. Macon's group started building railroad tracks with klim cans, which were milk cans made from tin. They would take the wood from wooden bed planks and wall planks in the barracks and place the tin over the wood tracks so the wheels could roll. They carved the wood into wheels, covered the wheels with tin to make the wheels move easier, and placed them on small boxcars made of wood. They confiscated wire, which they used to manipulate the cars back and forth through the tunnel. They also used the wood to bolster the tunnel, so that the tunnels would not collapse, possibly killing escapees.

Lieutenant Macon and the prisoners found the Germans adept at discovering tunnels and escape routes. The prison camp personnel would bring in sound equipment to measure density in the ground beneath the prisoners' barracks. When a tunnel was discovered, it was, according to Macon, usually refilled with human waste. In Macon's organization, two of the three escape tunnels were discovered.[14]

Many escapes were made from Stalag Luft 3. The most notable was the "Great Escape," which took place during the year prior to Macon's capture. One man in Lieutenant Macon's group had a British uniform made into a German outfit with insignia. German identification papers were forged, and pictures of German prison camp personnel were used for identification cards and orders for a mission. When he was ready to escape, the prisoners in Macon's barracks started a baseball game, and then started a fight over a disputed call. The guards enjoyed watching the prisoners play baseball, and even enjoyed watching them fight. The guards did not notice when the prisoner, dressed as a German soldier, walked out of the compound. The escapee was last seen by the prisoners working outside of the barbed wire fence surrounding the camp measuring a distance from the gate to some point outside the fence, as if he was on duty. The prisoners watched him salute one of the prison guards and leave the camp, never to be seen again.[15]

Lieutenant Macon and his fellow prisoners were liberated by Patton's army on 29 April 1945. The prisoners knew Allied artillery was near because they could hear the shells going overhead. By that time, the prisoners had learned that a shell you could not hear was the most dangerous. They were able to judge how far the Allies were progressing and how far the Germans were retreating from the noise created by the bombs. On the morning of the liberation, one of the prisoners sighted an American tank approaching the prison camp. Small arms fire developed as German soldiers fired at the tanks across the compound where the prisoners were housed. Many of the prisoners hid to avoid the gunfire. Lieutenant Macon hid in a chimney.

The prisoners came out of the barracks when the shooting stopped and after the tank crashed through the prison camp fence. General Patton, himself, was in one of the tanks and personally supervised the capture and arrest of the prison camp commander. When the liberated men saw their former jailer under guard, they asked him what was he going to do. He said to them what he would say to every prisoner entering the camp: "The war for me, she is over."[16]

Lieutenant Macon took leave and went back to America to see his wife and family. His orders, somehow, had an identification code indicating he was white. All through the embarkation points, the clerks kept giving Macon strange looks, because his orders said he was white. At that time, in 1945, white former prisoners of war were sent to the reception center on the Boardwalk in Atlantic City. Consequently, Macon and his wife registered at the Ritz Carlton. The manager said that they could not register there. Lieutenant Macon replied that he had an order indicating that he was to stay at the Ritz Carlton and that the manager could call the general who signed the order and explain it to him. The manager declined, and allowed Macon and his wife to stay at the hotel. Mr. and Mrs. Macon may have been among the first African Americans to, albeit accidentally, integrate the Ritz Carlton in Atlantic City.[17]

Another pilot from the 332nd Fighter Squadron had a different experience as a captive. While returning from a bomber escort mission in Hungary, Lt. William W. "Chubby" Green and members of his flight team spotted a target of opportunity in Yugoslavia. They took passes at a barn they believed to be an ammunition storage area. The flight team took three passes at the barn firing their .50 millimeter guns and, on the third pass, the barn exploded. The debris from the explosion hit Green's P-51 and the plane of his wingman, Lt. Luther Smith. Both pilots nursed their damaged fighters to about 5,000 feet and then bailed out.

Lieutenant Smith landed near a German unit and was captured and later sent to a prison camp. Lieutenant Green had a little more luck. He landed in Yugoslavian Partisan territory and was soon captured by the Partisans and transported to Partisan General Headquarters under the command of General Tito. Once the Partisans determined that they could use the skills of a combat pilot, they accepted Lieutenant Green as an honorary Partisan.[18]

The Partisans specialized in guerrilla warfare, using hit-and-run tactics against the German occupation force. With Lieutenant Green on board, they focused their attention on an ammunition dump in the Lake Balaton area of Yugoslavia. Lieutenant Green assisted in the planning of the attack and prepared some of the explosives used in the effort. The Partisans were successful in destroying the ammo dump, severely reducing the ammunition supply of the German occupation force.[19]

After the Lake Balaton mission, Lieutenant Green, who was reported as missing in action, was taken to a British Supply Mission and later returned by Russian pilots to Rametelli, Italy, home base of the 332nd. A short time later in October 1945, Lieutenant Green was awarded the Order of the Partisan Star, III Class.[20]

Notes

1. Francis, *The Tuskegee Airmen,* 123-25; interview with Woodrow Crockett; interview with Richard Macon; interview with Alexander Jefferson.
2. Interview with Woodrow Crockett; interview with Richard Macon,; interview with Alexander Jefferson.
3. Interview with Richard Macon.
4. Ibid.
5. Ibid.
6. Ibid.
7. Ibid.; interview with Alexander Jefferson.
8. Ibid.
9. Interview with Richard Macon.
10. Ibid.
11. Ibid.
12. Ibid.
13. Ibid.
14. Ibid.
15. Ibid.
16. Ibid.
17. Ibid.
18. Francis, *The Tuskegee Airmen,* 48; "Pilot Gets Yugoslav Award," *Godman Field Beacon,* 29 October 1943.
19. "Pilot Gets Yugoslav Award," *Godman Field Beacon,* 29 October 1943; interview with Harry Stewart, 27 February 1990, Detroit.
20. "The Catipillar Club," *Godman Field Beacon,* 24 December 1945.

Chapter 10

Epilogue: Before the Brown Decision

With the end of hostilities in Europe, the men of the 332nd came home to segregated reception centers and local separation stations. There were no New York ticker-tape parades, such as those given in honor of the Negro soldiers of World War I, and no marching through Manhattan.

At that time in America, in 1945, Negro soldiers and veterans of World War II were not wanted, and were mistreated by white civilians, especially in the South, and not wanted by, or protected by, the military. There were several instances of mob and attacks on Negro soldiers and their families that matched the violence experienced after World War I. In Walton County, Georgia, an honorably discharged Negro was allegedly involved in a fight with a white man who had been making inappropriate advances at the Negro's wife. The Negro veteran was arrested and the white suitor ended up in the hospital. A mob, stirred up over the Negro's alleged insolence, stormed the jail and drove him into the country to an area where his wife and another Negro couple were held prisoner. All four were brutally lynched. Although the NAACP legally intervened and were successful in attracting a federal grand jury, the leaders of the mob were never brought to justice.[1]

In Minden, Louisiana, another veteran of the war was kidnapped and burned to death by a blow torch even though he was found innocent of loitering charges and released. Fortunately, there was an eyewitness, and the NAACP intervened and managed to secure a federal grand jury, who handed indictments to the mob organizers. Unfortunately, a local jury found the indicted mob leaders innocent.[2]

In another incident, forty-two draftees on their way to Fort Benning, Georgia, were accosted, beaten with clubs and blackjacks, and jailed by

Columbus, Georgia, policemen. Their crime: playing cards and laughing loudly on their train. Although the men were just drafted into the military, the military police ruled, erroneously, that the men were, technically, civilians until they reached Ft. Benning, and, therefore, that the Columbus civilian police were responsible.[3]

In October 1946, the enlisted men at McDill, a base located outside Tampa, Florida, complained to the Negro press about the segregated recreational and mess facilities, and unequal distribution of work and leave time given to Negro enlisted men, when compared to whites.[4] Frustrated at the inability of the McDill commanding officer to address their concerns, a clash between the Negro servicemen and the base military police ensued after the MPs sought to break up a fight at a base dance. The fight with the military police escalated to the extent that the M.P.s fired shots into the crowd, injuring a Negro soldier. After the incident, the Negro soldiers regrouped and collected rocks, bottles, and other objects and sought to attack a white housing project near the base. They were met by the county sheriff and several armed deputies, who were successful in dispersing the Negro crowd. The alleged leader of the riot was arrested, court-martialed, and given one to twenty years of hard labor and a dishonorable discharge.[5]

The most publicized account of a Negro soldier brutalized at the hands of civilians was the case of Issac Woodard. Woodard, a veteran of the Pacific campaign, was just discharged from the army when he took a bus ride to North Carolina to see his family. According to NAACP Secretary White's account, Woodard was admonished and threatened by the bus driver for taking a long rest stop. Later on the trip, the bus driver contacted a South Carolina policeman and falsely accused Woodard of being drunk and disorderly. When Woodard objected to the charges, he was severely beaten about the head by the policeman. Woodard was put in jail without medical attention and, tragically, was blinded for life. The NAACP came to Woodard's aid and, after an FBI investigation and eyewitness accounts, the South Carolina policeman was indicted and tried for the offense. He, too, was found innocent by a local jury. The fact that the army denied his application for a disability pension only compounded Woodard's problems. Fortunately, the NAACP solicited contributions for an annuity for Woodard.[6]

The men of the 332nd who chose to remain in the Army Air Force were given leave and told to report to Tuskegee Army Air Field or Godman Field, Fort Knox, Kentucky.

At Godman Field, the 332nd was deactivated and made part of the 477th and a service group, the 387th, was organized. Equipped with a surplus of fighter pilots, the 477th was reorganized into the 477th

Composite Group. A fighter squadron, the 99th, was added and two bomber squadrons were dropped. Since Godman Field housed the only Negro Composite Group in the Army Air Force Tactical Air Command, the unit was referred to by the Negro press as "Ben Davis's Air Force."[7] This particular alias was given partially out of respect for Colonel Davis, Jr.'s capability, and partially out of their disdain for the War Department's segregationist polices.

The objective of the 477th Composite Group was to prepare itself for overseas duty in the Pacific theatre.[8] In a situation similar to the deployment problems encountered at Tuskegee in 1942 and 1943, the Army Air Force had difficulty finding a base suitable for segregation and acceptable to the AAF Command in the Pacific theatre and, equally important, one that would be militarily efficient for the AAF's Negro problem.[9] Before a decision could be made, the Japanese surrendered, ending the war in the Pacific and ending what could have been another dangerous and precarious position for Negro pilots and airmen.

Godman Field was always considered by the Training Command and the Tactical Air Command as an airfield with inefficient runway space and storage facilities.[10] The inefficiency of the air base and the surplus of airmen necessitated a move to a more efficient base. The AAF searched the country for an area that would be most accommodating to a segregated Negro unit the size of the 477th and an area that would have a large enough civilian population to absorb the unit's social, educational, and recreational needs which were crucial to morale. The AAF command settled on Lockbourne Air Base outside of Columbus, Ohio, despite the protest of some influential whites in the Columbus area. The major newspaper in Columbus carried editorials that made it clear that Columbus was not interested in Negro troublemakers and Negro servants of the Air Force. The AAF command persisted and the 477th Composite Group moved to Lockbourne in March 1946.[11]

Shortly after the 477th Composite Group relocated to Lockbourne, the War Department issued a reduction in troop strength. This order had an adverse affect on the 477th because the personnel reduction created a shortage in experienced officers at Lockbourne. To make matters even more acute, the War Department and the Selective Service issued an order to all induction stations informing them to stop accepting Negro enlistees. This order, which was perceived by the NAACP and the Negro community as unconstitutional, meant that, for a time, talented and highly educated African Americans, qualified in technical occupations, were barred from the Army Air Force.[12]

Although most of the Negro officers survived the reduction in force and chose to stay in the AAF, a significant number of experienced officers were separated from service. Consequently, the 477th was fifty pilots short of the postwar authorized level. This shortage of officers with command experience forced many officers to work out of class on assignments normally given to men of higher rank.[13] Promotions were almost impossible, since there were few vacant positions ever filled and virtually none available, outside of Lockbourne, in a segregated Air Force.

With the closing of Tuskegee as a training base in April, 1946, many of the pilots who were stationed there after the war and the pilots who graduated in the classes in late 1945 and early 1946, were assigned to Lockbourne. The Columbus base became home for about 260, or 75 percent, of the Negro officers in the AAF, and 100 percent of the Negro pilots on active duty in the Tactical Air Command.[14] The grouping of all Negro pilots on active duty at Lockbourne created a surplus of Negro pilots, and especially lieutenants and captains, effectively eliminating room for advancement.[15] Those individual officers involved in the Freeman Field Mutiny who were given administrative reprimands were also at a disadvantage when it came to acquiring promotions. An administrative reprimand could be used against an officer seeking promotion. In the immediate postwar Army Air Force, 9,800 officers were approved for promotion, and only thirty-one were Negroes.[16]

The mob attacks on Negro war veterans and soldiers and the unequal and segregated treatment afforded Negro servicemen in places such as McDill and Lockbourne caused Negro civil rights organizations, labor groups, churches, and educational groups to form a coalition called the National Emergency Committee Against Mob Violence.[17] The goal of the Committee was to counteract the increase in white mob violence and white hate groups. The interracial group lobbied House members and the Senate for legislation outlawing certain activities of hate groups.[18]

The committee formed a delegation, with Walter White as the spokesperson, and met with President Truman and Att. Gen. Tom Clark on 19 September 1946, to discuss the concerns shared by the group regarding mob violence. During an impasse in the meeting, according to an NAACP secretary, an aide to the president, David K. Niles, recommended a committee to investigate the violation of civil liberties of Americans. This particular committee, appointed by the president, would study the acts of violence against all minorities and recommend a plan for corrective action.[19]

President Truman accepted the recommendation, one that had been made on several occasions by his predecessor and used as a stalling tactic for delaying action. President Truman, however, pledged to sign an executive order establishing the group.[20]

According to White, President Truman wanted the committee established and a report completed for the opening of the 80th Congress in January 1947. When the president asked the delegation for recommendations for committee membership, White and others mentioned that the committee membership should include business and financial leaders, so that the committee would not be viewed as a special interest group or as influenced by the communists. President Truman followed through with his pledge and appointed the President's Committee on Civil Rights. Charles E. Wilson, president of the General Electric Corporation, was selected as the chairman and Franklin D. Roosevelt, Jr., son of the late president, was named vice chairman. African Americans were represented on the fifteen-member President's Committee by Dr. Channing Tobias and attorney Sadie T. Alexander. Two of the members were prominent businessmen, and the balance of the committee represented labor, education, and the church.[21]

To convince the Negro civil rights community of his sincerity and to lay the groundwork for a Democratic party push for the Negro vote in the 1948 election year, President Truman, in June 1947, became the first president to appear before the NAACP National Convention.[22] Although his speech was not filled with specific proposals for a civil rights program, he did state that the federal government should be the defender of equal rights of all Americans.[23] Publicly, he went further than his predecessor in affirming the government's role in protecting the rights of its minority citizens. This position pleased the Negro press, the NAACP, and the Negro community as a whole.[24]

There were some Negro leaders, however, who continued to push President Truman and his administration to contemplate the end of discrimination in the military establishment. In the fall of 1947, A. Phillip Randolph and Grant Reynolds organized the "Committee Against Jim Crow in the Military Service and Training."[25] In the early months of 1948, Randolph and Reynolds lobbied the president and Congress for the elimination of segregation and discrimination in the draft bills before Congress. The two civil rights workers and labor activists threatened civil protest and unrest, something the president and the Democrats did not want in an election year. President Truman arranged meetings for Randolph and Reynolds with officers of the four branches of the military, to discuss the feasibility of integration. The two activists applied pressure, until Truman issued his executive order ending discrimination in the Armed Services.[26]

In tandem with the "Committee Against Jim Crow in the Military Service and Training," the NAACP, cognizant of the president's precarious position with the Southern leaders of the Democratic party and the

United States' delicate position in the free world, presented the Negro's case to the United Nations on 23 October 1947, asking for their influence in persuading the American government to protect the rights of their citizens at home.[27] One week later, President Truman responded by releasing the report from the President's Committee on Civil Rights' investigation of civil rights violations. The conclusions and recommendations for corrective action formed the report entitled: "To Secure These Rights." The committee's report included the following recommendations, with relevance to the Negro community and the Negro airmen:

1. Establishing a permanent Commission on Civil Rights, a joint Congressional Committee on Civil Rights, and a Civil Rights Division in the Justice Department;
2. Strengthening existing civil rights statutes;
3. Providing federal protection against lynching;
4. Establishing a Fair Employment Practices Commission to prevent unfair discrimination in employment;
5. Protecting the right to vote; and
6. Ending all forms of discrimination and segregation based on color, race, or creed, in the Military.[28]

The report was hailed by the civil rights community as being the most courageous document since the Emancipation Proclamation.[29] President Truman supplemented the release of the Civil Rights Committee report by asking, in his message to Congress in February 1948, for civil rights legislation based on the recommendations from the Civil Rights Committee report. President Truman also asked for the abolition of segregation in the use of transportation facilities by public officers and employees of private corporations, but stopped short of asking for the end of segregation in the federal government and the military.[30] It appeared that Truman planned to use the Civil Rights Committee's recommendations and his request for the abolition of segregation in federal and public employment in the 1948 Democratic platform, without endangering the southern Democratic vote.

What was clear, no matter what President Truman proposed, was that the 477th was still a segregated Negro unit in 1947 and 1948. The unit had developed a track record of proficiency in war games with their bombers and fighters and was praised by Gen. Peter Quesada, commanding general of the Tactical Air Force Command for the scores that the unit made in Aliso Canyon, California, during a mock invasion that simulated the conditions of the "D" Day invasion.[31] In July 1947, however, the 477th Composite Group was redesignated as the 332nd

Fighter Group, the bomber squadrons were dropped, and two fighter squadrons, the 100th and 301st, were added, thus giving the new unit three fighter squadrons, including the 99th.[32] The P-47 became the primary fighter plane.

The mission of the new 332nd was to continue preparing for combat readiness and peacetime efficiency, however, since the bomber squadrons were phased out, the bombardier-navigators had no jobs to perform. Due to the segregationist policies of the War Department, they had nowhere else to go. Fortunately, they were able to retain their flying status by flying C-47s. The bomber pilots were trained in the P-47 and were phased into the fighter squadrons.[33]

Since there was a shortage of pilots of advanced rank (beyond captain), many of the officers had to work out of their specialty area. In addition, the officers of rank could not take advantage of the advanced training offered by the Army Air Force, because of the shortage of rated Negro officers to take over command or the advanced occupation. Because of the Air Force's segregationist policy, even white officers could not replace the Negro officers. Therefore, the Negro officers had difficulty keeping their ratings current. Once the ratings were frozen, advancement in the Army Air Force was virtually impossible.[34]

The following month, August 1947, the War Department designated the AAF as a separate and independent branch of the military, along with the army and the navy. With the newly designated United States Air Force, fifteen new groups were established and the 332nd became the 332nd Fighter Wing, even though the new wing was the size of a fighter group. The Air Force did not assign new squadrons to the 332nd Fighter Wing.[35] The Air Force, however, quietly transferred the Negro flying cadets from Tuskegee to Randolph Field, in Texas, where the Negro and white cadets took classes together. This was integration by necessity, since it was too expensive to operate Tuskegee, given the few cadets who received training after 1945.[36]

By 1948, according to Defense Department documents, 50 percent of the officers at Lockbourne were employed out of their military occupational specialty. Captains commanded the three tactical units, when lieutenant colonels were required. In addition, Randolph Field, the only training base with Negro cadets, could only turn out nine Negro cadets at the end of 1947. Consequently, the wing was undermanned by, at least forty officers.[37]

In addition, the War Department lifted their ban on Negro enlistees and the Air Force received more than its 10 percent quota. A significant number of the enlistees tested at the lower levels of the AGCT and were, therefore, relegated to the low-skilled occupations. The 332nd Fighter

Wing had its share of nonskilled enlistees. Almost 35 percent of the enlistees at Lockbourne scored in the lower levels of the AGCT.[38] Consequently, skilled African Americans from other installations were transferred to Lockbourne to keep the wing efficient. Segregation proved to be an inefficient and expensive policy for operating a fighter wing.

The year of 1948 was also an election year, and a watershed year for Civil Rights. President Truman, who was considered a moderate Democrat, ventured out on a delicate political limb by proposing civil rights legislation, especially legislation that might bring an end to segregation. Truman expected, and received, negative feedback and political threats from the Southern hardliners in the Senate. His concern, however, was keeping the moderates from the South, who were opposed to desegregation, from leaving the party. According to his memoirs in "The Years of Trials and Hope," President Truman felt that he owed the people with no clout in Washington a right to be heard.[39] In Truman's opinion, people with no clout included Negroes. By supporting what was, in his opinion, a strong civil rights agenda, President Truman believed he was protecting a principle more important than a political campaign.[40] However, as a savvy politician, President Truman wanted his civil rights legislation and his party intact in 1948.

In election year 1948, President Truman and his political advisors had much to be concerned about. His former secretary of commerce, Henry Wallace, whom Truman had fired, left the Democratic party and formed the Progressive party and announced his candidacy for the presidency. Wallace was expected to court and secure a considerable minority vote.[41] War Department Chief of Staff Dwight D. Eisenhower was courted by the liberals of the party from the Roosevelt cabinet, who were investing in Eisenhower's popularity as a war hero. Even Truman viewed Eisenhower as a darkhorse contender.[42] President's Truman's greatest threat, however, came from the Southern moderates and conservatives, who threatened to bolt the party if Truman pushed for a civil rights plank that included integration in the party platform.

Political advisors close to President Truman developed a strategy whereby the Truman campaign would seek support from the Negro voters in the North and in border states, from the farmers in the West, and from urban-centered labor. Truman's advisors expected the majority of the moderate southern vote to stay with the party.[43] With this particular strategy as the focus of his presidential campaign, President Truman entered the Democratic party convention in Philadelphia a shaky favorite to win the nomination of his party.

When it became clear that Southern Democrats might bolt the party over Truman's aggressive civil rights plank proposals, the President sought a compromise, by recommending the language of a moderate civil rights plank accepted at the 1944 Democratic Convention in the place of the more aggressive 1948 plank. Young Democrats, mostly members of the Americans for Democratic Action, led by Hubert Humphrey, then mayor of Minneapolis, forged a coalition with Negro civil rights organizations and forced President Truman and the party to accept more assertive civil rights plank.[44] As a result, Gov. J. Strom Thurmond of South Carolina led a delegation representing several Southern states, such as South Carolina, Alabama, and Mississippi, in a walk-out from the convention floor. Later, the delegation initiated the States Rights party, with Governor Thurmond as it's leader.[45] Fortunately for Truman, Eisenhower refused to be drafted for the nomination and Wallace's Progressive Party was tainted by communist infiltration making Wallace a nonfactor in the race.[46] President Truman was nominated by the convention to run for reelection against the Republican challenger, Thomas E. Dewey.

President Truman was given a tentative mandate to proceed with his civil rights agenda, which his advisors hoped would derail the Republican party's outreach efforts to the Negro community. Although the Republican party had received a significant number of Negro votes in the 1944 election, Negro leaders were concerned with the camaraderie shared between the moderate republicans and the conservative republicans from the South, who supported segregation.[47]

Consequently, President Truman acted quickly to show his support for the civil rights plank in the party platform. Truman issued two executive orders that underscored his intent to capture the Negro and traditional New Deal voter. Executive Order 9980 sought to eliminate discrimination in the federal civil service, and Executive Order 9981 attempted to eliminate discrimination in the military and would create a committee, later known as the Fahy Committee, to implement policy. Since neither executive order mentioned eliminating segregation specifically, Negro civil rights organizations, and the Negro and majority press sought clarification from the Truman administration. A short time later, Truman, after responding to the press regarding an assertion from Army Chief of Staff Gen. Omar Bradley, that the army had no plans to end segregation, stated that he meant to eliminate segregation in the military.[48]

The executive orders and the establishment of the Fahy Committee may have provided the margin of victory for Truman in the 1948 election. Truman followed his Executive Order ending segregation in the military by appointing a committee to develop a policy for equality of opportunity, and policy for ending segregation in the military. The

"Committee on Equality of Treatment and Opportunity in the Armed Services," which was appointed on 18 September 1948, was chaired by Charles Fahy, a former solicitor general. The committee became known as the "Fahy Committee."[49] The Negro community was represented by two African Americans, Lester B. Granger, of the Urban League, and John H. Sengstacke, editor of the *Chicago Defender*. This committee would later be instrumental in implementing desegregation of the military.

President Truman was reelected by a very slim margin. He did manage to win, as his advisors predicted, a sizable Negro vote, enough to cover the damage caused by the bolting of the southern states.[50]

The Fahy Committee convened its first meeting in January 1949. President Truman was present and was unequivocal in his expectations of the Pentagon. The secretaries of the branches, also members of the Fahy Committee, were present, and Air Force Secretary W. Stuart Symington told the commander in chief that the Air Force would eliminate segregation by dismantling the 332nd Fighter Wing.[51]

This appeared to be an incredulous statement, considering where the Air Force was on this issue in 1945 and 1946. In 1945, the success of the Tuskegee training and the subsequent success of the segregated 99th Fighter Squadron and the 332nd Fighter Group, along with the excellent training and safety record of the segregated 477th Medium Bombardment Group, proved to the War Department that skilled Negroes, if given the opportunity, could perform as well as whites with the same skill level and education. Consequently, the McCloy Committee sought to investigate, for future development, the participation of the Negro soldier and officer in the postwar military establishment.[52] The McCloy Committee, especially McCloy, Davis, and Gibson, intended to set the groundwork for the eventual integration of the highly skilled Negro into white units. Their rationale for the study was predicated on the improvement of military efficiency with the utilization of all available talent, not on social experimentation.

An integral part of McCloy's study was a questionnaire that was sent in late May 1945 to commanding generals stateside and to those stationed in combat zones. The questionnaire sought to secure the generals' thoughts on a variety of issues pertaining to the employment and training of the Negro, Negro response to hostile training environments, the effectiveness of Negro officers in combat situations, the extent and effect of segregation and integration of Negro units with white units, and what to do with the Negro soldier after the war ended. The survey also requested recommendations on the subject of segregation and the integration of Negro troops.[53] The responses were capsulized by the commanding generals of the service, ground, and air forces and the admirals of the navy.

The Army Air Forces command reported that they also utilized the majority of their Negro troops in nonskilled occupations. The Air Forces, however, trained and employed more highly skilled Negroes. African Americans employed in skilled positions were comparable to whites in education and AGCT scores.[54] The Air Forces reiterated that it took longer to train African Americans in specialties such as navigation/bombardier, because of the difficulty encountered in finding Negroes who qualified for the training, even after the Air Forces lowered its eligibility requirements.[55]

The Air Force command also reported that racial disturbances and unrest, such as the Selfridge and Freemen Field incidents, disrupted training requiring the Negro bombardier/navigators to endure almost twice the training time allowed to whites.[56] The commanding general of the Air Forces attributed the racial disputes to professional agitators from the NAACP, the Negro press, and northern-born African Americans who did not understand the ways of the South.[57] This position on Negro disturbances was shared the commanding officer of the Air Force organization administering the 477th. According to Allen Gropman's *The Air Force Integrates, 1945-1964*, General Hunter, commander of the First Air Force, stated in his report that the Army Air Force was being used as a social laboratory by professional Negro agitators bent on social equality that did not exist in civilian life in America.[58]

Hunter's report was prepared, in late May 1945, by Colonel Selway, former commanding officer of the 332nd Fighter Group and, at the time of the report, the commanding officer of the 477th Bombardment Group. This particular report, which was submitted to Gen. Hap Arnold, included one of the most negative responses to future plans for the utilization of African Americans in the Air Force. Colonel Selway attacked the Negro officer's intellect, integrity, and credibility. He concluded that the Negroes in his command were lazy and without a sense of pride and duty. According to Selway, even the brightest of Negroes, such as the Negro officers in the two Negro flying units under his command, were incapable of assuming positions of authority and responsibility. He maligned the Negro units for lacking in proficiency, and for their inability to learn skilled occupations within standard time periods, and praised white officers for being the only men with the leadership traits necessary to draw a satisfactory performance from their units. Consequently, Selway recommended that the Air Forces eliminate the Negro flying units in the postwar military establishment. He also recommended that

Negro enlisted men be retained in the postwar Air Force, employed in low-skilled occupations in small, segregated nonflying units commanded by white officers.[59]

After consolidating all of the reports from the Air Forces organizations, including General Hunter's brief, the Air Forces commanding general recommended that the Air Forces employ a 10 percent quota of African Americans, provide Negro personnel with the same training as whites, employ Negroes in units no larger than a group equaling three squadrons, and, unlike the other forces, provide Negro officers with the opportunity to command Negro units.[60]

Although the 99th Fighter Squadron and the 332nd Fighter Group performed satisfactorily in combat under the yoke of segregation and inexperience, the Air Forces Command believed that white units outperformed the Negro units. Therefore, the Army Air Force commanding general recommended that Negroes in flying units of a postwar Air Force be thoroughly screened, selected, and matched with occupations that matched their skills and aptitudes.[61]

All commanding generals, including General Arnold of the Army Air Force, supported the War Department's standing policy of segregation, despite the fact that they admitted segregation was an impediment to Negro efficiency and morale. The generals of the War Department, however, felt that they were morally and militarily correct in placing priority on the efficiency and morale of the white majority.[62] Segregation of troops by race in combat, mess, and social activity ensured the maintenance of that efficiency. According to the commanding generals, Negro soldiers would participate in the postwar military establishment in a limited and segregated capacity equal to, and possibly worse than, their employment in World War II.

The McCloy Committee, however, recommended deliberate and gradual desegregation of small Negro units.[63] McCloy agreed and concluded that the War Department's Special Planning Division must examine the damaging effects of segregation on its troop personnel and plan for the most productive use of Negro personnel in a post-war military establishment. In addition, McCloy advised the secretary of war, Robert Patterson, to appoint a board of general officers to investigate the employment of Negro troops in World War II for the purpose of developing a new Negro troop policy. [64]

The secretary of war appointed a board of four general officers, headed by Gen. Alvan C. Gillem, for the purpose of developing a policy for the utilization of Negro soldiers during the postwar era, and to develop a strategy for building the most efficient fighting force that could be assembled, in the event of war. The group of officers, who were known as the Gillem Board, convened in the summer of 1945 and within several months, interviewed over fifty persons, including prominent African Americans, and read volumes of data and reports on the merits of and the arguments against the utilization of Negro troops in a postwar military establishment.[65]

The Army Air Force, in particular, supported segregation and used the combat performance records of the 99th Pursuit Squadron, the 332nd Fighter Group, and the training record of the 477th Medium Bombardment Group, which the Air Force Command felt were inferior to whites, as evidence that Negro units were not proficient. The new AAF commander, Gen. Carl Spaatz, predicted that the integration of Negro airmen and officers into white units would adversely affect the efficiency of those units. General Spaatz contended that Negro pilots and bombardier/navigators could not compete with their white counterparts. The Air Force commander also rejected the notion that Negro officers could command white airmen.

If integration was forced on the Army Air Force, General Spaatz stated, the AAF would recommend limited use of Negro officers as technical specialists in white units, provided the number of Negroes was small enough to segregate eating and sleeping quarters. According to the AAF commander's testimony, integration could be implemented on a limited scale in pilot training schools, provided that the training sites were carefully selected.[66]

After six months of reviewing documents, holding interviews, and group discussion, the Gillem Board submitted its study, including recommendations, entitled: "Report of Board of General Officers of the Utilization of Negro Manpower in the Post-War Army," to the chief of staff in November 1945.[67]

The Gillem Board concluded in their report that most of the army's Negro problems, such as, poor performance, racial disturbances, alleged unsatisfactory response to training, and assignment difficulties, stemmed from a lack of planning in the selection, training, and employment of Negro troops.[68] The board advised the War Department not to repeat the same mistake in the postwar military establishment. It strongly suggested that the War Department initiate planning for the optimal utilization of Negro manpower in the postwar period. The board also concluded that the deficiencies of Negro leadership could be eliminated by expanding the Negro base of officers and enlisted men to assist in the training in the postwar army that would establish a cadre of qualified leaders to employ in case of a war emergency.[69]

The board's report offered eighteen recommendations for corrective action and future War Department policy. Although all of the Gillem

Board recommendations intended to impact War Department policy regarding the optimal use of Negro manpower, a few of the recommendations had special implications for African Americans in the Army Air Force. Those recommendations, printed and distributed as "Circular No. 124," were as follows:

1. The proportion of Negro to white manpower, 1:10 or 10 percent, that exists in the civil population shall be the accepted ratio for creating a troop basis in the postwar army;
2. All officers, regardless of race, should have access to equal rights and opportunities for advancement and professional improvement;
3. In camps, posts, and bases, where Negroes and whites are stationed, the War Department policies regarding the use of recreational facilities and memberships to officers' clubs, messes, and other social agencies shall be in effect, and that commanders at these installations be cognizant of their responsibilities to follow War Department policy;
4. The War Department should take steps to ensure the education and indoctrination of all ranks in the Service of the necessity of unreserved acceptance of the provisions of the policies; and
5. The War Department should approve and promulgate a policy for the utilization of Negro manpower in the postwar army as soon as such policy is practicable.[70]

The War Department, and certainly the Army Air Force, did not intend to implement any of the recommendation's in 1946, nor was "Circular No. 124" an order that was enforceable. Instead, the War Department implemented the recommendation in "Circular No. 124" that pertained to the education and indoctrination of all troops on the War Department policies on recreational facilities, officers' clubs, and mess halls located on bases where whites and Negroes were stationed. The War Department distributed a pamphlet on the Negro soldier entitled: "Army Talk 170."[71] Later in 1947, the War Department issued "Circular 76," which was to be used with a three and one-half hour workshop that included a history of successful Negro units in World War II, discussions on race relations, and the need for efficient Negro manpower in the postwar army.[72]

The Air Force, however, was apparently was involved in the planning stages of their desegregation plan as early as May 1948. Secretary of Defense James D. Forrestal, a future member of the Fahy Committee, convened a conference on Negro affairs for Negro leaders who needed answers from Defense Department officials on the department's racial policies. Gen. Idwal H. Edwards, the Air Force deputy chief of staff, told the group of Negro leaders that segregation was unnecessary and that integration would eventually occur in the Air Force. General Edwards mentioned the integrated setup at Randolph Field as an example of Air Force progress toward integration.[73] Later in the same month, the Air Board, a group responsible for the review and recommendation of policy to the Chief of Staff, began a feasibility study of integration. The personnel of the Air Board included the Assistant Chiefs of the Air Staff, the Air Inspector, the Air Comptroller, the Director of Information, the Deputy Assistant Chief of Staff for Research and Development, and others, as needed.[74]

J. C. Evans, the former coordinator of the CPTP project at West Virginia State College for Negroes, was then the advisor to the secretary of defense. It was Evans's idea to convene the conference on Negro affairs. He was asked to consolidate the questions and recommendations from the Negro leaders who attended the meeting and to forward them to the Secretary of the Air Force Stymington for study.[75] Evans recommended that Colonel Davis, Jr. be sent to advanced military training to prepare him for command of diversified units. Evans recommended that a white officer be sent to relieve Colonel Davis. Evans also felt that the Air Force should dissolve the Negro fighter wing and distribute the Negro personnel to other Air Force installations on the basis of specialty and technical training. In addition, he recommended diversification in the training and occupational specialties available to African Americans for the purpose of promoting proficiency.[76] Evans sent a copy of the recommendations to General Edwards, and the general discussed the recommendation with the Air Board, then involved with the evaluation of Negro employment.[77]

Based on the results from discussion of Evans's recommendations at the Air Board meeting, Gen. Richard E. Nugent, the director of Civilian Personnel, was assigned to head a research team to evaluate the Air Force's racial policy. Nugent's study. written by Col. Jack F. Marr, a member of the Air Staff, concluded that Air Force racial policies were inconsistent with those recommended by the Gillem Board and that the Gillem Board recommendations for racial policy would not work in the Air Force. The report stated that Negroes were employed in a wasteful, militarily deleterious fashion. The report admitted that some white commanding officers had employed African Americans in specialty occupations alongside whites and that the African Americans had performed comparably. The Nugent Report recommended that full integration not be implemented, but that a limited plan of integration be

adopted. Negroes and whites above an accepted age would be discharged. Certain Negro units, such as the 332nd Fighter Wing, would
be dropped, the 10 percent quota would be eliminated, and a Negro
integration quota of 1 percent in the technical, combat, and service
units would prove functional. Negroes and whites would compete for
jobs based on their abilities and qualifications. Integration of sleeping
quarters would be handled by the construction of separate barracks or
barracks with separate cubicles.[78]

Although the Nugent Report recommended limited integration, the
Air Force officers opposed any form of integration. General Edwards,
Eugene Zuckert, the assistant secretary of the Air Force, and J. C.
Evans continued to lobby for the Nugent recommendations for limited
integration in the Air Force. Their opportunity came when President
Truman enacted the executive order outlawing discrimination in the
armed services and with the establishment of the Fahy Committee to
implement the enactment of armed forces policy of racial equality
that, according to the president, included integration. General
Edwards simply fined-tuned the previous recommendations from the
Nugent Report. He had the quota dropped and retained Negro units
for individuals who were ineligible for transfer to white units or for discharge from the service. Also added was a plan for sleeping quarters, a
critical point in the discussions regarding integration. Integrated sleeping quarters would be constructed, with individual cubicles for privacy,
or separate barracks would be constructed. Negro and white officers
would have access to all of the recreation and social facilities at all
installations.[79]

General Edwards submitted the reworked recommendations to
Secretary Symington for approval in early January 1949.[80] Symington
approved the plan as being militarily sound and economically efficient
and sent it to Secretary of Defense Forrestal and the Fahy Committee.[81]
The committee had few problems with the proposal and made recommendations for the elimination of Negro quotas and a provision that
would have allowed base officers the authority to assign African
Americans to all-Negro units.[82]

The Fahy Committee and the Personnel Policy Board approved the
Air Force's revised plan for integration. On 11 May, Colonel Davis
reported to the Defense Department to receive his orders and instructions on the review process to be employed in determining who in the
332nd Fighter Wing would be reassigned, which men required
advanced training, who would receive training in their current occupation, and who would be separated from the Air Force.[83] The Personnel
Redistribution Board, chaired by Colonel Davis, arrived at Lockbourne

on 14 May and, during a ten-day period, the officers and enlisted men of the 332nd were interviewed and put through a battery of aptitude tests.[84]

A significant number of the Negro personnel at Lockbourne were very concerned about the Air Force's integration plan. Many complained about the dissolution of Lockbourne and the scattering of Negroes, as opposed to the integration of Lockbourne by white airmen and officers.[85] As early as March of 1949, Negro officers of the 332nd Fighter Wing, including Spann Watson, Silas Jenkins, Charles Dryden, Andrew McCoy, George Ilyes, and Samuel Lynn, were lobbying the Negro press, the NAACP, and the Urban League to investigate the Air Force's integration plan and implementation procedures.[86] The NAACP was invited to Lockbourne to secretly evaluate the attitude of the men who would be affected by the integration plan. Roy Wilkins sent NAACP legal counsel Robert Carter. What Carter found was that the officers were not opposed to integration. Indeed, Carter found the officers concerned about an integration plan that would not rule out the phasing out of the Negro commanding officers at the rank of captain and above. The Negro officers could not envision an Air Force that would allow Negro officers to command whites.[87] Mr. Watson and his group maintained that the Air Force should retain the 332nd Fighter Group and integrate it with white pilots, while integrating other white units with African-American pilots.

The NAACP had officially endorsed the Air Force's plan. Since the plan was consistent with the NAACP integrationist agenda, the Carter report did not change the NAACP's position.[88]

The Urban League, also, reacted to the concerns of the 332nd. The officers had complaints about the screening process that was to be implemented and were concerned that a key determining factor was the screening committee's perception of the Negro officer's adaptability, skills necessary to work in an integrated situation. Since many of the officers were never in an integrated situation, with the exception of the members of the 99th Pursuit Squadron, who flew with the 79th Fighter Group in Italy during the invasion of Italy, the Negro officers felt that the screening committee had no objective criteria from which to make such a decision. Lester Granger raised this issue in a March 1949 Fahy Committee meeting and General Edwards confirmed that the Negro's attitude toward employment in an integrated unit would be observed and factored into the final decision. General Edwards assured Granger that he did not expect many Negro officers to be separated from the service because of an incorrect attitude toward integration.[89] Granger and the Urban League appeared satisfied with the response.

As a result of the screening of 192 Negro officers of the 332nd, ten were separated from the Air Force, 158 were reassigned in their occupational specialties, and twenty-four, including Colonel Davis, were recommended for additional training. The outcome of the screening, by most accounts in the military and in the Negro press, was fair and equitable. Most of the officers were reassigned to other installations in the country. A very small percentage were sent overseas to the Far East and to Europe. Colonel Davis was able to obtain the advanced training that had been denied him due to the segregationist policies of the Air Force.[90]

By the end of 1949, almost half of the African Americans in the Air Force were in integrated units. However, many flying officers were assigned nonflying administrative positions that came with no command responsibilities over white troops. In addition, there was a reduction in force in the fall of 1949 that also reduced the number of African-American flying officers in the 9th Air Force from 175 in 1949 to 35 in early 1950.[91]

It is important to note that representatives from the 332nd Fighter Wing participated in the Air Force's First National Gunnery Meet in May 1949 in Las Vegas. The competition included skip bombing, strafing, rocketry, and aerial gunnery at 10,000 and 12,000 feet. The 332nd placed first in its group of conventional class competition.[92] The showing proved Negro pilots had the capability, if given the opportunity, to compete favorably with whites.

The double victory achieved with the success of the Negro flying units in World War II and the eventual limited integration of the Air Force was bittersweet. Bitter because it took nearly twenty years, from the time the War Department reduced the proud Negro army units to housekeeping and horse training outfits and used their resources to expand the Army Air Corps that did not accept African Americans, to the advent of Air Force integration. Bitter, due to the fact that the Air Force integration plan was, in reality, desegregation and a dilution of Negro leadership in the military. Many officers of the defunct 332nd Fighter Wing were never given their just rewards for their performance and selfless courage in the defense of their country. The Negro airmen, just like the old ballplayers of the Negro Leagues, were victims of segregation and time. The two variables stole from them their greatness.

The double victory was sweet, because it proved to America that human beings, regardless of their race, had something valuable to contribute toward the greatness of their country. The victory was sweet because Negro men of military honor no longer had to endure the humiliation of second-class citizenship in the Air Force. Sweet because most of the Negro airmen survived to lead productive and successful careers in the military and civilian life. Despite the hardships, the airmen possessed enough grace to become judges, generals, mayors, teachers, doctors, and millionaires. Double victory was sweet because the civil rights organizations, the Negro press, the Negro church, educational institutions, fraternities, sororities, labor, aviators, and advocates formed a coalition that stood the test of time and endured to see the first fruits of its labor. As a result the Air Force was the first federal organization to integrate the races, five years before the Brown Decision of the Supreme Court in 1954.

Notes

1. White, *A Man Called White*, 322-23.
2. Ibid., 323-25.
3. Louis Lautier, "No Cause for Police Beating of Selectees," *Pittsburgh Courier*, 27 April 1946.
4. Gropman, *The Air Force Integrates*, 64.
5. Ibid., 65-67.
6. White, *A Man Called White*, 325-28.
7. McGovern, *Black Eagles*, 48; Gropman, *The Air Force Integrates*, 78.
8. R. M. Phillips, "Orders 477th Group to Pacific, Slated to Leave in Late Summer or Fall," *Baltimore Afro-American*, 30 June 1945.
9. Ibid.; Gropman, *The Air Force Integrates*, 30.
10. Osur, *Blacks in the Army Air Forces*, 110.
11. Gropman, *The Air Force Integrates*, 40; McGovern, *Black Eagles*, 48-50; Davis, *Benjamin Davis, Jr.*, 148.
12. MacGregor, *Integration of the Armed Forces 1940-1965*, 182-84, 186-87, 275; Gropman, *The Air Force Integrates*, 78.
13. Interview with Elmore Kennedy; Interview with Leroy Gillead; MacGregor, *Integration of the Armed Forces 1940-1965*, 275, 277. McGovern, *Black Eagles*, 50.
14. MacGregor, *Integration of the Armed Forces 1940-1965*, 277. Gropman, *The Air Force Integrates*, 81.
15. McGovern, *Black Eagles*, 50. Gropman, *The Air Force Integrates*, 81.
16. Interview with Elmore Kennedy.
17. White, *A Man Called White*, 329.
18. Ibid.
19. Ibid., 330-31.
20. Ibid.
21. Ibid, 332-33; MacGregor, *Integration of the Armed Forces 1940-1965*, 294-95; Harry S Truman, *Memoirs by Harry S Truman, Volume Two: Years of Trial and Hope* (Garden City, New York: Doubleday, 1955-1959), 180-82.

22. Truman, *Memoirs by Harry S Truman, Volume Two*, 181; MacGregor, *Integration of the Armed Forces 1940-1965*, 293.
23. Ibid.
24. White, *A Man Called White*, 348.
25. Gropman, *The Air Force Integrates*, 104-5; MacGregor, *Integration of the Armed Forces 1940-1965*, 300.
26. Gropman, *The Air Force Integrates*, 106; MacGregor, *Integration of the Armed Forces 1940-1965*, 302-9.
27. Franklin, *From Slavery to Freedom*, 605.
28. Ibid, 609; MacGregor, *Integration of the Armed Forces 1940-1965*, 295-96; Gropman, *The Air Force Integrates*, 103-4; Truman, *Memoirs by Harry S Truman, Volume Two*, 181.
29. White, *A Man Called White*, 348.
30. Gropman, *The Air Force Integrates*, 104; MacGregor, *Integration of the Armed Forces 1940-1965*, 296; Truman, *Memoirs by Harry S Truman, Volume Two*, 181.
31. "Airmen Praised for Battle Prowess," *Pittsburgh Courier*, 7 December 1946.
32. Gropman, *The Air Force Integrates*, 80; Interview with Harry Stewart.
33. Gropman, *The Air Force Integrates*, 80; Interview with Leroy Gillard; Interview with Harry Stewart.
34. Interview with Elmore Kennedy; Gropman, *The Air Force Integrates*, 81; MacGregor, *Integration of the Armed Forces 1940-1965*, 283-84.
35. Ibid.
36. MacGregor, *Integration of the Armed Forces 1940-1965*, 275.
37. Gropman, *The Air Force Integrates*, 81-82; Interview with Elmore Kennedy; MacGregor, *Integration of the Armed Forces 1940-1965*, 283.
38. MacGregor, *Integration of the Armed Forces 1940-1965*, 282.
39. Truman, *Memoirs by Harry S Truman, Volume Two*, 184-85.
40. Ibid.
41. Ibid.
42. Ibid., 182, 185-86.
43. Barton J. Bernstein, "The Ambiguous Legacy: The Truman Administration and Civil Rights," paper presented at the American Historical Association meeting 1966, reprinted in Sternsher, *The Negro in Depression and War*, 283.
44. Ibid., 287, 289.
45. Truman, *Memoirs by Harry S Truman, Volume Two*, 183.
46. Ibid, 184-87; Bernstein, "The Ambiguous Legacy," 288-89.
47. Bernstein, "The Ambiguous Legacy," 288.
48. Ibid., 290; MacGregor, *Integration of the Armed Forces 1940-1965*, 291, 312.
49. Bernstein, "The Ambiguous Legacy," 297; MacGregor, *Integration of the Armed Forces 1940-1965*, 310-14.
50. Bernstein, "The Ambiguous Legacy," 291-92.

51. MacGregor, *Integration of the Armed Forces 1940-1965*, 339-41; Gropman, *The Air Force Integrates*, 115.
52. Gropman, *The Air Force Integrates*, 130-31.
53. Ibid., 34; MacGregor, *Integration of the Armed Forces 1940-1965*, 339-41; Osur, *Blacks in the Army Air Forces*, 123-24.
54. MacGregor, *Integration of the Armed Forces 1940-1965*, 140; Gropman, *The Air Force Integrates*, 35-36.
55. Osur, *Blacks in the Army Air Forces*, 124-25; Gropman, *The Air Force Integrates*, 36-37, 38-39; MacGregor, *Integration of the Armed Forces 1940-1965*, 140.
56. Osur, *Blacks in the Army Air Forces*, 128-29; Gropman, *The Air Force Integrates*, 39-40.
57. Gropman, *The Air Force Integrates*, 43; MacGregor, *Integration of the Armed Forces 1940-1965*, 129.
58. Gropman, *The Air Force Integrates*, 39.
59. Gropman, *The Air Force Integrates*, 34-41; Osur, *Blacks in the Army Air Forces*, 127-28.
60. Gropman, *The Air Force Integrates*, 44-45; Osur, *Blacks in the Army Air Forces*, 128-29; MacGregor, *Integration of the Armed Forces 1940-1965*, 140-41.
61. Gropman, *The Air Force Integrates*, 44-45; Osur, *Blacks in the Army Air Forces*, 128-29.
62. Osur, *Blacks in the Army Air Forces*, 129; Gropman, *The Air Force Integrates*, 44-45; MacGregor, *Integration of the Armed Forces 1940-1965*, 150.
63. MacGregor, *Integration of the Armed Forces 1940-1965*, 142.
64. Gropman, *The Air Force Integrates*, 46; MacGregor, *Integration of the Armed Forces 1940-1965*, 150.
65. Gropman, *The Air Force Integrates*, 47; MacGregor, *Integration of the Armed Forces 1940-1965*, 153-54; Osur, *Blacks in the Army Air Forces*, 134.
66. Gropman, *The Air Force Integrates*, 54.
67. MacGregor, *Integration of the Armed Forces 1940-1965*, 155.
68. Ibid.
69. Ibid., 155-56.
70. "Circular No. 124," report of Board of Officers on Utilization of Negro Manpower in Post War Army, 26 February 1946 in Gropman, *The Air Force Integrates*, 240-42; MacGregor, *Integration of the Armed Forces 1940-1965*, 156-57.
71. Gropman, *The Air Force Integrates*, 59.
72. Ibid., 59-60.
73. Gropman, *The Air Force Integrates*, 89; MacGregor, *Integration of the Armed Forces 1940-1965*, 285-86.
74. MacGregor, *Integration of the Armed Forces 1940-1965*, 287.
75. Ibid., 286.
76. Ibid.

77. Ibid., 287.
78. Ibid., 288; Gropman, *The Air Force Integrates*, 87.
79. MacGregor, *Integration of the Armed Forces 1940-1965*, 340.
80. MacGregor, *Integration of the Armed Forces 1940-1965*, 341; Gropman, *The Air Force Integrates*, 115.
81. Gropman, *The Air Force Integrates*, 116; MacGregor, *Integration of the Armed Forces 1940-1965*, 341-48.
82. Ibid.
83. Gropman, *The Air Force Integrates*, 120.
84. Ibid., 120-21.
85. Interview with Leroy Gillead; Interview with Elmore Kennedy.
86. Interview with Spann Watson; Lem Graves, Jr., "332nd Objects, Integrated Air Force Stymied," *Pittsburgh Courier*, 5 February 1949.
87. Interview with Leroy Gillead; Gropman, *The Air Force Integrates*, 118.
88. Gropman, *The Air Force Integrates*, 119; Courier Press Service, "Armed Forces Integration Hope Hinges on Committee," *Pittsburgh Courier*, 16 April 1949.
89. Gropman, *The Air Force Integrates*, 120.
90. Ibid., 120-21; Lem Graves, Jr., "4000 Tan Airmen Will Be Shifted," *Pittsburgh Courier*, 21 May 1949; "Air Force Shift Underway, 66 Officers Moved," *Pittsburgh Courier*, 18 June 1949.
91. Gropman, *The Air Force Integrates*, 120.
92. "Fighter Up Again," *Air Force Magazine* (June 1949): A21-23.

Bibliography

Books

Angelucci, Enzo, and Peter Bowers. *The American Fighter: The Definitive Guide to American Fighter Aircraft from 1917 to the Present.* New York: Orion Books, 1985.

Bernstein, Barton J., ed. *Politics and Policies of the Truman Administration.* Chicago: The University of Chicago Press, 1970.

Carisella, P. J., and James W. Ryan. *The Black Swallow of Death.* Boston: Marborough House, 1972.

Carter, Kit C., and Robert Mueller. *The Army Air Forces in World War II: Combat Chronology 1941-1945.* Washington, D.C.: Office of Air Force History, U.S. Air Force, 1973.

Dalfiume, Richard M. *Desegregation of the United States Armed Forces.* Columbia: University of Missouri Press, 1966.

Davis, Benjamin O., Jr. *Benjamin O. Davis, Jr., American, An Autobiography.* Washington D.C.: Smithsonian Institute Press, 1991.

DuBois, W.E.B. *Dusk of Dawn: An Essay Toward an Autobiography of a Race Concept.* New York: Schockon Books, 1968.

Francis, Charles E. *The Tuskegee Airmen: The Men Who Changed a Nation.* Boston: Brandon Publishing Company, 1988. (Originally published 1955).

Franklin, John Hope. *From Slavery to Freedom,* 3d. ed. New York: Vintage Books, 1969.

Glinis, Carroll V., Jr. *The Compact History of the United States Air Force.* New York: Hawthorne Books Inc., 1963.

Gropman, Alan L. *The Air Force Integrates 1945-1964.* Washington D.C.: Office of Air Force History, U.S. Air Force, 1985.

Hall, James Norman. *High Adventure; A Narrative of Air Fighting in France.* New York: Houghton Mifflin Co., 1929.

Hall, James Norman, and Charles B. Nordhorr. *The Lafayette Flying Corps.* Boston: Houghton Mifflin Co., 1920.

Hardesy, Vaughn, and Dominick Pisano. *Black Wings: The American Black in Aviation.* Washington, D.C.: The American National Air and Space Museum, Smithsonian Institution Press, 1984.

Hastie, William H. *On Clipped Wings: The Story of Jim Crow in the Army Air Corps.* New York: NAACP Crisis Pamphlet, 1943.

Hughes, Langston. *The Big Sea: An Autobiography of Langston Hughes.* New York: A. A. Knopf, 1940.

Jablonski, Edward. *Wings of Fire, Air War Volume IV.* Garden City, New York: Doubleday, 1972.

James, C.L.R. *Fighting Racism in WWII.* New York: Monad Press, 1980.

Johnson, Hayden C. *The Fighting 99th Air Squadron 1941-45.* New York: Vantage Press, Inc., 1987.

Johnson, Jack. *Jack Johnson In the Ring and Out, Autobiography.* London: Proteus Publishing, 1977.

Lee, Ulysses G. *The Employment of Negro Troops.* Washington, D.C.: Government Printing Office, 1966.

Longstreet, Stephen. *The Canvas Falcons: The Story of Men and Planes of WWI.* New York: World Publications Company, 1970.

MacGregor, Morris J., Jr. *Integration of the Armed Forces, 1940-1965.* Washington, D.C.: Center of Military History, U.S. Army, Department of Defense, 1981.

Mason, Herbert Molloy. *The United States Air Force: A Turbulent History.* New York: Mason Charter, 1976.

————. *The Lafayette Escadrille.* New York: Random House, 1964.

Mauer, Mauer. *Air Force Combat Units of World War II.* Washington, D.C.: Office of Air Force History, 1983.

McGovern, James R. *Black Eagles—General Daniel Chappie James, Jr.* Tuscaloosa: University of Alabama Press, 1985.

McKee, Alexander. *The Friendless Sky: The Story of Air Combat in World War I.* New York: William Morrow and Company, 1964.

Motley, Mary Penick. *The Invisible Soldier: The Experience of the Black Soldier, World War II.* Detroit: Wayne State University Press, 1975.

Osur, Alan M. *Blacks in the Army Air Forces During World War II.* Washington, D.C.: Office of Air Force History, U.S. Air Force, 1977.

Parris, Grichard. *Black in the City; A History of the Urban League.* Boston: Little, Brown, 1971.

Patterson, Elois. *Memoirs of the Late Bessie Coleman Aviatrix: Pioneer of the Negro Peoples in Aviation.* Washington, D.C.: Library of Congress, 1969.

Roberts, Randy. *Papa Jack: Jack Johnson and the Era of White Hopes.* New York: The Free Press, 1983.

Rose, Robert A. *Lonely Eagles: The Story of American Black Air Force in World War II.* Los Angeles: Tuskegee Airman Inc., Los Angeles Chapter, 1976.

Scott, Emmet J. *Scott's Official History of the American Negro in the Great War,* 2d. ed. New York: Arno Press, 1969.

Spencer, Chauncey E. *Who is Chauncey Spencer?* Detroit: Broadside Press, 1975.

Sternsher, Bernard, ed. *The Negro in Depression and War; Prelude to Revolution, 1930-1945.* Chicago: Quadrangle Books, 1969.

Suchenwirth, Richard. *The German Air Force in WWII, Historical Turning Points in the German Air Force War Effort.* New York: U.S. Air Force Historical Studies, U.S. Air Force Historical Division, Arno Press, 1968.

Truman, Harry S. *Memoirs by Harry S Truman, Volume Two: Years of Trial and Hope.* Garden City, N.Y.: Doubleday; 1955-1959.

Tuskegee Airmen, Inc., East Coast Chapter. *The Tuskegee Airman Story.* Washington, D.C.: O'Dennis Associates, 1988.

Waters, Enoch P. *American Diary: A Personal History of the Black Press.* Chicago: Path Press, Inc. 1987.

Watson, George Sr. *Memorable Memoirs.* New York: Carlton Press, Inc., 1987.

Wheeler, Barry C. *Military Aircraft Markings and Profiles.* New York: Gallery Books, 1990.

White, Walter. *A Rising Wind.* Garden City, N.Y.: Doubleday, Doran and Company, Inc., 1945.

———. *A Man Called White: An Autobiography.* New York: Viking Press, 1948.

Whitehouse, Arthur. *Legion of the Lafayette.* Garden City, N.Y.: Doubleday & Company, Inc., 1962.

———. *The Years of the Sky Kings.* Garden City, N.Y.: Doubleday & Company, Inc., 1959.

Wynn, Neil A. *The Afro-American and the Second World War.* New York: Holes & Meior Publishers, 1976.

Periodicals

Bethune, Mary McLeod. "My Secret Talks with FDR." *Ebony* 4 (April 1949): 42-57.

Brewer, James H. "Robert Lee Vann, Democrat or Republican: An Exponent of Loose Leaf Politics." *Negro History Bulletin* 21 (February 1958): 100-3.

Dalfiume, Richard M. "The Forgotten Years of the Negro Revolution." *Journal of American History* 55 (June 1968): 90-106.

DuBois, W.E.B. "The Color Line." *The Crisis* 11 (December 1915): 65.

———. "The Horizon." *The Crisis* 16 (January 1918): 145.

———. "An Essay Toward a History of the Black Man in the Great War." *The Crisis* 18 (February 1919) 63-90.

———. "The Life of Monsieur Bullard." *Ebony Magazine* (December 1967): 121-28.

"Experiment Proved." *Time* 42 (20 September 1943): 66-68.

Fishel, Leslie H., Jr. "The Negro in the New Deal Era." *Wisconsin Magazine of History* 48 (Winter 1964): 111-26.

"Fighters Up Again." *Air Force Magazine*, June 1949, 21-23.

Gatski, John. "Enlisted History: Eugene J. Bullard, The First Black Combat Pilot." *Sargeants Magazine* (January/February 1988): 145.

Guzman, Jesse P. "The Negro in the Army Air Forces." *Negro Yearbook, A Review of Events Affecting Negro Life, 1941-1946*. Tuskegee, Alabama: Tuskegee Institute, 1947, 354-58.

Irwin, Will. "Flashes From the War Zone." *The Saturday Evening Post*, 15 June 1916, 12.

"National Defense." Army Section. *Time* 36 (12 August 1940): 15-16.

"99th." *Time* 38 (15 September 1941): 32-33.

Peck, James. "When Do We Fly." *The Crisis* 47 (December 1940): 376-78.

Smith, Mary A. "The Incredible Life of Monsieur Bullard." *Ebony* 23 (December 1967): 121-28.

Wilkins, Roy. "Editorials: First Bomber Pilots." *The Crisis* 52 (January 1944): 7.

———. "Hastie Resigns." *The Crisis* 50 (February 1943): 41.

———. "Farewell Speech to Our Pilots." *The Crisis* 50 (March 1943), 72.

———. "Air Force Progress." *The Crisis* 51 (August 1943): 231.

———. "How About Navy Pilots." *The Crisis* 51 (October 1943): 295.

———. "The Negro in the United States Army." *The Crisis* 49 (February 1942): 47.

———. "Army Air Corps Smoke Screen." *The Crisis* 48 (April 1941): 103.

Work, Monroe N. "Occupations of Negroes. Licensed Negro Aviators." *Negro Yearbook, An Annual Encyclopedia of the Negro, 1937-1938*. Tuskegee, Alabama: Tuskegee Institute, 1938. 279-81.

Newspapers

Baltimore Afro-American, 1942-1945.
Chicago Defender, 1930-1939, 1949.

Godman Field Beacon, 1945-1946.
Hawk's Cry, 1942-1945.
Louisville Leader, 22 February 1941.
Michigan Chronicle, 1944.
New York Amsterdam News, 1920-1937.
New York Daily Star, 1924.
New York Herald Tribune, 1961.
Pittsburgh Courier, 1920-1949.
Pittsburgh Post Gazette, 22 October 1936.

Unpublished Material

Carter, Robert. Memorandum to Thurgood Marshall, Testimony of Col. Robert R. Selway, 13 September 1945, NAACP Papers, Collections of the Manuscript Division, Library of Congress.

Coleman, William T, Jr., Lt., 118th AAF Base Unit, "C" Squadron, Letter to Commanding Officer Freeman Field, 10 April 1945 NAACP Papers, Collections of the Manuscript Division, Library of Congress.

Gillead, Le Roy. Letter to Louis Zollar, 19 April 1945, NAACP Papers, Collections of the Manuscript Division, Library of Congress.

Gould, Harold D. Letter to Walter White regarding Chicago Urban League's concern for Jim Crow training of pilots at Tuskegee Institute. 15 November 1940, NAACP Papers, Collections of the Manuscript Division, Library of Congress.

Hastie, William. Letter to Thurgood Marshall regarding Negro Licensed Pilots, 25 February 1941, NAACP Papers, Collections of the Manuscript Division, Library of Congress.

———. Letter to Thurgood Marshall regarding Eligibility for Aviation Cadets, 13 February 1941, NAACP Papers, Collections of the Manuscript Division, Library of Congress.

Houston, Charles H. Letter to General Douglas MacArthur, Chief of Staff, United Army, War Department, Washington, D.C. Regarding Attitudes of Negroes on National Defense, 9 August 1934, NAACP Papers, Collections of the Manuscript Division, Library of Congress.

———. Letter to the Afro-American, Associated Negro Press regarding MacArthur letter, August 1934, NAACP Papers. Collections of the Manuscript Division, Library of Congress.

———. Letter to Walter White Regarding War Department Army Discrimination. September 1934, NAACP Papers, Collections of the Manuscript Division, Library of Congress.

Marshall, Thurgood. Memorandum to NAACP Secretary Walter White, Discrimination Against Negroes in Certain Federal Agencies, 30

January 1939, NAACP Papers, Collections of the Manuscript Division, Library of Congress.

NAACP Press Service Release, NAACP to Represent 477th Officers in Trial, 28 June 1945, NAACP Papers, Collections of the Manuscript Division, Library of Congress.

NAACP Report on Civilian Pilot Training Program 1939-1940, February 1941, NAACP Papers, Collections of the Manuscript Division, Library of Congress.

Parks, William, J. Jr., 2nd Lt. Memorandum to Commanding Officer, Freeman Field, Seymour, Indiana, through Commanding Officer 477th Bombardment Group (M) Seymour, Indiana, 10 April 1945, NAACP Papers, Collections of the Manuscript Division, Library of Congress.

Perry, Leslie S. "Report to Walter White on the Investigation of Freeman Field, Indiana (477th Medium Bomb Group) 13-14 April 1945." NAACP Papers, Collections of the Manuscript Division, Library of Congress.

Scott, William. "Hubert F. Julian and the Italo-Ethiopian War: A Tragic Episode in Pan African Relations." Paper presented at the African Studies Association Meeting, Houston, Texas, November 1977.

Watson, Spann. Letter to Captain C. R. Landon, Headquarters, Second Corps Arena, Office of the Corps Area Commander, Govornors Island, New York, Application to Army Air Corps, 16 November 1940, NAACP Papers, Collections of the Manuscript Division, Library of Congress.

Webster, Grove. Letter to Roy Wilkins regarding Civilian Pilot Training Program, June 1940, NAACP Papers, Collections of the Manuscript Division, Library of Congress.

White, Walter. Memorandum to War Department regarding "Observations in the North African and Middle Eastern Theatres of Operation," 22 April 1944, NAACP Files, Collection of the Manuscript Division, Library of Congress.

————. Letter to All Negro Graduates of Civilian Pilot Training Program, 21 February 1941, NAACP Papers, Collections of the Manuscript Division, Library of Congress.

————. Letter to Henry J. Stimson, War Department, Officers of Freeman Field, 19 April 1945, NAACP Papers, Collections of the Manuscript Division, Library of Congress.

————. Straightwire to Henry J. Stimson, War Department, Arrest of 162 Officers of the 477th Medium Bombardment Group, 14 June 1945, NAACP Papers, Collections of the Manuscript Division, Library of Congress.

Wilkins, Roy. Letter to William H. Hastie regarding Enoch P. Water's concern regarding Jim Crow training of Negro pilots in CDAA Training at Tuskegee Institute, 15 November 1940, NAACP Papers, Collections of the Manuscript Division, Library of Congress.

———. Letter to William H. Hastie regarding Enoch P. Water's letter to Walter White on Tuskegee as Training Site for Air Corps, 15 November 1940, NAACP Papers, Collections of the Manuscript Division, Library of Congress.

Government Manuscripts

Department of the Army, United States Army Court of Military Review, Office of the Clerk. Court Martial Record, Milton R. Henry, HQDA (JAAJ-CC) 1944, Washington, D.C.

———. Court Martial Record; Shirley Clinton and Marsden Thompson, HQDA (JAAJ-CC) 1945, Washington, D.C.

———. Court Martial Record, Roger Terry, HQDA (JAAJ-CC), 1945, Washington, D.C.

Interviews

All interviews conducted by co-author Lawrence P. Scott

Anderson, C. Alfred, interview 10 June 1990, Tuskegee, Alabama.

Berry, Theodore, telephone interview, 12 October 1990.

Blair, Omar P., Captain 96th Service Group, 366th Air Service Squadron, 332nd Fighter Group; interview 8 August 1990, Los Angeles, California.

Cargill, Gilbert, Flight Instructor; Primary Flight Instructor, Tuskegee Army Air Field, interview 10 April 1990, Detroit, Michigan.

Carter, Herbert, Colonel (Ret), Engineering Officer/Maintenance Officer, 99th Pursuit Squadron, 477th Composite Group, 332nd Fighter Group, and 332nd Fighter Wing, interview 10 June 1990, Tuskegee, Alabama.

Coffey, Cornelius, interview 1 February 1991, Chicago, Illinois.

Crockett, Woodrow, Colonel (Ret), 100th Fighter Squadron, 332nd Fighter Group, 477th Medium Bomb Group, 477th Composite Group, 332nd Fighter Group, and 332nd Fighter Wing, interview 9 August 1990, Los Angeles, California.

Custis, Lemuel, Captain, 99th Pursuit Squadron interview, 10 August 1991, Detroit, Michigan.

Downs, Walter, Colonel (Ret.) Commanding Officer 301st Fighter Squadron, 332nd Fighter Group, interview 27 January 1990, Detroit, Michigan.

Dryden, Charles, Lieutenant, 99th Pursuit Squadron, Captain, 553rd Fighter Squadron, interview 14 April 1991, Atlanta, Georgia.

Gillead, Leroy, Flight Officer, 477th Medium Bomber Group; Composite Group; 332nd, Fighter Group; and Fighter Wing, interview 7-9 August 1990, Los Angeles, California.

Henry, Milton, 16 March 1991.

Holliman, William, Colonel (Ret), 302nd and 301st Fighter, 332rd Fighter Group, 477th Composite Group, 332nd Fighter Group, and 332nd Fighter Wing, interview, 5 May 1990, Detroit, Michigan.

Hurd, Harold, interview, 10 October 1990, Chicago, Illinois.

Hutchins, Fred, Colonel (Ret.) 302nd Fighter Squadron, 332nd Fighter Group, 477th Medium Bomber Group, 477th Composite Group, 332nd Fighter Group, 332 Fighter Wing, interview 8-9 August 1990, Los Angeles, California.

Jamison, Clarence, Lieutenant, 99th Pursuit Squadron, Captain 477th Medium Bomber Group, interview 11 May 1991, Columbus, Ohio.

Jefferson, Alexander, Lieutenant, 302nd Fighter Squadron, 332nd Fighter Group, interview, 19 April 1990, Detroit, Michigan.

Kennedy, Elmore, Colonel (Ret.), 619th Bomber Squadron Commanding Officer 447th Medium Bomber Group, 447th Composite Group, 332nd Fighter Squadron, and 332nd Fighter Wing, interview 5 June 1990, Detroit, Michigan.

Lee, Phillip, Primary Flight Instructor, Tuskegee Army Air Field, interview 8 August 1990, Los Angeles, California.

Macon, Richard, Lieutenant, 99th Fighter Squadron, 332nd Fighter Group, interview 2 February 1990, Detroit, Michigan.

Mitchell, Rufus, Mechanic, 99th Pursuit Squadron, interview 7 August 1990, Los Angeles, California.

O'Neal, Ira, Provost Marshall, 332nd Fighter Group, interview 7 August 1990, Los Angeles, California.

Pitts, Robert, Intelligence Officer, 332nd Fighter Group, interview 1 March 1990, Detroit, Michigan.

Polk, Wardell, Lieutenant Bombardier/Navigator, 477th Medium Bomber Group, 477th Medium Composite Group, interview 18 February 1990, Detroit, Michigan.

Richardson, E. E., Lieutenant, 477th Medium Bomber Group, interview, 9 August 1990, Los Angeles, California.

Rogers, John W., Lieutenant, 99th Pursuit Squadron, Captain and Major 477th Medium Bomber Group, Composite Group, interview 2 February 1991, Chicago, Illinois.

Shephard, Harry, Mechanic, 99th Pursuit Squadron, Officer/Pilot, 302nd Fighter Squadron, 332nd Fighter Group, B-25 Instructor,

Tuskegee Army Air Force, interview 9 August 1990, Los Angeles, California.

Stewart, Harry, Lieutenant, 302nd and 301st Fighter Squadron, 332nd Fighter Group, 477th Composite Group, 322nd Fighter Group, Fighter Wing, interview 27 February 1990.

Thompson, William, Armament Officer, 99th Pursuit Squadron, interview 10 October 1990, Chicago, Illinois.

Washington, Jenny, wife of Thomas Washington, Sargent, Mechanics instructor, Tuskegee Army Air Field, interview 10 May 1990. Lansing, Michigan.

Watson, Spann, Colonel (Ret.), 99th Pursuit Squadron, 553rd Fighter Squadron, 477th Medium Bomber Group, 477th Composite Group, 332nd Fighter Group, and 332nd Fighter Wing, interview 9 March 1991, Washington D.C.

Whitehead, John Colonel (Ret.), 301st Fighter Squadron, 477th Composite Group, 332nd Fighter Wing, interview 8 August 1990, Los Angeles, California.

Womack, William M., Physical Education Instructor, Army Air Corps, Southeast Training Command, Tuskegee Army Air Field, Officer, 332nd Fighter Group, interview 1 March 1990, Detroit, Michigan.

Index

A

Abbott, Robert, 21; aviation supporter, 64, 65, 66, 72; and Coleman, 26, 27, death of, 108; motivated Negro migration, 109; successor, 109. *See also Chicago Defender*
Acres Airport (Illinois), 44, 45
Adams, Emory E., 97
Addis Ababa, 31, 52, 53
"Adequate National Defense Plan" (Roosevelt), 87-88
Aduwa, Ethiopia, 52
Advisory Commission on Defense, 119-21
Advisory Committee on Negro Troop Politics. *See* McCloy Committee
Aeronautical University, Chicago, 138
Africa, 3
African Americans: as aviators, 2, 7, 8; in battle, 9; life in Europe, 8; limitations on, 5, 6. *See also* Bullard, Eugene; discrimination
African Patriotic League, 65
Africans: as aviators, 12; as WW I soldiers, 10-11, 12
Afro American Life Insurance Company, 84
AGCT. *See* Army General Classification Test

Agricultural and Technical College (Greensboro, N.C.), a CPTP school, 96
Air Force: first Negro general (Davis, Jr.), 243
Air Force Integrates 1945-1954 (Gropman), 281
Air Force Racial Policy Study. *See* Nugent Report
air mail, 85-86
air races, 37-38
air shows: all Negro, 35, 36-37; Baltimore, 90; Chicago, 90; Cleveland, 90; Dayton, 90; Fort Wayne, 90; at Harlem field, 85; New York, 90, 92; Pittsburgh, 90, 92; Washington, D. C., 90, 92; West Virginia State College, 90. *See also Chicago Defender*
aircraft types. *See* specific plane name
Airtech Flying School (San Diego), 39
Alexander, Sadie T., 275
Algerians, 10
Allegheny Airport, 92
Allegheny Mountains, 38
Allen, Thomas: Banning's mechanic, 37-38, 42
Amberg, Julius, 193
Amenia Conference (1933), 62